JUNG AND INTUITION

JUNG AND INTUITION

On the Centrality and Variety of Forms of Intuition in Jung and Post-Jungians

Nathalie Pilard

LONDON AND NEW YORK

First published 2015 by Karnac Books Ltd.

Published 2018 by Routledge
2 Park Square, Milton Park, Abingdon, Oxon OX14 4RN
711 Third Avenue, New York, NY 10017, USA

Routledge is an imprint of the Taylor & Francis Group, an informa business

Copyright © 2015 to Nathalie Pilard.

The right of Nathalie Pilard to be identified as the author of this work has been asserted in accordance with §§ 77 and 78 of the Copyright Design and Patents Act 1988.

All rights reserved. No part of this book may be reprinted or reproduced or utilised in any form or by any electronic, mechanical, or other means, now known or hereafter invented, including photocopying and recording, or in any information storage or retrieval system, without permission in writing from the publishers.

Notice:
Product or corporate names may be trademarks or registered trademarks, and are used only for identification and explanation without intent to infringe.

British Library Cataloguing in Publication Data

A C.I.P. for this book is available from the British Library

ISBN 9781782201304 (pbk)

Edited, designed and produced by The Studio Publishing Services Ltd
www.publishingservicesuk.co.uk
e-mail: studio@publishingservicesuk.co.uk

CONTENTS

ACKNOWLEDGEMENTS vii

ABOUT THE AUTHOR ix

INTRODUCTION xi

PART I
JUNG'S NOTION OF INTUITION
AND ITS CONTEXTS IN HIS PSYCHOLOGY

CHAPTER ONE
Plurality of meaning in Jung's notion of intuition   3

CHAPTER TWO
Contexts of the birth of intuition in Jung's psychology   23

PART II
AFTER 1896: INTUITION IN THE UNDER-CONSCIOUS

CHAPTER THREE
Supernatural intuitions, religion, science, and philosophy   61

CHAPTER FOUR
Psychological intuitions   95

PART III
AFTER 1912: INTUITION IN THE UNCONSCIOUS

CHAPTER FIVE
Anschauung and archetype 141

CHAPTER SIX
Archetype, intuition, instinct, and empathy (1) 155

PART IV
AFTER 1913: INTUITION IN JUNGIAN AND POST-JUNGIAN PRACTICE

CHAPTER SEVEN
Intuitive methods and empathy (2) 169

PART V
AFTER 1921: INTUITION IN JUNGIAN AND POST-JUNGIAN CONSCIOUSNESS

CHAPTER EIGHT
Psychological types 205

PART VI
LATE JUNG, EMPATHY (3), AND THE NATURE OF INTUITION

CHAPTER NINE
Suggestions for further research 233

APPENDIX I
Indexations of "-intuition" 239

APPENDIX II
CW and *GW 6*, indexing of "-intuition" in Chapter Two 243

NOTES 245

REFERENCES 277

INDEX 293

ACKNOWLEDGEMENTS

I would like to thank Robert Segal for his talent and generosity, Sonu Shamdasani and Tomas Bokedal for their expert comments, my parents for their support, the French Ministère des Affaires Étrangères et Européennes and the University of Glasgow for my scholarship, the Department of Divinity and Religious Studies of the University of Aberdeen for the various financial support I received during my PhD.

Thanks are also due to Paul Bishop, John Beebe, Antoine Faivre, Leslie Gardner, Lucy Huskinson, Roderick Main, and Martin Rueff for their advice and lively conversation, all the members of the International Association of Jungian Studies weblist for keeping me aware of the Jungian debate, Pete Gunter and John Mullarkey for their philosophical help, Greg Richter and Charles-Henri Discry for their help in German and linguistics, and Yvonne Voegeli and Marion Wullschleger for their warm assistance at the *Jung Arbeitsarchiv* of the Eidgenössische Technische Hochschule (ETH) Zürich.

I am grateful to my friends for their patience, and especially Paul Midjord. I would like to thank Cécile Chavel, Frances Milne, and John Callender for their help and for the deepest motivation that lies beneath this work: health care.

I thank the Foundation of the Works of C. G. Jung, Zürich: (c) 2007 Foundation of the Works of C. G. Jung, Zürich for permission to reproduce from Jung's unpublished manuscripts.

For permission to quote from the *Collected Works* by C. G. Jung © 1983 *CW 1*; © 1991 *CW B*; 1970 © *CW 1*; 1973 © *CW 2*; 1960 © *CW 3*; 1971 © *CW 6*, I thank T&F and PUP editions. Reproduced by permission of Taylor & Francis Books (UK, worldwide), and Princeton University Press (USA, Canada).

For permission to cite Corinna Treitel *A Science for the Soul: Occultism and the Genesis of the German Modern*, pp. 32–33, Table 2.1, I thank Johns Hopkins University Press © 2004 Johns Hopkins University Press.

I thank Pantheon Books for permission to quote from *Memories, Dreams, Reflexions* by Jung–Jaffé, translation copyright © 1961, 1962, 1963 and renewed 1989, 1990, 1991 by Random House LCC.

ABOUT THE AUTHOR

Nathalie Pilard was born in Paris, where she started her studies in history and religion at the universities of Panthéon-Sorbonne, Denis Diderot, and the Ecole Pratique des Hautes Etudes. Her thesis on C. G. Jung and the Confucian *Changes* was subsequently published in France. She then joined the University of Aberdeen, Scotland, where she completed her PhD on C. G. Jung and intuition. An independent scholar, she is also a collagist and an artist, currently working on a tarot deck.

For Théotime

Introduction

Intuition, Eingebung, Einfall, Einfälle, Vorahnung, clairvoyance, *Anschauung, Analogie, intellektual Intuition,* and *Visionen* are ten of the more than two dozen terms used by Jung to describe the multiplicity and the complexity of the epiphanies of the notion of intuition in his writing. In my previous study, I used intuition as a method through which to approach Jung's introduction to Richard Wilhelm's translation of the *Book of Changes*, or *I Ching* (see Pilard, 2010). Now I wish to move from the specific to the general, asking myself whether intuition had a single meaning for Jung. Single became multiple, and five years later the compilation started to take shape.

This polymorphic aspect of intuition is more than a preliminary issue to be addressed before reaching the heart of the topic. It is the teething issue itself. I invite the reader to examine Jung's definition of intuition in Part I and to read it again having reached the end of the book. As is too often the case with Jung's three-dimensional writing, a first reading of his work is bound to be flat. Jung writes from somewhere that he rarely depicts. The Jung of *The Red Book*, unmistakeably deep, is the Jung of his entire work. Yet there, the task of finding the third dimension, depth, is left to the reader and to the hermeneut. Hence, this work, and the work of other academics who try to elevate Jung's words and restore their shadow.[1]

Beyond the study of Jung, a topic as large as intuition requires the possession of data to prevent shortcuts, to energise an old philosophical debate, and to name phenomena that exist in religion, in philosophy, in literature, in languages, in science, and in psychology. This acquirement of knowledge clarifies the necessity for multi-disciplinary intuition and, to some extent, defines it. The analysis of precise data concerning intuition in Jung and post-Jungians avoids the mistake of confusing ungraspable with vague.

This last crucial differentiation has already been questioned within a correlated field of research, esotericism, and has found a solution, which is to elevate the topic to the level of an academic *discipline*.

Connected to a great extent, the umbrella terms "esotericism" and "intuition" provoke different perceptions.[2] While the term "esotericism" can still be taken negatively, "intuition" does not offend the ear. Yet, the existence of esotericism as an academic discipline, albeit young, has been established thanks to the numerous and continuing contributions regarding the definition of both the term and the discipline.[3] Intuition does not yet enjoy this privilege. Everyone understands that esotericism can be ungraspable and, thus, no one suspects esotericism of being vague. Sadly, the situation is the opposite concerning the term intuition, not to mention the absence of a discipline devoted to the study of it.

Defining both "esotericism" and "intuition" is a hard task, since, nowhere more than in those specific areas, the object and the subject of study can easily be conflated. Resorting to paradigm or theory is insufficient if we examine Pierre Riffard's portrayal of the esotericist:

> The esotericist is not a believer. He does not adhere. He unsticks. An esotericist does not work with faith or knowledge but . . . with reflexion on the correspondences, and by returns on ideals. Everything interpenetrates in intelligence, and the one who thinks that participates in that meaning and communicates it. In this type of contemplation . . . one does not gain laws, dogmas, things, but a global vision of life . . . The esotericist knows that he is duped. He is no more sceptic than dogmatic; he situates. (Riffard, 2001, p. 810, translated for this edition)

Likewise, the intuitive person that Jung was needed never be trapped inside anything that he could mistake for "his" intuition in order to gain some hasty present from it. He states, "We can never reach the level of our intuitions and should therefore not identify ourselves with them" (Jung, *CW 12*, par. 148). The task, the neverending work, is hard and weighty. Jung's work, his psychology, represented such a global and circular vision of living. It was like an encyclopaedia, the entry in which would always remain Jung's "personal equation" instead of any dogma or faith (Shamdasani, 2003, pp. 18–22). Afraid of being duped, Jung tried to "unstick" and to situate intuition, most famously in his intuitive type and function.[4]

Many people at least know of Jung's psychological types. Yet, intuitive types and functions are much more complex than they might appear to the readers, who see only the visible part of the iceberg, that of the intuition in consciousness, whereas intuition in Jung's theory comes from the abysses of the deepest unconscious of psychology. More important, intuition is present everywhere instead of just in types and functions.

To try to untangle all the forms of intuition present in Jung's writing is to expose its central and pivotal position in his psychology. This work uses three means to show the centrality of intuition. First, it devotes a whole section, Chapter One, to the exposition of all the manifestations of intuition written by Jung. Second, it systematically contextualises the occurrence of the terms that stand for intuition in Jung's work and examines more precisely in Chapter Two the general context of the birth of intuition in Jung's work. Third, it discriminates among four areas of Jung's work to study the specificity of intuition in each of them. Those domains are Jung's psychology of the "underconscious" (a term to be defined precisely at the end of Chapter Two and which is the frame of Part II), Jung's psychology of the unconscious in Part III, the psychology that is concerned with Jungian and postJungian practice in Part IV, and Jung's psychology of consciousness in Part V. A very short Part VI introduces late Jung with regard to the complex notion of empathy (3) and recapitulates the most significant theoretical aspects of the book that could open new avenues of research. The complexity of intuition induced this thematic organisation, yet Parts II to VI, apart from simultaneities, appear in a chronological order.

Jung's psychology of the under-conscious—this state in between the unconscious and consciousness that favours the appearance of intuition—overflows with terms beneath which the most spectacular kinds of intuitive epiphanies happen. At the turn of the twentieth century, the scientific community was thrilled by the ways of reaching the unconscious. The intuitive gift was one of them, when it was employed, for instance, by mediums during spiritist sessions.[5] Like many other intellectuals, Jung benefited from the then current general enthusiasm of the scientific community towards esotericist phenomena. Yet, Jung's keen and lifelong interest in the *Esoterik* would quickly suffer from the limitations of a vogue abandoned for the sake of science.[6] From the lectures that he delivered as an undergraduate student to the intuitive experiences that he recorded in his "private cosmology" *Liber Novus*, or *The Red Book* (Shamdasani, 2010, p. 36), early Jung considered and experienced many extraordinary intuitions.

Intuition that stemmed from patients I call "psychological intuitions". Framed within psychiatric contexts, intuition was analysed and classified. Jung's cousin, Helene Preiswerk, with whom he experienced spiritism before 1900, for instance, became "the case S. W." in his medical dissertation.[7] No longer as "clairvoyante" as the famous eighteenth-century clairvoyante of Prevost, Helly rather had "teleological hallucinations". At the Burghölzli lunatic asylum of Zürich, Jung was also testing patients with his technique of word association (to one word, one must react with another word) and prompted *Einfälle* in the answers. All those unfamiliar terms, and others that will appear in Part II, designate intuition.

In Jung's psychology of the unconscious, intuition does not manifest itself in multiple forms—or rather pre-forms, since they are unconscious—but into two aspects of the utmost importance. On the one hand, and borrowing the French anthropologist Lévy-Bruhl's locution, Jung writes of the *participation mystique* of the "primitive" (Lévy-Bruhl, 1923). On the other hand, he equates intuition with the German term *Anschauung*.

According to Jung, from the mid-1910s on, the unconscious was not only the reservoir of memories and of repressions of the individual. That part, Jung called the "personal unconscious". At a deeper layer of the unconscious of each individual, one could find the "collective unconscious", that is, access to the past and future of the whole of humanity through the images of the archetypes.[8] Those archetypes, or universal patterns of behaviour, belonged to myth, fairy-tales, religion, and other means used by humanity to perpetuate its memory. Consciousness, for Jung, was not the origin of the unconscious, as it was for Pierre Janet and Sigmund Freud. Instead, the origin of consciousness was the unconscious. The collective unconscious had always preceded consciousness. At the start there was the unconscious, which was the state of the "primitive". The attitude of the "primitive" towards the world was intuitive. Therefore, it was one of total identification with it. This *participation mystique*, described by Lévy-Bruhl and endorsed by Jung, we call empathy (1).[9]

The centrality of the *Anschauung* in Jung's psychology historically started with the first appearance of the term "archetype" in 1919. Jung did not write of the (German) *Archetypen*, but of the *Archetypen des Anschauungen*, "the archetypes of intuition". To my knowledge, no one so far has commented on that appendix to the most central notion of Jung's psychology. The question will be dealt with in Part III and will have significant repercussions on Part IV (intuition in Jungian and post-Jungian practice) and Part V (intuition in consciousness).

In Jungian practice, more specifically that which concerns dream material, intuition historically appeared during the crucial time of Jung's rift with Freud around 1912.

According to Freud, neurotic individuals unconsciously realised their unfulfilled desires in their dreams. Their affects could be deciphered through the "distortion" of reality in their dreams, the "work" of which consisted in "displacements", or "condensations", for instance (see, for example, Freud (1900a, Chapters Two to Six)). Another powerful guise in Freud's theory between reality and dream was the symbol. What Freud called a symbol, Jung called a sign—a mere sign. A sign, for Jung, was any element (of a dream, for instance) that referred to something—or many things—in consciousness, in the experience of the person. By contrast, a symbol was, for him, the only means and the best possible form that the collective unconscious had found to express the affect of the dreamer.[10]

Dissatisfied with Freud's "analytic method" of dreams, Jung decided in the mid-1910s to use a new method, the "constructive method", which he equated with Henri Bergson's philosophical intuitive method. Instead of deconstructing the multiple signs of the dream and finding out to what they referred in consciousness, the constructive method looked for the symbols that the experience of the dreamer could not explain and the origin of which, therefore, had to be unconscious. From the mid-1910s on, Jung evoked the natural and primeval language of the dream. Instead of distorted dreams, he wrote of modern people disconnected from their roots.[11] The intuitive connection among the dreamer, the symbol, Bergson's duration, and the collective unconscious will be studied in detail in Chapter Six.

Another method that was concurrently employed by Jung (and is used by his followers) that used intuition was active imagination. Instead of dreams, or in addition to them, active imagination required tools, or supports for the painful elements of the collective unconscious to find room to express themselves intuitively. Those tools included dance, automatic writing, drawing, crystal gazing, and painting. Jung himself painted, and the major contemporary outcome of this method was Jung's masterpiece, *The Red Book*.

Jungian and post-Jungian practice finally displayed intuition through its most common phenomenon, transference. This kind of intuition we call empathy (2).

As seen earlier, intuitive types and functions belong to Jung's psychology of consciousness. Both wholly depend upon the *Anschauung*, which mediates the archetype into consciousness. All four functions and types (intuition, thinking, feeling, and sensation) in fact depend upon the processes of the *Anschauung*. In turn, the differentiation of the functions describes the major part of what Jung calls the "individuation" of the person, which is the goal of Jung's psychology.[12] Post-Jungian research on types is hardly scarce. Research concerned with intuition is examined in Part V, section headed "Critiques and variants to Jungian types".

Also important concerning types is the study of their genesis. Exceeding a mere well-informed chronological description of Jung's sources, the genetic research deals with the validity or invalidity of Jung's premises. Numerous discussions on intuition at the Psychological Club of Zürich during the 1910s allowed Jung to examine his ideas and to hear those of others. Emulation can be the natural tendency of a charismatic, introverted, intuitive type such as Jung. Debate constitutes a necessary exercise for that particular type if one wants one's sparks of intuition to take shape in the world.[13]

So far, examined historically, empathy will be observed through its theoretical aspect in Part VI as empathy (1), or *participation mystique*, empathy (2), or intuition in transference, and empathy (3), or intuition in synchronicity.

* * *

The three problems that we encountered with the sources are discussed in Parts I, II, and V. First, what has been published so far of Jung's work does not appear identically in German, English, French, and Italian. Apart from historical disagreements concerning editions and corrections are intrinsic and insuperable cultural issues of translation. Because the goal of this work is to know what intuition means for Jung, this issue is hardly a linguistic detail. *Anschauung*, for instance, might well be grammatically translated into "insight", yet "insight" does not render the notion of intuition. The first two sections of Chapter One address those issues.

Second, some unpublished works by Jung are only accessible in archives. The analysis of the third section of Chapter Two is based on the discrepancies that exist between Jung's published psychiatric treatment of his spiritist experience with his cousin (Jung's medical dissertation) and the unpublished protocols of the sessions possessed by the ETH Bibliothek in Zürich.

Third, insurmountable obstacles can only be bypassed. Before examining Jung's *work* on intuition, I wanted to account for the possible *presence* of intuition in Jung's young life and, consequently, report on the influence of Jung's personal experience on his writing. Yet, for the time frame of the 1890s, the most important documentation concerning Jung's life is his diary, which is currently in a bank vault and is not available for study.[14] Aniela Jaffé's psychobiography of Jung, *Memories, Dreams, Reflections* (MDR), is too strongly edited *vis-à-vis* the protocols of her interviews with Jung. I have, therefore, restricted its use to the specific purpose of illustrating intuition in Jungian practice and theory, which was itself one of Jaffé's initial goals.

* * *

Between source and literature, we find the first generation of works which were not written by Jung, but which are concerned with Jung and intuition. Those works have been composed by Jung's colleagues, analysts and probable intuitive types themselves, as well as by early analysands of Jung.

In his correspondence with Jung from 1915 to 1916, Jung's Baselian psychiatrist colleague, Hans Schmid-Guisan, notably discussed Bergson's intuition (Iselin, 1982). The German correspondence was translated last year by the historian, specialist in Freud, and translator of Jung, Ernst Falzeder, and edited by the Jungian analyst, specialist on the subject of types, and an intuitive type himself, John Beebe (Jung & Schmid-Guisan, 1915–1916).

Jung's assistant Antonia Wolff was another person who helped Jung define the four psychological types. In 1934, she proposed her own typology to describe four feminine psychological types (Wolff, 1934, pp. 77–90). Less famous are the contributions about intuition from the late 1910s of Emilii Medtner, in German and in limited edition, and of Maria Moltzer, the latter only recently published by Sonu Shamdasani.[15] Both of them also supported Jung's psychology of the unconscious by contributing their ideas to the definition of empathy (1) and (2) before Jung read of Lévy-Bruhl.

Literature by analysts on types is not scarce. Two remarkable contributions are Marie-Louise von Franz's 1971 "The fourth function" and John Beebe's 2004 "Understanding consciousness through the theory of psychological types" (Beebe, 2004, pp. 83–115; Von Franz, 1971, pp. 1–72). Von Franz was one of Jung's assistants, and she, together with another assistant, Aniela Jaffé, has written on several topics linked to intuition.[16] Von Franz's positioning, bolder than Jaffé's, is that of a follower in a strict sense. After Jung's death, rather than applying or elucidating Jung's work, she wrote what she believed had not been written by Jung himself of valuable contributions on alchemy and synchronicity. One exception among Jaffé's writings that follows this daring spirit is *MDR*. In this generation, we can also count the writings of the psychiatrists Heinrich Karl Fierz and Verena Kast, who present the various relationships between intuition and psychiatry (Fierz, 1991; Kast, 1980).

A second kind of literature, stemming from scholars, is constituted by a more contemporary generation in religious studies (such as Robert Segal, Leon Schlamm, Antoine Faivre, and Lucy Huskinson), in psychoanalytic studies (such as Roderick Main), in cultural studies (such as Christine Maillard, Paul Bishop, and Véronique Liard), or in history (such as Sonu Shamdasani, Corinna Treitel, Jacqueline Carroy, Régine Plas, Pytlick Priska, Eugene Taylor, and Henri Ellenberger). Intuition is not directly presented by those specialists but all do offer hindsight, contexts, and analyses not found in some of the preceding "intuitive works" by Jungians. In that category we also find methodological works, philosophical, religious, and psychological dictionaries.[17]

Among, finally, the works in progress at the time of my writing is Christian McMillan's work on "Jung, Bergson, and Intuitive Knowledge"[18] and some literature, perhaps, on *Liber Novus*, which has not yet prompted extensive research because of its recent publication but could, and I dare say will, inspire remarkable work on intuition.[19]

PART I

JUNG'S NOTION OF INTUITION AND ITS CONTEXTS IN HIS PSYCHOLOGY

CHAPTER ONE

Plurality of meaning in Jung's notion of intuition

The circumscribed value of the indices of the Collected Works

The plural of the entry "Intuition(s)" in the *General Index* of the *Collected Works of C. G. Jung* (the last and twentieth volume) bears witness to the problematic nature of the study of intuition. In Jung's published work, there is neither a single term for intuition nor a single intuition. Jung's work offers challenges to the micro-lexicologist, whose labour is threatened by three primary factors: translations, editions, and auto-revisions.

Routledge and Kegan Paul in London and the Bollingen Foundation in Princeton, New Jersey first published Jung's *Collected Works* in the 1950s (before the German publisher, Rascher) (McGuire, 1982, pp. 123–127).[20] In his investigation of the correspondence between Jung and Rascher, Paul Bishop discovered that Jung "did not want to rush the preparation of the 'Gesamtausgabe' [collected edition] . . . [arguing] that it would in fact be better to leave the bulk of the work up to the editors of the English edition" (Bishop, 1998b, p. 374). Tensions ensued between Jung and the two publishers. In 1953, for instance, Jung expressed to the British–American editorial committee "in the strongest possible terms", reports William McGuire, the

American Bollingen house editor, "his dissatisfaction with the progress in the publication of the *Collected Works*, accusing his publishers of the virtual suppression of his work" (McGuire, 1982, p. 127). In the long term, thinks Bishop, the intellectual disadvantages of this financial strategy of spreading the Jungian message in English-reading countries with no adequate professional care outweighed its practical benefits (Bishop, 1998b, p. 375).

In agreement with Bishop, Shamdasani[21] (2007, p. 117) writes of the "insufficient coordination between the two editions". (See also the detailed chapter, "The incomplete works of Jung", in Shamdasani (2005).) Characteristically, and as the first hindrance to our attempt at defining intuition in the work of Jung, the English *General Index* was edited in 1979, whereas the German *Gesamtregister* was published only in 1994. The Foreword of the latter, while noting the reliance on the indices of each of the eighteen other German volumes, made no mention of the English *General Index*. These unco-ordinated efforts gave free rein to editorial preferences and to entwined linguistic and cultural penchants. Knowing whether "intuition" means something different in German and in English is not the purpose of this section. Here, intuition is outlined within the precise context of Jung's writing, something made possible by the comparison of German and English general indices, that is, Volume 20 and Band 20 of Jung's *Collected Works* and *Gesammelte Werke*, respectively.

A careful study of all the references concerned with the entry "Intuition"[22] in the general index of Jung's *Collected Works* and *Gesammelte Werke* reveals discrepancies between the index-linking in German and the English index-linking.[23] I present in Appendix I four tables listing the similarities and differences between the German and the English indexing of the (English and German) term "intuition", the terms of its family, and all their cross-references found under the entries "intuition", "intuitive", and "intuitive type". Appendix I, therefore, brings together the German and English indexing of Jung's *Collected Works* and *Gesammelte Werke 1 to 18*.[24]

These tables first reveal that if the major references to intuition generally belong to *both* German and English indices (Appendix I, Table 1, the Swiss editors either are more interested in the notion or are more serious in their indexing, for they select more than twice the number of paragraphs in the eighteen volumes than the British–American editors did. Some of the paragraphs index-linked either only in German (that is, missed in English (Appendix I, Table 2 or only in English (that is, missed in German (Appendix I, Table 3) reveal clear editorial penchants.

If we temporarily ignore the numeral issue, the first striking dissimilarity is raised as early as the index-linking of what is termed the "definition" of intuition.

The German index refers the definition of intuition to the lecture of 1919, "Instinct and the unconscious", which belongs to Jung's *Psychology of the Unconscious*. The English index refers to the 1921 *Psychological Types*, which, historically, introduces Jung's psychology of consciousness.[25] These two texts are the chief sources for Jung's theoretical approach to intuition, but they have little in common in the way that they depict it. This discrepancy seems secondary to Jung, whose reference in a footnote in the first text to the mentioned paragraphs of the other gives priority to the coherence that he sees in the notion of intuition in the two texts, and we shall see why in the last section of this chapter.

"Instinct and the unconscious" comprises only ten pages out of the 600 of Volume 8 of Jung's *Collected Works*. Like *Psychological Types*, it is the result of decades of research. Several reasons, of form and content, justify the German indexing of paragraph 269 as the place to find the "definition" of intuition. The third sentence, which starts "Intuition is", is a formal presentation of the notion that runs to the end of the paragraph. There, intuition is depicted in the unconscious, by stressing the differences and similarities existing between the interlinked processes of intuition and instinct on the one hand and the central notion of *Anschauung* on the other.

Psychological Types is not, despite the table, a work on types, that is, on types only, but it also represents the sum of Jung's psychology in 1921. The fact that it is the single work of Jung's that contains a section (of nearly eighty pages) on "Definitions" shows the author's contemporary desire to undertake a comprehensive setting of his psychology.[26] The entry "Intuition", which runs to one and a half pages, offers all the facets of the notion of intuition (those of intuition in consciousness as much as those of intuition in the unconscious), yet only after careful analysis.[27] So far, therefore, whereas the Swiss index has a clear penchant towards Jung's psychology of the unconscious regarding intuition, the English indexation seems to refer neutrally to the single place where one can find that which Jung, indeed, names the "definition" of intuition. Yet, "Definitions" belongs to *Types*, some chapters of which technically and precisely refer to Jung's psychology of consciousness. These chapters have been unusually abundantly referred to in the English index. This is no longer impartial.

In my final table (Appendix II, Table 1), I compare the German and English indices on a smaller scale: Chapter Two of *Psychological Types*. The micro-format confirms the general one: the same two German and English editing preferences for Jung's psychology of the unconscious and for Jung's psychology of consciousness reappear respectively.

The hundred pages of "Schiller's ideas on the type problem" in *Psychological Types* offer a study of Friedrich Schiller's correspondence with Johann Wolfgang von Goethe. There, Jung entwines a description of the naïve and sentimental poets with both his own typology of consciousness and his theory of the unconscious.[28]

The term "intuition" and related terms appear fifteen times in the chapter, but are indexed only eight times in German and seven times in English. While common in the English index, this oversight—seven German and eight English references out of fifteen missed—is noticeable with the Swiss editors and is explicable only by the fact that *Psychological Types* here treats Jung's psychology of consciousness.

Among the few recorded paragraphs, only four of them are common to both the German and the English indices. The content of the remaining four German and three English references gives credence to my earlier association of German with the unconscious and of English with consciousness concerning intuition. All four paragraphs found only in German describe Jung's psychology of the unconscious. Paragraph 184 refers to the archetype by describing "these intuitions [which] contain a living power". Paragraph 171 portrays the relationship between intuition and symbol. Both paragraph 123 and paragraph 195 discuss "the religious problem of the primitive". Archetype, symbol, and "primitive" thinking all belong to Jung's psychology of the unconscious.

Thorny problems with the psychology of consciousness are developed in the two notes of paragraphs 143 and 148, which are selected only in the English index and expressly catalogued under the sub-entry "Intuitive type, extraverted feeling" for paragraph 143*n*, and "Intuitive type, introverted thinking" for paragraph 148*n*. Schiller, for Jung, belonged to the introverted type and intuited the differences between introversion and extraversion, the main topic of the psychology of consciousness, through his relationship with the extraverted Goethe. The two notes brilliantly illustrate the reverse tendencies, which might explain the English choice. Yet, one could argue that introversion and extraversion are only indirectly linked to intuition and that it is, therefore, far-fetched for them to be included in the index. The third paragraph, which is selected only in English, neutrally refers to Goethe's "intuition" and again testifies to another German oversight or omission.

Even the four paragraphs selected both in German and in English leave room for distinct editorial penchants. Paragraphs 117 and 219 describe intuition in the unconscious as well as in consciousness. Paragraphs 103 and 104 clearly indicate a German reference to the psychology of the unconscious and an English reference to the psychology of consciousness in the way that they are indexed. Paragraph 103 is catalogued under the English sub-entry "Intuition, in Schiller" and under the German entry "*Intuition, bei Goethe*". Here, Jung uses Schiller to illustrate types and functions of consciousness but accounts for "[Goethe's unconscious] overriding intuition". Paragraph 104 refers, in the German index, to the entry "*Intuitivismus*", or Schiller's [unconscious] intuitiveness. The German index, therefore, pinpoints exceptions to the main concern of the chapter. Only the paragraphs covering the psychology of the unconscious have been saved.

Translation issues and cultural biases

In order to know what intuition means for Jung, one needs to stick to a precise terminology, even if it is long and incomplete. Jung's desire to remain ambiguous in order for his psychology to remain open to the richest variety of interpretation compels us to try to clarify. Jung's versatility in writing also needs to be appreciated through his extraordinary awareness of the significance of the precision of language. School and high school, for Jung, had meant *Gymnasium*, or "grammar school" in the international micro-city of Basel, where Latin and Greek were taught. Hence, Jung's frequent recourse to etymology, for instance. As Marie-Louise von Franz described in her own terms, "The other voice [the unconscious] could be heard in Jung's special way of reviving the original etymological meanings of words and allowing both feeling and imaginative elements to enter into his scientific exposition of each term" (von Franz, 1975, p. 4). Precision, imagination, intuition, and unconscious are never at odds. Intuition itself is not vague, but our capacity to understand it can be. As he was an extremely intuitive person, this was not the case with Jung.

Jung's concern for precision in language is not restricted to his specific use of etymology in dead languages. Next to Jung's wish to spread analytical psychology in the most effective and sometimes fastest way were his struggles to obtain precise translations.[29]

One example belongs to the history of the *Collected Works*, reported by Shamdasani. Editing and translating involved choices that often divided people into camps. Translation issues came between those, on the one hand, who cared first for the final language—English in this case—and its style (its readability), and those, on the other hand, who cared for the first language, German, and its precision. This split corresponds to the central issue of contemporary translation. The poet Richard Hull, who directed the translation, belonged to the first group, whereas the Doctor of Philosophy Gerhard Adler belonged to the second one. Shamdasani writes,

> Jung suggested that Gerhard Adler be appointed to check the translations. Jung considered it absolutely necessary to have this done by a native German-speaker. For Jung, the manner in which he used language was an integral part of his psychology. (Shamdasani, 2007, p. 173)

Respect for German was, indeed, crucial for Jung. Yet, his knowledge of the *living* languages—also learnt at the Gymnasium, and later spoken and written, of, for example, English and French—left him aware of the fact that his *living* psychology sometimes needed more than literal translation. In 1998, Paul Bishop questioned Jung's favour for Roland Cahen-Salabelle's anthological—rather than systematic—presentation of his work for the French reading public, notably through *L'homme à la découverte de son âme*.[30] If this question is still open, I shall try to address the issue here.

A charismatic individual and a controversial figure as a psychologist, Cahen-Salabelle was a great admirer and fine practitioner of languages. A psychiatrist after the Second World War, he had left his language studies—his pursuit of the *aggregation* for German—to embrace Freud's and then Jung's psychology.[31] Pointing, as here, to resemblances to Jung's profile—and character—is unavoidable and explains, for one thing, Cahen-Salabelle's liberties in his "adaptation" of *L'Homme à la découverte de son âme*. Beyond the critiques he received for his work, I leave Cahen-Salabelle to describe his approach to his translation of Jung's work. In 1951, he writes,

> As for us, we endeavoured to effect a translation that was both faithful and flexible. The author's thoughts are often expressed in such shortcuts that, in order to render the *substantifique moelle* ["true substance"], one needs to make them explicit and comment on them somewhat. We endeavoured not to transcribe any thought, irrespective of how complex and deep it might be, without linking it to an expression that would be immediately accessible to the cultured reader. When we came up against a difficult translation, we asked ourselves, "how would we have said that in French?", "how do things happen in analytical reality and practice?", and the linguistic solution burst upon us.[32]

Linguistic issues being, for Cahen-Salabelle, secondary considerations to those who, as experts, commit themselves to bringing to another culture the shocking novelties of foreign thought, he adds,

> If Jung never prided himself on being a writer, we became translators only through the necessity to help to reveal a better knowledge of the human soul, to enable a deeper comprehension of the patients and of their unhappy and troubled consciousness ... the medical and social renovation promoted by modern medical psychology must triumph. These are the reasons that, it seemed to us, one must be daring, for the human psyche hardly tolerates vegetating.[33]

Cahen-Salabelle's expertise as a psychiatrist, as well as a psychologist and, finally, as a former Freudian, already enlightens the second question triggered by Paul Bishop, who writes:

> In response to Rascher's suggestion for a German version of *L'Homme à la découverte de son âme* [given its editorial success], Jung rejected this idea, on the basis that some of the material contained in this collection had already been published in German. Instead, Jung said he would rather consider publishing the "Basler Seminar", extracts from which had appeared in Cahen's anthology. (Bishop, 1998a, p. 272)

Crucial, here, is the fact that one of the main topics of the then unpublished "Basler Seminar" in Cahen-Salabelle's anthology is intuition.

Paul Bishop continues,

> Strangely enough, two years later in his letter to Rascher of 7 November 1949, Jung used the argument that, precisely because it had already appeared in *L'Homme à la découverte de son âme*, he had no intention of reworking the "Basler Seminar" and instead congratulated Cahen-Salabelle for having undertaken such a revision himself. (Bishop, 1998a, p. 272)

Cahen-Salabelle had reworked and revised (*"überarbeitet"*) the seminar given by Jung in 1934 at the French-speaking Swiss Société de Psychologie. Jung's congratulations were not faked, and his choice was wise for two reasons. Cahen-Salabelle was not, indeed, a translator in the modern interpretation of the term: that is, someone who cares for the text, the author, and the precision of the original language. He reworked a seminar—that is, notes which invite changes once written down, incorporating his personality and French culture.

As explained by Bishop, Jung expected much from the French book market. Entwined religious (the French *laïcité*) and politically historical (the French government of Vichy, which collaborated with the German Nazi government) reasons did (and continue to) militate against a proper spread of Jung's work in France. Yet, in the country of the *Méditations* of Descartes and of the Enlightenment, on the one hand, and of Henri Bergson, the French modern philosopher of intuition, on the other, the dichotomy opposing Reason (rationality) to Intuition (irrationality) is a central, because cultural, issue stemming, for example, from school manuals. Thus, there was no one better than Cahen-Salabelle to revise the Basler Seminar, except for Jung himself. The men simply met in a common and central (culturally for Cahen-Salabelle, psychologically for Jung) concern.

Cahen-Salabelle, like his French counterpart, Dr Yves Le Lay, the translator of both "Instinct and the unconscious" and *Psychological Types*, belonged to a generation and to a kind of translators favouring the language of reception. This traditional way of translating favours readability and *les belles lettres*. Their English counterpart was the poet Richard Hull, who took care of the translation of Jung's *Collected Works*. One difference distinguished the French from the English translators. Whereas, in Shamdasani's words, Hull was "an ardent rationalist" (Shamdasani, 2005, p. 50), both Le Lay and Cahen-Salabelle had chosen the *pro* intuition camp of their cultural background. This sensibility to intuition could give rise to other editorial penchants.

If a systematic comparison between the German, the English, and the French over intuition is a titanic enterprise, since the French does not possess a general index, one can examine some specific and revelatory passages. One French bias appears in *Psychological Types*, entry "Intuition", of the set earlier evoked. In the German original edition, Jung refers to Bergson by using a footnote to compare his psychology to Spinoza's. The footnote reads: *Ähnlich Bergson*, literally "similar to Bergson".[34] Le Lay's French translation reintegrates the footnote in the main body of the text by adding an entire sentence, which reads, "In modern philosophy, the same viewpoint is represented by Bergson (*dans la philosophie moderne, le même point de vue est représenté par Bergson*)" (Jung, 1950[1921] in French, p. 454). The English Baynes–Hull translation offers putting "and Bergson" in brackets in the main core of the text, thereby masking Jung's conspicuous mention, yet "rejection", of Bergson in a footnote (Jung, *CW 6*, par. 770). These are not details but approaches.

Let us come back, after this French detour, to the potential means that were sought to link the German and English *Collected Works*. Gerhard Adler never was appointed to check the translations. Shamdasani (2007) informs us that Adler "was also supposed to establish the equivalents for the German terminology" (p. 174). His work would have been of great value to researchers, to Jung's followers, and, perhaps, to Jung himself, through his involvement in the task. This episode echoes the correspondence between Rascher and Jung about the rewriting of "Definitions" in *Types*. Jung rightly estimated years of work when he declined the "re-engineering" of the set and accurately described his anxiety about underestimating "the full value of certain words".[35]

Adler and Jung would have been well advised, for example, to write down English equivalents for the German terms *Einfall* and *Anschauung*, both absent in the English *General Index* because directly untranslatable. Jung's use and apprehension of these two terms are equally hard to grasp. Yet, *Einfall* (Part II, section headed "Intuition from pathological *Einfälle* to general *Einfall*") and *Anschauung* (see all of Chapter Five) are the intuitive core of Jung's psychology of the under-conscious and of the unconscious, respectively, and, thereby, allow their understanding.

The several forms of intuition in Jung's work

A very simple German term, *Einfall* is easily graspable, as Jung noted in the 1935 Tavistock Lectures, given in English, thanks to etymology. *Ein* means "in" and *fall* "fallen". *Einfall* is also *plötzlich*, "sudden". Jung writes, "The Germans call this an *Einfall*, which means a thing which falls into your head from nowhere. Sometimes it is like a revelation . . . [a]ctually intuition is a very natural function" (Jung, *CW 18*, par. 26). Depending on the context of its use, the term *Einfall* and its plural *Einfälle* does not seem so straightforward. The entry *Einfall* in the *Gesamtregister* is divided into sub-entries referring to (1) *Kryptomnesie*, (2) *pathologische Einfälle*, and (3) *Einfallsmethode* "method of free association".[36]

Above all, these entries reveal the chronological evolution of the use of the notion in Jung's work. *Einfall* is a neutral term describing an incidence. If one considers that the "things that fall" essentially fall by repression, then one can use Freud's "method of free association" (number 3, above) in order to reveal them. If one considers that that which falls is a (1) "cryptomnesia", that is, a forgotten perception that none the less has been unconsciously registered, one then refers to Flournoy's coined term. If one uses the plural *pathologische Einfälle* (2), one refers to the *Eingebungen*, the "inspirations" or strange utterances of some patients, when they were asked, in psychiatric conditions, to react with the French "method of free association" (3). Jung's description of *Pathologische Einfälle* betokens his use of the term *Einfall* next to or for that of intuition in his psychology of consciousness, when the English translates it into "hunch", for instance.

Theoretically speaking, the *Einfall* is central to the under-conscious state, as it mechanically portrays in the simplest terms what happens there. On the one hand, something "happens", or falls; on the other hand, the state of receptiveness characteristic of the (Janetian and then) Jungian under-conscious permits that this thing, an uncontrolled automatism, happens. This structural basis is probably more relevant for Jung than the three other kinds of intuition to be found in this area—the intuitive faculty, the results of this intuitive faculty, and any kind of intuitive method using analogue—since all three kinds derive psychologically from the structure *Einfall*-under-conscious.

As a psychologist, Jung never denied any kind of intuitive gifts as soon as he could check the results (patients' *Vorahnungen* ("premonitions"), *Todesahnungen* ("presentiments of death"), precognitive dreams, visions) through experience and sometimes self-experience. His early focus of study on occult phenomena also displays a keen interest in the matter (see Part I, section headed "Experiencing intuition through spiritist séances" and all of Chapter Three). Any intuitive faculty, be it pathological, supernatural, or normal, passes through this under-conscious structure, which redirects intuition either to the unconscious, as we shall see, through the *Anschauung*, or to consciousness to become a proper intuition instead, for instance, of an under-conscious vision. Likewise, Jung's constructive method (Part IV, Chapter Seven, section headed "Intuition in the constructive method") and active imagination (Part IV, Chapter Seven, section headed "Intuition and active imagination") start with this non-obstructive quality of the structure and then use analogy between the personal of the patient and the collective of myth (see Part IV, Chapter Seven, section headed "A paradigm: Jaffé's *Mythosanschauung*") to be found in the unconscious. Analogy is not intuition itself, but it derives and is dependent from intuition. The constructive method is not intuition, but an intuitive method.

The term *Anschauung* is as hard to grasp as it is easy to grasp the term *Einfall*. *Einfall* is used in either common or scientific contexts, whereas *Anschauung* has been used for centuries in scientific, philosophical, aesthetical, poetic, or literary contexts (Part III, all of Chapter Eight) and is now nearly obsolete in common language. Jung is attached to this term due to the radical *schau*, from *schauen*, "to see".

Jung's hypothesis of a collective unconscious that encompasses the past and future of any space as well as the myths of any cultures is feasible only in early Jung through the "imaginal" nature of this unconscious.[37] However pleased with Pierre Benoit's novel *L'Atlantide* Jung was, for instance, he did not believe in the materiality of any lost kingdom under the waters. This imaginal nature of the collective unconscious is the psyche itself, which in Greek means the human "soul, mind, or spirit".

If the Atlantide never existed, the women who led the kingdom continue to impress unconsciously, and in the most patent and material ways, the French people just as Goethe's Mothers unconsciously impress the German-speaking people, for instance, or the Amazons impress everyone. All these feminine characters, whether real or not, and many others such as Eve, Sophia, Helen of Troy, Mary, Queen Elizabeth, and the French Marianne, are historical, mythical, religious, and cultural representations, or archetypes, of women, and also in 1921, the soul-images of men, their anima.[38]

This unconscious impression of the archetype on the present consciousness of humanity is allowed by the *Anschauung*, on the one hand, or the instinct on the other, or both together. Thanks to their *Anschauung*, human beings "see" the (collective) myth in order to live it with their own personal images in a situation which is theirs and which is psychologically needed. Sometimes, human beings directly "enact" the myth. In this case, it is directly their instinct that reaches the archetype, which is also "a pattern of behaviour".

Living the myth, for Jung, is as real as living any reality of consciousness. There is no "as if" or "like", such as in Freud, where humans live their Oedipus complex "as" Oedipus lived it. For Freud, Oedipus unconsciously wanted to kill his father to have sex with his mother. Freud's analysis precedes and precludes any personal experience of the myth by the patient. By contrast, Jung believes that any myth is reachable, reached, and directly experienced by *Anschauung*. Living the collective myth *personally* is what allows the patients' psychological progression.[39] Respect for the integrity of both the personal and the collective is permitted by intuition, *Anschauung*.

The difficulty with the term *Einfühlung* does not stem so much, as was the case with *Anschauung* and *Einfall*, from its absence in English as from its general polysemous use and from the polysemous use of *Einfühlung* in Jung's work itself. *Einfühlung* was translated into English by the word "empathy" for the first time in 1909 by the American psychologist, Edward Titchener, a student of one of the founding fathers of experimental psychology, the German Wilhelm Wundt (Titchener, 1910, pp. 21–22). It is less easy to determine who coined the original term *Einfühlung*. As Jung did in *Psychological Types*, so psychologist Gustav Jahoda traces the origin of the term in nineteenth-century Germany aesthetics without singling out a name (Jahoda, 2005, notably the Bibliography; Jung, CW 6, pars 484–504). Rather, he convincingly shows that empathy was of interest to many fields of research, not to mention the fact that nineteenth-century psychologists such as Wundt or William James were also philosophers. A generation later, Bergson as well as Janet and Flournoy (the three of whom strongly influenced Jung's psychology, as seen in Table 1), having received both a philosophical and a psychological education, were referred to as psychologists or philosophers.

Table 1. (Contexts) or forms of intuition integrated in Jung's early work.

	Main sources	Energy	Form	Function	Container	Natural process or method	Tools
Under-conscious	Kerner (*Gnostics Swedenborg du Prel Romantics*)	Faith	Clairvoyance, divine spark, visions, gnosis	*All-Sinn* (universal sense lost after the Fall)	*Grund, Weltseele* ("world soul")	Magnetic somnambulism, philosophical and theological interest	Magnetic passes, rapport, mystical ecstasies
	*Janet	Fixation (obsession)	*Idée fixe*, negative automatism	Passive apprehension	The subconscious	*Abaissement*, moral and scientific exorcism	Suggestion
	Flournoy (Hélène Smith)	Multiple personality	Glossolalia and faith	Mythopoetic function	The subliminal	Spiritist sessions, intellectual interest	Suggestion, ritual with "power word"
	(Miss Miller)	Variations and modalities of personality	Positive automatisms audio-visual hallucinations	Mythopoetic function	Waking dream, dream	Cenesthesia, creative imagination hypnagogia by rhythm	Instantaneous self-suggestion poetry, hypnagogic poetry
	(Myers) James	Mediumship, faith	The supranormal, the paranormal	Intuitive capacity, gift ...	The subliminal, the floating threshold	Psychical research	Observation, experiment
Unconscious	*Freud	Freudian libido	Everyday slips and parapraxes	Repression, the forgotten	Pre-conscious	*Einfallsmethode* ("association method")	Psychoanalysis
	(Bergson)	*Élan vital*	Highest form of knowledge	Instinct then intuition	*Durée créatrice* ("duration")	Intuitive method	Metapsychology, pragmatic philosophy
Conscious-ness	(Kant)	*Vernunft* (pure reason)/ *Verstand* (discursive reason)	*Intellectus Archetypus* (original)/ *Intellectus ectypus* (copy with images)	*Intellektual Intuition*	Unreachable *Ding an sich* (thing in itself)	*Anschauung*	
	Nietzsche	Genius/disease	Cosmological vision	*Ahnung* ("presentiment")	Aesthetics	*Philosophie des Kommenden* ("what is to come")	Human as the bridge (*Brücke*) to superhuman

*There are no "forms" of intuition in either Janet or Freud's works, but their methods or frames are part of Jung's early work.

History being of no help, let us turn to etymology again. Whereas *Einfall*, or "what falls into", describes only a movement, *Einfühlung* expresses "the act of *feeling* (oneself) into". Feeling and intuition are distinct in Jung's psychology of consciousness. There, Jung essentially uses the term *Einfühlung* to designate the basic function of feeling among the four vital functions of intuition, feeling, thinking, and sensation. Yet, three other areas of Jung's work differentiate between what belongs to *fühlen* and which is invariably of a feeling order and what belongs to *ein* and which is mixed with intuition. This differentiation is the key of successful transference between analyst and patient in the area of Jungian and post-Jungian practice.[40] This relationship, I refer to as empathy (2) in Table 3. More broadly, the relationship between a person and the Other, that is, a person to other persons, to the inner or outer world, I refer to as empathy (3). Empathy (3) is linked to Jung's late notion of synchronicity. Nevertheless, Jung had his first glimpses of synchronicity through his reading of the Confucian classic *Book of Changes*, or *I Ching*, in the late 1910s. Synchronicity will be dealt with here in Jung's area of metapsychology (Part VI) and within the realm of Jungian practice.[41] Empathy (1) appears in the unconscious, where Jung associates it with anthropologist Lévy-Bruhl's notion of *participation mystique*. In the almost undifferentiated "primitive" state of mind, objects and subjects are felt as identical. The *participation mystique* reveals the presence of analogy not, this time, as a tool implying an intuitive method, but more directly as an intuitive-analogue state. Before Jung read Lévy-Bruhl, Maria Moltzer and Emilii Medtner developed their ideas for the practical use of types (Part V, section headed "Genesis: *Psychological Types* and the Zürich Club").[42]

The final form of intuition, that which now properly carries the name "intuition", is intuition in consciousness, as in the final row of Table 2. There, all direct forms of intuition have been chronologically ranked from top to bottom. Table 2, the "Direct forms of intuition described in early Jung," is also informed by Table 1, the "[Contexts of] forms of intuition integrated in early Jung". In other words, Jung's 1921 definition of intuition in *Psychological Types* arises after years of research. These tables are guidelines and a simplification of a more elaborated picture. Their content will run throughout the entire book, but the two tables may already help to clarify intuition in Jung's early work and, in turn, Jung's early work itself.

Table 2. Direct forms of intuition described in Jung and post-Jungians.

		Main sources	Energy	Form	Function	Container	Natural process or method	Tools
Under-conscious		Zofingia Lectures		Precognitions, prophecies, double-sight...	Intuitive gift	Soul	Occult practices	Diverse
		MD dissertation Helene Preiswerk	Freudian libido and faith	Teleological hallucination, speaking in High German, embodiment of persons, mild gnosis and telepathy, "Ivenes" as future personality	Intuition (yet not extra-ordinary), cryptomnesia, repression	Conflicting polar sub-personalities	Puberty and physical factors linked to light hypnagogia, psychic contamination, spiritist sessions	Suggestion, self-induced trance, semi-somnambulism, mediumistic faculty, table turning
		Word Association Tests	Neurosis, psychosis	Pathological Einfälle (Eingebungen, "inspirations")	(Janetian) abaissement	Complexes	Word association tests in psychiatric context	(French) free association
		Psychology of the Unconscious (Processes)	Jungian libido	Symbols of transformation		Dominants, Urbild (primordial image)	Constructive method (amplification)	Anamnesis, analogy
		Red Book	Loss of myth, numinous	Jung's visions, precognitive dreams of WWI	Jung's intuition as introvert intuitive	Jung's dreams and fantasies	Writing down	Liber Primus
Unconscious				Symbol	Passive/active apprehension	Jung's fantasies	Active imagination Introversion/introversion of libido	Painting, mandalas of Liber Secundus
		Instinct and the Unconscious Zurich Club	Vital energy	Archetypes of Anschauung/(Instinct)	Anschauung (intuition, visual)	Collective unconscious	Natural compensation, analogy	
			Mana (later)	Empathy (1)	Sensation/intuition	The "primitive", the child		
Three states		Practice (Jungian and post-Jungian)	Attachment	Empathy (2)	Feeling/intuition	Patient/analyst	Transference/countertransference	Care
			Dao	Empathy (3)	Resonance	Cosmos	Synchronicity	I Ching
Consciousness		Psychological Types	Religious (transcendent) function	Thought, sensation, feeling	Intuition	Life	Individuation (for everybody), intuitive attitude (for intuitive type)	Natural i individuation or analytical psychology

Intuition in consciousness, therefore, becomes clear for Jung once his psychology of the unconscious is itself mastered by practice with empathy and by theory with the archetypes of *Anschauung* (the expression will be commented on in Part III, Chapter Five, section headed "The dependency of archetypes upon Jung's *Anschauung*"). Intuition in the unconscious, central in this area, was itself grasped by Jung thanks to his psychology of the under-conscious elaborated in earlier years. Most regrettably for the understanding of Jung's work, his psychologies of the unconscious and of consciousness were developed while his psychology of the under-conscious essentially remained implied in his later writings.

In consciousness, intuition is both a function and a type. Everybody shares the function. It starts with the *Anschauung* in the unconscious, crosses all kinds of intuitions in the under-conscious, and sometimes appears in consciousness in the form of a thought, a feeling, or a sensation. The type—that is, those persons whose general actions are above all guided by intuition—belong to it. Some of the intuitive types are introverted. Some are extraverted. By introversion, Jung means the psychological mechanism that introverts the libido and fills archetypes (or complexes).[43] Extraversion proposes the opposite mechanism. As a result, extraverted people favour the object while introverted people favour the subject. This opposition proves the most insuperable in the understanding of the other and strongly separates introverted from extraverted intuitive types, who are mysteries to one another in the way they function (see Part V, Chapter Eight, section headed "Specificities of introverted and extraverted intuitive types"). In terms of functions, intuition and sensation are opposed, yet similar. They are the two poles of the irrational functions, themselves opposed to the two polar rational functions of feeling and thinking.

Jung's single definition of intuition

The various forms of intuition introduced in the previous section guide the reading of Jung's entry "Intuition" of 1921. Table 3 will help analyse the main features described in Jung's definition:

> INTUITION (L. *Intueri*, 'to look at or into'). I regard intuition as a basic psychological *function*. It is the function that mediates perceptions in an *unconscious way*. Everything can be the focus of this perception, outer or inner objects, or their relationships. The peculiarity of intuition is

that it is neither sense perception, nor feeling, nor intellectual inference, although it may also appear in these forms. In intuition a content presents itself whole and complete, without our being able to explain or discover how this content came into existence. Intuition is a kind of instinctive apprehension, no matter of what contents. Like *sensation*, it is an *irrational* function of perception. As with sensation, its contents have the character of being "given," in contrast to the "derived" or "produced" character of *thinking* and *feeling* contents. Intuitive knowledge possesses an intrinsic certainty and conviction, which enabled Spinoza (and Bergson) to uphold the *scientia intuitiva* as the highest form of knowledge. Intuition shares this quality with *sensation*, whose certainty rests on its physical foundation. The certainty of intuition rests equally on a definite state of psychic "alertness" of whose origin the subject is unconscious.

Intuition may be *subjective* or *objective*: the first is a perception of unconscious psychic data originating in the subject, the second is a perception of data dependent on subliminal perceptions of the object and on the feelings and thoughts they evoke. We may also distinguish *concrete* and *abstract* forms of intuition, according to the degree of participation on the part of sensation. Concrete intuition mediates perceptions concerned with the actuality of things, abstract intuition mediates perceptions of ideational connections. Concrete intuition is a reactive process, since it responds directly to the given facts; abstract intuition, like abstract sensation, needs a certain element of direction, an act of the will, or an aim.

Like sensation, intuition is a characteristic of infantile and primitive psychology. It counterbalances the powerful sense impressions of the child and the primitive by mediating perceptions of mythological images, the precursors of *ideas*. It stands in a compensatory relationship to sensation and, like it, is the matrix out of which thinking and feeling develop as rational functions. Although intuition is an irrational function, many intuitions can afterwards be broken down into their component elements and their origin thus brought into harmony with the laws of reason.

Everyone whose general *attitude* is oriented by intuition belongs to the intuitive *type*.* Introverted and extraverted intuitives may be distinguished according to whether intuition is directed inwards, to the inner vision, or outwards, to action and achievement. In abnormal cases intuition is in large measure fused together with the contents of the *collective unconscious* and determined by them, and this may make the intuitive type appear extremely irrational and beyond comprehension.

*The credit for having discovered the existence of this type belongs to Miss M. Moltzer.[44]

Table 3. Synthesis of Jung's 1921 entry "intuition". *Source*: Jung, CW 6.*

	Form of intuition	Category of intuition	Keyword in Jung's entry
Jung's psychology of consciousness	• Function	One of the four basic psychological functions and types	• *irrational [1]* function, as sensation has the character of being "given", [not] "derived", "produced" of feeling and thinking, rational functions*
	• Type Extraverted Introverted		• *intuitive type, introverted . . . intuition directed inwards, extraverted . . . outwards* • *abnormal intuitive types are irrational [2]* and beyond comprehension*
	• Knowledge as that which secures the efficacy of the function		• *the "highest form of knowledge" for Bergson and Spinoza*
	• Intuitive function more or less mixed with other functions		• *concrete, abstract intuition*
Jung's psychology of the unconscious	• *Anschauung* (Instinct)	A biological and psychological link	• *mediates perceptions in an unconscious way* • *kind of instinctive apprehension*
	• Empathy (1) the "primitive" and the child		• *characteristic of primitive and infantile psychology*
Jungian practice	• Empathy (2) intuition in transference	A bond to the other	• *subjective or objective intuition, concrete and abstract intuition*

*Despite Jung's single definition of "irrational" as the following entry of the set after that of "intuition", it seems better here to differentiate between "irrational [1]", which means "immediate, without mediation", and "irrational [2]", which means "what is outside reason".

Jung does not display any feature of intuition in the under-conscious in his definition, even though I presented how vast this area was. Two vestiges remain where Jung evokes the extreme irrationality of some intuitive types and when he uses the term "subliminal", borrowed from Flournoy, who himself borrowed it from his teacher, F. W. H. Myers. It seems that, by 1921, Jung had integrated all that relates to intuition in the under-conscious and did not want to elaborate further on the topic. Rather, he might have wanted at that moment to use that knowledge in his practice or integrate it in his psychology of consciousness to describe the function of intuition, by far the most developed aspect of the definition (first paragraph), if not the more comprehensible compared to that, extremely clear, of the intuitive type in the last paragraph.

Jung's psychology of the unconscious is evoked only in the key first two sentences, which emphasise the role of link played by intuition there. The "unconscious way" (*Weg*) is that of the *Anschauung*. Also, it is important that the focus of intuition is "everything, outer or inner objets, or their *relationships*" (my italics). The German original also uses the term *Anschauen* for the English "inner vision" and, thereby, points to the inwardness of the unconscious. An entire paragraph, the third one, is dedicated to the description of what we named "empathy (1)", the *Einfühlung* in the unconscious.

The second paragraph is best understood if we place it in the context of Jungian practice, that which emphasises the role of bond to the other played by intuition in issues of transference and empathy (2).

CHAPTER TWO

Contexts of the birth of intuition in Jung's psychology

Spiritualism and science at the end of the nineteenth century

Jung's first work has been grouped as *The Zofingia Lectures*. Between 1896 and 1899, Jung gave five lectures at the student Zofingia Club of the University of Basel, a club that he had joined in 1895 while an undergraduate student. Jung's first two lectures—November 1896 on "The border zones of exact science" and May 1897 on "Some thoughts on psychology"—give an accurate picture of the contemporary conflict between science (which Jung took to be too narrow through being materialistic) and spiritualism, the novelty of which appealed the young scientist.[45]

Marie-Louise von Franz noticed Jung's coherence and sense of progress in his five lectures, which we can summarise as follows. The too restricted border zones of exact sciences (Lecture I) opened up the realm of the occult (Lecture II), the necessary independence of the researcher and the citizen (Lecture III), epistemology (Lecture IV), and the quest for meaning in religion (Lecture V).[46] The improvised superstructure of these three-year student lectures almost constitute the whole of Jung's work and life. Therefore, in the way they comprehend Jung's future, the *Zofingia Lectures* are strikingly, as well as unintentionally, prophetic in their progression.

Commenting on the orator's aim in her introduction, von Franz writes,

> The first lecture stops short ... and only opens the door for what he really wants to say in his second lecture. Thus the first lecture must be understood as a deliberate preparation of the way for showing what he had in mind [some thoughts on spiritist phenomena, the background for Jung's dissertation], which—he knew well—would be shocking for his audience. (Von Franz, 1983, p. xvii)[47]

Von Franz's term "shocking" needs contextualisation. The scientific study of spiritism was then common, as revealed, for instance, in the abundant medical literature quoted in Jung's dissertation.[48] Moreover, Basel was a cosmopolitan and bourgeois city, two favourable ingredients for developing spiritist circles.

Esotericist John Patrick Deveney explains both the "recurrent" meaning of Spiritualism and its historical context:

> In its most basic form, Spiritualism is simply the belief that living men can and do hold intercourse, usually through an intermediary, with 'spirits' of the dead. It is thus both a recurring possibility of human experience in all ages and a specific, historically defined phenomenon with roots in mid-19th century America. ... By 1855 the number of Spiritualists in the United States was estimated to be between 1 and 11 million people—in a country of only 28 million. (Deveney, 2006, pp. 1074–76)

The movement rapidly reached England and spread across European circles. Spiritualism's accessible eschatology seduced war-widowed Christians and Jews, whose beliefs had recently been shaken by the Enlightenment. The wide spread of the religious movement soon attracted the tenants of the new science of the psyche.[49] Shamdasani writes,

> At the end of the nineteenth century, many of the leading psychologists—Freud, Jung, Ferenczi, Bleuer, James, Myers, Janet, Bergson, Stanley Hall, Schrenck-Notzing, Moll, Dessoir, Richet, and Flournoy—frequented mediums. It is hard today to imagine that some of the most crucial questions of the "new" psychology were played out in the séance, nor how such men could have been so fascinated by the spirits. What took place in the séances enthralled the leading minds of the time, and had a crucial bearing on many of the most significant aspects of twentieth-century psychology, linguistics, philosophy,

psychoanalysis, literature, and painting, not to mention psychical research. (Shamdasani (1994) introducing the new translation of Flournoy (1994)[1899])

Curiously enough, those aspects rarely were applied to the study of religion. The psychologists had a prior technical interest. By making contact with spirits, mediums, in fact, accessed the unconscious.

On the other hand, that which Jung described as conservative portrayed not only the possible mentality of his fellow students, but referred to the state of science and, in his field, to the late nineteenth-century scientific ideal of Emil DuBois-Reymond, the leading advocate for a purely mechanistic psychology (Hogenson, 2012, p. 258).[50] As Eugene Taylor explains,

> The issue at hand for Jung was why the medical literature on psychiatry focused almost exclusively on diagnostic categories of mental illness, evolving a classification scheme that did not even resemble the diagnostic categories of general medicine, while at the same time the psychiatric literature reflected the general orientation of reductionistic science, in which the whole of personality was understood exclusively through the rational ordering of sense data alone. (Taylor, 2012)

Jung's critique pointed towards Wilhelm Wundt's shift in the history of psychology from metaphysical psychology to "physiological psychology" (Shamdasani, 2003, p. 32).[51] Wundt's model copied that of natural science, yet included experimentation with observation. Only experimentation could analyse the dynamic process of the psyche.[52] Thus, in these early years, according to Taylor, Jung already wished to expand psychiatry towards psychology to find a "language that would express the dynamic aspects of human consciousness in all their vagaries, from the psychopathic to the transcendent" (Taylor, 2012) to immateriality.

As two examples of the innovative study of the "immaterial", Jung mentions Kant's *Dream of a Seer-Spirit* and "the triumphal entry of hypnotism into the domain of German science". (Jung, CW A, par. 63) Part II, Chapter Three, section headed "Jung versus Kant and Ritschl on intuition and epistemology" will examine Jung's reading of Kant through Karl Du Prel's pre-critical analysis.[53] Let us first clarify what Jung could have had in mind when he evoked the scientific study of the immaterial. Treitel's table (Table 4) allows a first contextualisation.

Table 4. A timeline of important dates related to the early German occult movement. *Source*: Treitel, 2004, pp. 32–33.

Date	German publications	German events	Publications and events outside Germany
1779			F. A. Mesmer, *Memoir on the Discovery of Animal Magnetism* (Fr.)
1781	I. Kant, *Critique of Pure Reason*		
1816		Prussian state creates university chairs of animal magnetism (Berlin, Bonn)	
1829	J. Kerner, *The Seeress of Prevorst*		
1843			J. Braid coins *hypnotism* (UK)
1845	K. von Reichenbach, *Researches on Magnetism and Related Topics*		
1851	A. Schopenhauer, *Essay on Spirit Seeing*		
1853		Table-turning craze begins in Bremen	
1855	L. Büchner, *Force and Matter*		
1860	G. T. Fechner, *Elements of Psychophysics*		
1868	*Spiritualism Library for Germany*, Ed. G. K. Wittig		
1869	E. von Hartmann, *Philosophy of the Unconscious*		
1874	*Psychische Studien* founded		W. James founds first experimental psychology laboratory at Harvard
1877		K. F. Zöllner investigates Slade	
1878			J.-M. Charcot begins using hypnosis at the Salpêtrière (Fr.)

(continued)

Table 4. (continued).

Date	German publications	German events	Publications and events outside Germany
1879		W. Wundt founds Germany's first institute for experimental psychology in Leipzig	
1882			L' Académie des Sciences accepts Charcot's paper linking hypnosis to hysteria (Fr.)
			Society for Psychical Research founded (UK)
1884	E. von Hartmann, *Spiritualism*	Theosophische Societät Germania founded in Elberfeld	
1885			W. James begins experiments with the medium Leonora Piper (US)
1886	*Sphinx* founded	Psychologische Gesellschaft founded in Munich	Seybert Commmission report lambasts spiritualism (US)
			Nancy School of Psychiatry emerges under H. Bernheim (Fr.)
1889	C. Du Prel, *Philosophy of Mysticism*	Gesellschaft für Experimental psychologie in Berlin	
		M. Dessoir coins *parapsychology*	
1890	A. Aksakov, *Animism and Spiritism*		W. James, *Principles of Psychology*
1896	*Metapsychische Rundschau* replaces *Sphinx*		
1899			S. Freud, *Interpretation of Dreams* (Austria)
			T. Flournoy, *From India to the Planet Mars* (Sw.)
1902			C. G. Jung, *On the Psychology and Pathology of so-called Occult Phenomena* (Sw.)

Although not exhaustive, Treitel's table gives a first historical background that partly explains Jung's words. When Jung mentioned the triumphal "entry" of hypnotism in Germany, he must, therefore, have been aware of its use in other countries as well. William James had indeed founded the first experimental psychology laboratory, where he had experimented with the medium Leonora Piper. Jean-Martin Charcot had used hypnosis at the Salpêtrière hospital in Paris. The psychological publications of K. von Reichenbach, *Researches on Magnetism and Related Topics* and *Psychische Studien*, also imply the same use of hypnotism.

Familiar with the various geographical offsprings of the method, Jung also knew its history from the Marques of Puységur, himself a disciple of Mesmer's animal magnetism, to its then recent European and American extension.[54] "From 1784 to about 1880", writes historian Ellenberger (1970, p. 112), "artificial somnambulism was the chief method of gaining access into the unconscious mind. First called the perfect crisis by Puységur, magnetic sleep, or artificial somnambulism, was given the name of hypnotism by Braid in 1843". Pytlik writes, *"Es war seine [Mesmers] Schüler und Mitarbeiter Graf Puységur, der seine Aufmerksamkeit auf die somnambulen Zustände richtete"* ("It was his student and assistant, the count of Puységur, who directed his [Mesmer's] attention to the somnambulic states" (Pytlik, 2005, p. 30).

Problematically, if Treitel's table gives a picture of the most advanced and prestigious researches, it does not display that which caused the tenants of the mainstream "conservative materialist" science to be rebuked by the study of the immaterial, which is belief on the one hand (the belief in spirits, for instance) and swindle (of so-called mediums, of stage hypnotists, etc.) on the other. Before the end of the century in Europe, these two factors were also to provoke an unbridgeable gap between some of the scientists of the immaterial themselves and their own subjects.

If mediums were the centre of attention of scientific psychology, only a few psychologists believed in spirits at the end of the nineteenth century. Despite this fact, spiritists were invited to submit papers to the first International Congresses of Psychology. These congresses, the first of which had been organised in Paris in August 1889, gathered an incredible number of luminaries. Their reports constitute the work of the founding Fathers of the discipline. That same year, 1896, when Jung gave the lecture, the Third International Congress of

Psychology had taken place in Munich in early August, where no fewer than five hundred participants had attended. Ellenberger describes the event:

> One hundred and seventy-six papers were read in four languages (German, Spanish, English, and Italian). Among the participants were the best-known philosophers, psychiatrists, and psychologists of that time. Many of the papers were of high quality, and a few of them remain of particular interest in retrospect. . . . The number, variety, and originality of the contributions must have given the participants the feeling that psychology was on the verge of a breakthrough. (Ellenberger, 1970, p. 774)

The participants were divided into sections. One of them held the spiritists; another gathered the "telepaths promoting hypnotism" (Armand, 1896, p. 428, translated for this edition). Hypnotism was indeed triumphant.

Yet, four years later, in 1900, the Fourth International Congress of Psychology took place in Paris, as well as other congresses of importance, among them the International Congress for Medicine, which attracted eight thousand participants, and the Second International Congress of Hypnotism (see Ellenberger, 1970, pp. 779–780 for a general description). As physicians and scientists, most of the psychologists attended all three congresses. In four years of political and social instability in Europe, conservative values had regained the foreground of research and Spiritualism was soon to be abandoned as an object of study.

Although the Fourth International Congress of Psychology gave rise to many excellent papers, the tensions between materialistic science and the scientific study of the immaterial created irreparable divisions, which came down in favour of the former despite the attempts of the latter to remain scientific by dissociating themselves from the belief of their subjects.

Henri Piéron enumerates the personalities present during the congress: "Baldwin, William James, Morton Prince, Munsterberg . . . Stanley Hall, Titchener . . . Théodule Ribot, Charles Richet, Pierre Janet . . . Oskar Vogt . . . Claparède . . . Bergson . . . Théodore Flournoy . . . Hyppolyte Bernheim" (Piéron, 1954, pp. 400–401). The list was so long that Piéron, albeit French, even omitted Jules Séglas, Auguste

Forel, Binet, Gabriel Tarde, the French poet and essayist François René Sully Prudhomme, and F. W. Myers and Wilhelm Wundt.

To the disadvantage of the spiritualists, Frederick Myers and Henry Sidgwick, the co-founders of the Society for Psychical Research in London, were both invited, but only Myers came. Sidgwick died eight days after the opening of the congress on 28 August 1900. Myers died the following year.

In his report of the key events and papers, Piéron writes,

> Théodore Flournoy, *à propos* his beautiful analysis of the so-called "Martian" language of the medium Hélène Smith, was asked to talk with tact of spiritism in one of the general sessions, but, during a section presided over by Professor Bernheim from Nancy, entitled "Hypnotism, suggestion and closely related questions [*"questions connexes"*], some too convinced spiritists intervened and provoked strong reactions: Ebbinghaus declared himself "scandalised" and Oskar Vogt instigated a vigorous protest "against spiritism". (Piéron, 1954, p. 401, translated for this edition)[55]

Oskar Vogt's career as a physician and neurologist typically fits the scheme of a reasonable interest in the study of the immaterial followed by a definitive shift to materialism. Having conceived and used the method of "partial hypnosis" until 1903, Vogt cannot be dismissed as a purely materialist scientist.[56] Yet, in 1914, he created the Kaiser Wilhelm Institute for Brain Research, the future Max Planck Institute for Brain Research. The two earlier papers given by Vogt during the congress, "La psychologie du sentiment" and "L'anatomie du cerveau et la psychologie", testify to his contemporary interest in both immaterial psychology and materialism.

Animosity grew between the camps during the congress. One of the participants, Félix Krüger, reports Piéron, would keep vivid memories from the event and describe it some thirty-six years later as a *"vielstimmige Harmonie"*, a "polyphonic harmony" (Piéron, 1954, p. 401). Both Krüger and Piéron write with understatement. Piéron's qualification of Flournoy's "tact" towards the spiritists is debatable in view of the following extract from his paper. Flournoy writes of spiritist studies,

> studies which are so compromising, as everybody knows, that one only talks of them in veiled terms, and that a self-respecting Congress

like ours, when it does not manage to close its door completely to them, conceals them cautiously under the ingenious section of *Closely related questions* ["*Questions connexes*"]. Nobody admires the delicate art of keeping up appearances more than me. But since this is between us, you will forgive me for calling a spade a spade and for admitting that under the closely related questions actually lurk spiritism, occultism, and other *bêtes noires* of contemporary scientific psychology. (Flournoy, 1900, pp. 102–103, translated for this edition)[57]

"Bête noire" is not exactly tactful, and neither is the act of closing one's door to someone. In return, these sentiments must have closed the doors of spiritist circles to many psychologists. However, we see clearly how Flournoy's paper is a survival reaction, reflecting a determination to keep the study of the immaterial within the scientific field.[58]

If Flournoy's research with mediums had reached its climax thanks to the creativity of Hélène Smith, one short article published some six years later in Flournoy's journal *Les Archives de Psychologie* by a certain Miss Miller would attract Jung to Flournoy's research for a second time.[59] In Europe, science had left Spiritualism. The science of the spiritual had not said its last word.

Jung's teachers: Bleuler, Janet, Freud, Flournoy

In the Editor's prefatory note to my article, it is stated that I started from the teachings of Freud. I did not start from Freud, but from Eugen Bleuler and Pierre Janet, who were my immediate teachers. When I took up the cudgels for Freud in public, I already had a scientific position that was widely known on account of my association experiments, conducted independently of Freud, and the theory of complexes based upon them. My collaboration [with Freud] was qualified by an objection in principle to the sexual theory, and it lasted up to the time when Freud identified in principle his sexual theory with his method. (Jung, *CW 10*, par. 1034*n*)

Jung made this readjustment after a "Freudocentric" view of his career in 1934. Some prejudices die hard and, despite the advancement of historical research, such statements are still worth mentioning today. (For a critical review of this research, see Monahan, 2009.) These declarations need to be detailed not only concerning Freud's role, but also Bleuler's and Janet's. Théodore Flournoy is not mentioned. Indeed, he was never Jung's official teacher. Yet, among the four huge personalities who helped the early Jung grow, he is arguably the one from whom Jung learnt the most (see Shamdasani (1994) introducing Flournoy (1994)[1899] translation; Witzig, 1982). The work of the philosophers Henri Bergson and William James, also decisive for Jung, will be discussed in connection with specific issues.

In December 1900, Jung had not yet written his medical dissertation but had already left the University of Basel to begin work at the Burghölzli psychiatric clinic near Zürich, where he had been appointed assistant physician by its director, Eugen Bleuler, who also held the chair of psychiatry at the university. There, Jung's denunciation in the Zofingia Lectures of the rationalist diagnostics currently applied in psychiatry found its first resonances in the goals and methods of his superior.

Just as Jung, in his student lecture, had attacked the materialism of "Papa DuBois Reymond" in Berlin, so Bleuler, through his work, opposed Emil Kraepelin, who, "from the beginning, had strongly emphasised a somatic/biologic etiology of mental disorders and strongly de-emphasized possible social or psychological causes" (Roelcke, 1997, p. 383). Kraepelin was—and remained—famous for his concepts of diagnostic categories, derived from the *Zählkarten* (literally "census cards") that he used for each of his patients to briefly describe their symptoms (see Kraepelin, 1987; also Weber & Engstrom, 1997). Moskowitz and Heim portray how different Bleuler's methods seem to have been from those of Kraepelin:

> Bleuler was motivated to become a psychiatrist because of the frustration the local people of his Canton in Switzerland felt towards the foreign (primarily German) doctors, who could not understand their dialect and were unfamiliar with the local culture.... [H]is elder sister was hospitalised at Burghölzli when he was a teenager (and remained chronically ill throughout her life, living with Bleuler and his family for most of her later years). Bleuler ... thought he could do his best by spending as much time as possible with [his patients] and taking copious notes on their speech and behaviour. (Moskowitz & Heim, 2011, p. 473)

This method had its drawbacks. Bleuler was as demanding with his employees as he was with himself. Just like Jung, Karl Abraham,

Franz Riklin, Max Eitingon, and Hermann Nunberg had to spend all their time with the patients and be aware of the most recent state of the art research in the fields of psychopathology and psychology. Emma Jung, Jung's wife since 1903, soon became his secretary when the couple moved into a flat in the building of the Burghölzli (McGuire, 1988[1974], p. xvi).

Soon after the release of Freud's *The Interpretation of Dreams* (1900a), Bleuler asked Jung to review it and present it at the clinic. Bleuler himself had already authored a favourable review of Breuer and Freud's *Studies on Hysteria* (1896d), declaring it "one of the most important recent publications in the field of normal and pathological psychology", which calls to mind Falzeder, for whom "Bleuler's support for Freud can hardly be overestimated. He was indeed the first university professor to endorse Freud's views" (Falzeder & Beebe, 2007, pp. 344–345). Falzeder continues, "It seems safe to say that Bleuler's interest [in Freud] was mainly a scientific and practical one: a wish to understand his psychotic patients better, to find meaning in their hallucinations, delusions, and other symptoms" (p. 345).[60]

"Normal" is key here. Freud, Bleuler, and Jung were interested in (normal) people. Their patients were people with diseases and were not just pathological cases. This view was very modern when compared with the "diagnostic cards" of the German school, on the one hand, and with Janet's "figure cases" in Paris, on the other. Known for his integrity and humanity, Janet was also the physician able to name the sub-personalities of his first patients "Lucie 2", "Léonie 3", or elect a first name of *his* choice, sometimes against their will (Janet, 1886, pp. 318, 320, 330, 1889, p. 589).[61] Rather than subjects of science, Janet's patients appeared as objects, which were labelled.[62]

If, unlike Bleuler, Jung had not perceived the significance of Freud's *The Interpretation of Dreams* immediately, he later provided Freud with examples for the reprinting of his *Psychology of Everyday Life* in 1907 (Freud, 1901b). In his review of the enlarged edition, Jung praised Freud for his clarity and ability to provide lay persons with an understanding of complex psychological processes (Jung, *CW 18*, par. 906) Clarity was highly valued by Jung. As we shall see, he acclaimed Henri Bergson, William James, and Théodore Flournoy for having that same quality. In these early years of his career, Jung reviewed the work of his peers. From what is published, it is possible to comment on the fact that clarity was always a leading criterion for him (Jung, *CW 18*, pars 884–921). There is no doubt that Jung, through Bleuler, had found in Freud the strongest ally he would ever find in going beyond the pathological, one of Jung's highest goals.

The reverse also proved true. Through Bleuler—or rather, in collaboration with him, but we must not forget that Bleuler was Jung's superior—Jung would early recognise in Freud an enmity to some of his other ideas.[63] When Jung writes that his collaboration with Freud "lasted up to the time when Freud identified in principle his sexual theory with his method", he summarised a situation for the sake of a short reply. Central points of Freud's theory did not systematically fit Jung's experience at the Burghölzli, among them that of repression.

If Jung and Bleuler disagreed on the possible aetiology of schizophrenia—a vexed question still today—neither could possibly accept an explanation (repression) that was not consistently observed in their dealings with the patients. Moreover, as we shall see, theories opposed to those of Freud's existed in France, which seemed to have more to offer to Bleuler and to Jung's experiments in word association than Freud's theories. Moskowitz writes,

> Pruyser (1975) notes that Bleuler's 'splitting,' as well as Breuer's 'hypnoid states' and Janet's 'dissociation' (but not Freud's 'repression') 'just happens . . . without a causative agent' (p. 28) and concludes that Bleuler's term was closer to dissociation than repression. In addition, except for a brief period during his association with Breuer, Freud was distinctly uncomfortable (i.e. Breuer and Freud, 1895) with the notion that consciousness *itself*, as opposed to the contents of consciousness, could be split (Pruyser, 1975). (Moskowitz, Schäfer, & Dorahy, 2009, pp. 45–46)

In short, in the war opposing the dissociationists—born out of the philo-psychological collaboration in France—and the associationists (notably the German School, but also Freud), Bleuler leaned towards the first camp. For associationists, what could be structural was the disease, but symptoms occurred one after the other, sometimes repeating themselves, within a single psyche. Nosologies were established by associationists, such as Kraepelin. For dissociationists, in contrast, what was structural was that no one had a single self. Dissociationism encompassed not only Janet and all the French psychopathologists, but also Bergson, Myers, and Flournoy, for all of whom dissociation was the basis of their work, whether approached positively or negatively.[64] Jung, during all the time that he spent at the Burghölzli, navigated between the poles. His ties to both Bleuler and Freud might not be at odds with this fact.

Chronologically, the second figure next to that of Freud who influenced Jung was Myers' disciple—and friend of William James—Théodore Flournoy. Founder of the Chair of Psychology at the University of Geneva, Flournoy was first a student of Wundt in Leipzig, yet never practised medicine. He was devoted to teaching. Philosophy was as central as psychology for him. In a letter to James, examined by Witzig, Flournoy reveals how he happily neglected his experimental academic laboratory—thereby left at the disposition of his cousin and associate Édouard Claparède—to investigate mediums (Witzig, 1982, p. 132). Jung proposed to Flournoy that he should translate into German his highly praised 1899 *Des Indes à la planète Mars: Étude sur un cas de somnambulisme avec glossolalie*, where Flournoy had observed the trances of the medium Elise Muller, self re-baptised Hélène (Smith) after the first name of Flournoy's daughter. At that time of Flournoy's fame, Freud was not recognised at all. Jung had discovered Flournoy by himself. In contrast, he had been invited to read Freud by his superior.

The translation by Jung did not happen. Instead, Jung, who had recorded the trances of his cousin, medium Helene Preiswerk, during his undergraduate years, would use the protocols of the spiritist séances as a basis for his medical dissertation, *On the Psychology and Pathology of so-called Occult Phenomena: A Psychiatric Study*.[65] His methodology would also follow that of Flournoy. Jung was grateful to his Genevan "fatherly friend" in many respects and without reservation. Jung writes,

> With [Flournoy] I could really discuss all the problems that scientifically occupied me—for example, on somnambulism, on parapsychology, and the psychology of religion. I had no one else who shared my interests in these matters. Flournoy's views lay completely in my line and gave me many a suggestion. His concept of the "imagination créatrice," which particularly interested me, was an idea I adopted from him. I learned a great deal from him—above all the way and manner to consider [*betrachten*] a patient, the loving absorption [*Vertiefung*] in its history. This was how I borrowed one of his cases, namely that of Miss Miller in *Transformations and Symbols of the Libido* (1912), and subjected it to careful analysis.[66]

Witzig, who called Flournoy *vis-à-vis* Jung "a friend indeed", reminds us all what Jung owed to him (Witzig, 1982, p. 131). Not only did Flournoy allow Jung's psychiatric study of spiritualism, offering him a canvas for his dissertation, but also he provided Jung with Miller's fantasies, the origin of Jung's *Psychology of the Unconscious* (1917a), with techniques to enter and interpret the under-conscious, that is, Jung's future active imagination, the method that he used in the *Red Book, Liber secundus*, and, above all, with some means to deal properly with the relationship with the patient! The very question seems to be whether Jung needed any other teacher than Flournoy. Had Flournoy agreed to Jung's proposal of translation—lost among letters of many other translators and publishers in the wake of the book's success—Jung's career might have not taken so many theoretical detours, through Bleuler, Freud, and Janet.

Jung became directly acquainted with the French psychopathologists in the winter semester of 1902–1903, which he spent in Paris following Janet's lectures, *Les émotions et les oscillations du niveau mental*, at the Collège de France (Janet, 2004, pp. 37–40 for his summary in French). Pierre Janet was first educated as a philosopher. He was a student, like Bergson, of the Parisian Ecole Normale Supérieure. His 1889 *L'automatisme psychologique* was his philosophical doctoral thesis. Janet was in constant contact with philosophy thanks to his close friendship with Bergson. Bergson notably enabled Janet to meet and work with Jean-Martin Charcot, the founder of the French School of the psychopathologists located in the Parisian hospital of La Salpêtrière. Two of Charcot's other famous pupils were Freud and Alfred Binet, both of whom influenced Jung. While Jung appreciated Binet, he was not impressed by Janet as a person.

1902 proved important for both Janet and Binet. At stake was their rival applications for the prestigious Chair of "*psychologie expérimentale et comparée*" at the Collège de France previously occupied, and for the first time, by Théodule Ribot. Serge Nicolas informs us,

> During the election in 1902, Binet did not succeed in dethroning Janet because Janet had the determining support of his reporter Henri Bergson (1859–1941). Bergson accepted the idea of a pathological psychology [like Janet's] because it did not go against his philosophical convictions, but he certainly could not reconcile himself to supporting an experimental laboratory of psychology [like Binet's]. (Nicolas, 2004, p. 5, translated for this edition)

Bergson declares, indeed, "that which characterises French scientific psychology is that it essentially relies on pathology, whereas German psychology is more interested in laboratory researches and in mensurations on normal personalities" (Bergson, 1910, p. 347, translated for this edition).[67] Bergson wrote these words with the benefit of hindsight, in 1910. Whoever in Germany practised these methods—they were numerous, as we shall see—Jung in Switzerland with his word association tests belonged to this category, as did Binet in France. It is precisely in the non-pathological arena that the two scientists met.

If we examine Jung's early work, Janet probably offered more to Jung than Binet. Yet, Nicolas does mention Bergson and Janet's closeness. The fact that they were *élevés dans le serail*, that they both belonged to the very private club of the Ecole Normale Supérieure, is of major importance as it allowed Janet to obtain a prestigious position.

In 1907, Jung went to Paris for the second time. His career was then established, and he wished to meet Janet in person. Freud was well aware of Janet's potential to convince Jung and was apprehensive about the encounter. He had brilliantly summarised the situation in a letter to Jung on 14 June 1907, before his departure, by naming Jung's two competing complexes the "Vienna complex" and the "Paris complex" (McGuire, 1988[1974], p. 65). In his reply to Freud on 28 June 1907, Jung explained how disappointed he had been by Janet:

> My experience of the trip was *pauvre*. I had a talk with Janet and was very disappointed. He has only the most primitive knowledge of Dem pr. Of the latest happenings, including you, he understands nothing at all. He is stuck in his groove and is, be it said in passing, merely an intellectual but not a personality, a hollow *causeur* and a typical mediocre bourgeois. . . . It got on my nerves so much that I gave up the idea of going to London, where far, far less is to be expected. Instead, I devoted myself to the castle of the Loire. No question of a Paris complex. (McGuire, 1988[1974], p. 67)

I do not believe that Jung was lying in order to please Freud in this letter—something that Jung did frequently.[68] I also think that what he presents "in passing" was important for him. With a single *causeur* talk in French (Jung was fluent in French, yet did not practise it in Zürich[69]), Janet succeeded in relegating France to a venue for tourism and closed forever any further relationship with Jungian psychology.

Experiencing intuition through spiritist séances and Liber Novus

To understand the following extract, we must picture Jung, then twenty-one and nicknamed "Walze" (Jung's nickname is mentioned in Shamdasani, 2005, p. 87), and his fellows gathered around a table, each touching with a finger an upturned and moving glass and trying not to touch the letters of the alphabet displayed on that same table. Those are the first sentences of the *Protokoll der Sitzung in Walzes Wohnung am 19 Marz 1897 91/2 Uhr Vormistags*, the "protocols of the [spiritist] séances in Walze's place 19 March 1897, 9.30 a.m." handwritten by Jung/Walze in a notebook:

> *Das Glas will viel bewegen. Fex fragt: 'Welche Person hinderlich?' Das Glas bewegt sich gegen Stegel hin. Dieser entfernt hierauf seine Fingerspitzen vom Glas. Nur beginnt das Glas sich nach zu bewegen und berührt der Reihe nach die Buchstaben zu dem Satze: sich ganz ruhig halten (d. h.: nachdem der Buchstabe erschienen war, schlossen die Teilnehmer die Augen, nur Stengel beobachtete die Wege, die das Glas beschrieb.*

> The glass moves a lot. Fex asks: 'Who is hindering?' <u>The glass moves back close to Stengel</u>. Stengel then removes his fingers from the glass. Only after that the glass begins to move and touch the letters in turn to [form] the sentence: <u>keep totally steady and calm</u> (that is, after the letter had been chosen, the participants closed their eyes; only Stengel observed that which the glass spelled out).[70]

Undoubtedly, Jung was involved in his researches. Two months after this spiritist experience, he gave his second lecture at the Zofingia Club on experimental psychology and Spiritualism with enthusiasm. Who would not be enthusiastic? When experienced for the first time, seeing a glass move by itself on a table, touching letters one by one to form a sentence, would seem amazing to anyone. Jung wrote these notes. He was not lying. The protocols of that session might not describe Jung's first ever session, but soon enough he must have found it useful to take notes. Only three days afterwards, at the same place and at the same time, Kneipp, Walze, Fex, Icarus, Joseph, and, this time, Bebbi and Elsi tried once more to contact "spirits". All wanted to repeat the experience except for Stengel, who was not present.

These first two minutes exactly constitute what Jung describes in the *Zofingia Lectures* as the scientific experimentation with unlimited borders regarding the object of study.[71] The precision of the report testifies to Jung's scientific method. Everybody respects the protocol of any spiritist session. Questions are posed to a "spirit" (*Geist*), that is, the spirit of a dead person, who answers through one of two means: the "letters" (*Buchstaben*) to produce words and sentences, or the "three-legged table" (*Tisch mit drei Füssen*) to obtain yes's or no's.[72] Jung/Walze, indeed, understood from the "spirit" that when the table tilted twice after a question, that meant "yes", whereas thrice meant "no".[73] Another medium was used during the second séance, that of the "water basin" (*Wasserbecken*).[74]

Sessions I and II described first gatherings as the participants sought not only for the right procedure to follow, but also for the "spirit"'s identity. During the second session, the "spirit" answered "NIUGGK" ("es ist K. G. Jung" [C. G. Jung's grandfather]) when directly asked about its name. A first succession of letters, somehow similar to the series "NIUGGK", that of "SQJJGRB", had appeared during the first session and might have led the participants to this interpretation:

> Es würden zwei weitere Fragen gestellt, blieben aber unbeantwortet. Das Glas berührte die Buchstaben <u>SQJJGRB</u>. Die Teilnehmer stellten keine weitere Frage mehr. Waltze wundert sich, dass kein befriedigende Resultat herausgekommen war. Darauf began das Glas sich zu bewegen [and indicated with the letters that it needed a stronger medium, hence the resort, in the second session, to the water basin].

> Two more questions were posed, but remained unanswered. The glass touched the letters <u>SQJJGRB</u>. The participants did not pose any more questions. Walze was surprised that no satisfactory result had come out. Then [or, consequently] the glass started to move [and indicated with the letters that it needed a stronger medium, hence the resort, in the second session, to the water basin].[75]

From the three-legged table to the water basin, this extract reveals the learning-through-experience of the participants. All of them had some knowledge of spiritist sessions, yet nobody knew beforehand what would ensue. When Jung was disappointed, surprised at the bad result, he did not do anything to change fate but merely reported that he was disappointed.

Jung's rigorous scientific integrity belonged to a larger phenomenon, clearly perceptible as early as the second session, when the group passed from the letters "NIUGGK" to the interpretation "es ist K. G. Jung", that of *folie à plusieurs*. Describing the problem in the wider context of psychiatry and psychiatric history in general, Borch-Jacobsen explains its components:

> [T]heir [psychiatrists and therapists] intervention is part of the 'etiological equation' of the syndromes that they claim to observe from the outside. [As well as the historians of psychiatry] they must, if they want to remain faithful to their improbable 'object,' study the complex interactions from which those syndromes and those theories emerge, somewhere between the doctors, the patients and the society that surrounds them. In short, they must study the *making* of psychiatric history, and understand that they participate in it. (Borch-Jacobsen, 2001, p. 19)

In our situation, the spirit of Jung's grandfather is clearly an improbable object of study. It is born out of the prevailing society, since spiritist sessions were then *à la mode*. It is also the construction of a group of students, the result of their interaction. Finally, and this is where the minutes are such valuable testimonies, this object is in the making. In session I, the spirit does not exist. In session II, it is produced.

The second of the *Zofingia Lectures* in May 1897, introducing empirical psychology, reveals how this experience had made Jung confident about spiritist phenomena:

> In the second part of my talk, which deals with empirical psychology, I will supply documentary evidence [on Spiritist literature] which should satisfy those many people who were not entirely happy with the theoretical reflections in the first part [Rational Psychology]. On the other hand, this same factual evidence will put off many who were, in principle, satisfied with the theoretical exposition [of the immortality of the soul] in Part One. (Jung, CW A, par. 112)

We do not possess the minutes of Session III, yet those of Session IV, on 18 August 1897, reveal that Jung's enthusiasm and involvement grew with the appearance of another, stronger medium, his cousin, Helene Preiswerk.

So far, the participants had essentially enquired about issues of a physical order to establish the spirit's ability: for instance, to know what time it was, or the place where some person, not present, found himself (an answer to be checked afterwards).[76] The presence of Helene Preiswerk and that of Jung's mother in Session IV transformed what could be qualified as spiritist experimentations to a specific kind of religious Spiritualism. Here were the first three questions and answers of the session:

> 1 Frage: Was hältst du von der Sünde?
>
> Antwort: Sie ist das Verderben der Menschen „schon Anfangs gewesen".
>
> 2 Frage: Ist die Stelle F. Moses 18, 11 gegen den Spiritismus gerichtet?
>
> Antwort: Nein.
>
> 3 Frage: Hat diese Stellebedeutung für uns?
>
> Antwort: Sie geht euch gar nichts an.

Question 1: What is your opinion on sin?

Answer: It has been the bane of Humankind "since the Beginning."

Question 2: Is Deutoronomy 18,11 [Don't let anyone try to control others with magic, and don't let them be mediums or try to talk with the spirits of dead people] directed against spiritism?

Answer: No.

Question 3: Does this signify anything for us?

Answer: It has nothing to do with you.[77]

Questions now were addressed to the spirit of the grandfather of the medium, Samuel Preiswerk, Jung and Helly's grandfather. Comparing Jung's two grandfathers, Gerhard Wehr writes,

> Jung's maternal grandfather, Samuel Preiswerk (1799–1871), was also [like Jung's paternal grandfather, or else K. G. Jung] a striking personality who enjoyed great prestige in Basel. A preacher in the parish of Leonhard there, he had presided over the reformed clergy as the so-called Antistes, or head-vicar. ... [He] had qualified as a senior lecturer in Hebraic languages and was the author of a Hebrew grammar that was circulated as far as America. In the monthly journal *Morgenland*, which he edited, he expressed his interest in the resettlement of Palestine by the Jews. (Wehr, 1988, pp. 17–18)

Wehr's pieces of information clarify the religious turn of the séances and the medium's knowledge of the Old Testament. As for her leaning towards Spiritualism, Wehr adds,

> Preiswerk was . . . "a visionary who experienced whole dramatic scenes, complete with conversations with spirits" . . . [He believed that his daughter Emilie, Jung's mother] was endowed with "second-sight". (Wehr, 1988, p. 18)

Official religious duties were not at odds with spiritism in Jung's maternal family, to which his cousin Helly belonged. This was not the case on Jung's paternal side. Pastor Paul Jung would not have allowed such practices, but the man was dying as Jung started the séances.

Jung's genuine interest can be traced in the subsequent second *Zofingia Lecture*, where he uses the words of one of his "allies" in the spiritualist cause, David Strauss, to describe not "her" medium yet (Helly), as he will later do in his medical dissertation, but Friedericke von Hauffe, Justinus Kerner's famous medium.[78] Jung reports,

> He [Strauss] writes concerning the Seeress: . . . Her conversation with or about blessed or accursed spirits [was] conducted with such truth that we could have no doubt that we were truly in the presence of a prophetess who partook of communion with a higher world . . . We in no way share the opinion of those who attack the truth of Kerner's account, in part accusing the sick woman of dissimulation, in part imputing to the physician a consistent failure to perceive what was really going on—a supposition which not only eyewitnesses like the author, but also all unbiased readers of Kerner's account, can recognize as groundless. (Jung, CW A, pars 74–75)

Strauss's words and tone could indeed have been Jung's. The *Zofingia Lectures* reflect how highly involved Jung was in his experiences and how he then had the highest hopes concerning his cousin, whom he saw as a new Fredericke von Hauffe.

After some time, however, Jung's expectations were no longer met by his cousin's accomplishments. He claimed that he caught her cheating, an accusation later denied by the medium's family. Whatever the reality of the end of the sessions, Jung's first enthusiasm, apart from some notable exceptions to be studied later in Jung's text, disappeared from the report that he wrote for his medical dissertation.

Henri Ellenberger was the first historian who closely studied these events from the medium's side. His task represented a paradigm of a historian's challenge. The first stumbling block here is that too much is at stake: the beginning of a career for Jung, a reputation in the case of Helene Preiswerk. From the start, the (Gadamerian) hermeneutical rules—taking into account the context, the necessary prejudice of the authors of sources, our own prejudice, and anything the authors of sources can take advantage of—are biased (see Gadamer, 1975[1960]). The second stumbling block ensues from the first one: sources have hardly any value *per se* in such states of conflict. As a result, even though research can shed light on the events, the task of interpretation is left to the readers themselves.

Ellenberger identified four sources: (1) Jung's version of the story as recorded by him in his medical dissertation in 1902; (2) the family version, or, "family tradition and hearsay"; (3) the "corrected findings based on documents and the testimony of reliable persons"; (4) the "unknown history: that side of the biography which escapes our awareness and which we often do not even suspect" (Ellenberger, 1991, p. 41). Hewison (2006, pp. 383–403) argues that Jung himself shifted from a scientific method based on proof and illustrated by "case history" to the hermeneutics of human sciences illustrated by "case story".

Category (1) presents the first drawback, that of being incomplete. The protocols that we just examined and compared to Jung's contemporary statements in the *Zofingia Lectures* proved essential. Jung's later works or statements on spiritualism could have been added here, too.[79] Unpublished seminars and letters by Jung are concerned with the topic. Category (2) reveals the other side of the conflict, mainly constituted by the book written by Helene Preiswerk's niece, *C. G. Jung's Medium. Die Geschichte der Helly Preiswerk* (Zumstein-Preiswerk, 1975). A necessary counter-balance to Jung's writing, Zumstein-Preiswerk's version is no more objective than Jung's and is a second-hand source.

Concerning the positioning of the historian, Ellenberger partly solves the problem by presenting his final synthesis in a remarkable twelve-page article of 1991. He first draws attention to Jung's version, then to Zumstein-Preiswerk's, and, finally, to the social and cultural context. Analysis and comments are reduced to a minimum. Instead, he focuses on the admittedly meagre category (3) by trying to find new documents or testimonies by third persons, and category (4) filled with his contextual study. Yet, the library of the E. T. H. Zurich possesses in the Archives a file—also dated 1991—which contains Zumstein-Preiswerk's material used as the basis of her book and which reveals Ellenberger's unavoidable involvement.[80]

The nineteen-page inventory of the file is divided into four sections: manuscripts, correspondence, dossiers, and photographs. Among the fourteen manuscripts, three directly concern us. While the first eleven manuscripts are written in German, the three-page Manuscript Twelve suddenly announces in English, "New title and new preface. A girl C. G. Jung loved in his youth—his medium Helly" and *eine englische Ausgabe* [release] *von "C. G. Jungs Medium"*.[81] Manuscript Thirteen constitutes the 150-page document in question—a translation by Zumstein-Preiswerk's sister and niece of *C. G. Jungs Medium*—with a three-page supplement: "Preface from Henry F. Ellenberger author of the Discovery of the Unconscious".[82] Manuscript Fourteen is one of Ellenberger's annotated by Zumstein-Preiswerk. It comprises eleven pages of notes on the Goethe Legend of C. G. Jung—one of *C. G. Jungs Medium*'s sections—constituting a preface of the planned translation into English.[83]

The correspondence reveals twenty-five letters by Ellenberger to Zumstein-Preiswerk dated 1975 to 1989, and another one from Ellenberger to Zumstein-Preiswerk's sister dated 1983. Correspondence with English-speaking publishers mentions Pantheon Books, New York (1983–1984), Princeton University Press, and University of Chicago Press (1981).[84]

From this document dated 1991, no definitive conclusion can be drawn concerning the reason that prevented the English publication of *C. G. Jungs Medium*. That Ellenberger died in 1993 might be one of them. Still, many documents of even scientific experiences with spiritism remain unpublished in Swiss archives today.

In 1991, Ellenberger wrote a critical study that he named the "story" of Helene Preiswerk. This term brings to mind that fiction and construction are unavoidable in making sense of this episode. As will be examined later, Jaffé's *Memories, Dreams, Reflections* clearly built on Jung's "story" of the realisation of the unconscious. Here, I would rather call the spiritist experience an opera, the end of which, however, would not be as happy as Vincenzo Bellini's 1831 *La Somnambula*.[85]

From 1895 to 1902, Jung's goal changed. In the *Zofingia Lectures*, he wanted science to be informed by spiritualism. In his medical dissertation, science clarified the "so-called occult phenomena". Importantly, one aspect of Jung's method remained the fact that he relied on experience, assumed by the title of his dissertation *On the Psychology and Pathology of so-called Occult Phenomena: A Psychiatric Study*. (Shamdasani, 1998b, p. 118, amended the usual translation of Jung's work by adding "A psychiatric study" to the title.)

Through the phenomenon of *folie à plusieurs* and the capacities of the medium, Jung experienced intuition in the form of empathy (*Einfühlung*). The same thing happens between patient and analyst and constitutes an important part of the transference. This part is not of a sexual nature, but is based on synchronic analogy. We will study in Part IV, Chapter Seven, section headed "Empathy (2): intuition and transference", how Jung might have linked his later theory on transference with his experiences with his cousin.

Undertaken some decades afterwards, *Liber Novus*, or the *Red Book*, constitutes another experience for Jung—a journey from 1913 to 1929 that he called his "confrontation with the unconscious" and that contains the *prima materia* of his entire future psychology. The *Red Book* came from Jung's *Black Books*, which contained drawings and texts.

It is easier to find a correspondence in Jung's state of mind between his spiritist experience and the *Zofingia Lectures* than between his spiritist experience and his medical dissertation. *The Red Book*, by contrast, was the equivalent to the *Black Books* on that matter. Whereas Jung's *Occult Phenomena* uses an experience, *The Red Book* describes the experience itself, hence Jung's expression "*prima materia*".[86] Furthermore, whereas *Occult Phenomena* applies an external psychological theory (essentially Flournoy's), *Liber Novus* engenders Jung's own theory.

In *Liber Novus*, Jung not only praises experience, but also changes perspective on its use. Whereas *Occult Phenomena* is a psychological reduction of spiritism, *The Red Book* does not contain a single psychological analysis. As a psychiatrist, Jung had already described many cases. That, as a psychologist, he nearly stopped doing so might have come from the fact that, with *The Red Book*, he learned to differentiate between the impossibility of rendering the wealth of experience and the reductive intentionality of a case.

Jung's "under-conscious" (Unterbewusste): historical definition

The adjective *unterbewusst* [under-conscious] appears for the first time in Jung's medical dissertation (1902) in the expression "*unterbewusste Persönlichkeit*" (Jung, GW 1, par. 93), which refers to, and in this context is synonymous with, Pierre Janet's subconscious [personality]. While the *Collected Works* translate the term with the English "unconscious", Shamdasani re-established the term "under-conscious" (2001a, p. 9). Jung's later infrequent use of the term "under-conscious" does not systematically refer to Janet and always renders the idea of an in-between state, which, on the one hand, is not a collective unconscious (be it Jung's or Carus's), and, on the other, is not a personal unconscious either (be it Freud's, Janet's, or Bleuler's).[87] Beyond the term "under-conscious" is a state that Jung describes but does not systematise. The challenge of the next part (Part III) of this work is to show that Jung's historical psychology of the under-conscious—that is, the psychology of the pre-collective unconscious—theoretically exists and presumably represents one part of a Jungian theory of intuition.

Historian and analyst Wendy Swan tells how "at a symposium in 1910, several psychological researchers [among them Pierre Janet and Morton Prince] came together to explore and attempt to define subconscious, or unconscious, phenomena". Swan continues, "At the end of the day, they were able to generate six definitions of subconscious phenomena, not one" (Swan, 2008, p. 185). In the 1910s, many scientific researches on the topic had been carried out around the world; the participants must have been aware of the possibly titanic aspect of the task. Here is Swan's sixfold presentation of the definitions:

(1) a region of diminished attention
(2) a region of split-off ideas
(3) a region where to find a self active in every human mind
(4) a region filled with forgotten experiences
(5) the region of the subliminal
(6) a region of pure neural processes without any mentation. (Swan, 2008, pp. 185–186)

Uniting at least (1) and (2)—that is, Janet's system—with (4)—that is, Freud's system—and (3) and (5)—that is, Myers' system with the ideas of many other psychologists present at the symposium (such as

Morton Prince) or absent such as (6)—that is Binet's system—was a generous, yet unrealistic attempt. Point (6) alone repeated the definition of the unconsciousness, *l'inconscience*, collectively proposed during the first International Congress of Psychology held in Paris 6–10 August 1889. The nominated general secretary of the congress, the physiologist Charles Richet, wrote in his report:

> *Unconsciousness*: state of the mind in which there is no consciousness, that is, where the present acts and ideas are not perceived from the *self*, or else withdraw from the memory as they manifest. The intellectual work that presides over these acts is probably of the same nature as conscious intellectual work. There can be *multiple consciousnesses* which coincide in the same individual, that is, *multiple personalities*; these multiple consciousnesses can be either successive or simultaneous. In this case, there is partial rather than total unconsciousness. The state of total unconsciousness is one of psychological fatality, because deliberation implies consciousness, that is, the simultaneity in the mind of several ideas that can seesaw and fight against each other. (Richet, 1889, pp. 14–15, translated for this edition)[88]

To be accepted, this definition needed to please all the members of the congress. Presided over by Théodule Ribot, with vice-presidents Hyppolyte Taine and Antoine Magnan, the first International Congress of Psychology was, above all, remarkable for the list of its 203 participants, since "the history of science has consecrated the names of many of the members" (Piéron, 1954, p. 398). Janet and Binet were to be found next to the famous name of Charcot. Piéron continues,

> Among the physiologists, Helmholtz, Hering . . . Bechterew . . . Henri Baunis. . . . William James and Jastrow, Wilhelm Wundt and Münsterberg. Flournoy and Auguste Forel . . . Delboeuf . . . Freud, Brissaud, Bernheim . . . Meynert, Oskar Vogt . . . Lambroso and Manouvrier, Galton . . . Alfred Espinas . . . Emile Durkheim . . . Richet . . . Ochorowicz . . . Sidgwick. (Piéron, 1954, pp. 398–399, translated for this edition)

From a single agreed-upon approach in 1889 from which to start any research in any direction, we arrive in 1910 at six different definitions.

In his early work, Jung used one or more of the six features, some more than others. What follows focuses only on Jung's reception of the opposite negative and positive (examined in that order) approaches to the patently undefined "unconscious/subconscious".[89]

For Janet, "subconscious" was different from "unconscious". He writes,

> The studies of the unconscious are very ancient: they are metaphysical studies on the possibility of some intelligence, which would be different from human intelligence, independent from consciousness and from its conditions as we assess them in ourselves. The researches on the *subconscious* are, by contrast, much more recent: they are purely psychological studies, which were born out of the difficulties of interpreting certain peculiar mental troubles. The term "subconscious", if we limit ourselves to the signification that I gave when I proposed its usage in 1889, restricts itself to summarising the singular characters that present to the observer some personality disorders. (Jastrow, 1908, p. I)[90]

Janet belonged to the first generation of psychologists, many of whom were also educated in philosophy. Answering a question from Vitalis Norström in 1910, Bergson sheds light on the vitality of philosophy in France. In the French educative system, philosophy was taught as early as high school and was divided into the four sections of "psychology, logic, moral philosophy, and metaphysics".[91] Bergson writes,

> One must first set apart psychology, which has constituted itself as an independent science and does not want to show solidarity with any philosophical system. It is principally represented by Ribot, Pierre Janet, Binet, Dumas, etc.; it has its specific journals and its specific chairs. What characterises French scientific psychology is that it essentially relies on pathology, whereas German psychology endeavours to practise laboratory researches and measurements on normal personalities. (Bergson, 1910, p. 347, translated for this edition)[92]

The independent *science* of psychology wanted to break all ties with *speculative* philosophy. Hence, Bergson and Janet's definitions. "Psychology", writes historian Nicole Edelman, "broke away from philosophy, the efforts of which to preserve supremacy of knowledge about human thought and action had failed" (Edelman, 2001, p. 22, translated for this edition). Many histories of psychology have told the story of the formation of a science relying on physiology and breaking altogether with philosophy. This story has been revisited by new scholars, revealing a more complex picture of the reality, independent of the will of the main agents.

Pathology leads us to Janet's definition of the subconscious. Refinements in the description of the disorders of the personality represented the only changes that occurred between Janet's statement dated from 1908 in the extract below and his first enunciation of the definition of the subconscious. Janet's subconscious described some "disintegration of the personality", "alteration of the personality", and a *rétrécissement du champs de la conscience*, a "restriction of the field of consciousness". The state was either perceptible, such as in catalepsy, or hidden and, thereby, only reached through the use of techniques. Here is how Janet, in 1889, described the restricted consciousness:

> It is precisely a consciousness of this sort, purely affective, reduced to sensations and to images, with none of those links, those ideas of relationship which constitute personality and judgment, that we believe it is legitimate to presuppose in catalepsy and analogous states. Neither total absence of consciousness and pure biological working [*mécanisme*], nor conscious awareness capable of comprehension and obedience seem to us likely here; on the contrary, it is a question of a particular form of consciousness intermediate between these two extremes. (Janet, 1889, p. 79, cited and translated by Monahan, 2009, p. 38)[93]

That the mere capacity of comprehension was the good side of the two extremes shows how negatively the state was perceived by Janet. In the second case, when the subconscious state was hidden, the state could be reached either by the patient's self-induced trances of somnambulism or by the duplication of the process when provoked by the suggestion of the physician. These two techniques will be further examined in detail. I single out only Janet's negative approach to the subconscious in his early work.

As a philosopher, Janet relied on Charcot's expertise as a neurologist and teacher of anatomy for the physiogenesis of mental disease. Hysteria, which was seen as a neurological condition, was the condition of the majority of Janet's subjects in his early work.[94] Hysteria was then also at the centre of a debate between Charcot in Paris and Hippolyte Bernheim in Nancy (the Nancy School) (see Carroy, 1991, pp. 56–64; Ellenberger, 1970, p. 143). At stake was Charcot's allegation that only hysteric patients could be hypnotised, a view contradicted by Bernheim's practice. For Shamdasani, the fact that for Charcot "the capacity to be hypnotized was a symptom of hysteria [also] crucially shaped the view of Freud" (Shamdasani, 1994, p. xxiii). Since Freud translated some of Bernheim's work into German, we must, therefore, at least acknowledge Charcot's charisma. In 1882, Charcot had indeed convinced the French Academy of Science of the need for the modern medicine of old hypnotism.

Following Ellenberger,[95] hypnosis stemmed from hypnotism, itself rooted in Franz Anton Mesmer's animal magnetism and the magnetic sleep of Mesmer's disciple, the Marques of Puységur. Ellenberger writes,

> Mesmer's system [of] 1779 can be summarised in four basic principles. (1) A subtle physical fluid fills the universe and forms a connecting medium between man, the earth, and the heavenly bodies . . . (2) Disease originates from the unequal distribution of this fluid [animal magnetism] in the human body . . . (3) With the help of certain techniques, this fluid can be channelled, stored, and conveyed to other persons. (4) In this manner, "crises" can be provoked in patients and diseases cured. (Ellenberger, 1970, p. 62)

Mesmer, because he possessed the "fluid", was the one, he believed, able to provoke the patients' crises—asthma, epilepsy, and so forth, in which we recognise the later organic symptoms of hysteria: from the crises came the cure.

Puységur, by adding magnetic sleep to Mesmer's theory and technique, transformed (1) the relationship between the magnetiser and the magnetised and (2) the crisis that he renamed "perfect crisis". Once hypnotised, the subjects experienced the state of "magnetic sleep" or "artificial somnambulism", and became themselves the "physicians". "Once they were in that state, they were able to diagnose their own diseases, foresee its course of evolution (which Puységur called the *pressensation*), and prescribe the treatments" (Ellenberger, 1970, p. 71).

These opposite approaches to Mesmer's (organic, physical) "crisis" and Puységur's (mental, spiritual) "perfect crisis", respectively, resonated in the negative approach to the subconscious and, in its most positive aspect, in Frederic Myers' spiritual "dissolutive or evolutive *subliminal*",[96] one of the six "definitions" of the subconscious–unconscious accepted by the 1910 symposium.

To summarise, on one side stood at least Charcot, Janet, and Freud, for all of whom the content of the unconscious–subconscious was negative and had, therefore, to be (scientifically) exorcised, as in the case of Mesmer. Even if hypnosis or later psychoanalysis did not provoke crises any more, the three scientists aimed at exteriorising symptomatic or traumatising content in order to delete or reject it. Like Mesmer, all three scientists were attached to the biological aspect of mental disease, since both Charcot and Freud were neurologists. That Jung was a psychiatrist is crucial and leads us to examine the second psychic–spiritual side.

At the same time, on the other side, stood the followers of the "perfect crisis" of Puységur, who had a positive view on the experimented-upon liminal state.[97] Whereas hypnosis was *used* by the scientists, somnambulism was *observed* without their intervention. During the second half of the nineteenth century, the study implied the participation in spiritist sessions led by mediums who, unlike hysterical patients, were highly esteemed, before they became themselves new objects of science and classified as other hysterics, thanks notably to Jung.

Technically, the *self*-induced trance of spiritism recalled the *self*-cure of Puységur's experimenters who became "physicians". Instead of being exorcised, the content produced by the trance, highly regarded by the spiritists and by the "psychics", had to be cultivated, or raised up, by the medium.[98]

"Psychics" were intellectuals involved in psychical research, that is, in the study of the paranormal activities or capacities developed during the liminal, subconscious states. Institutes and societies for psychical research welcomed their researches in Boston (the American Society for Psychical Research was co-founded by William James), London (in 1913, Bergson became president of the London-based Institute for Psychical Research, where Myers had undertaken his work), Paris (Institut Métapsychique International), and Geneva (with Flournoy's academic laboratory). This "French–Swiss–English–American Alliance", to use Eugene Taylor's expression, was the second and opposite influence to Jung's under-conscious (Taylor, 1996, p. 550).

As mentioned, when Jung met the philosopher and psychologist William James in 1909 during his first visit to the USA with Freud, the two men appreciated each other. Jung reports that he was "tremendously impressed by the clearness of his mind and the complete absence of intellectual prejudices" (Adler & Jaffé, 1973, p. 531). Since the main content of their exchange was psychical research, "intellectual prejudices" meant prejudices against parapsychology and intuition. Taylor explains,

> The Boston psychopathologists refined the French ideas of dissociation into the theory of *co-conscious states of awareness*; they investigated their own cases of neurasthenia [depression], hysteria and multiple personality, and they submitted numerous psychotherapeutic techniques to clinical trials to determine the most effective ones. As well drawing on the work of the committees within the American Society for Psychical Research, they adapted such techniques as crystal gazing, light hypnosis, and automatic writing to diagnosis and treatment of the psychoneuroses. (Taylor, 1996, p. 552)

While designating the same liminal area of the subconscious, these co-conscious states of "awareness" were the opposite of Janet's *restriction* of consciousness. In that respect these states equalled Myers' positive conceptions.

"Myers was not only a parapsychologist," writes Ellenberger, "but also one of the great systematisers of the notion of the unconscious mind" (Ellenberger, 1970, p. 314). His influence on Jung is demonstrated by what can be considered one of Jung's greatest tributes: his attribution to Myers the discovery of the unconscious (Jung, *CW 8*, par. 336, citing James (1905 [1902], p. 233). Jung's permanent adoption of Myers' term "subliminal" next to that of unconscious reveals more than a conspicuous faithfulness. It displays a certainty, an unshakable foundation for one, Jung, who believed his ideas went against the mainstream. Writing of the "subliminal", Myers writes,

> The idea of a *threshold* (*limen, Schwelle*) of consciousness—of a level above which sensation or thought must rise before it can enter into our conscious life—is a simple and familiar one. The word *subliminal*—meaning "beneath that threshold"—has already been used to define those sensations which are too feeble to be individually recognised. I propose to extend the meaning of the term, so as to make it cover *all* that takes place beneath the ordinary threshold, or say, if preferred, outside the ordinary margin of consciousness ... which seldom emerges into that *supraliminal* current of consciousness which we

habitually identify with *ourselves*. . . . I feel bound to speak of a *subliminal* or *ultra-marginal consciousness*—a consciousness . . . uttering or writing sentences quite as complex and coherent as the supraliminal consciousness could make them. (Myers, 1903, p. 14)

In this extract, Myers pinpoints the collective character of the subliminal, to be differentiated with what "we habitually identify with ourselves", that is, consciousness. He then identifies the floating "threshold" and the "marginal". In Myers' system there is no strict unconscious, on the one hand, and consciousness on the other. The complexity of the subliminal state, in which progress, decay, and the exceptional can be observed, is what is lacking in Jung's theoretical psychology—the focus of which is either consciousness or the collective unconscious.

Janet's previous description of the restriction of the field of consciousness is fought against here in Myers' italics *all* ["that takes place beneath . . . consciousness"]. Myers attributed Janet's reductionism to Charcot and to Janet's faithful but wrong positioning on Charcot's side against Bernheim. Like Bernheim, Myers challenged Charcot and Janet's assumption that only insane individuals could be hypnotised, an assumption that resulted, in Myers' opinion, "in a cramp in Janet's conceptions" (Shamdasani, 1993, p. 120). For Myers, the state reached during hypnosis was neither pathological nor even lower than the conscious state, which required, in Janet's *L'automatisme psychique*, the high faculty of attention. Myers writes,

> I believe, in short, that we have no right to go a whit beyond actual observed facts in any judgment which we may pass as to the relative superiority of 'normality' of any of man's different states. I refuse to call my actual waking state 'normal' or 'natural' in any sense except that of habitual or ordinary.[99]

Instead, this liminal state was highly regarded by Myers as it permitted a kind of awareness beyond consciousness, intuitive faculties—such as telepathy—broadening the scope of ordinary intelligence. Myers emphasised the necessity of further investigations with regard to the relationship between subliminal and consciousness. His hopes were high when he wrote, "and we shall come, perhaps to find super-conscious as necessary a term as sub-conscious, if we would indicate the true relation to each other of the processes in which our being consists".[100]

The theoretical definition of the under-conscious corresponding to the liminal state between the unconscious and consciousness in Jung's psychology does not exist. In addition to psychology, philosophy, especially metaphysics, epistemology, aesthetics, the philosophy of religion, and the philosophy of science, would be required for this task.

When John Mullarkey attributes to Bergson, in reference to his intuitive method, "the idea that 'true empiricism' is the 'true metaphysics'" (Mullarkey, 2008, p. 597) he—without intent—properly frames a suitable theoretical approach to Jung's psychology of the under-conscious, since it enlarges the debate of what really is at stake. In other words, that in Jung's work intuition belongs to both empiricism and metaphysics and can be studied in both fields is less important than the question of how intuition makes empiricism become metaphysics and vice versa. Archetypes, synchronicity, "occult" phenomena, to cite only few among many examples, are more than either just empirical observations or just metaphysical claims. Addressing this latter issue would open up the theoretical study of Jung's psychology of the under-conscious to researchers outside the fields of psychology, history, and esotericism. Jung's psychology needs to be articulated by philosophers, if they themselves are able to grasp the ever-dynamic dimension of psychology.

Hypotheses and directions have already been proposed in the work of Robert Segal, Paul Bishop, Antoine Faivre, Leon Schlamm, and Roderick Main, for example. Some structures in Jung's work displayed by Segal have been challenged in order to find different boundaries and perspectives of the study of Jung's theory. Within Segal's fourfold description of Jung's history of the psyche (primitive, ancient, modern, and contemporary ages) (Segal, 1992, pp. 11–18),[101] Bishop reframed the diachronic role of the archaic *Einfühlung* (empathy, empathy (1) here) observed by Segal in Jung's timeless synchronicity (Bishop, 2008). Both historical and a-temporal views contain problematic elements pertaining to the theory of the under-conscious. I will study them in detail in Part III, Chapter Six.

As well, Roderick Main's work on synchronicity brings to mind Jung's intellectual and scientific challenge to postulate the necessity of one a-causal connecting principle. For Jung, the most decisive evidence for a-causal events "ha[d] been provided by the parapsychological experiments of J. B. Rhine . . . [which showed that] under certain psychic conditions time and space can become relative" (Main, 2004, p. 37). These psychic conditions belong to the under-conscious. That esotericism and science are at odds is a cultural prejudice.

Examining Segal's compendium and analysis of Jung's writings on Gnosticism, Schlamm addresses issues concerning the relationship between the unconscious and consciousness, therefore, the under-conscious (Segal, 1992, pp. 27–48). Schlamm writes that Jung believed some Gnostic teachings "anticipated his own work on the relationship between consciousness and the unconscious" (Schlamm, 2008). For Schlamm, Jung, after 1944, distanced himself from Gnosticism and the goal of the return to an undifferentiated state of divine plenitude to embrace the Kabbalist view that the godhead creates the world and humankind to realise itself fully. The Kabbalah provided Jung with other means and symbols for a collective as well as divine individuation in consciousness.[102] Jung's work in that regard is, in Schlamm's words, "an invitation, even a challenge, to consciousness to further explore its unknown psychic background, thereby extending its boundaries and understanding" (Schlamm, 2007, p. 403). I take Schlamm's "extension" of the comprehension of consciousness to be the necessary understanding of the under-conscious.

What follows can be described as theoretical points concerning terminology. It is important to clarify the distinction between the "personal unconscious" and the "under-conscious". The under-conscious and the personal unconscious are opposite in terms of libido—in Jung's terms, "psychic" or "vital energy" (Jung, CW 8, pars 26–33).[103] For example, some intuitions, such as those in precognitive dreams, are conscious but not yet differentiated and, therefore, belong to the under-conscious. Their origin is unconscious, but their possible direction consciousness. By contrast, forgotten and repressed material lead the libido onwards, as their origin is conscious.

These opposing directions explain why a "state" better designates the under-conscious than either *just* an area or *just* a time. In terms of terminology, Charles Tart's 1968 "altered *states* of consciousness" (see Tart, 1968[1990]), therefore, seems to express progress in the grasp of the under-conscious phenomena. Tart notably encompasses extrasensory perception, hypnosis, mania, daydream, delirium, trance, panic, sleep, and meditation.[104] For him, all these active states are open to the most acute function of intuition. Tart writes,

> An altered state of consciousness for a given individual is one in which he clearly feels a qualitative shift in his pattern of mental functioning, that is, he feels not just a quantitative shift (more or less alert, more or less visual imagery, sharper or duller, etc.), but also that some quality or qualities of his mental processes are different. Mental functions operate that do not operate at all ordinarily, perceptual qualities appear that have no *normal* counterparts, and so forth. (Tart, 1990[1968], pp. 1–2, my italics)

"Altered" in Tart's expression "altered states" defines the scope of his study: some initial states, which have been (actively) modified. Other contemporary researches are, by contrast, based on Janet's psychic (static) dissociated states (Mancini & Faivre, 2012).[105] Research on intuition must find its way between its inherent active (actively modified state) and its passive (static) characters. It sometimes implies, as in Silvia Mancini's work, the historical as well as the anthropological distinction between the natural and the cultural. Tart, in this extract, finds no "normal" counterpart to the states he depicts. By definition, "ordinary" and "normal" cannot belong to the liminal. By definition, therefore, the under-conscious is, to borrow Myers' term, "supernormal". For me, this term describes intuition in the most accurate way.

Myers' term "supernormal" characterises the intuitive phenomena occurring in the under-conscious. The term points, as I will attempt to show, to one reason that prevented Jung from theorising on the under-conscious. A second reason relates to Jung's personal experience.

Myers' parapsychological research and that of his colleagues were collected after his death in 1901 in the two encyclopaedic volumes *Human Personality and Its Survival of Bodily Death* (Myers, 1903). There, next to personal data and ideas, can be found one reliable source for the general understanding and practice of the nascent psychology, especially in his "Glossary", where the term "supernormal" appears as follows:

> Of a faculty or phenomenon which goes beyond the level of ordinary experience, in the direction of evolution, or as pertaining to a transcendental world. [In either case they are above the norm of man rather than outside his nature]. The word *supernatural* is open to grave objections; it assumes that there is something outside nature, and it has become associated with arbitrary interference with law [laws of such a kind that they may hold good in a transcendental world as fully as in the world of sense]. (Myers, 1903, p. xxii)

"Supernormal", or "above the norm", was always meant positively by Myers. It could relate to our "world of sense", such as in the telepathic phenomenon, or to a transcendental world, such as the supernormal faculty of communicating with dead people. Myers' differentiation between "supernormal" and "supernatural" legitimated the scientific aspect of his research. What needed to be studied were not external and inexplicable phenomena, but real human abilities such as intuition. The term "parapsychology", coined by the German Max Dessoir in 1889, survived its creator, whereas "supernormal" did not. Yet, from "parapsychology" arose "paranormal", that is, what is "next to" ("para-") the normal, or else what is inexplicable and, thus, does not interest science. "Supernormal" might sound quaint, yet it contains in its form the essence of its content: antinomy, ambiguity.

To some extent, Myers' transcendental world describes Jung's under-conscious. The prefix "trans-", or "beyond, across, crossing, on the other side", defines the necessary in-between condition for the supernormal to occur. Likewise, Jung's under-conscious is a state in between the unconscious and consciousness, where symbolical and literal are equivalent—the very moment, for instance, when someone has a vision. On this border occurs the extraordinary. For Myers, the other side of the border sometimes corresponded to life after death and the realm of spirits. For Jung, who did not deny this possibility, the other side rather corresponded to a momentary state before a psychological change, such as in the "transcendent" function experienced during active imagination (see, for example, Jaffé, 1989, p. 105). In any case, that state engendered the mysterious, that is, that which could not be explained without an interpretation implying choices embedded with the strongest affects, whether the affects are conscious or otherwise. There lay the reason for Jung's keeping his study of the under-conscious private.

The first concrete effect of this secrecy was the postponement of the publication of an important work of Jung's. The 1916 article, "The transcendent function", Jung's only theoretical work on active imagination, was published only in 1957 by the C. G. Jung institute, see explanations in *CW 8*, par. 131). *The Red Book*, Jung's own experience of active imagination (1912–1929) and paintings (Shamdasani, 2009), and the 1930–1934 seminar on Christiana Morgan's active imagination *Visions* (Douglas, 1997), were published only after his death.

Jung displayed ambivalence towards this esoteric (intentionally kept secret) production. A so-called "youthful sin", the *Seven Sermons to the Dead* pertaining to *The Red Book* were "at Jung's request excluded from the Collected Works" (Segal, 1992, p. 181), and remained broadly unpublished until 1962 (after producing them, Jung merely distributed some printed copies).[106] Yet, Jung also described the *Sermons* as "a memory of limpid nights", which "fell quite unexpectedly into my lap like a ripe fruit at a time of great stress and has kindled a light of hope and comfort for me in my bad hours" (Adler & Jaffé, 1973, p. 34).[107] Christine Maillard also reveals that Jung had consigned his copy of the *Sermons* to his personal library in Küsnacht under the acronym "JU 0" for "zero-origin of Jung's work". Using this information, she demonstrates how the *Seven Sermons* "constituted Jung's first attempt at exposing his thought in a systematic and global way ... [and] the further developments of his work would be born, for the most part, out of the intuitions revealed during this visionary period" (Maillard, 1993, p. 33, translated for this edition).

After having intimately "confronted" the unconscious from the limbo of the under-conscious, Jung wanted to build his theory of consciousness. Intuition in the under-conscious was Jung's laboratory, a private matter that would never find any central theoretical place in its publications. Attempting to translate into scientific and objective language the results of his discoveries was his priority when he was, at the same time, "confronting the unconscious". By working (privately) on intuition in the under-conscious, Jung had been able to outline clearly his system from the collective unconscious to consciousness. However, by keeping the under-conscious undisclosed, he omitted the central part of the system in his writing.

PART II

AFTER 1896: INTUITION IN THE UNDER-CONSCIOUS

CHAPTER THREE

Supernatural intuitions, religion, science, and philosophy

Supernatural intuitive gifts in the second Zofingia Lecture

Roderick Main explains that "the second of the lectures [Jung] delivered to his student fraternity, the Zofingia Society, consists largely of an impassioned and informed appeal for the serious scientific study of spiritualist phenomena" (Main, 2004, p. 67). To interest his fellow students in this quest, Jung presented the literature of the field, testifying to, as we shall see in the next table, many forms of intuition. Main informs us of important details that contextualise Jung's statement and render this presence of intuition natural:

> Living in the Swiss countryside, [Jung] continually heard stories of uncanny happenings such as 'dreams which foresaw the death of a certain person [see Table 5, next page], clocks which stopped at the moment of death, glasses which shattered at the critical moment' (Jung, 1963: 102). The reality of these events, he says, was 'taken for granted in the world of my childhood' (ibid). . . . Jung's grandmother Augusta, Preiswerk's second wife, was believed to be clairvoyant [see Table 5]. (Main, 2004, p. 66)

Stories or hearsay, even though taken for granted in the family and the vicarage, could not satisfy a young scientist and an assembly of students. In the part of his lecture titled "Empirical psychology", Jung aimed this time at providing *proof* of occult phenomena, of "facts" concerning extrasensory data. I have examined *all the examples that Jung supplied*—and they are numerous—and have ordered them into three categories in Table 5. Strikingly, one can see from all examples at least one corresponding intuitive gift that they each require (my second column).

All the examples chosen from Jung's selection require intuition. In contrast, by no means did occult phenomena necessarily require this capacity. Tracing back the historical development of the occult, we meet with the medieval occult "qualities"—defined in contrast to the "manifest qualities"—such as "the force of magnetism (different from animal magnetism), the influences emanating from the stars, and the curative virtues of herbal, animal and mineral substances" (Hanegraaff, 2006, p. 885). None of these qualities was linked to intuition. Occult

Table 5. Intuitive gifts and the various occult phenomena for which they are required. *Source*: Jung, CW A, pars 112–134.

Occult phenomenon	Intuitive gift at stake
(1) Past made present: Materialisation of souls (spirits)	Mediumship
Telekinesis: • Hypnotism	Sensitiveness to the rapport (the link to the hypnotist)
• *Doppelgänger* (ghostly haunting double)	Sensitiveness to (link with) the dead person
(2) Higher present: Telepathy: • Clairvoyance	Faculty of seeing/hearing things which are outside the reach of the five senses
Clairvoyance (strict term: access to "ultimate realities") Second sight	The highest level of mediumship
(3) Future made present: Premonitions Prophetic dreams Prophecies	Pure intuition and temporal annihilation of all functions modifying its cognition (access to Kant's noumenon)

philosophy emerged with the German theologian Heinrich Cornelius Agrippa's 1533 *De occulta philosophia* and gave rise to the occult sciences, which were divided into the various arts and practices of natural magic, astrology, and alchemy. Once again, if natural magic and alchemy could, to some extent, be connected to intuition, astrology did not require it.

These examples of non-intuitive occult phenomena reveal by opposition the angle of Jung's paper and one of his main interests in the occult, intuition, through which Jung wished to prove the eternity of the soul in this paper. Paul Bishop writes ("ZL" for *Zofingia Lecture*),

> Furthermore, [Jung] asserted that the soul is both intelligent (ZL §116) and is independent of time and space (ZL §119). To support such claims, Jung provided 'documentary evidence' such as telekinetic phenomena (including the experience of the *Doppelgänger* or double), telepathic phenomena (including clairvoyance), and prophetic phenomena (exemplified by the "second sight" of the Scots'—according to Jung, 'a gift that actually afflicts vast numbers of people on the solitary isles of Northern Scotland'!) (ZL §123 and §134). (Bishop, 2000, p. 85)

Let us examine the kinds of intuition described by Jung.

In section (1) of Table 5, I collate phenomena in which the past is rendered present by intuition or else by "retrocognition"; that is, "the knowledge of the Past, supernormally acquired" (Myers, 1903, p. xxii) in Myers' glossary. When presenting them, Jung rather insisted on the overcoming of spatial laws during these events. Overcoming spatial issues, indeed, can deal only with past events. To identify a higher present, as in section (2) of Table 5, one must overcome causality. To discern the future, as in section (3) of Table 5, one must overcome time—and also causality. Therefore, I could otherwise title the three sections of the table (1) space, (2) causality, and (3) time. In any case, the table renders Jung's presentation from the least to the most spectacular phenomena of intuition.

"Mediumship" (Table 5, second column) indicates the presence of a medium, "a person through whom communication is deemed to be carried on" (Myers, 1903, p. xviii), whose intuitive quality defines the person's function. "Quality" refers first to a status and only to a certain extent to a personal gift: "[the term medium] is often better replaced by automatist or sensitive", writes Myers (1903, p. xviii).[108] By the same token, in this context intuition means, first, relationship or rapport and, second, capacity. In other words, the medium (who mediates) is an intermediary being: this position alone allows communications with, for example, the soul of the dead in Spiritualist sessions. In this last case, for example, as soon as the medium was designated by the little group that participated in the séance, the individual played the role of intermediary to the other world. If the medium was particularly intuitively gifted, she could attract more attention, but intuition as a link to the dead was first performed by the group.

From automatic writing to visions, many events could occur during or in between séances. For his lecture, Jung selected one spectacular performance that at the time was called the "materialisation of souls". Spiritualists believed that the soul, or the spirit, could be materialised in bodies or parts of bodies next to the mediums who called them. "Proof" of these manifestations existed in the form of photographs of fairies or angels, several of which Jung had in his possession. These beautiful pieces of art became famous at the end of the nineteenth century.[109] If the pictures could not provide evidence, they emphasised the embodiment of intuition, which is precisely the role played by the medium.

Fairies, angels, and demons, like mediums, have, ever since antiquity, been considered intermediary beings. "The belief in angels, demons and other intermediary beings has become", writes Roelof van den Broek, "an important aspect of Western religious thought and imagination, in mainstream Christianity as well as in esoteric currents" (van den Broek, 2006, p. 616). Intermediary beings, either disincarnated entities or elements, presented general features that constantly reappeared in different religions. The role of spiritual tutors and divine messengers constituted a pattern to be found in both traditional disincarnated intermediary beings and physical (in the sense of real person) mediums. Jean-Pierre Brach explains that during the Renaissance "the traditional role of guide into the divine presence was simultaneously perceived as the penultimate rung of the cosmological ladder, and the uppermost spiritual intermediary in the contemplative ascent of the soul" (Brach, 2006, p. 624).

Hierarchies constituted a second of these recurrent and inherent patterns. The status of "intermediary" forced the hierarchies of entities—for example, between Hell and Earth, Earth and Heaven, Hell and Heaven—which had never belonged to either one or the other place but instead remained in between both. In Spiritualism, mediums evoked the expanse of different levels, often visualised as planetary spheres, such as some visions already recorded in medieval liturgy.[110]

Like spirits, who belonged neither to the divine nor to the human, the mediums were neither in nor outside society, but at its margin. Just as mediums in trance experienced an in-between state, so they had a transversal status in society. The nineteenth-century's photographs revealing mediums next to fairies and angels actually united entities who were considered to be closely related in nature. Van den Broek reminds us that "the Hebrew word [for "angel"] *mal'ak* is used to designate both a human and a divine messenger. The term primarily indicates a function" (van den Broek, 2006, p. 618). Here, the function of intuition in the intermediary state of the under-conscious unites mediums and intermediary beings.

Through hypnotism, his second example, Jung wished to reveal the relativity of space laws through the independence of the "soul" (with no further explanation) from space. Agents and percipients (hypnotisers and hypnotised people, thus designated in their roles of intermediaries) could be separated by several steps or be in different rooms while continuing to communicate. The hypnotist's suggestion would be obeyed by the percipient even though the hypnotist was some distance away. For this reason, Jung classified hypnosis under a twisted version of the phenomenon of telekinesis, currently accepted as a term "used of alleged supernormal movements of objects, not due to any known source" (Myers, 1903, p. xxii). In Jung's example, the source of the movement was known, yet the movement could be considered as supernormally produced. Intuition again appeared as a link, through the rapport, or relationship, created between agent and percipient. Hence, the rapport, which chronologically preceded the transference in psychoanalysis, first appeared in Jung's writings in connection with intuition rather than linked to feelings or erotic bounds (the usual description).

Jung's third example featured another intermediary being: the *Doppelgänger*, or *eidölon*, which the Pythagoreans understood as "the recognisable unsubstantial shape of the deceased in the underworld, and identified with the preexistent soul" (van den Broek, 2006, p. 619). Adopted in many traditions, the heavenly twin, or guardian angel, was generally perceived positively. Here, Jung presented the *eidölon* as the double of a dying person that could be seen in hallucination by a relative. Thus, he emphasised intuition as the extraordinary relationship existing between the dying individual and the relative who would remain on earth. The *eidölon* appeared in order to replace his earthly twin next to the relative or the friend by creating a new, immaterial, relationship with him that would overcome death.

Describing the same phenomenon, Jung later wrote of the *Todesahnung* (see Jung, *CW 8*, pars 850, 857, 964), or the "premonition of death". Jung himself reported having had a vision, or *Todesahnung*, of the man whom he considered to be his spiritual friend or brother, Richard Wilhelm, who died in the 1930s. Wilhelm was a missionary pastor who translated the *Book of Change*, or the *I Ching*, the first of the five classics of ancient China, into German. Jung's interest in Chinese thought was supported by (living) Wilhelm, but it is his *Todesahnung* that renewed and changed his relationship with (dead) Wilhelm and China and that gave Jung the very meaning of their encounter. As Jung wrote,

> A few weeks before his death, when I had had no news from him for a considerable time, I was awakened, just as I was on the point of falling asleep, by a vision. At my bed stood a Chinese in dark blue gown, hands crossed in the sleeves. He bowed low before me, as if he wished to give me a message. I knew what it signified. The vision was extremely vivid. Not only did I see every wrinkle in the man's face, but every thread in the fabric of his gown. (Jung, 1995, p. 410)

Jung recognised Wilhelm in the old Chinese, in the appearance of someone bowing low to deliver a message of the utmost importance for both Wilhelm and Jung. This message represented their link, their intuition, or the reason for their encounter: Wilhelm's mission was now transferred to him. Jung "knew what it signified": he knew that his friend would soon die and leave him with the duty of spreading the wisdom of the *I Ching* in the Western world. A decade later, the *Book of Changes* would be translated into English by one of Jung's pupils, Cary Baynes.

After a description of intuition as a link within a relationship, Jung investigated intuition with regard to causality and time laws. Jung distinguished two levels of clairvoyance. He identified the first level with telepathy and the second with the independence of the soul from time, which he considered more complex than the independence from space studied earlier in section 1 of Table 5. Myers, who coined the term "telepathy", directly identified telepathy with Jung's second level:

> [Telepathy is] the communication of impressions of any kind from one mind to another, independently of the recognised channels of sense. The *distance* between agent and percipient which the derivation of the term—"feeling at a distance"—implies, needs, in fact, only be such as to prevent the operation of whatever known modes of perception are not excluded by the other conditions of the case. Telepathy may thus exist between two men in the same room as truly as between one man in England and another in Australia, or between one man still living on earth and another man long since departed. (Myers, 1903, p. xxii)

In his definition, Myers emphasised the overcoming of causal laws to the detriment of spatial considerations. What proved extraordinary in the telepathic phenomenon was not that people could communicate over distances as far apart as continents, but that the mode of perception was different from any of the *known* five senses. Telepathy and intuition as a sixth sense defied not only spatial laws, but also causality.

Jung's first level of clairvoyance corresponds to Antoine Faivre's first and second kinds, as described in the extract below. Faivre's third category announces what Jung called "clairvoyance in the strict term":

> 1) A faculty of seeing/hearing things which are normally outside the reach of the clairvoyant's five senses (like being able to read sentences from a book although it is closed) but which do not extend beyond the domain of our common reality.
>
> 2) A "higher" faculty, which consists in seeing/hearing entities like spirits of the dead, angels, demons etc., and occasionally in having a personal contact with them.
>
> 3) A "highest" faculty, of a noetic ("gnostic") character, which extends beyond the first two and consists in being able to have access to some sorts of "ultimate realities": the visions [*Ahnungen*] thus imparted to the subject bear on ontological mysteries that concern, for example, the divine world, the cosmos, the hidden sides of Nature, etc. (Faivre, 2008, p. 191)

Clairvoyance, "in the strict term", surmounted temporal laws, the ultimate intuitive achievement for Jung. Here, again, a hierarchy existed in the *Ahnungen* among mere premonitions, prophetic dreams, and, finally, prophecies, which implied a whole vision of the world. Jung gave a single and very specific example of prophetic dream. He writes, "One special form is the 'second sight' of the Scots, a gift that actually afflicts vast numbers of people on the solitary isles of northern Scotland" (Jung, *CW A*, par. 134).[111] Jung here merely reproduced from memory, with no critical reading, Justinus Kerner's account in the *Seeress of Prevorst*:

> It is well known that the gift of second-sight is endemic in certain places—or in some parts of Scotland and Denmark, for example. People who have this second-sight are remarked to have a piercing look. . . . At the moment that the faculty is in exercise, the body of the seer is rigid; his eyelids are up-raised, and he is blind and deaf to all besides. If the seer, in the moment of second-sight, touches another person, or animal, this person or this animal is endued with the same faculty also. A horse will break into a sweat and refuse to advance, when his rider sees a vision; and horses frequently see these things when the rider does not. (Kerner, 1845[1829], p. 85)

Kerner's somewhat dated description provided images of raised eyelids that we can associate with both the earlier and the later trances of mediums.

Jung finally declared, "The Old Testament prophets may also be described as clairvoyants" (Jung, *CW A*, par. 132). Although remaining undeveloped, the example concluded the lecture in order for Jung to leave his audience with deeper perspectives. To explain and justify these extraordinary phenomena, Jung quoted Schopenhauer's reading of Kant's categories in *Parerga and Paralipomena*:

> Consequent upon Kant's doctrine of the ideality of space and time we understand that the *Ding an sich*, in other words the only reality in all phenomena, being free from these two forms of the intellect (intellectual categories), knows nothing of the distinction between near and far, between present, past and future. Accordingly the divisions based on these modes of viewing the world show themselves not to be absolute, but instead, in terms of the mode of cognition we speak of, which is substantially altered by the modification of the organ [of cognition], no longer present any insuperable barriers. (Schopenhauer, 1851, p. 280, quoted in German by Jung, *CW A*, par. 132)

Schopenhauer's critique of Kant's categories certainly interested Jung more than Kant did. Jung also read Kant through another person, Karl du Prel, on another work, Kant's *Dreams of a Spirit-Seer Illustrated by Dreams of Metaphysics*, studied in my next chapter.

Jung vs. *Kant and Ritschl on intuition and epistemology*

Between November 1896, the date of his first lecture at the Zofingia Club, and January 1899, the date of his last talk, Jung experienced dramatic changes. The death of his father had occurred some months before the first lecture, in early 1896, leaving Jung with pain and guilt over having grown apart from him. Yet, the distance from Pastor Jung was necessary for Jung to be able to make career choices. Against his so far financially supportive family's recommendation to follow his father's career, something that his father had also done in the same financial circumstances, Jung decided to study psychiatry and, after researching brain anatomy, to conduct researches on paranormal phenomena (Bair, 2004, p. 41; Wehr (1988, pp. 45–50). In his last two lectures, Jung's penchant for the irrational (here, what rationality rejects but cannot explain)[112] will find a first adversary in Kant as well as in the theologian Albrecht Ritschl.

Here, I attempt to establish a parallel with the opposition between Immanuel Kant and Emanuel Swedenborg in the eighteenth century and that of Jung and Albrecht Ritschl one century later, where religion, science, and philosophy find various ways to co-exist.

Dreams of a Spirit-Seer Illustrated by Dreams of Metaphysics (hereafter *Dreams*), published in 1766, represents a key text in Kant's life: a mid-life publication announcing his critical period. *Dreams* is itself a strong critique of another mid-life turning point, that of Emanuel Swedenborg, who felt elected by God after a spiritual crisis. Swedenborg, writes Jane Williams-Hogan,

> believed he was called to reveal the internal sense of the Bible and to announce a new True Christianity [because, as he wrote in *Arcana Cælestia*] he had had direct experience of the spiritual world: *vidi, audivi, sensi* 'I have seen, I have heard, I have felt'. (Williams-Hogan, 2006, p. 1097)

The young Swedenborg was a researcher in astronomy, engineering, biology, and philosophy, especially metaphysics. His father was a

Lutheran priest with a strong belief in the supernatural. A great traveller, Swedenborg craved knowledge insatiably. The scientific work of the first half of his life, rather than opposing his later inspired writing, furnished the first systematic basis of his theology that would be later refined by his study of Scripture. From the summer of 1743 until the autumn of 1744, Swedenborg experienced his life-altering crisis. "The crisis began simply enough, with dreams that were sufficiently disturbing for Swedenborg to wake up and record them. . . . He believed that they were communications to him about his spiritual state of health" (Williams-Hogan, 2006, pp. 1100–1101) first given by his guardian angel and then by Jesus Christ himself. In this revelatory episode appears the link between Swedenborgians and spiritists. Soon after, Swedenborg began his voluminous, extraordinary, and radical religious work, which was anonymously written until 1768 but which became, from 1759 onwards, more commonly attributed to the famous clairvoyant who had foreseen the fire of Stockholm. If Swedenborg himself never attempted to organise a new religion, many Swedenborgians, or New Church, organisations were established and still exist worldwide today.

It was the precise visions of the fire in Stockholm in 1759, reported from a distance of about 300 miles away, that first drew Kant's attention to Swedenborg, since "the witnesses of these 'sightings' were for Kant absolutely reliable" (Kuehn, 2001, p. 158). Yet, it was only after having read the eight volumes of Swedenborg's *Arcana* that Kant held a definitive opinion on the man. As a result, Kant rejected with the greatest scorn the revelations of his Swedish contemporary in the pamphlet *Dreams of a Spirit-Seer Illustrated by Dreams of Metaphysics*, an exceptional book in Kant's *oeuvre*. Cosmology and metaphysics might have been the main interests of both Swedenborg and Kant before their radical change. Yet afterwards, whereas Swedenborg felt called by God, Kant antithetically chose Reason to become the greatest philosopher of the Enlightenment.

The title of Kant's work announced the ambiguity of both its topic and its readership. "Metaphysics", then taken to be the scholarly study of "the articulation of the general principles of all that is" (Rossi, 2009), was meant to be an illustration of spirit seeing. It was, therefore, as Kuehn analyses, "a book for everyone and for no one" (Kuehn, 2001, p. 173). In his Foreword, Kant writes, "Thence originated the present treatise, which, we flatter ourselves, will fully satisfy the reader; for the main part he will not understand, another part he will not believe, and the rest he will laugh at" (Kant, 1900[1766], p. 39). The satirical tone of Kant's book was settled, borrowed from two French masters of the genre: the Baron of Montesquieu, author of the *Persian Letters* (2004)[1721] and, even more, Voltaire, author of *Candide, or Optimism* (2003)[1759], which Kant expressly imitated.

Like the French writers, who aimed at enlightening their reader in the actions of their main naïve characters against the avowed enemies of Reason, Kant identified here both readers and enemies. His enemies were, on the one hand, those who did not understand—that is, his fellow contemporary metaphysicians—and, on the other hand, those who believed in spirits. His elected readers had no other choice but to appreciate his tone and laugh at his wit or wry sense of humour when Kant compared, for instance, Swedenborg's "heavenly inspiration" with some "hypochondriacal wind raging in the guts".[113] Comparably, as Alfred Aldridge has analysed, Voltaire's goal was "to bring amusement to a small number of men of wit" (Aldridge, 1975, p. 251) Voltaire's enemies in *Candide, or, Optimism* were, on the one hand, philosophers, specifically Leibniz, and, on the other hand, religion and (candid) theologians. "Illustrated by" in Kant's title *Dreams of a Spirit Seer Illustrated by Dreams of Metaphysics* explicitly refers to Voltaire's "or" in his title *Candide, or Optimism* in order to link contemporary religion with philosophy.

Voltaire opens his book by presenting Candide:

> In the country of Westphalia, in the castle of the most noble baron of Thunder-ten-Tronckh lived a youth whom nature had endowed with a most sweet disposition . . . a solid judgment joined to the most unaffected simplicity. (Voltaire, (2003)[1759], p. 11)

Candide's tutor, Master Pangloss, is described as "the oracle of the family" who taught the "metaphysico-theologo-cosmonigology" (Voltaire, (2003) [1759], pp. 11–12). "Nigo" inside "cosmonigology", without which we read "cosmology", referred to the French "nigaud" (same pronunciation), which means "fool". From the start, religion and metaphysics are ridiculed in the character of Pangloss. In the following extract, Pangloss, by reversing cause and effect, exposes to Candide the final proof of the existence of God entwined with Leibniz's theory of pre-established harmony:

"It is demonstrable," said he, "that things cannot be otherwise than as they are; for since all things have been created for some end, they must necessarily be created for the best end. Observe, for instance, the nose is formed for spectacles, therefore we wear spectacles. The legs are visibly designed for stockings, accordingly we wear stockings." (Voltaire, (2003)[1759], p. 12)

In the same way, Kant mocks at once Swedenborg's belief in spirits and, at the same time, Leibniz's monads by mixing the belief in life after death with crude material issues:

From these considerations no valid reason can be brought forward, why my soul should not be one of the substances of which matter consists. . . . In that case, however, there would remain no peculiar characteristic of the soul by which it could be surely recognised and distinguished from crude elementary matter, and the jocose suggestion of Leibnitz would not be laughable anymore, that in our coffee we swallow, perhaps, atoms which are to become human souls. (Kant, (1900)[1766], p. 52)

Pangloss is like Leibniz and Swedenborg. All three embodied the enemy of Reason. This extract and the following one reveal how Kant had somehow entered the character of Candide and enacted his journey. Kant had gone through a process, and to explain why one should not laugh at these jocose suggestions, he wrote,

It is at times necessary to frighten the thinker who is on the wrong path, by the consequences, so that he may pay more attention to the principles by which he has been led off as in a dream. I confess that I am very much inclined to assert the existence of immaterial natures in the world, and to put my soul itself into that class of beings. (Kant, (1900)[1766], p. 52)

Kant saw himself in need of being frightened since a part of him was inclined to believe in the immateriality of his soul. That part of him was naïve, in need of education and of morality. Paul Bishop convincingly defended the thesis, also acknowledged by Robert Butts, of Kant's ambiguity towards mysticism and paranormal activity. Both Bishop and Butts discovered and commented on other such statements by Kant, revealing how the philosopher pushed to the limits what he considered the lower tendencies of his mind to suppress them (Bishop, 2000, pp. 222–228, 286–290; Butts, 1986, p. 35).

With Kuehn, we learn that Kant, exceptionally, wrote *Dreams* piece by piece: it was an extraordinary procedure which looked like an extraordinary process, the goal of which could not be the mere intellectual content of the book (Kuehn, 2001, p. 171). In the face of his friend Moses Mendelssohn's severe reaction to *Dreams*, Kant argued that he had "learned to do without as well as to scorn most of the things that tend to corrupt one's character" (Kant to Mendelssohn, quoted in Kuehn, 2001, p. 172). "Scorn" referred to the tone of *Dreams*. "Learned" referred to the journey he had gone through. "One's character" was, for Kant, the goal to acquire through moral rebirth:

> [Character] must always be acquired. We may also assume that the foundation of this character and its beginning must be unforgettable. It is like a kind of rebirth, like a kind of solemn promise to oneself. ... It comes about only through an explosion, as it were, which follows all at once upon the dissatisfaction with the state of vacillation of instinct. They will be perhaps only few who have tried to accomplish this revolution ... before the age of forty. (Kant, quoted in Keuhn, 2001, p. 144)

Kant turned forty on 22 April 1764, two years before the final publication of *Dreams*. In "the dissatisfaction with the state of vacillation of instinct" we recognise Kant's inclination to assert the immateriality of his soul—a belief that, even though it "appear[ed to Kant] very obscure" (Kant, (1900)[1766], p. 52), was present and was corrupting the accomplishment of Kant's revolution. We can also—and was Kant here referring to one and the same thing?—outline here Kant's vacillating credulity in the wake of the report of Swedenborg's visions during the fire of Stockholm.

In the same year as that of *Candide*'s publication, in 1759, Swedenborg described from 300 miles away the fire that was taking place in Stockholm, a fire that miraculously stopped just before reaching his house. It was also in the year of Kant's turning forty, in 1764, that he and all the inhabitants of Königsberg helplessly witnessed the fire that broke out in their city and that lasted one week, taking hundreds of lives, rendering thousands homeless, and leaving all the survivors with a deep feeling of the precariousness of life (Kuehn, 2001, p. 158). Voltaire wrote *Candide* after the earthquake that had occurred in Lisbon in 1755. During Candide's journey around the world, he and Pangloss went through all the horrors and abominations of Voltaire's time. Even in the middle of Lisbon on fire, with all its cadavers, Pangloss remained optimistic, claiming that "Leibniz could not be wrong, and besides pre-established harmony is the finest thing in the world" (Voltaire, (2003)[1759], p. 123). Voltaire's caustic tone in describing this precise event might have definitely created vacillations in Kant's heart in favour of Voltaire/Candide against optimistic Pangloss/Swedenborg, who believed God had miraculously spared his house from the flames.

When Kant challenged Reason before Swedenborg's visions, he was "as in a dream", the dream of a seer-spirit-Swedenborg—and of a metaphysician—Kant before his critical period. The process of writing *Dreams*, like the fire of Königsberg, awakened its author from this dream, like a rebirth coming about only through an enormous explosion.

At the end of his journey, Candide retreated from travelling the world to settling and cultivating his garden:

> Pangloss sometimes would say to Candide: "All events are linked together in the best of possible worlds; for after all, had you not been kicked out of a fine castle for the love of Miss Cunégonde, had you not been put into the Inquisition, had you not travelled across America on foot, had you not stabbed the Baron with your sword, and had you not lost all your sheep which you brought from the good country of El Dorado, then you wouldn't be here eating preserved citrons and pistachio-nuts." "Excellently observed," answered Candide; "but we must cultivate our garden." (Voltaire, (2003)[1759], p. 130)

Pangloss's enumeration recalled the long process of his "sophistries", at the end of which Candide had learnt the famous maxim "we must cultivate our garden". In the same way, Candide/Kant concluded his process of writing *Dreams* by answering Pangloss/Swedenborg:

> Human reason was not given strong enough wings to part clouds so high above us, clouds which withhold from our eyes the secrets of the other world. The curious who inquire about it as anxiously may receive the simple but very natural reply, that it would be best for them to please have patience until they get there. But as our fate in the other world probably depends very much on the manner in which we have conducted our office in the present world, I conclude with the

words with which Voltaire, after so many sophistries, lets his honest Candide conclude: "*Let us look after our happiness, go into the garden, and work.*" (Kant, (1900)[1766], p. 122)

Kant/Candide is honest: he cannot know. The irrational must be rejected not because it is false, but because it is unknowable. Only after this admission could "work" begin, a work, in Kant's case, precisely relating to the limits of epistemology.

What would definitely counter Swedenborg's revelation, this time not with scorn but with thinking, would take a decade to be delivered. It was Kant's argument of the opposition between sensual and (unreachable) intellectual intuition in his first *Critique*, the *Critique of Pure Reason*.

Better informed now of the content of *Dreams*, let us return to 1897 and to Jung's first lecture at the Zofingia club. Through his reading of Kant's *Dream* via du Prel's reading of him, Jung first mistook Kant's intentions in *Dreams*, turning him into an "ally" of spiritism and Swedenborg. Paul Bishop recalls how "Jung completely overlook[ed] the sarcastic tone of this tract, ignoring, for example its description of Swedenborg as . . . 'candidate for the asylum'" (Bishop, 2000, p. 86).[114] Two years later, in his last Zofingian lecture, Jung would not fail this time to recognise that Kant had publicly chosen the camp of "free and moral religion" against "mystic and miraculous religion". The duel between Swedenborg and Kant finds an echo in the duel between Jung and the Kantian and liberal Protestant theologian, Albrecht Ritschl.

The son of a theologian, Ritschl (1822–1889) was one of the most prominent figures of Protestant liberalism, the positivism of which brought about both criticism and fame in Germany during the forty years preceding the First World War. Greatly influenced by Kant, Ritschl aimed at integrating Pietism with the humanism of the Enlightenment. Therefore, the moral nature of religion had to be emphasised over doctrine. Religion as *practised* by Jesus had to be taught, rather than religion *about* Jesus, such as the Trinity and the Incarnation. All forms of mysticism were banned and miracles were ignored: religion had to be enlightened rather than in any way mystical.

Unlike Kant, who concluded the final chapter of *Dreams* with the futility of the quest for the occult of philosophy, medical student Jung maintained that the occult needed to be investigated by science. Jung's final lecture was delivered in January 1899, two years before he wrote his dissertation on occult phenomena. In this last lecture, Kant was no longer Jung's "ally" but now the ally of Jung's enemy, Ritschl. There, Jung fought against the Kant of *Dreams* using the same weapons: wit, anger, and disdain for a figure to be ridiculed. This figure had been Swedenborg for Kant. It became Ritschl for Jung.

Kant's influence on Ritschl was not limited to epistemology: it stemmed directly from Kant's writing on religion. In *The Conflict of the Faculties* (1794), Kant criticises "Pietism, which provides a 'completely mystical' solution to the problem of religion and morality ... and [also criticises] Orthodoxy, which declares 'belief in dogma to be sufficient for religion'" (Kuehn, 2001, p. 382). Not without sarcasm, Kant, for instance, analysed the Pietistic rebirth:

> This radical change, therefore, begins with a *miracle* and ends with what we would ordinarily consider natural, since *reason* prescribes it: namely a morally good course of life. But even in the highest of a mystically inclined imagination, one cannot exempt man from doing anything himself ... what man has to do is *pray* fervidly and incessantly ... and only from this can he expect that supernatural effect. (Kant, (1996)[1794], p. 278)

Kant positioned himself against miracles and mysticism—both of which, in contrast, were unproblematically integrated in the field of esotericism and the occult. So did Ritschl, providing Jung with an occasion to show his wit. In his lecture, Jung quoted Ritschl's criticism of mysticism:

> They posit [the mystics, as for Ritschl], as the reality of things, what are nothing more than unauthenticated and unstable images in the memory ... For an exact memory is the medium of personal relationships ... and in the broadest sense this is true of the bond, in religion, between our lives and God, effected through our precise remembrance of Christ. (Jung, *CW A*, pars 272, 274)

In this extract, Jung identified one of the theologian's weaknesses. Ritschl's "precise remembrance of Christ" implied, in fact, complex mediations, as, for Ritschl, Christians could not have a direct relationship to God or directly speculate on the Holy Scriptures, where correct, conscious, "sensual memory" opposed "hallucination". At home in the medical field, the vocabulary that Ritschl clumsily used for his demonstration, Jung did not hide his pleasure when ridiculing the theologian:

> But I must say that the technical terms employed by the modern theologian are so abstruse and misleading that even educated people must engage in an abdication of the intellect in order to understand what is meant, on the symbolic or magical level, by a phrase like "religious-ethical motive". And when, finally a Ritschlian construction is placed on an idea which continues to be addressed under the same old names, one can only gape in amazement and patiently endure the incredible spectacle. At the end one will probably say to one's neighbour: "I suppose that's how it must be?!" (Jung, CW A, par. 257)

The second target of Ritschl was the awkward miracle opposing his positivism. Jesus did not have to be venerated as one entity among the three of the (miraculous) Trinity, but Jesus' moral conduct on earth did have to be emulated. Swept of the learning of the Christian doctrine, the historical figure of Jesus described in the New Testament was, for Ritschl, the concrete and objective foundation of religion. Against this human presentation of Jesus, Jung lyrically opposed Jesus the (intuitive) prophet, one of these "supramundane being[s] who relates to the historical conditions just enough to be understood" (Jung, CW A, par. 243).

> Their [such men as Jesus of Nazareth] truths are new ... they know ... that we have been waiting for them, that we have awaited them a long time, and that it is for them alone that causal sequence of the world's historical development has ploughed the fields and prepared them to receive the seed ... They know that they are the meaning and the end toward which the labour of many centuries has been directed ... They *are* their own idea, untrammelled and absolute among the minds of their age, and not susceptible to historical analysis ... They have not evolved from any historical foundation, but know that in their inmost natures they are free from all contingency ... the image of Christ must be restored to the idea he had of himself, namely as a prophet. (Jung, CW A, pars 243, 288)

For Jung, Ritschl's historicism wrongly reduced Jesus to a time-bound historical figure. Jung indirectly criticised Kant's time category, which, therefore, could not concern prophets, their life, and their prophecies.

However, later in his lecture, Jung's tone changed to anger and a strong attack against the theologians such as Ritschl whose historicism was merely an example for him of what would kill religion: the assimilation of rationalism into faith. In so doing, for Jung, Ritschl was mistaking faith for masquerade:

> We may make light of Ritschl's God, but we can feel nothing but pity for Ritschl's Christian. Every pagan has his gods to whom he can cry out when he feels sorrowful and afraid, even if this god is nothing but a brightly polished boot, a silver button, or a stick of wood. But Ritschl's Christian knows that his God exists only in church, school, and home and owes his efficacy to the subjectively determined power of motivation supplied by memory. And it is to this powerless God that a Christian is supposed to pray for salvation from bodily and spiritual want? God cannot lift a finger for he exists only historically, in tradition, and in strictly limited sense. (Jung, CW A, par. 278)

In these words, Jung appeared strongly affected. This was no longer Kant or Ritschl's trial, who hardly claimed that God exists only historically or in tradition. These words seemed to project Jung's unassuaged rage against his dead father. Jung's father, the pastor, as had his son, had "struggled desperately to keep his faith [and] was entrapped by the Church and its theological thinking . . . [which] had faithlessly abandoned him" (Jung, 1995[1961/1963], p. 113). The "shaken and outraged" child, who had been in pain in the face of his father's "hopelessness", was now trying to find the intellectual source of his father's anguish. It was Jung's father's trial, Jung's denouncement of his father's and faith's enemies.

Far from being a traditional obituary to his father, who had died three years earlier, this lecture constituted a necessary battle for life. Prior to having any rational meaning for his audience, Jung's words had an immediate (intuitive, through *Anschauung*) efficiency for him. They acted on him. Jung had learnt that irrational and rational are opposites and so cannot be mixed. In his attempt to do it, Jung's father, as well as his son, had lost faith. Jung's mother might have intuited the importance of this lesson for her son when, in the voice of her Personality Number 2, she told her son about his father: "*Er ist zur Zeit für dich gestorben*", "He died in time for you" (Jung, 1995[1961/1963],

p. 116).[115] Jung's mother's intuition, personality, and family were about to play a direct role in Jung's doctoral dissertation.

Clairvoyance and Gnosticism in Occult Phenomena

Another document, *Aufzeichnungen über positive, relative und negative Kräfte*, "On positive, relative, and negative forces", written in Jung's hand, relates to his spiritist experience with his cousin Helly. This document and its retranscription in Jung's medical dissertation can be divided into the author's positive and negative comments on the medium's feats. The archive constitutes two circular diagrams (Figures 1 and 2 reproduce their main features) and a text that Helly dictated to Jung. Jung's dissertation fairly reproduces the text, yet draws a system diagram (the third and last system) (Figure 3), which is at odds with the two systems that he draws some years earlier.

The fact that the third system is closer to Helly's explanations could justify Jung's drawing of another diagram. Yet one element, present here and absent in the previous systems, could well be the reason that led Jung to create this new figure and to hide the first two. This element is the names of the forces, such as "Magnesor", "Connesor", "Mannus", "Fixus", "Persus" ... Those names link Jung's work to Flournoy's *From India to the Planet Mars*, the literature on which Jung's medical dissertation was partly based and a work that was not yet published when Jung had realised his spiritist experiences:

> The curious names of the mystical system can mostly be traced back to known roots. Even the circles remind one of the planetary orbits found in every school atlas. ... In this way the names "Persus", "Fenus", "Nenus", "Sirum", "Surus", "Fixus", and "Pix", can be explained as childish distortions of "Perseus", "Venus", "Sirius", and "fixed star" ... "Magnesor" is reminiscent of "magnetism". ... The frequent endings in "-us" and "-os" are the signs by which most people distinguish between Latin and Greek. ... Naturally the modest glossolalia [speaking in foreign tongue] of our case cannot claim to be a classic example of cryptomnesia [coming into consciousness of a memory image which is not recognised as such but as foreign and present], for it consists only in the unconscious use of different impressions, some optical, some acoustic, and all very obvious. (Jung, *CW 1*, par. 144)

80 JUNG AND INTUITION

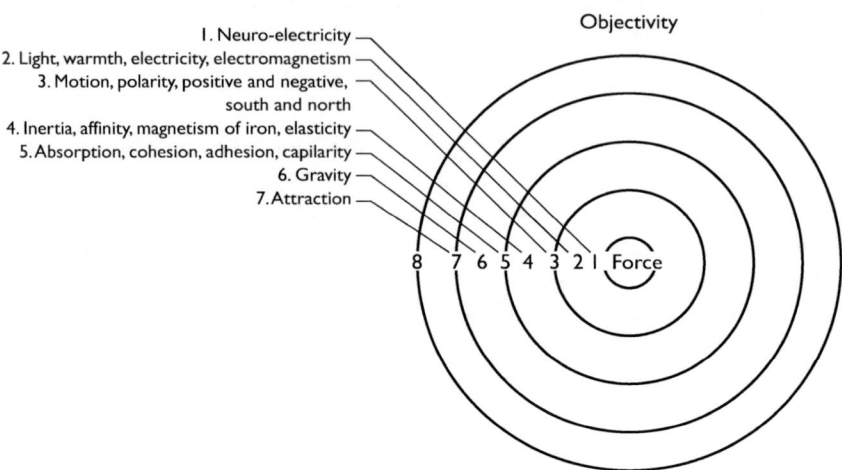

Figure 1. Jung's reproduction of Helly's explanations in *Occult Phenomena* (1).

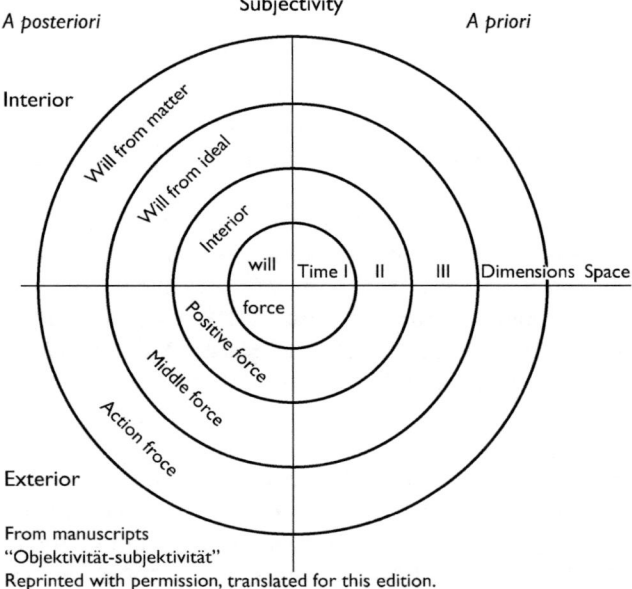

From manuscripts
"Objektivität-subjektivität"
Reprinted with permission, translated for this edition.

Figure 2. Jung's reproduction of Helly's explanations in *Occult Phenomena* (2).

SUPERNATURAL INTUITIONS, RELIGION, SCIENCE, AND PHILOSOPHY

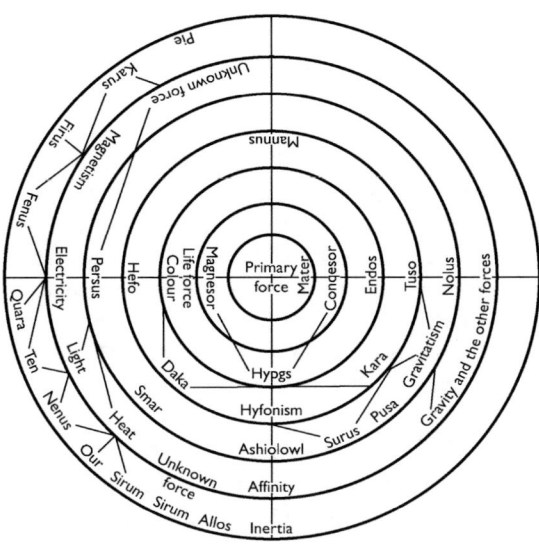

Figure 3. Jung's reproduction in *Occult Phenomena*. Reprinted with permission.

In 1902, Jung recognises cryptomnesia in Helly's system and probably emphasises his discovery in a new drawing (Figure 3). This psychologisation constitutes the only negative comment by Jung on his cousin's system. If Jung clearly changed his mind between the moment when he experienced spiritism and the time of this writing down of the dissertation, this did not happen concerning Gnosticism.

Jung always maintained a positive attitude towards Helly's system. Yet his involvement, which began with him as a strict believer at the Zofingia Club backing up Gnostic theories, turned to his being an open-minded scientific observer in his medical dissertation. Jeromson writes,

> In the fourth [Zofingia] lecture, Jung reflects on the existence of an infinite number of worlds relating to each other 'like concentric and eccentric circles.' Jung's circular worlds are occupied by species with increasingly complex sensory systems as one moves outwards from the centre. Ultimately, the world of man is reached, contained in turn within the Kantian world of the noumena or things in themselves. (Jeromson, 2012)

In 1902 Jung this time focused on Helene Preiswerk and on the possible origin of his cousin's knowledge. The suggestive part of the system for him arose from some conversations during the sessions and from Helene's reading of Kerner's *The Seeress of Prevorst*. Yet Jung adds,

> This exhausts my knowledge of the sources used by the patient. Where the root idea came from she was unable to say. Naturally I waded through the occult literature so far as it pertained to this subject, and discovered a wealth of parallels with our Gnostic system, dating from different centuries, but scattered about in all kinds of works, most of them quite inaccessible to the patient. Moreover, at her tender age, and in her surroundings, the possibility of any study must be ruled out of account. (Jung, CW 1, par. 149)

Helly had two kinds of vision: personal visions—visions that were linked to her ego—whether teleological or linked to the future, to be studied in the next section, and visions that went beyond herself. In the second case, she attained clairvoyance, which Antoine Faivre, as seen earlier, defines as follows:

> A "highest" faculty, of a noetic ("gnostic") character, which consists in being able to have access to some sorts of "ultimate realities": the visions [*Ahnungen*] thus imparted to the subject bear on ontological mysteries that concern, for example, the divine world, the cosmos, the hidden sides of Nature, etc. (Faivre, 2008, p. 191)

This last case of *Vorahnungen* raised the issue of the unknowable origin of its content for Helene. Because she could not have any memory of works or studies inaccessible to her, given her social environment and age, Helene had indeed an "intuitive knowledge" incomprehensible for the author. "Gnostic (system)", interchangeable in Jung's text with "Mystical (system)", focused on the status of her cousin and her sudden intuitive knowledge. Helly could not have obtained the gnosis (term derived from the Greek "knowledge" or "understanding") other than by revelation, one of the three main features of Gnosticism. Jung describes Helly's revelation from her testimony, where we can appreciate the perceptive aspect of intuition:

> S. W. [Helly] sees Magnesor as a shining white or bluish vapour which develops when good spirits are near. Connesor is a black fuming fluid which develops on the appearance of "black" spirits. On the night

before the great visions began, the shiny Magnesor vapour spread round her in thick layers, and the good spirits solidified out of it into visible white figures. It was just the same with Connesor. (Jung, CW 1, par. 70)

Segal (1992) and Rudolph (1998) remind us of the other striking features of Gnosticism, such as the antithetical dualism of immateriality and matter, the central place of the knowledge to be revealed to humans, that is, "the redemption of man from the constraint of earthly existence . . . thanks to the presence in man of a divine 'spark' linking man to the divine realm" (Segal, 1992, p. 3). This noetic knowledge "rests upon one's own investigation but on heavenly mediation" (Rudolph, 1998, p. 55).[116]

All these points are to be found in Helene Preiswerk's system, where hierarchy, combination, and opposites appeared for her as the three main means to represent the inexpressible content of the spirits' scientific messages. For example, the second circle "combine[d] with the Primary Force [of the first circle] and from this combination ar[o]se other spiritual forces: on one side the Good or Light Powers [Magnesor], on the other side the Dark Powers [Connesor]" (Jung, CW 1, par. 66). Light and Dark are traditional representations of Gnosis, divine *vs.* matter, body, and human.

Jung mentioned that affinities existed between this system and that of the Seeress of Prevorst. Indeed, in 1829, Justinus Kerner writes that

> in order to describe these [hardly expressible] perceptions, Mrs Hauffe constructed figures, which she called 'her sun-sphere', 'her life-sphere', and so forth. On the life-sphere rested a totally different world. Hence the existence in each human being of the intuitions [*Ahnungen*] of a superior world. (Kerner, 1845[1829], p. 124)[117]

Those intuitions are the Gnostic "sparks" present in each human, their divine part.

A final element of convergence between Gnosticism and Helly's system consisted in her description of a dualism, yet not this time between Dark and Light, but between the visible and the sensible and the invisible, or else the unknown God of the Pleroma (see Rudolph, 1998, p. 58). This dualism also has intuition as a perception at its centre:

With the sixth circle the visible world begins; this appears to be so sharply divided from the Beyond only because of the imperfection of our organs of sense. In reality the transition is a very gradual one, and there are people who live on a higher plane of cosmic knowledge because their perceptions and sensations are finer than those of other human beings. Such "seers" are able to see manifestations of force where ordinary people can see nothing. (Jung, CW 1, par. 70)

Jung's use of the register of Gnosticism to describe what, for him, constituted Helly's brightest intuitive demonstration appears in his last chapter, which is entitled "Heightened unconscious performance". If, wrote Jung, his cousin's productions hardly reached the "rarer and incomparably more astonishing cases of intuitive knowledge displayed at times by somnambulists", he was, none the less, "inclined to regard the mystical system devised by [his] patient as just such an example of heightened unconscious performance that transcend[ed] her normal intelligence" (Jung, CW 1, par. 148).

Here, perhaps, Jung also had in mind Helene's two other circular systems (the first two presented here, dated from the sessions), where, instead of the funny names given to the spheres, she (or Jung, since he had reproduced the systems) had rather articulated concepts of another and brighter level, such as:

A posterior–A priori
Time–Space–Dimension
Interior–Exterior
Subjectivity–Objectivity
Will–Intention.

For Jung, Helene Preiswerk's achievement could "be regarded as something quite out of the ordinary" (Jung, CW 1, par. 149). This last sentence was given emphasis, for it was the end of Jung's thesis apart from a short paragraph of polite thanks to his teacher, Eugen Bleuler.

We are familiar with Jung's use of literary effects to convince the reader. Only a few years before writing his medical dissertation, he had composed the poem *"Gedanken in einer Frülingsnacht"*. As analysed by Paul Bishop, Jung there employed numerous poetic strategies to reveal the author's *Naturmystik* experience—understood as the intuition of God evoked and generated through the contemplation of the Creation (*Naturwelt*) (Bishop, 2003, p. 341). When Jung titled the last chapter of *Occult Phenomena* "Heightened unconscious performance" and ended his work by evoking his cousin's most intuitive achievement, he applied the same formula to call attention to another form of intuition.

After having put emphasis on the content of Helly's achievement, Jung used a second literary device to single it out. Not only did the performance appear at the end of the work, but it left the author speechless, unable to explain the phenomenon. Jung could not finish, or, rather, chose not to finish, therefore highlighting the mystery of the intuitive performance.

Jung's third literary device, the expression of his powerlessness at the very end of his work, is one version of a literary effect of surprise that we find amplified in "The Sleeper in the Vale", by Arthur Rimbaud (1895). There, the poet depicts the peacefulness of nature in harmony with the young sleeper of the sonnet until the very last verse: "He has two red holes on his right side", revealing the (unexpected and deeply affecting) death of the soldier. This surprise expresses the powerlessness of life in the face of war, which the poet could not understand. Jung used this identical form to account for his interest in intuition, even though he felt incapable of describing it better than with the terms "something quite out of the ordinary" at the end of his work. Both Rimbaud and Jung invited a critical reading: "Do not blindly believe in what you read" was implied in both endings. Jung's last ambiguous statement about intuition and Helly's achievement contradicted the eighty-eight pages of his work in order to stir the reader's own "taste", his own reflection. Taking up a position against war in 1870 was more dangerous, and no less controversial, than positioning favourably towards intuition when scientifically studying spiritist circles twenty years later. In other words, Jung expressed his incapacity to explain intuition not only because of its intrinsic mystery, but also because of the restrictions implied by "a psychiatric study".

Similarities also united Helene's circles with what Jung would later describe as the culmination and the end of his journey through *Liber Novus* with the making of a mandala. Jeromson analysed Jung's interest in mandalas and writes about Helly's Gnostic system,

This is the earliest image of a mandala in the *Collected Works*, although Jung did not refer to it as such at the time. Writing in 1929, he recalled this diagram, referring to it as a mandala of a somnambulist. He compared the medium's primary force with the white light of the Tibetan Buddhist Bardo and the unity of the Tao. (Jeromson, 2012)[118]

In *Memories, Dreams, Reflections*, Jung told how, in 1928, he painted a mandala "with a golden castle in the middle" and then had a dream, "which brought with it a sense of finality. . . . The goal had been revealed. One could not go beyond the centre. . . . After this dream, I gave up drawing and painting mandalas". Mandalas, for Jung, were magic circles, "the symbol of the centre goal or of the self, a self-representation of a psychic process of centring, and the production of a new centre of personality" (Jung 1995[1961/1963], pp. 415–416). "The dream depicted the climax of the whole process of development of consciousness" (Jung, (1995[1961/1963], pp. 222–224). The final words of the legend under the mandala were "*Aeon finitus*", "The end of an aeon". In 1950, Jung commented, "The ground round the castle is laid with black and white tiles, representing the united opposites . . . The Taoists call this centre 'the land of ancestors or golden castle'" (quoted in Shamdasani, 2009, p. 320).[119] Likewise, Helene's production of her mandala had been judged by Jung, as early as 1902, the climax of her mediumnistic productions.

Helene Preiswerk's opposites, combination, and hierarchy somehow became united opposites, and progress in Jung's pictorial representation of the "land of ancestors". For both Helly and Jung, the end of an epoch was reached through an enigmatic revelation. The text that followed Jung's mandala, extremely hermetic, displaced terms and topics to be found in Helene's circles, such as "Matter", "Force", "Light", "Life", "Affinity", and "Inertia" (Shamdasani, 2009, pp. 321–322). As in Helene's context, their use had no link with science or rationality but, instead, with a psychological and spiritual growth.

Prophecies vs. *liberal Protestantism in* Liber Primus

We saw how Jung disagreed with Ritschl's theology. If Jung's psychology and liberal Protestantism had one goal in common, that is, to take into account secular needs and issues, different were their means of reaching this goal. Central to the nineteenth and twentieth centuries' theologian thought was science and modernity. Segal distinguishes three positions:

> The first, the fundamentalist view, pits religion against modernity and opts for religion. It denies modernity, or at least the inescapability of modernity. . . .
>
> The second view, which I call 'rationalist,' is like the fundamentalist view in one key respect: it, too, pits religion against modernity. For both fundamentalists and rationalists, there can be no modern religion. The term 'modern religion' is a contradiction. But antithetically to fundamentalism, rationalism opts for modernity over religion. . . .
>
> The third view, which I call 'romantic,' breaks with both fundamentalism and rationalism in its refusal to oppose religion to modernity. Rather than forcing a choice between the two, it strives to reconcile them. (Segal, 1999, p. 548)

Through the threefold classification, we recognise that both Ritschl and Jung belong to the third category of "romantics". Let us now examine the means to the reconciliation between religion and science. Segal explains,

> In fact [for the "romantics"], the conflict with science gives religion the opportunity to rid itself of its explanatory baggage and to make explicit for the first time its non-explanatory core. Far from threatening religion, science abets religion by obliging it to show that it has always been other than an explanation, even if its non-explanatory core is recognised only now. A virtue is made out of a necessity. (Segal, 1999, p. 549)

One of Ritschl's scientific issues can be traced back to David Hume's 1748 *Essay on Miracles*, which demonstrated the evidential impossibility of miracles. Science, therefore, had rid religion of the supernatural life of Jesus. Instead, the exemplary moral life of Jesus had to be taught and followed by Christians.

For Jung, in contrast, everything that was supernatural in the character as well as in the life of Jesus was inseparable from Jesus and was the core of the Christian religion. In 1897, Jung had written of the danger of a religion devoid of the supernatural. He never changed his mind. In 1938, he added that, more generally, the supernatural aspect of religion could itself define religion. Main writes,

> Jung provides his broad definition of religion as 'a careful consideration and observation of certain dynamic factors that are conceived as "powers" (1938/40: §8), as 'the attitude peculiar to a consciousness which has been changed by experience of the *numinosum*' (ibid.: §9), and as 'a relationship to the highest or most powerful value, be it positive or negative' (ibid.: §137). (Main, 2004, p. 130)[120]

"Numinous", in Jung's writings, originated in his understanding of the theologian Rudolf Otto's use of the term in 1917 in *The Idea of the Holy*.[121] For Jung, a numinous experience depicted the tremendous effect of a sensory intuition. He would later write of the numinosity of archetype. The "numinous", therefore, always reveals in Jung's writings the presence of an archetype, and, as a consequence, of intuition in the form of *Anschauung*. Although simultaneous, *Anschauung* and numinous are not equivalent. The numinous also points to the primacy of experience (over creed) in religion. Shamdasani writes,

> Flournoy conceived of the source of religion experience to be the subconscious or subliminal. As [William] James put it, 'if there be higher powers able to impress us, they may get access to us only through the subliminal door' (James, 1902, p. 243). In his work, Jung took over these principles. He affirmed ... the nomination of the unconscious as the source of religious experience. The further step that Jung took was that of linking these questions to the practice of psychotherapy. (Shamdasani, 1999, p. 541).

Jung's experience that preceded the undertaking of the *Red Book*—his premonitory visions of the First World War—constitutes, following Segal's classification, one of Jung's "romantic" reconciliations of religion with secular issues. War did happen. Nevertheless, as we shall see, Jung's visions did not lose either (1) their supernatural aspect or (2) their numinous aspect. We are, therefore, in the presence of (1) a religious experience, (2) embedded in the most important secular issue, war, (3) intuition, in the form of premonitions. Now, as announced in Sonu Shamdasani's last sentence, we shall see, by examining Jung's experience carefully, how Jung links this experience to the practice of psychotherapy.

Giving a talk in Aberdeen on "The importance of the *unconscious* in psychopathology" (my emphasis) just before the First World War, Jung, then invaded by dozens of blood and death visions, the origin of which were *unconscious*, believed that he barely described himself in his speech. Learning the following day of the breaking out of war, he understood he was not schizophrenic, but that the world outside was becoming mad: he had had premonitory visions of the war. Thus, he believed his prophecies needed to be conserved and used. Hitherto, *Black Books* would become *The Red Book*. "It is not an exaggeration to say that had war not been declared, *Liber Novus* (*The Red Book*) would in all likelihood not have been compiled," writes Shamdasani (2009, pp. 201–202). To support his claim, Shamdasani shows how Jung's pre-war visions were the rationale of the undertaking of *Liber Novus* by writing,

> It is important to note that there are around twelve separate fantasies that Jung may have regarded as precognitive:
>
> 1–2. OCTOBER, 1913
>
> Repeated visions of flood and death of thousands, and the voice that said that this will become real.
>
> 3. AUTUMN 1913
>
> Vision of the sea of blood covering the northern lands.
>
> 4–5. DECEMBER 12, 15, 1913
>
> Image of a dead hero and the slaying of Siegfried in a dream.
>
> 6. DECEMBER 25, 1913
>
> Image of the foot of a giant stepping on a city, and images of murder and bloody cruelty.
>
> 7. JANUARY 2, 1914
>
> Image of a sea of blood and a procession of dead multitudes.
>
> 8. JANUARY 22, 1914
>
> His soul comes up from the depths and asks him if he will accept war and destruction. She shows him images of destruction, military weapons, human remains, sunken ships, destroyed states, etc.

9. MAY 21, 1914

A voice says that the sacrificed fall left and right.

10–12. JUNE–JULY 1914

Thrice-repeated dream of being in a foreign land and having to return quickly by ship, and the descent of the icy cold. (Shamdasani, 2009, p. 202)

Jung's precognition is emphasised in the strongest possible way. Shamdasani numbers and dates the twelve successive visions and dreams and introduces them with "it is important to note". The twelve intuitions also appear conspicuously at the end of the first part of the introduction.

As seen earlier, prophetic dreams and visions did not constitute a new topic in Jung's writings in 1913. Jung had commented on these intuitive faculties as early as 1897 in the *Zofingia Lectures*. For the first time, however, he wrote of his own visions, where we can decipher the use of religious experience, here in the form of prophecy, *for* psychology. Christine Maillard brings our attention to what she calls the "connecting thread" of *The Red Book*: its opening words, "Der Weg des Kommenden", "The way of what is to come" (Maillard, 2011, pp. 119–131). "The way", such as the "journey", for Jung, is an active process. This activity is rendered in the second part of the expression "what is to come". Maillard explains,

> The very expression "what is to come" (*das Kommende*) and his way (*der Weg des Kommenden*) is quite distinct from the more usual expression "the future" (*die Zukunft*), which is also present in the texts of *The Red Book*, even though they really are related to one another. And actually they sometimes appear as antinomical: the future, as a representation of the aftertime, is not what interests the speaker of *The Red Book*. "The future," he says, "must be left to those of the future" (LR and RB, p. 306). The point is not to project oneself into a future, which is the object of all expectations, to the detriment of the present instant, but to return to what is essential: "I return to the small and the real for this is the great way, the way of what is to come" (LR and RB, p. 306). (Maillard, 2011, p. 122, translated for this edition)[122]

With Maillard, we understand that the prophet is not great because he can foresee the future, but because he carries in himself the way—or, to use another image, the seed—of what is to come. This way is paved with symbols. The symbol is the link between religious experience and psychotherapy. Maillard later clarifies,

> It is through the symbol that what is to come can be perceived, [that is,] what is not yet, but what is already the object of an intuitive presentiment (*Ahnung*). Symbols trace this "way of what is to come", whereas signs (*Zeichen*) only evoke what is already known, the meaning of which is fixed. Thus, under its poetic surface, *The Red Book* formulates a theory of the symbol, which will be developed in *Psychological Types*, the work of which is in preparation during these same years. . . . "If one accepts the symbol, it is as if a door opens leading into a new room whose existence one previously didn't know of" (LR and RB, p. 311). The "symbolic life" in question here is first the life of the individual engaged on the way that Jung, in the frame of his psychology, will call "individuation", and which designates a process of emancipation of the subject, who escapes, therefore, the collective determinations. (Maillard, 2011, pp. 130–131, translated for this edition)[123]

In the first extract, Maillard develops Jung's idea of the difference between what we could call a passive esoteric future (*Zukunft*) and what we could call an active psychological "way of what is to come". In the first case, the prophet, no more than any seer predicting the future to some clients, would inevitably, for instance, provoke the passive projection of the same clients into some expected future. Opposite this merely passive reaction stands the psychological and active way, the seeds of which are to be found in the present. In this second case, the individuals are not told anything by anyone. Instead, they must create their own way. The way of what is to come, above all, is theirs, and it starts now, in the present of its enunciation. Jung does not feel any urge to enlighten the world with *his* revelations. As early as the first pages of *Liber Primus*, he writes, "*You seek the path I warn you away from my own. It can also be the wrong way for you. May each go its own way*" (Jung, in Shamdasani 2009, p. 231, original italics).

In the second extract, Maillard this time clearly links prophecy to Jung's later psychotherapy and present practice, or, rather, present testing of the method with himself. She describes the means from the present to what is to come, not just for Jung, but for everybody. This means is the symbol. The method is no less than Jung's psychology. Jung's "*May each go its own way*" becomes the motto of the analytical psychologist, and individuation its goal, as will be detailed when we examine the place of intuition in Jungian and post-Jungian practice.

Another point of importance is the difference between prophecies and the prophet in *Liber Primus*. That Jung experiences prophecies does not make him a prophet.[124] If we wanted to call Jung a prophet, then we should refer to Nietzsche's conception, free of metaphysics and *a priori*. Huskinson explains that, according to Nietzsche, "we must seek experience of life and our own interpretation of the world. We arrive at an interpretation through our feelings, sensations and intuitions, and these constitute what is fundamentally 'real'." Huskinson uses the telling expression of Nietzsche's conception of life as "a fleeting world of becoming" (Huskinson, 2004, p. 23). This fleeting world of becoming corresponds to Jung's first sentence of *The Red Book*, "the way of what is to come" and to Jung's addition (and injunction) that his way is nobody else's. As early as the first pages of *Liber Primus* appears the Soul, who guards Jung against the rationalist "spirit of the time". In 1928 Jung writes,

> I would not like to deny in general the occurrence of real prophets, but as a precaution I would first doubt each individual case, since it is too questionable a thing to casually decide to take someone for genuine without further ado. Every proper prophet strives at first manfully against the unconscious imposition of this role. (Jung, "The relations between the ego and the unconscious", quoted in Shamdasani, 1998a, p. 81)

If Jung were temporarily to assume the total defeat of his ego by the Soul, this act would not lead to the establishment of a cult with Jung as its prophet. Certainly, Jung fought against the Soul in the matter of the unconscious imposition of this role, even though he listened to her to learn and psychologically progress. Jung's use of religion had a different goal. Shamdasani proposes that "Jung attempted to develop a psychology of the religious-making process. The task was to depict the translation and the transposition of the numinous experience of individuals into symbols, and eventually into the dogmas and creeds of organised religions" (Shamdasani, 1999, p. 543).

A symbol potentially carries the future of the dreamer when it appears during the night. For Jung, this does not make the dreamer a prophet, but makes him a candidate for either active imagination or for Jung's constructive method, as will be studied in Part IV.

CHAPTER FOUR

Psychological intuitions

Non-intuitive hallucinations and visions in the SW case

As a future physician, Jung carefully observed every physical phenomena occurring during Helene Preiswerk's trances. The literature of his thesis, such as the references to the work of the neurologists Freud, Binet, and Claparède, all of whom he would later meet, showed Jung's consideration for the organic side of his work. Here are some of his descriptions:

> I witnessed the first attacks of somnambulism. Their course was usually as follows: S. W. grew very pale, slowly sank to the ground or into a chair, closed her eyes, became cataleptic, drew several deep breaths, and began to speak. ... The ecstasy [the second stage] was generally followed by a cataleptic stage with *flexibilitas cerea*, which gradually passed over into the waking state. An almost constant feature was the sudden pallor which gave her face a waxen anaemic hue that was positively frightening ... her pulse was then low but regular ... the breathing ... barely perceptible ... S.W. predicted her attacks beforehand; just before the attacks she had strange sensations, became excited, rather anxious, occasionally saying ... that she would probably die in one of these attacks. ... On one occasion after the

cataleptic stage, tachypnoea was observed, lasting for two minutes with a respiration of 100 per minute. (Jung, *CW 1*, pars 39–40)

Self-induced trances were hardly a merely psychic phenomenon. Body and mind were involved together in the extraordinary spiritist process. Strong sensations existed. All the apperceptions (thoughts and feelings) were transformed into perceptions by the medium. Helene's "feelings" of anxiety and "thoughts" of death were, in fact, perceptions of the fading of the external world—and of some of its elements—to enter another one. Only the medium's intuitions were accurate—when Helly predicted her attacks, for instance. If some hallucinations had to do with intuition, not all did. Paul Bishop reminds us that "Jung cites the distinction made by M. M. A. Macario between 'intuitive halluzinationen' ['intuitive hallucinations'] and other ordinary hallucinations (JGW 1/JCW 1 §106)" (Bishop, 2000, p. 98).

Psychic and physical depictions shared one trait: most of them occurred during in-between states. Outside of sessions, Helene Preiswerk had hypnagogic (between wake and sleep) and hypnopompic (between sleep and wake) visions.

Jung distinguished between visions, hallucinations, and teleological hallucinations. Hallucinations did not match "the plastic clearness" (Jung, *CW 1*, par. 43) of visions, and some hallucinations did not possess any teleological character. Whereas three of the sisters of Helene Preiswerk started to hallucinate at night—one of them, for example, awoke after a nightmare seeing "a black shadow with human outlines, and near it a cloudy white figure" (Jung, *CW 1*, par. 43)—Helene had almost no such rudimentary hallucinations but instead had visions of spirits that she could even touch.

Exceptionally, when Jung described Helly's (clear) vision of the two grandfathers, Preiswerk and Jung the elder, arm-in-arm, he wrote of hallucination,

> These two factors, darkness [which descended] and a remarkable occurrence [a brusque interruption of a communication from the spirit grandfather] seemed to have caused rapid deepening of hypnosis, which enabled the hallucinations to develop. The psychological mechanism of this process seems to be as follows: the influence of darkness on suggestibility, particularly in regard to the sense organs, is well known. Binet states it has a special influence on hysterical subjects, producing immediate drowsiness. (Jung, *CW 1*, par. 97)

Jung then spends almost six pages, using the current scientific literature, to support his claim on the physiogenesis of Helene's hallucination. One chapter accounts for a possible psychical origin, yet only mentions the possible (sexual) repression of the medium towards him.

What we learn from Jung's quoted literature is that stimuli and conditions of sight and hearing were considered responsible for the hallucinations. In other words, in-between physical states played a large role. Jung mentions Alfred Maury, Myers, and George Trumbull Ladd, who had described hypnagogic and hypnopompic hallucinations. Flournoy and Justus Hecker supported Jung's views that "complex hallucinations do not belong to the waking state but occur as a rule in a state of partial waking" (Jung, CW 1, par. 106). Jung's use of the term "complex" before "hallucinations" shows how, in fact, the frontier between "hallucination" and "vision" did not clearly appear in his work. In the same way that Jung wrote of "automatisms" only *à la Janet*, negatively depicting the timid automatic writing of the medium and the tilting of the table, he was driven by the negative and positive connotations of, respectively, "hallucination" and "vision".

Multiple personalities and teleological hallucinations in the SW case

Another physical in-between state, which could also be called an in-between stage, was then considered central by the psychiatrists to the appearance of trances: puberty.

Jung reconstructed the long chain of research on somnambulists and on cases associated with puberty, among which the double personality of Mary Reynolds stood out. This time, physiogenesis and double personality will bring Jung to intuition.

At the age of nineteen, Mary Reynolds suddenly lost all memory and found herself in a new state, opposite in character (gay and eccentric) to her normal one (sober, prone to depression, and devoid of imagination). After many changes between her first and second states, she definitely remained in her second positive state at age thirty-five (see, for example, Ellenberger, 1970, p. 128). Roderick Main writes,

> While analysing his cousin's trances psychiatrically, Jung did not dismiss the psychic dissociation as simply pathological. The secondary

personalities she was manifesting could also be therapeutic, representing 'attempts of the future character to break through' (1902: §136). (Main, 2004, p. 67).[125]

In the following extract, in which by "future character" Jung implied "after puberty", he writes,

> In view of the difficulties that oppose the future character, the somnambulisms sometimes have an eminently teleological significance, in that they give the individual, who would otherwise succumb, the means of victory. Here I am thinking of Joan of Arc, whose extraordinary courage reminds one of the feats performed by Mary Reynolds in her second state. This is also perhaps, the place to point out the like significance of "teleological hallucinations", of which occasional cases come to the knowledge of the public, although they have not yet been subjected to scientific study. (Jung, *CW 1*, par. 136)

Jung's "somnambulisms" referred broadly to the entire production of one's somnambulist, such as Mary Reynolds, mentioned after Joan of Arc and before the teleological hallucinations. Jung's grammatical construction allows us to link both women to the teleological hallucinations and, thereby, supports Jung's favourable approach. Jung's "occasional cases" referred to Flournoy, who had described the teleological hallucinations of Hélène Smith. Here follows Flournoy's presentation and analysis—second paragraph of the extract—of one incident experienced by Hélène Smith during her teens, an incident involving, for the Genevan psychologist, an "evident connection with a phase of development of major importance" (Flournoy, (1994)[1899], p. 25), that is, puberty. Flournoy writes,

> At about the age of seventeen or eighteen, Hélène was returning from the country one evening, carrying a fine bouquet of flowers. During the last minutes of the journey she heard behind her a peculiar cry of a bird, which seemed to her to warn her against some danger, and she hastened her step without looking behind. . . . She went tired to bed, and in the middle of the night awoke in great pain, but was unable to cry out. At that moment she felt herself gently lifted, together with the pillow on which she lay, as if by two friendly hands [those of Léopold], which enabled her to recover her voice and call her mother, who hastened to comfort her and carried the flowers, which were too odorous, out of the room.

The incident belongs to the category of well-known cases where a danger of some sort not suspected by the normal personality, but which is subconsciously known or recognised, is warded off by a preservative hallucination, either sensory (as here—the cry of the bird) or motor (as in the lifting of the body). (Flournoy, 1994[1899], pp. 21–22)

Hélène Smith's sensory hallucinations had the goal of protecting her from the dangerous smell of flowers during her sleep. The young woman under-consciously intuited the danger that her conscious state could not fathom. Likewise Mary Reynolds, Joan of Arc, and Helene Preiswerk were under-consciously guided by their visions, or by their spirits (like Léopold for Hélène) in critical situations. Unlike Jung's use of the term "hallucination", Flournoy's deployment of it in this context is clear. The bird did not cry out, and Hélène Smith was not lifted by two invisible hands. Hallucination, thus described, has neither positive nor negative connotation. It means that what Hélène saw and felt did not happen.

It is in such a way that Jung more clearly described teleological hallucinations six years later, when he experienced them first hand at the Burghölzli:

(1) A patient in the first stages of progressive paralysis wanted in desperation to kill himself by jumping out of the window. He jumped on to the window-sill, but at that moment a tremendous light appeared in front of the window, hurling him back into the room.

(2) A psychopath who was disgusted with life because of his misfortunes wanted to commit suicide by inhaling gas from an open jet. He inhaled the gas vigorously for a few seconds, then suddenly felt an enormous hand grasp him by the chest and throw him to the floor, where he gradually recovered from his fright. The hallucination was so distinct that the next day he could still show me the place where the five fingers had gripped him. (Jung, CW 3, pars 305, 306)

If the patients did see a light and did feel a hand, there was neither light nor hand. It was, therefore, a hallucination. Presented by Jung as the expression of under-conscious ("repressed", yet not in a Freudian sense) complexes, one is here rather driven to write simply of a primal, collective, survival instinct. At the same period, in 1907, Flournoy published "Automatisme téléologique anti-suicide: un cas de suicide empêché par une hallucination", in which he acknowledged the teleological character of one anti-suicidal teleological automatism.[126]

Let us come back to Jung's medical dissertation. The last and central in-between state depicted by Jung was Helene's "semi-somnambulism ... some time before and after the actual somnambulistic attack" as she left or re-approached consciousness. Semi-consciousness was again both a physical and a psychical state:

> [Helene] lent only half an ear to the conversation around her, answered absent-mindedly, frequently lost herself in all manner of hallucinations; her face was solemn, her look ecstatic, visionary, ardent. Closer observation revealed a far-reaching alteration of her entire character. She was now grave, dignified. ... one almost had to ask oneself: Is this really a girl of 15½ [in fact 13½]? (Jung, CW 1, par. 77)

Out of these physical and mental transformations, Ivenes (Helene's spirit self) was born.

Helly's report of her visions recounted many travels and sojourns in the "Beyond", in "that space between the stars which people think is empty, but which really contains countless spirit worlds", or else once in "a wonderful moonlit valley that was destined for generations as yet not born" (Jung, CW 1, par. 59). Before her, Hélène Smith had travelled from India to the planet Mars. Like Hélène Smith and other spiritist mediums, Helene Preiswerk also travelled through time, from earlier reincarnations as a medium between humans and the Beyond to her earliest incarnation as an ordinary Jewess back in the time of King David.

Jung writes that "she anticipates her own future and embodies in Ivenes what she wishes to be in twenty years' time" (Jung, CW 1, par. 116). Helene, indeed, became adult less than five years later. He depicts Ivenes as "a serious, mature person, devout and right-minded, full of womanly tenderness and very modest, who always submit[ed] to the opinion of others" (Jung, CW 1, par. 62). Truly impressed, he continues,

> When she spoke, the theme was always an extremely serious one. In this state, she could talk so seriously, so forcefully and convincingly ... that one almost had the impression that a mature woman was

being acted with considerable dramatic talent. The reason for this
seriousness, this solemnity of behaviour, was given in the patient's
explanation that at these times [of semi-somnambulism] she stood on
the frontier of this world and the next. (Jung, *CW 1*, par. 77)

Helene Preiswerk's explanation implied that she stood on the frontier between this world and the Beyond. So far, "beyond" had meant "past", through incarnations in previous lives. Now "beyond" meant "future". Helene was no longer hallucinatory, but now visionary: she had a *Vorahnung*, a prescience, of her future. Freed from the expectations of the other participants (such as her mother, who saw in Carl a perfect son-in-law), she answered and intuitively visualised her own destiny.

This prospective aspect of spiritism remained central to Jung's interest. In 1909, he would boldly write to Freud about some "first-rate spiritualist phenomena". Jung had the feeling that there existed a universal complex having to do with "the prospective tendencies in man". "If there is", he wrote, "a 'psychoanalysis' there must also be a 'psychosynthesis' which creates future events according to the same laws". Dated 2 April 1909, the letter arrived in Freud's hands just after Jung's "spookery" (while Freud and Jung were talking about parapsychology, Jung predicted a second loud report from the bookcase that did occur) (McGuire, 1988[1974], pp. 215–216). These kinds of statements would appear too audacious to Freud. In contrast, Jung's association tests, thanks to which he had gained his peers' recognition, had Freud's approval and Jung used them to meet his future mentor.

Associations: between Janet and Freud

Sir Francis Galton is credited with having invented the first word association test. In 1883, he wrote these conclusions in his *Inquiries*:

> Perhaps the strongest of the impressions left by these experiments regards the multifariousness of the work done by the mind in a state of half-consciousness, and the valid reason they afford for believing in the existence of still deeper states of mental operations, sunk wholly below the level of consciousness, which may account for such mental phenomena as cannot otherwise be explained. (Galton, 1883, p. 145)

Galton's state of half-consciousness shows once more how the royal road to the unconscious, where mental operations took place, was not yet exclusively dream analysis but, instead, the various methods undertaken in the under-conscious. Word association was the new experimental method of the under-conscious state, since hypnosis had fallen out of favour at the turn of the twentieth century. Galton's use of the terms "states" and "level" evinced his belonging to the family of the psychodynamic experts that included Myers, Flournoy, and Janet.

The "new" technique had roots as old as the tenth century, in the work of Avicenna. Part III of Avicenna's *Canon* dealt with disorders of the nervous system and the psyche, among which the "disorder of love" needed to be treated as follows:

> Avicenna stated that the identification of the beloved one is the cornerstone of the management of such patients. As a diagnostic tool, numerous names should be spoken while monitoring the patient's pulse. A change in the pulse rate and the quality upon naming the appropriate name might indicate the name of the beloved one. The test also should be repeated for different titles, vocations, places, and cities together with the liable name to further locate the suspected person. This name and pulse test is a classic example of a psychosomatic reaction. (Shoja & Shane Tubbs, 2007, p. 229)

Replacing "beloved one" with "complex" allows us to see one of Jung's aims during the tests: identifying the complex lying behind the words uttered by the subject.

This twofold but not exhaustive presentation of the origin of the word association experiment reveals two possible avenues of research for Jung: the psychodynamic of the psyche that he found in his approach based on that of Janet, and the qualitative components that he found in his approach based on Freud.

Word association tests were instigated at the Burghölzli by the director, Eugen Bleuler. Bleuler asked Jung and Franz Riklin to undertake word association, which Riklin had already done in Germany with Gustav Aschaffenburg (see Bair, 2004, p. 64). Simply, the test "consisted in enunciating to a subject a succession of [a hundred] carefully chosen words ["stimulus-words"]; to each of them the subject had to respond with the first word that occurred to him; the reaction time was exactly measured" (Ellenberger, 1970, p. 691). After a break, or else in different and generally disturbing conditions, the individual was given the same stimulus-words and had to start the exercise again. Repetitions and forgetting were as significant as the time lag. Each "suspicious" answer—when the link between the stimulus-word and the reaction was not obvious—prompted the examiner to ask the subject which exact context had given rise to the word.

Published in 1904–1906, the series of articles such as "The reaction-time ratio in the association experiment" and the essay "The associations of normal subjects" constituted Jung's first attempt to bring together the results of his collaborative research.[127] This extensive, rigorous publication (volume 2 of Jung's *Collected Works*) methodologically represents the most reliable of Jung's studies in word association. Jung critically reviewed and used the literature of his German, Swiss, French, and English-speaking esteemed colleagues, among them Emil Kraepelin, Gustav Aschaffenburg, Georg Theodor Ziehen, Édouard Claparède, Hugo Münsterberg, Benjamin Bourdon, and Wilhelm Wundt. Of great importance for Jung were Aschaffenburg's and Kraepelin's distinction between internal (by meaning) and external (by forms of speech, by sound) associations and Ziehen's discovery of the relationship between the length of reaction and the emotionally charged complex of representations (*gefühlsbetonter Vorstellungskomplex*) (Ellenberger, 1970, p. 692).[128] In "The associations of normal subjects", Jung announced his method and outcomes with clarity and remained careful, almost circumspect, about interpretation.

Two parts divided the work into the procedures and the results, both of which amounted to precise classifications. There, one can find the *methodological* origin of Jung's *Types*. Jung organised the word-reactions of the subjects in eight categories:

1. Internal (meaningful) associations, such as predicative, causal relationships, contrast.
2. External associations, such as linguistic–motor forms
3. Sound reactions, such as rhymes.
4. Miscellaneous, among which are the important failures to react or the repetition of the stimulus-word.
5. Perseveration: when a reaction-word is given more than once.
6. The egocentric reaction, as opposed to an objective reaction, where the word has almost nothing to do with the subject.

7. Repetition of the reaction.
8. Linguistic connection, such as the same grammatical form or the same ending (paraphrased from Jung, CW 2, par. 113).

The eight groups were not mutually exclusive. Each provided the examiner with complementary data. For example, the association of "blessed" with the stimulus-word "pious" alone could seemingly only belong to Category 1 (a meaningful reaction). But if the reaction "blessed" had already appeared five times in a set of a hundred reaction words, then it would also belong to Category 5 (perseveration) and probably to Category 6 (egocentric reaction) or Category 7 (repetition of the reaction). If the reaction "blessed" occurred as a fifth perseveration in a row, then the reaction would not even belong to Category 1.

Jung concludes, "The associations show normal variation, principally under the influence of (A) attention; (B) education; (C) the individual characteristics of the subject" (Jung, CW 2, par. 488: (A), (B), and (C) added for clarity). Of primal importance, point (A) will be studied alone later. Point (A) is directly linked to the state, underconscious, of the subject. Point (B) recalled that the division of the subjects into male and female, and educated and uneducated, persons had proved necessary. Historical and sociological data, thus, hierarchically preceded individual data. Point (C) organised eight types of subjects deduced from the calculation of the percentage of their types of reactions, the calculation of the percentage of the time ratio of their reactions, and the observation of their attitude during the tests.

Jung ended the examination with a precise summary:

I. *Objective type*. The stimulus-word is taken objectively, that is:
   (α) mainly according to its objective meaning [internal objective type]
   (β) mainly as verbal stimulus [external objective type]
II. *Egocentric attitude*. The stimulus-word is taken subjectively (egocentrically).
   (α) *Constellation type*. The personal elements used in the reaction belong to one or more emotionally charged complexes, there being two possibilities:
      (αα) The complex-constellations are spoken without concealment.
      (ββ) The complex-constellations appear in veiled form as a result of a not always conscious repression.

(β) *Predicate type*. This type has presumably the psychological particularity of particularly vivid (plastic) inner images, by which its particular mode of reaction can be explained. This type also shows at best an abnormally low ability to divide attention. (Jung, *CW 2*, par. 490)

To illustrate Jung's theory, we take an example of what could have been eight typical reactions (italicised) to the stimulus "to find". An *internal objective* type's reaction could be "to search" (causal relationship) where an *external objective* type could react with "found" (grammatical variation). Both reactions are meaningful and are only remotely, if at all, related to the subjects. Provided that these kinds of reaction happen to a great extent during the experiment, they would be *objective* types.

Egocentric types' reactions, in contrast, accounted for elements of a personal order. Since suspicious (that is, not obvious), the reaction "brooch" to the stimulus "find" would require, for example, the subject's explanation that he had recently found a brooch on the street. It would, therefore, describe what Jung called an "egocentric attitude". In this context, "egocentric" means only "linked to the subject", instead of ego-centred. This type Jung also called "simple constellation type" (Jung, *CW 2*, par. 414).

This was not the case with the three remaining types, *predicate* and the two kinds of *complex-constellation* types, who display ego-centred traits. "Is a blessing" would be a predicate reaction to "to find". "Is a blessing" describes the stimulus with a predicate, which implies vivid inner images and is an ego-centred overreaction. The reactions of predicate types often implied "I think that" or "I feel that" before what they considered to be an answer rather than a reaction to the stimulus.

To "to find", the objective type could react with the general thought "key". By contrast, the reaction "key" of a *complex-constellation type spoken without concealment* would appear after a long time-reaction (symptomatic of the presence of a complex) and with the subject's explanation of his anxiety about the real experience of losing his keys.

A typical reaction of a *complex-constellation type following a repression* would be a failure to react to the stimulus "to find". Long time-ratios and failures are complexes in veiled forms.

As clear as Jung's methodology is, one point requires clarification. In a footnote of this summary of types, Jung referred to Freud's work. We are, therefore, apparently invited to link Jung's use of the term "repression" with Freud's. Yet, Shamdasani (1998b) notes that in his 1905 "Experimental observations on the faculty of memory", Jung this time clearly states the difference between his and Freud's employment of the term "repression". Jung writes,

> The concept of repression, which I use on many occasions in my analyses, requires a brief explanation. In Freud's work this concept . . . has the meaning of an active function, frequently a function of consciousness. . . . In the area of normal subjects it might, however, be a question of a more passive "sliding into the background"; at least here repression seems to be something unconscious. (Jung, CW 2, par. 619n, quoted in Shamdasani, 1998b, p. 121)

Jung's presentation of Freud's repression stems from Breuer and Freud's 1893 "Preliminary communications" in Freud's *Studies on Hysteria* (1895d, pp. 4–21). There, indeed, repression can be read as an intentional, conscious forgetting, "identical with the 'not wanting to remember' unpleasant impressions" (Jung, *CW2*, par. 639). Even though Jung refers once, in a contemporary study published in 1905, to Freud's "The neuro-psychoses of defence" (1894a), to Freud's "The psychical mechanism of forgetfulness" (1898b), and crucially to Freud's more elaborated "Screen memories" (1899a), Jung here conflates wish—which is Freud's concern—with will (Jung, *CW 2*, par. 639). Will was linked to consciousness. Wish, as the first factor of repression, was more complex, and certainly not the product of a function of consciousness in Freud's work, since it was connected as early as 1900 to instincts and drives (*Triebe*). (For a historical perspective on Freud's concept of repression, see Boag, 2006, pp. 74–86.)

What Jung described as "his" employment of the term "repression" against Freud's was indeed distinct and, as Shamdasani observes, was Janetian. What, for Jung, was the opposite of the *active* hiding of a distressful memory was a *passive* withdrawal into the background, to be connected to Janet's *abaissement du niveau mental*.

To the stimulus "to find", an unemployed subject could have reacted, for instance, with a failure, therefore revealing the complex of his unemployment. When stimulated by the word "to find", the unemployed person would have under-consciously—that is, not exactly consciously but not wholly unconsciously either—constellated *Einfälle* (images would have fallen into the subject's mind) around the emotionally charged idea of "finding a job". The subject would have known very well that he was unemployed. His complex would have been conscious, but he would not necessarily have been willing actively to hide it. That is what Jung called the passivity of the subject, that is, the *temporary* absence of the ego in the face of the independence of the complex at the moment following the stimulus word. That very moment was what the test was all about: a necessary lack of attention leaving room for anything to come from behind, from under, from the sub-, the under-, or the un-conscious, and by one single means, intuition (*Einfall*).

During the entire experiment, Jung's subjects had to respond with the first word that occurred to them. This process implied that ideally they answered instinctively and that their reactions were not mediated by any apperception. Point (A) of Jung's conclusion reinforced what Jung had already claimed and what he emphasised in his Foreword—that "among the psychic factors that exert the main influence on the mechanism of association, *attention* is of cardinal importance" (Jung, CW 2, par. 3, original italics). If Jung had previously dedicated "Occult phenomena" to Flournoy, this time by stressing the importance of attention Jung dedicated "The association of normal subjects" to Janet, whose seminars in Paris he had recently attended. Thereby, Jung also reminded his readers of the frame of the experiment: the intuitive realm of the under-conscious more or less disturbed by attention, since "all associations taking place in the subconscious [are] outside the range of attention" (Jung, CW 2, par. 451).

Jung explains,

> Münsterberg maintains that, in order to stimulate associations, the external excitation does not first have to be converted into a conscious process, but that, between external excitation and conscious central excitation, there is a non-conscious stage in which an association process takes place that does not reach consciousness. (Jung, CW 2, par. 88*n*)[129]

Crucially, the first stage of the association test took place in the under-conscious, where the subject is deprived of attention, of pure forms of thought, feeling, or sensation.

Jung, for instance, described what he called "indirect associations", which consisted in unexpected reactions that had emerged from an intuitive perception. To the stimulus "white", a subject reacted with "far". The "indirect" association in this case was the perception "snowfield" (Jung, CW 2, par. 83), which instantly fell into the subject's mind (*Einfall*) after the stimulus "white". Albeit "suspicious", not obvious, indirect associations were not revelatory of any (qualitative) complexes but, instead, displayed (quantitative) intuition, the invisible perception that allowed the test to make sense.

To grasp that "infinitely complicated mechanism" of attention, Jung had closely followed Janet's work, as testified by the numerous references to Janet. He had particularly read Janet's 1903 *Les Obsessions et la psychasténie*, where the correlated notion of *fonction du réel* was described. Central in Janet's work, the *fonction du réel* theoretically links Janet, Bergson, and Jung.[130] Janet writes,

> [The *fonction du réel* consists in] the psychological operations that allow humanity to enter into contact with reality, to act on it, and to grasp its existence with certainty. The *fonction du réel*, with the operations of will, the feeling of the real, the feeling of the present, holds the top position in the hierarchy of psychological phenomena. (Janet, 1903, p. ix, translated for this edition)[131]

Attention was one of these psychological operations. It was one of Janet's "higher" functions, next to concentration, or "mental synthesis". At the other extreme stood the "lower" psychological functions, the automatisms, resulting from the narrowing of the field of consciousness, and leading to dissociation. Janet's system was primarily psychodynamic. As Haule writes, "by the turn of the century, the dominant theme in Janet's works was that of ... lowering the mental level (*abaissement*)" (Haule, 1984, p. 642). This *abaissement* brought a person from the higher to the lower functions. In Jung's work on association, Janet's *fonction du réel* is translated into "acting up to realities", or "the psychological adaptation to the environment" (Jung, CW 2, par. 1066). The entwined concepts of Janet's system—the style of which we recognise in the thought of his colleague from the Ecole Normale Supérieure and friend, Bergson—show some fundamentals of Jung's word association typology.[132]

Objective types, as well as the uneducated subjects who were willing to answer the stimulus word instead of reacting to it in order to show that they understood the word, displayed mental synthesis. A meaningful reaction required Janet's higher functions. Equally important was the major factor that distinguished complex-constellation types from predicate types. We saw that all three types were egocentred, yet attention divided them. When the predicate type registered "to find—is a blessing", he was attentive, since he was eager to reveal his view, opinion, or taste. In contrast, the complex-constellation type's psyche, when registering a failure, passively lowered his mental level and repressed any reaction (see Shamdasani, 1998b, p. 121 concerning repression).

Indirect associations were not the sole expressions of intuition, that is, intuitions (*Einfälle*) *as a result*.[133] Jung observed another interesting automatism of the lower functions occurring in the under-conscious. It was the *audition colorée*, or synaesthesia, where one person, Subject Three, reacted to sounds with colours as follows:

> to kiss (*küssen*) yellow
> *ü* is yellow for the subject.
>
> misery (*Elend*) something red
> *e* is red.
>
> indolent (*träge*) blue
> *ä* is blue. (Jung, CW 2, par. 139)

The *audition colorée* had, at this time, as many definitions as explanations for its occurrence. Physio- or psychogenesis, circumstances or heredity—there was no agreement on its aetiology (see Claviere, 1898, pp. 161–178). This experiment first reminds us of Arthur Rimbaud's 1871 sonnet, "Vowels", which says: "A black, E white, I red, U green, O blue: vowels / I shall tell, one day, of your latent births".[134] In the stream of Charles Baudelaire's *correspondances*, the theory of Rimbaud *"le voyant"*, the visionary, literally "the one who sees", appeared as even more direct, immediately and palpably intuitive. Likewise the reactions of Subject Three displayed an automatic perception, intuition, which was not disturbed by any kind of apperception or mental synthesis. When subjects such as Subject Three reacted with motor automatisms, Jung classified them "motor types" (Jung, CW 2, par. 141).

Finally, Jung's resorting to experimenting with the subjects when they were fatigued or under distraction lowered attention and furthered the *abaissement*. More permanently in an under-conscious state, the subjects could use intuition.[135] These conditions gave rise to another type, the "blunt-reaction type" (Jung, *CW 2*, par. 170):

> In our interpretation, sound reactions, which are only on a slightly higher level than mere repetitions of words, are the most primitive of associations by similarity. After early childhood they are no longer used but, always called up . . . they are repressed [that is, under-conscious] and usually exist outside consciousness. We call the increase of linguistic–motor forms and sound reactions the blunting of the reaction. (Jung, *CW 2*, par. 119)

A typical "primitive" repetition of word would be the child repeating "mum" after her mother's own uttering of the term. Empathetic and analogical, this process is, therefore, intuitive. A sound reaction is different from an external objective reaction such as "to find—found", where the essential connection is meaning. "To find—fine" would be a sound reaction by alliteration. When they were fatigued, educated people tended to produce a growing number of blunt reactions. Commenting on his own results (Jung was Subject Nineteen), Jung writes,

> In the last third of the experiments [that occurred late when the subject was fatigued by a full working day] with internal distraction the subject became uninterested, as if hypnoidal . . . the sound associations increased [from 3 sound associations during the first third to 18 during the last third of the experiment]. (Jung, *CW 2*, par. 204)

Just as the *motor* type connected *audition colorée* to medium's *motor* automatisms such as glossolalia, Jung's *hypnoidal* condition linked word association to *hypno*tism—*hypno-* for "sleep"—as a voluntary obtained state. All four elements implied an under-conscious state and intuition.

At the turn of the century, a clear-cut divide between consciousness and the unconscious did not exist. The environment of their work was the under-conscious (see Jung, *CW 8*, pars 194–219. *Auditions colorées*, indirect associations, blunt reactions, motor reactions, automatisms, were all intuitions. They were *Einfälle*, elements that suddenly and intuitively fell into one's mind.

Janet's system did not favour intuition more than Freud's, but it provided Jung with a frame where intuition had room. If we look at

Freud's free association, *Einfallsmethode*, from a later Jungian point of view, it is hard to find a more intuitive method. Just like word association, Freud's *Einfallsmethode* required the analysand to associate an image, a thought, or an element of a dream with anything that came (fell into) to his mind without intellectual "censorship". In this instantaneity, Jung would later recognise intuition and derive his intuitive (analogical) method of amplification from it. Freud, who thought of intuition as irrational, simply did not introduce intuition into the picture. For Freud, common mistakes and lapses resulting from this instantaneity revealed psychic determinism and the natural process of repression by default (see Freud, 1901b).[136] In other words, if Jung was interested in *perceptions*, such as *audition colorée* or blunt reactions as just seen, Freud stressed *apperceptions*. Where Jung showed interest in intuition, Freud cared about feelings and their disturbances resulting from intellectual censorship. Jung did not underestimate emotion and also referred to Freud's work at length throughout his work. Yet, as Haule states, "The careful reader discovers only the loosest connection between these studies [the word association experiments] and the contemporary works of Freud" (Haule, 1984, p. 648).[137]

The widespread idea of the scientific character of the word association experiment, which *therefore* corresponds to Jung's Freudian period, needs readjustment. Jung's scientific *methodology* existed *before* Jung had met Freud. Jung's *success* with this method and not its scientific character was then outstanding, since that same scientific character was to be found in the contemporary word associations tests carried out in Germany, England, and France, as the numerous references to Jung's work testify. As the next section shows, Jung's word association tests lost their scientific character just as soon as Jung used them for the main purpose of endorsing psychoanalysis. Even today, some psychiatrists use the experiment initially framed in Jung's later theory. Their clinical applications display the structures and dynamics of complexes–archetypes, of anima and animus, and pay attention to the relationship established between the examiner and the patients (see, for example, Vezzoli, Bressi, Tricarico, et al., 2007, pp. 89–108).

Just as Jung's *Occult Phenomena* had been dedicated to Flournoy, and just as *The Associations of Normal Subjects* had been dedicated to Janet, so Jung's third main work, *The Psychology of Dementia Praecox*, intended to reach Freud. If the association between Jung and Freud could for both parties, with the benefit of hindsight, qualify as a theoretical detour, it remains the most successful strategic decision they ever took. That historians still struggle today trying to tell fact from fiction shows how convenient the fiction was for both men and how they both were themselves satisfied with keeping the legend of the significance of their scientific collaboration alive (see Shamdasani, 2000, pp. 459–472).

The collaboration started from an initial misunderstanding. While Freud was happy to disseminate psychoanalysis inside mental hospitals, Jung perceived them (the mental hospitals) as a time in his career of professional frustration. For Jung, Freud's ideas

> pointed the way to a closer investigation and understanding of individual cases . . . [while in hospitals, to him] patients were labelled, rubber-stamped with a diagnosis, and, for the most part, that settled the matter. (Jung, 1995[1961/1963], p. 135)

"For us, then young psychiatrists," explained Jung, "it was . . . a source of illumination, while for our older colleagues it was an object of mockery" (Jung, 1995[1961/1963], p. 169).

If the links between psychology and psychiatry were then, as they are still now, far from obvious, Jung's—or Jaffé's—statement carries less weight. Bleuler entered into contact with Freud before Jung did, and he required his staff to take care of the patients twenty-four hours a day. We saw how his life at the Burghölzli was "monastic", a strong accompanying motive to quit psychiatry for the novelties of psychoanalysis (see Bair, 2004, pp. 66–69). Jung's goal now was clear: seducing the leader of the Viennese school to enter the world of dreams and psychoanalysis, mentored by the greatest pioneer of the field. The success of his word association experiment constituted his best possible introduction. Along with some previous researches, Jung's article of 1906, "Psychoanalysis and association experiments", was sent to Vienna, Berggasse 19. Freud answered in a letter dated 11 April 1906:

> Dear colleague,
>
> Many thanks for sending me your *Diagnostic Association Studies*, which in my impatience I had already acquired. Of course your latest paper, "Psychoanalysis and Association Experiments", pleased me most, because in it you argue on the strength of your own experience that everything I have said about the hitherto unexplored fields of our

discipline is true. I am confident that you will often be in a position to back me up, but I shall gladly accept correction.

Yours sincerely, DR. FREUD (McGuire, 1988[1974], p. 3)

This first letter reveals the striking feature and one of the main topics of the correspondence that would follow between the two psychologists until 1914: strategic understandings.

Now encouraged by Freud, Jung had to precisely expose the links between psychoanalysis and pathological cases. *On the Psychology of Dementia Praecox: An Attempt* met this requirement. Shamdasani notices that this publication "marks a turning point in the mode in which Jung presented his work, as it was during the period of its composition that he commenced his association with Freud" (Shamdasani, 1998b, p. 122). "Presentation" is the key element here. Whereas Jung in *The Association of Normal Subjects* had exhaustively presented all his results and maintained a scientific caution in his small number of analyses, he now did the exact opposite in *Dementia Praecox*, where only one paradigmatic case provided the reader with "an attempt": explaining psychiatry with psychoanalysis.

As revealed by the correspondence between Freud, Jung, and Bleuler, as well as Jung's introduction of *Dementia Praecox*, Bleuler enthusiastically supported the introduction of psychoanalysis at the Burghölzli. As the director of the *Klinik*, he took the responsibility of the outcome of the experience and this way contributed to the dissemination of psychoanalysis through the success of its "Zürich style" offspring (Shamdasani, 2001, p. 13). In the front line with *Dementia Praecox*, Jung's involvement proved different in style and method. Starting from the psychoanalytic hypothesis, Jung boldly attempted to prove its validity from his observations.[138]

By "paradigm", Jung, in fact, meant a case "which could fit psychoanalysis". Before Bleuler changed "dementia praecox" into "schizophrenia" in 1909, the disease qualified the three states of catatonia, where motor activities were disrupted, hebephrebia, characterised by inappropriate emotional reactions, and paranoia, where delusions of grandeur and persecution played a large role (see Kraepelin, 1883–1899). Bleuler's modification of Kraepelin's formulation (correcting the assumption that the term "dementia" implied a final deterioration that did not necessarily occur in schizophrenia), albeit important, did not challenge Kraepelin's classification. Particularly,

Bleuler never disagreed on the physiogenesis of the disease. Kraepelin noticed that "there is as it were a hierarchy of clinical signs. As one ascends the hierarchy the more typical is the sign of schizophrenia" (Kraepelin, 1992, p. 505). In other words, for any psychiatrist, including Jung, diagnosis was a hard task since the manifestations of insanity were various, more or less pronounced, and steady.

Before Kraepelin's precise differentiations stood Jung's paradigmatic case of paranoid dementia to represent dementia praecox. Albeit fascinating, the case could not, against Jung's claim, testify to any relevance of psychoanalysis for catatonia or for cases of hebephrebia.

Dementia Praecox was to prove how schizophrenics, just like hysterics and even like sound (normal) persons, were under the sway of repressed feeling-toned complexes, the main topic of four out of the five chapters of the book, one of which being the paradigm in question. Repression this time was not *presented* as different from Freud's, even though many examples given by Jung could only be explained thanks to a lowering of the level of consciousness. Repression here constituted the most frequent symptom to be observed during psychoanalysis. It had been described by Freud in his works on hysteria and his analyses of the everyday life of sound persons. The task of proving Freud's legitimacy was impossible since Jung had to discard cases, thereby invalidating Freud's theoretical universality.

In his article of 1905 on "An analysis of the associations of an epileptic", Jung had, for instance, "excluded those cases who were not congenitally mentally defective and those who only contracted epilepsy after ... puberty ... [since these cases had] the tendency to 'define' the stimulus-word" (Jung, CW 2, par. 512) in their associations. These reactions did not disclose any repressed memory, leaving Jung incapable anyhow of accounting for the feeling-toned complexes of the entire population of the epileptics. Likewise, the highly varied traits and behaviours of schizophrenics could not all fit Jung's pattern. Hence, his resorting to a supposed paradigm.

Extremely clear, Jung's presentation of the paradigm left almost no room for anything foreign to psychoanalysis, and, therefore, for anything which could be linked to intuition, intuition being absent from Freud's theory. Here was Jung's plan:

A. Wish-fulfilment   B. The complex of injury   C. The sexual complex
D. Summary   E. Supplement (Jung, *CW3*, pars 198–316)

Jung's patient was a case of paranoid dementia. The woman was sixty-two, had been admitted to the asylum twenty years previously, and had remained there ever since. She had been suicidal. Delusional, she heard voices, which were "invisible telephones" that called her out (Jung, CW 3, par. 198). Part A related to the constellations that revealed the wealth and the treasures—material and immaterial—that the poor patient dreamt of. For instance, the patient displayed the oddest and "most extraordinary comical" reactions concerning the payments that the hospital—which she believed was a place where she worked—owed her. She believed that she was "triple owner of the world [*dreifache Weltinhaberin*]" or that she was "Germania and Helvetia of exclusively sweet butter" (Jung, CW 3, pars 224, 225, 232).

These wonderful reactions were offset by ones that revealed the complex of grievance, as described in Part B. For example, the stereotypical reaction "There is such a great discord" was explained by Jung thus:

> "Discord" seems to express something like "disagreeable circumstances". The patient finds it particularly disagreeable that the doctor never wants to hear anything about the payment she demands at every visit. She then complains mostly about the selfishness of people who only think of themselves and "only go on working" without thinking of the payment. (Jung, CW 3, par. 263)

The two interrelated complexes of Part A and Part B "mainly show[n] us the bright and dark sides of the patient's social striving, [now Part C would reveal] the commonest and most frequent manifestations of the complex, namely the sexual manifestations" (Jung, CW 3, par. 277). For example, the stereotypic neologism "amphi", sometimes associated by the patient with snakes, pork sausages, or hedgehog, "so broad and so long", constituted for Jung crude coitus symbols through obvious condensations and displacements such as "eating" for "kissing", for "having sex", etc. (Jung, CW 3, pars 282–286) A spinster, the patient wished—and fulfilled her wish through her constellations, the equivalent of the content of dreams—to have sexual intercourse.

Part D summarised the analysis, therefore implying that the main points had been developed. Problematically, one of the most striking elements of the patient's disease—that she heard voices—was treated only in Part E, the "supplement". There, Jung analysed the voices as teleological hallucinations, the intuitive character of which has been shown earlier in this work. We remember that teleological hallucinations had saved patients from critical and liminal situations (the "tremendous light" and the "enormous hand" that had prevented two suicides). It is in this section that Jung presents the two cases in order to link them to the efficacy of "correcting" voices that the paradigmatic patient heard by telephone. One day, the patient was associating words with Jung. Jung narrates and then analyses:

> Suddenly, to the great chagrin of the patient, the telephone [that is, another of the patient's 'voices'] called out, "The doctor should not bother himself with these things." [Another association presented difficulties] whereupon the telephone said "She is embarrassed and therefore can say nothing." Once when she remarked during analysis that she was "a Switzerland" and I had to laugh, the telephone exclaimed [understanding why Jung had laughed] "That is going a bit too far!" [The patient then became unclear through other word reactions.] The following dialogue then developed:
>
> Telephone: "You're leading the doctor round the whole wood."
>
> Patient: "Because this also goes too far."
>
> Telephone: "You're too clever by half!"
>
> [Then Jung continually misunderstood her for the patient whispered, as a result of which both patient and doctor became impatient.] At this moment the telephone called out: "Now they're getting in each other's hair" . . .
>
> In all these examples the "telephone" has the character of an ironically commenting spectator who seems to be thoroughly convinced of the futility of these pathological fancies and mocks the patient's assertions in a superior tone. This kind of voice is rather like a personified self-irony. (Jung, pars 310–313)

Those voices mocked the patient's delusions and, thereby, had a propensity to allow psychical progress. The patient herself intuited how she could get rid of her disease. Once more, Jung left little room, yet still in a distinctive place—the end of the book—to address what could not, in his opinion, be treated head-on: intuition, here in the form of teleological hallucination.

Intuition from pathological Einfälle
(Eingebungen) to general Einfall

Intuition as *Einfall* was defined in Part I as something that suddenly falls into the head. In 1907, Jung also used the terms *Eingebungen*, or "inspirations", and *pathologische Einfälle* to designate the same phenomenon. Jung's most famous shift from the pathological to the normal—from complex to archetype—was concurrent with that from pathological *Einfälle* to *Einfall* since pathological *Einfälle* reveal complexes and the *Einfall* an archetype.

We must first examine what is and what is not an *Einfall* with regard to some mistranslations of the *Collected Works*. In a letter dated 13 July 1953, Jung writes of R. F. C. Hull, the "ardent rationalist" translator of the *Collected Works*, about one of his works: "It is absolutely necessary that somebody who understands the arguments of my paper, as well as German, should go with a fine tooth comb through [Hull's] translation" (Shamdasani, 1995). Because of his rationalistic leanings, Hull mistranslated many passages of the first part of *Dementia Praecox*. Correcting Hull seems to be the best method of explaining Jung's approach to pathological *Einfälle*.

Hull's first mistake stemmed from his mistranslation of the German *Vorstellung* into "idea" (ten times in the first thirty paragraphs).[139] An umbrella term in the common language, *Vorstellung*, the most common translation of which is "imagination", sees its employment limited in a psychiatric context. *Stellung* means "position". The prefix *vor-* means here "before, in front of". A common spatial translation of *Vorstellung* is a (theatrical) "representation", which "positions itself in front of" the audience. "Imagination" embraces both spatial and temporal aspects of *Vorstellung*. Spatially, it is what presents itself "in front of" the mind. Temporally, it implies some mental activity that happened "before" this *re*-presentation, and which deals in the conditional mode with past, present, and future.

This last aspect is crucial in psychiatry, where temporal processes were closely examined as in the time ratio to reaction to each word given to the patient. The same prefix *vor-* previously appeared in the term *Vorahnung*, the anticipation of the future, when Helene Preiswerk saw herself in Ivenes. *Vorausahnung* and *Vorkenntnis* can also be translated into "precognition", *Vorhersage* into "prophecy", and *Vorhaussage* into "prediction". One cannot disregard time and processes in psychiatry as well as in psychology. Hull did so, and with significant consequences.

When German-writing psychiatrists such as Jung used the term *Vorstellung* in the word association context, they meant "what presents itself in front of both the patient and the doctor as the result of the mental activity that preceded it". That Hull called it an "idea" is a big mistake.[140] For example, Hull equated "the ideas (*Vorstellungen*) and sensations" with "these pathological perceptions" (Jung, *CW 3*, par. 4). Ideas are not perceptions. They are, on the contrary, the result of apperception. Embedded in the same misleading rationality, Hull translates *Erkennens* (gen.)—referring to the work of the French psychopathologist André Masselon, as well as Kant in a footnote— with "the realm of apperception". *Erkennen* is the means to reach (the unattainable) *intellectual intuition*. It is not an apperception, but the perception of intuition.

Stemming from his disregard of time, Hull (six times in the same thirty paragraphs) also mistranslated the German *Störung* into "disturbance" instead of "disruption" (Jung, *CW 3*, pars 10, 16, 17, 18, 24). For example, Jung described how, as a result of a sudden disruption in the process following the doctor's utterance of the stimulus word, there occurred a strange *Vorstellungsverbindungen*. If *Verbindungen* could be translated into "combinations", *Vorstellung* was no more an idea here than it had been before. *Vorstellungsverbindungen* was not a "combination of ideas" (Jung, *CW 3*, pars 9, 10). Strange combinations of "ideas" might result, perhaps, from "disturbances". Ideas can be disturbed. Yet, there were neither ideas nor disturbances here. Rather, there appeared *perceptions* strangely mixed together as a result of a *disruption* in the mental process that followed the utterance of the stimulus word. This described the mechanical explanation of the apparition of a pathological *Einfall* as the third reaction of the series provided by Jung:

dark	green
white	brown
black	"good day, William"
red	brown (Jung, *CW 3*, par. 9)

"Good day, William" was the opposite of an idea that would have stemmed from a "process of ideation". If English readers cannot, in the *Collected Works*, decipher that an *Einfall* is not an apperception but a perception, what follows will show that they are simply prevented from grasping what the *Einfall* is. The expression "*pathologischen Einfälle*" (five occurrences, and the central topic of the first thirty paragraphs) is, following Hull's mistaken logic, translated into "pathological ideas" (Jung, CW 3, pars 7, 10). We saw that *Einfall* means "what falls into". To describe the sudden appearance of "good day, William" in the middle of the other reactions, Jung writes of its sudden *Einbrüche* ("incursion") and then of its *einbrechende* ("breaking in"). *Einfall*, *Einbrüche*, and *einbrechende* share the same prefix, implying a movement. This movement is not rendered by Hull, who twice used the term "irruption" to translate *Einbrüche* as well as *einbrechende*. "Irruption" creates an ascending motion in the mind of the reader, whereas *Einfall* is a fall (Jung, CW 3, par. 10).

Other mistranslations also prevent the linking of *Einfall* to its intuitive nature. When Jung writes of *plötzlische* ["sudden"] "*Einfälle*", or simply of *Einfälle*, Hull translates it into "whims" (Jung, CW 3, pars 10, 17). Jung wished to bring together the various expressions of his peers in order to describe the *Einfall* phenomena. "*Pathologischen Eingebungen*" was one of these expressions (Jung, CW 3, par. 10). A common way to describe intuition, *Eingebung* ("inspiration"), again shares its prefix with *Einfall* and reveals the "out of nowhere" falling origin of the intuitive inspiration.

If Hull did translate *Eingebungen* into "inspirations", he found a way not to link it to *Einfall* in the following sentence covering *Einfall* phenomena, which contains various other mistranslations hiding intuition. Hull translates:

> they are the 'autochtonous' ideas, sudden impulses, hallucinations, influencing of thought, obsessive sequences of strange ideas, stoppage and disappearance of thought (aptly termed by one of my patients "thought deprivation"), inspirations, pathological ideas, etc. (Jung, CW 3, par. 56)

When Jung *identifies* "inspirations" with "pathological ideas" by putting "pathological ideas" within parentheses (*Eingebungen (pathologische Einfälle) usw*), Hull removes the parentheses and adds a comma. Likewise, if one wonders what "influencing of thought" might be, one can instead read the German, where Jung writes of the

Erscheinungen ("the apparitions", "the emergences", a term which also designates phantoms) of the influencing of thought in grasping the intuitive factor of the influence, absent in English. Full of mistranslated "ideas"—except for the "autochtonous" ideas, which are real *Ideen* but not of an apperceptive nature—the short passage also includes another mistranslation of *Vorstellung*, this of *Vorstellungsreihen* into "sequences of ideas".

Thus, English readers have either no access to the meaning of the German term *Einfall*, or receive the wrong notion of its meaning. However, Jung provided them with the *Einfall* itself through an example—a succession of *Einfälle*, to be precise. Problematically, it was in French, not translated. Hull, who translated into English everything that Jung had written hitherto in French, which Jung had left in French in the original version, made one exception in the example in question. After merely copying the French passage, Hull then forgot to translate Jung's term *schöne*, "beautiful", which qualified it, and so came back to his usual mistranslations of *Störung*, *Vorstellung*, etc. (Jung, CW 3, par. 23).[141]

The poetic and religious content of the pathological *Einfälle* described in the French thesis of Pelletier (1904) did not escape Jung. To link them to the strange sequences of the images—the symbols—in dreams, he quoted the entire sequence. Pelletier reports,

> *Je suis l'être, l'être ancien, le vieil Hêtre*, que l'on peut écrire avec un H. Je suis universel, primordial, divin, catholique, apostolique, Romaine*. L'eusses-tu cru, l'être tout cru, suprumu*, l'enfant Jésus*. Je m'appelle Paul, c'est un nom, ce n'est pas une négation*, on en connaît la signification* . . . Je suis éternel, immense, il n'y a ni haut ni bas, fluctuat nec mergitur, le petit bateau*, vous n'avez pas peur de tomber.* (Jung, CW 3, par. 22, quoting Pelletier, 1904, p. 142)

> I am the being, the ancient being, the old Beech, the one we can write with a B [in French "H" for *hêtre*, the pronunciation of which is the same as *être*]. I am universal, primordial, divine, Catholic, apostolic, Roman. Would you have believed, the being all believed, the bestus [neologism *suprumu* following the assonance in [y] rendered by this in [b]], the baby Jesus. My name is Paul, Paul is a name, it is not a negation, one knows what it means . . . I am eternal, immense, there is neither high nor low, *fluctuat nec mergitur*, the little ship, you do not fear to fall. (Pelletier, 1904, p. 142, translated for this edition)

The French method allowed the patients to react to a stimulus with more than a single word. Jung called this method "continuous associations", or "ongoing associations" [*fortlaufende Assoziationen*] and employed it himself when patients uttered terms or expressions that he could not understand and that he thought hid complexes.(Jung, *CW 3*, par. 215). With his paradigmatic case, for instance, Jung describes, "I got the patient to tell me all her associations to a stimulus-word. In this way the idea can be associated in all directions and its various connections discovered" (Jung, *CW 3*, par. 215). Uncovering all the connections, since they were intuitive and stemmed from an under-conscious state, was impossible. Jung wished to single out the complexes of the patients, the origin of which was consciousness. However, by doing so, Jung always selected among the continuous associations of his patients those which, as in the case of Pelletier, revealed the most evident links with his later psychology, those, in other words, which described an under-conscious state, *Einfälle*, intuitively driven from the collective unconscious to reach consciousness.

If "good day William" might have appeared as nonsensical but certainly was not, Pelletier's patient's associations could not have seemed meaningless to Jung after his experience with his cousin. Having attributed some Gnostic foundation to his cousin's system, Jung must have interpreted the origin of the *Einfall* "there is neither high nor low" of Pelletier's patient, who probably had never heard of the *Emerald Tablet*, as mysteriously—that is, intuitively—Hermetic.

Inspired by Pelletier, Jung introduced some thoughts on the symbol and its importance for the interpretation of dreams, as Freud had abundantly demonstrated in his *Interpretation of Dreams* (1900a). Pelletier indicated, for instance, that "'immense' suggested 'ocean', then the ship and the motto [*fluctuat nec mergitur* ("it is tossed by the waves, but does not sink")] that form[ed] the coat-of-arms of Paris" (Jung, *CW 3*, par. 22). Jung's *Psychology of the Unconscious*, which propounds at length his views on symbols through hundreds of examples, and which famously goes against Freud's views, can already be traced here. Jung writes, "We are indebted to her [Madeleine Pelletier] for a valuable observation on the symbols and symbolic relationships that are so very common in dementia praecox". Jung repeated this sentence in three separate occurrences in his book, with "valuable" later becoming "admirable" (Jung, *CW 3*, pars 25, 73, 136). Jung writes of "indistinct" symbols, "a very inferior form of thought", and of "primitive languages", which he sets *"in contraction to"* (my emphasis) clearer "allegories" [that he would soon call "signs", against Freud] (Jung, CW 3, pars 136, 29). This very inferior form of thought excluded the memories of what he would also later call, against Freud "the personal unconscious". By contrast, the *Einfälle* "I am *universal, primordial, divine,* Catholic, *apostolic, Roman*" (my emphases) strongly echoed Jung's retrospective views on his work with schizophrenics, such as those referred to in this passage, where Jung writes,

> If the unconscious were only personal, it would in theory be possible to trace all the fantasies of an insane person back to individual experiences and impressions. No doubt a large proportion of the fantasy-material could be reduced to his personal history, but there are certain fantasies whose roots in the individual's previous history one would seek for in vain. What sort of fantasies are these? They are, in a word, mythical fantasies. (Jung, CW 10, par. 11)

If Jung did not describe here *any* conscious origin of the *content* of the patient's *Einfälle*—the word "complex" was not even mentioned—he took, in contrast, great care to describe the under-conscious *form* of the associations by referring, for example, to Janet's *abaissement du niveau mental*. Quoting Pelletier, he also kept all her indications of form—the five asterisks—by adding five footnotes in his text. The asterisks in Pelletier's original text indicate the assonances, contiguities, or similarities of sounds. These instantaneous, intuitive, poetic forms connect the various sequences of *Einfälle* and create its natural flux in the under-conscious state of the patient. This sound-to-sound relationship between the *Einfälle*, rather than a sound-to-meaning relationship, defines the essence of both the archetype and the symbol: an intuitive relationship. Phonologist Paul Kugler writes,

> Symbolism in the archetypal sense does not reside in the relation between . . . sound and . . . meaning. While the relation between sound and meaning may not be symbolic, what we are suggesting is that there is a symbolic (archetypal) level in language that is to a certain extent nonarbitrary. This level, however, does not reside in the sound-to-meaning relationship, but in the sound-to-sound relationship. (Kugler, 2002, p. 60)

Sound-to-sound relationship is studied in phonology. "Phonology," writes Kugler, "is the study of the relation between sounds. [It] seeks to identify systems of sound *relations* which are essentially unconscious" (Kugler, 2002, p. 42, my italics; see also the next section). The sound of a word is its form. Sound itself, even without word, is form. Grasping that form is more important than content in grasping the archetype. The archetype is the emergence of an intuitive relationship.[142] As Jung writes in 1935, "archetypes are not determined as regard their content, but only as regard their forms ... the archetype itself is empty and purely formal, nothing but a *facultas præformandi.*" (Jung, CW 9(i), par. 155). The under-conscious, especially of some patients and intuitive people, is a direct window to that intuitive faculty, since that state favours the emergence of the intuitive links, images, or sounds. Unlike under-conscious images, under-conscious sounds can be recorded.

Jung evokes some *flachen Associaziontypus*, a "flat" kind of association, to reveal the continuity, the repetitive flow of what appears as a single utterance of Pelletier's patient's successive *Einfälle* (Jung, CW 3, par. 23).[143]

In the ongoing association of Pelletier's patient, five rhythmical repeated sentences appear. Here they are, numbered:

1. *Je suis l'être, l'être ancien, le vieil Hêtre, que l'on peut écrire avec un H.*
   ("I am the being, the ancient being, the old Beech, the one we can write with a B".)
2. *Je suis universel, primordial, divine, catholique, apostolique, Romaine.*
   ("I am universal, primordial, divine, Catholic, apostolic, Roman".)
3. *L'eusses-tu cru, l'être tout cru, suprumu, l'enfant Jésus.*
   ("Would you have believed, the being all believed [or crude], the bestus, the baby Jesus".)
4. *Je m'appelle Paul, c'est un nom, ce n'est pas une négation [nom pronounces non "no"], on en connaît la signification.*
   ("My name is Paul, Paul is a name, it is not a negation, one knows what it means".)
5. *Je suis éternel, immense, il n'y a ni haut ni bas, fluctuat nec mergitur, le petit bateau, vous n'avez pas peur de tomber.*
   ("I am eternal, immense, there is neither high nor low, *fluctuat nec mergitur*, the little ship, you do not fear to fall").

Following Jung when he writes of the primitive symbol, we can interpret that, repeated five times, the patient's message is a *single* message of identity. Phrases (1) to (5) are five aspects, five symbols, five records—since they concern voice and sounds—of the same archetype, of the same "primitive language", a litany.

The personal pronoun "I", which starts four of the five sentences, stands for the present of the patient. Schizophrenic, the patient intuitively navigates between many states. In the first sentence of the litany, "I" is followed by the auxiliary "to be" and three (dependent) subject complements, the first of which is "the being". What seems a strong affirmation of personal identity is diluted in the collective, when the patient mixes "I am the being" with "I am the Beech", the tree of her life in a collective symbolic dimension. The progression towards the collective reaches crescendo in the second movement, where the patient mixes (independent) adjectives with (dependent) subject complements. "I" becomes "universal, primordial, divine, Catholic, apostolic, Roman". The patient is a woman. The fourth move refers to Paul the apostle. "It's a name, one knows what it means" objectifies the function of Paul, who is at once far from and close to her, since she says "My name is Paul".

Phrases (3) and (5) add two other subjects. The familiar "you" (*tu*) appears in (3) and the collective or polite "you" (*vous*) appears at the end of (5). Sequence (3) constitutes the longest contiguity, with eight assonances in [y], the French "u", three alliterations in [l], [s], and [t] in *L'eusses-tu cru, l'être tout cru, suprumu, l'enfant Jésus*. The patient under-consciously plays. This play is an intuitive means to a limit, a paramount, "the baby Jesus". The movement is regressive—from under-conscious to collective unconscious. Too numinous a state, too numinous an identity, and too close to a possible inflation, the mind of the patient therefore shifts to the next move (4), where the identity is "lowered" to that of Paul in a diminuendo. In sentence (5), the identity appears in the collective, but this time seems lost in the impersonal subject "there", in the "immensity" of the ocean, in the "fluctuations" of the ship, in between high and low, and the fear of falling from on high. What falls, the *Einfall*, does not seem as pregnant with a colourful future. Yet, tossed by the waves, the little ship—the patient—does not sink.

We saw briefly how stereotypies consisted in repeated expressions representing for the patient explanations of the experience she lived, yet in a condensed and often unintelligible form for the doctor. *Einfälle* stemming from the tests had become frozen and the motto of the patients, such as "Germania and Helvetia of exclusively sweet butter", "triple owner of the world", and "amphi".

Jung writes, "By stereotypy in its widest sense we mean the persistent and constant reproduction of a certain activity (verbigeration, catalepsy, stock phrases, perseveration, etc.). These phenomena are among the most characteristic symptoms of dementia praecox" (Jung, CW 3, par. 182). Stereotypies for Jung were *Einfälle*, which expressed how "stuck" the patient was. Their reappearance showed the strength of the complex preventing psychological development. In France, André Masselon and Jules Séglas, whose work is largely quoted by Jung in Chapter One of *Dementia Praecox*, had then examined the relationship between language and insanity (see Jung, CW 3, pars 14–20, 74–76; Berrios, 1999; Obler & Albert, 1985). Acknowledging Masselon's precision in his description of the pathological *Einfälle*, Jung, however, formulates a criticism:

> Masselon tested the associations experimentally, finding numerous repetitions of stimulus words and frequent pathological *Einfälle* of an apparently quite fortuitous nature. The only conclusion he came to from these experiments was that the patients were unable to pay attention. The conclusion is right enough, but Masselon spent too little time on the pathological *Einfälle*. (Jung, CW 3, par. 17; I reintroduced the original German where Hull had translated it into "whims")

Jung's criticism is itself right enough. Jung, who did spend more time on the *Einfälle*, examined their content, as in his paradigmatic case, in order to find the origin of the *Einfälle* in the complexes of the patients. He could have—systematically rather than occasionally, as in Pelletier's case—spent more time looking at their intuitive form, a result indeed of the inattention of the patient. Contemporary (from today) psychiatric studies show how attention remains one of the most important factors in the various impairments in the language of schizophrenics, next to the "cognitive deficits of action planning, ordering, and sequencing" (Marini, Spoletini, Rubino, et al., 2008, p. 144; see also Huguelet, Nicastro, & Zanello, 2002). Perseverations, stereotypies, neologisms, "derailment, incoherence", and many other *forms* are the imprint of the lack of attention, that is, the room left for intuition (Bazin, Lefrere, Passerieux, et al., 2002, p. 109). Once Jung's intention was to prove that the patient had this or that complex, the origin of which was consciousness, he could not himself pay attention to the pathological *Einfälle*. Pathological *Einfälle* happened, emerged, in a present under-conscious, whatever their origin, an origin which needed to be excluded, or sought only after observation.

In his paradigmatic case Jung emphasised the patient's complexes—of sex, of grandeur, and of injury—that for him explained the emergence of the stereotypies such as "Germania and Helvetia of exclusively sweet butter", "triple owner of the world", and "amphi".

This time, my analysis goes against Jung's Freudian one and is much closer to Jung's use of Pelletier's case. The repetition, the stereotypy of "amphi", for example, could semantically constitute its own origin. The prefix "amphi-" means "on both sides, around", as in "amphitheatre". It could describe the position of the patient, who was, at one and the same time, with the doctor in consciousness and in the under-conscious. Sometimes, she could also be both in the under-conscious and in the unconscious. She was around, in no firm position, in between. In his previous chapter, Jung's own terms could have paradoxically supported this analysis:

> Many schizophrenics who ... will not react to the questions show "etymological" leanings: instead of answering ... they divert attention [*ablenken*, "distract"] to its phonetic aspects ... they are very fond of dissecting [*Zergliedern*, "analysing"] and interpreting words. [Auguste] Forel's patient felt compelled to make many such interpretations; thus she interpreted the name "Vaterlaus" as "pater laus tibi". [Glory to you Father.] (Jung, *CW* 3, pars 157, 157*n*)

Stereotypies also suggest endless repetitions of the term by the patient. Perhaps the patients wanted their stereotypies themselves to be heard by the doctors.

"Germania" and "Helvetia" also possessed numinosity by themselves, that is, through their form, through their sole enunciation. A sequence among continuous associations, "I am Germania and Helvetia of exclusively sweet butter" was followed by the association "that is life-symbol" (Jung, *CW* 3, par. 224). In this instance, as in many others, the patient literally gave Jung the *substantifique moelle* ["true substance"] of his later psychology. Certainly the patient had no "sweet butter" to eat at the Burghölzli (the complex of grief). More important, perhaps, the physical aspect of the *Einfall participated* in its apparition. In addition, the patient could have had a sexual complex. Yet, it did not *explain* the *Einfälle* themselves—that is, what constituted a *life-symbol*. Intuition precedes, or appears instantly. Intuition does not follow as a result of (a cause).

The patient *was* "Helvetia", the *name*, the identity of Switzerland, that is, her under-conscious inflationary identity from the collective unconscious. Likewise, "Germania" was feminine and possessed a Latin origin, close to some numinous archetype of a primal language transposed in the symbols at hand. Jung comments,

> Her speech is interesting. She does not say 'I make' but 'I *am* . . . she 'condenses' or identifies herself with this object too [the patient *is* many things, persons, or states] . . . 'I am' seems to be an *intensified* form of 'I have' or 'I make'. (Jung, *CW 3*, par. 222, second italics are mine)

Intentionally not specified by Jung, the patient's "condensation" has nothing to do with Freud's condensation in the work of the dream. The result of the condensation is not, as with Freud, the loss of the signified (the meaning of the sign) through the signifier (its form, here its sound) (see de Saussure, 1972[1903], p. 65). By contrast, condensation here describes how the signifier helps finding again-intuitively— the lost signified and the consequent intensity she experiences either close to inflation or through inflation.

Carried out with the conceded goal of discovering the complex hidden behind the stereotypy, the tests needed the patients not to be aware of this aim. Instead, the patients were asked to explain what they meant by their stereotypies in associating them with successive words. Jung, thereby, left the realm of the scientific. Hitherto, patients were all given the same series of words. Comparatively examined, each reaction was related to the ninety-nine other reactions of the patient in a set of hundred stimuli as well as to the reaction to the same stimulus given to hundreds of other patients. This scientific methodology is inapplicable here with the single personal *Einfall* "I am Helvetia", for instance. Most important, if the expected genuine reaction of the patient could follow a set of terms imposed by the psychiatrists, there was no such reaction to assume from a stereotypy.

The patients were personally required to give other words for one word descriptive of them, central in their *Weltanschauung*. They were given the opportunity to express not what they perceived as their complexes, but themselves. The expression, however, must not be articulated. No (apperceptive) explanation was demanded. Synonym uses, equivalents, analogical and direct (intuitive) links, whatever their forms, constituted the successive *Einfälle*, which, thus, appeared as a direct reading of the stereotypy and a direct entry in the patient's world.

In that context the religious and poetic tone of the patients' *Einfälle*, as well as the patients' etymological leaning, reminds us of what Faivre describes as "The art of Memory" practised by Western hermetists in the Renaissance:

> [The Art of Memory was] a manner of reading the world by interiorising it and subsequently writing it from inside the self . . . [It could] reorient us towards an anagogic[144] hermeneutic of Nature, human activities, and texts, thanks to modes of reading suitable for revealing the metalanguages or living structures of signs and correspondences. Reading in this way means seeking the depth of things in the right place, not in socio-economic infrastructures, nor in latent contents of the unconscious, but beyond them, in Nature itself. This is a reading that is necessarily plural [which refuses] objectifying the problem of the spirit under the form of reductive or abstract concepts [and which] transcends the illusion of the banal and finds meaning in the concrete again. (Faivre, 1994, p. 43)

If patients were not hermetists, the task that they were given with ongoing associations was understood as a reading of their own metalanguage, where stereotypies and neologisms represented as many signs as correspondences in their *Mythosanschauung*. Associated to stereotypies appeared other stereotypies in a closed system. Nobody knows what "Helvetia and Germania of exclusively sweet butter" meant for the patient, but to her, it was concrete. It was a life-symbol, a memory interiorised and written from inside the self.

The following continuous associations were stimulated by the patient's stereotypy "I am Socrates" or "I am Socratic". There, Jung recognised the appearance of empathy in its most intuitive form. Here are the successive *Einfälle*:

> Socrates: "Pupil – books – wisdom – modesty – no words to express this wisdom – is the highest ground-pedestal – his teachings – had to die because of wicked men – falsely accused – sublimest sublimity – self-satisfied – that is all Socrates – the fine learned world – never cut a thread – I was the best dressmaker, never left a bit of cloth on the floor – fine world of art – professorship – is doubloon – 25 francs – that

is the highest – prison – slandered by wicked men – unreason – cruelty – depravity – brutality. (Jung, *CW 3*, par. 216)[145]

Jung comments,

> All these things are analogies of the life and death of Socrates. [The patient] therefore wants [German *will*] to say: "I am like Socrates, and I suffer like him." With a certain poetic licence ... she says outright: "I am Socrates." The really pathological element is that she is so identified with Socrates that she can no longer get away from him; she takes the identification as its face value and regards the metonymy as so real that she expects everybody to understand it. (Jung, *CW 3*, par. 217; Hull had translated "will" into "wishes"]

The patient *was* Socrates. The link was immediate, direct, without mediation, hence of identity. Hence, its power and the patient's impression that she "was" Socrates. It was a perception. It was intuition in the strongest form of empathy, which we will later describe as *Einfühlung* (1). During her ongoing associations, she left impressions, in waves, intuitively shifting from personal memories "pupil ... modesty" to collective memories "no words for ... all Socrates", and then back to personal memories "the fine learned world", to finally making bridges, "that is the highest", and finding the symbol "prison – slandered by wicked men – unreason – cruelty – depravity – brutality". That form of intuition, empathy, here called "poetic licence", reappeared in Jung's writing when he outlined his own evolutionist story of humankind. In this case, the patient was not a "primitive" without ego, but a pathological case, whose ego was lost, inflated, in the collective unconscious.

While some stereotypies were expressions consisting of existing terms such as "triple owner of the world", some patients repeated real neologisms. Just as Jung had devoted an entire section of *Dementia Praecox* to the study of stereotypies, so he examined neologisms almost exclusively in the long section "continuous associations" of his paradigmatic case (Jung, *CW 3*, pars 182–196, 215–296).[146] Jung writes,

> In normal people and hysterics we find striking or linguistically odd reactions always at the critical places, and especially words from foreign languages. These correspond here [in schizophrenia] to the neologisms, which are nothing but peculiarly forceful and ponderous

expressions of thought-complexes [*Komplexgedanken*]. We can also understand why the patient describes her neologisms as 'power-words'. Wherever they appear they hint at the whole system hidden behind them, just as technical terms do in normal speech. (Jung, *CW* 3, par. 208)

"Forceful and ponderous" described the significance and the strength of the neologisms when compared with simple stereotypies. Neologisms were "power-words" (*Machtwörter*), as were words in foreign tongues (glossolalia). Pillars in the world of the patients, they ranged from totally abstruse impressions and the equivalents of obsessive gestures to substitutes for technical terms, which aimed at imitating the language of the doctors in order to find a means of communication. When uttered, *Machtwörter* empowered the patients, filling their mind, body, and soul with a sudden clear comprehension of "the whole system", of their universe, of their *Mythosanschauung*.[147]

Machtwörter expressed "thought-complex", or "thought *deprivation*". Because the patients could not express their ideas, they resorted to "power-words". In other words, *Machtwörter* were not apperceptions, but perceptions. They were intuitions, and their origin was dreams or hallucinations themselves. They came from second states rather than from consciousness. Also revelatory was that both expressions "power-words" and "thought deprivation" directly stemmed from one of Jung's patients (Jung, *CW 3*, par. 217).

The vociferation "I, the Grand Duke Mephisto, shall have you treated with blood vengeance for orang-outang representation" was closer, for example, to what Jung designed as an "exorcistic formulæ" and to the register of instinct, or, of perception, than of apperception (Jung, *CW 3*, par. 155). Jung later gave a definition of "power-words":

> Man's advance towards the Logos was a great achievement, but he must pay for it with loss of instinct and loss of reality to the degree that he remains in primitive dependence on mere words. Because words are substitutes for things, which of course they cannot be in reality, they take on intensified forms, become eccentric, outlandish, stupendous, swell up into what schizophrenic patients call "power words". (Jung, *CW 11*, par. 442)

Whatever the outlandish "orang-outang representation" meant, it had no correspondence in reality, but it did fuel the patient with the power that he wished to gain over the psychiatrists. Above all, "power words" acted on the patients themselves when the *Einfälle*, in the epiphany of a neologism, fell in the under-conscious.

Among more "easily decipherable" technical terms, the neologism "I suffer hieroglyphical" was employed by the patient, whom Jung described in his paradigmatic case (Jung, CW 3, pars 260–261). "Sacred" "inscriptions", or hieroglyphs, were the mysterious signs of a primal language before Jean-François Champollion deciphered them fully. In 1822, Champollion revealed his discovery to the French *Académie des Inscriptions et Belles Lettres* and explained his decisive contribution to Egyptology and, importantly for us, how hieroglyphs needed to be approached. "It is a complex system, writing figurative, symbolic, and phonetic all at once, in the same text, the same phrase, I would almost say in the same word" (Agazzi & Pauri, 2000, p. 97). What Champollion describes is an intuitive approach, which pictures or hears the totality of the text, its tonality, and then understands that this impression, this sound, this sign, is to be found again everywhere in any other sign or word.

This extraordinary approach is within the capacity of geniuses like Johann Sebastian Bach, whose compositions constitute a wide and complex system. Jung's introduction of *Occult Phenomena*, and, therefore, Jung's official professional introduction, called attention to the various under-conscious states such as somnambulism. While pathological, certain features of these states "point[ed]", wrote Jung, "beyond pathological inferiority to something more than a merely analogical relationship with the phenomena of normal psychology, and even with the psychology of the supranormal, that of genius" (Jung, CW 1, par. 3).

Jung's statement was then neither shocking nor original. It did not mean that patients were geniuses. Our example reveals the extent of the similarity. Whereas Champollion *approached* the sacred inscriptions, the patient lived them and was never outside of them. She *suffered* hieroglyphically. What she experienced was to find herself embedded in the middle of the countless intuitive links of a mysterious language. Whereas hieroglyphs constituted a real language, the impression of the Egyptian *Weltanschauung*, her sacred language was an impression of her *Mythosanschauung*. If ever *Welt-* and *Mythosanschauung* were intuitively linked, she could not tell how. If, as Jung had suggested with Helly, she had access to a kind of

Gnosis, she had not the genius to express it. Gnosis, for Jung, was an experience, an im-pression, whereas a language was also an ex-pression. Neologisms were impressions.

"I suffer hieroglyphically" can be connected to a passage in a letter of discharge (refused) that the patient addressed to the *Direktor* of the clinic: "What I have to suffer secretly through the novelties [which I am getting in touch with] in all areas is unfortunately known to me alone and is too shattering for my health as well as for my mind" (Jung, CW 3, par. 199).[148] "I suffer hieroglyphically" meant that the psychiatrists could not understand her sacred language—that is, her neologisms—and neither could she herself. Her neologisms were powerful and sacred. Of a religious nature, they were beyond grasp.

Evoking the "unconscious liking for new word formations (cf. the "heavenly languages" of the classic somnambulists)", Jung continues,

> In experiments with automatic writing ("psychography") we can see very clearly how the unconscious plays with *Vorstellungen* [equivalent to *Einfälle* here]. Often the words are written with the sequence of letters reversed, or there are strange conglomerations of words in otherwise clear sentences. Rudiments of new languages are also made under the constellation of spiritist convictions. (Jung, CW 3, par, 157, translation amended for this edition)[149]

Jung uses the passive form ("words are written, new languages are made") to describe the result, the *Einfälle*, in the under-conscious. "The unconscious"—which plays with words, which has got a liking for new word formations—and "there" were the mere subjects of the action taking place during the spiritist sessions. In this passage, Jung describes the status of emergence of intuition, when and where things "happen (as by themselves)".

Among the neologisms described in Jung's paradigmatic case appeared "ground-pedestal" and "oleum", to be linked with the stereotypical expressions "I am Socrates", "I am the universal", and "I am Schiller's *Bell* and the monopoly".

During the initial phase of simple—and not continuous—association tests, to the stimulus "pray", the patient reacted with "is a ground-pedestal". She had, thus, to explain her "suspicious" reaction and said that "without religion no one can do anything great", to which Jung added "ground-pedestal is one of her favourite neologisms" (Jung, *CW 3*, par. 207). In the second type of tests, among the successive *Einfälle* stimulated by "Socrates", falls "is the highest ground-pedestal". Her stereotypy "I am Schiller's *Bell* [from Schiller's poem *The Song of the Bell*] and the monopoly" had given rise to the ongoing associations stirred by "Schiller's *Bell*", during which "that is a governmental ground-pedestal" fell (Jung, *CW 3*, pars 216, 274).

Like all other symbols (in Pelletier and Jung's sense), the two terms of the *Einfall* "ground-pedestal" gathered opposites together. Just as Pelletier's patient had eliminated, or merged the opposites in that "there is neither high nor low", so the underneath "ground" and the beyond "pedestal" were conglomerated, fused into one impression, in one powerful word. So were "I am the monopoly" uniting mono- ("one") and -poly ("many", "much"). "I am universal" united into "the one and single (*unus*), which revolves" and the collective "universal".

The symbols unified extremes and paradoxes, thereby provoking numinous, painful experiences. These extraordinary limit states could describe the everyday life of certain severely ill patients, who were constantly living in fear and anxiety, never conscious but underconscious.

The nature of this power was religious since it appeared spontaneously after the stimulus "to pray". Just as performing ongoing associations constituted litanies, so uttering the power-word "groundpedestal" was a religious rite, a prayer for the patient. To the stimulus "miracle", she reacted with "peak" and explained "it is not conceivable for others that I created the highest mountain peak [stereotypy]" (Jung, [1907], *CW 3*, par. 207). "The highest mountain peak" was a metonomy for the pain she endured. A dressmaker, the patient had "mended enough linen to make a whole mountain" (Jung, *CW 3*, par. 246). In her mind the one who performed miracles probably was Jesus, with whom she empathised. Jung also mentioned that she "identified herself with 'Mary the mother of God'" (Jung, *CW 3*, par. 244). This form of empathy Christians call love.

Finally, as for the *Einfall* "oleum", Jung writes, "Where the word 'Oleum' came from I do not know. The patient claims to have heard it from the voices, just as she heard 'monopoly'" (Jung, *CW 3*, par. 269).[150] Jung emphasised his ignorance as well as the extraordinary character of the origin of the *Einfall*. Asked to perform ongoing associations with "oleum", the patient went on, and Jung commented,

Oleum: "Belong to [*gehört zu*: also "to be part of"] the title 'eternal' – it is for one old age – when I die, the title is gone [*aus*: also "out"], everything is gone [*aus*: also "out"] – it is a somewhat longer official length of life – Oleum serves for prolongation – it belongs to [or "is part of"] me but I don't know what it is made of – the age is established [*stellt fest* (stereotypy, the patient establishes)] – ever since 1886.

"'Oleum' seems to be a sort of elixir which is to prolong the precious life of the patient" (Jung, CW 3, par. 268). 1886 corresponded to the epoch of the woman's internment, something that both Jung and the patient knew. In contrast, the patient did not know that *oleum* existed in Latin.

Here is my analysis, keeping in mind Jung's emphasis on symbols. *Oleum* means "olive oil" (a perfect basis for an elixir). It is linked to the idea of effort, as in the modern expression "elbow grease". It is also linked to the idea of time and how effort and time are connected, as in the Latin expression *oleum et operam perdere*, "to waste time and effort". *Oleum* also means "palestra". The palestra was the public place for training and exercises in wrestling. Figuratively, the "palestra" was the *gradus ad parnassum*, the perpetual exercising of the poets asking for the Muses' help.

Here were the movements of the ongoing *Einfälle*. The first impulse after *oleum* was the association with a second neologism, "title eternal". "Oleum" is part of the "title eternal". Then comes a second phrase composed with the *Einfälle*: "it is for an old age – when I die the title is out – everything is out". Then comes "it is a somewhat official length of life – oleum serves for prolongation – it is part of me but I don't know what it is made of". And, finally, the fourth sentence echoes the second movement: "the age is assessed – ever since 1886".

As seen by Jung, "oleum" is an elixir of life, something that is part of a "title eternal". This "title", as "everything", is "out" as the patient dies. The "title" is "somewhat official" and "serves for prolongation". The elixir is part of the patient, but she does not know "what it is made of". "Ever since 1886", the woman has been a patient.

Ever since her internment at the Burghölzli, the woman had tried hard—yet had wasted time—to understand her hieroglyphical disease. She did not know what it was made of. Her effort fuelled the elixir of life, which was part of a somewhat official title eternal. This elixir was her ongoing associations, her prayers, her rites. The repetitive effort was a metonymy for the harassment of the Muses, which were the patient's voices. They sent their *Einfälle* in the under-conscious of the patient in such original forms that Jung would record them, unaware that he would execute the Muses' order to set their productions "out" for publication under the "official" "title eternal", *The Psychology of Dementia Praecox*, the pillar of which is his paradigmatic case, the patient's effort, her "oleum", as well as her official posterity.

What Jung's patient at the Burghölzli named "power-words" corresponded to what Flournoy had described as "magic words" in *From India*. Magical, the words were intuitive passwords, that is, they played the linking role of *Anschauung* to the unconscious, yet not necessarily from consciousness, as with *Anschauung*. Without them, no access was authorised into the under-conscious creative state of the somnambulist, or into "the system hidden behind", in Jung's terms. In his paradigmatic case, Jung enquired into the stereotypy "I am the master-key" of the patient, who explained that it was the key that opened all doors (Jung, *CW 3*, par. 230).

Flournoy related how, during a séance, Élise Müller (Hélène Smith), through automatic writing, had composed an epistle addressed to Flournoy in the handwriting of her guide, Léopold. The last three Alexandrine lines described the way she was able to write or to speak Martian. She and Flournoy had to follow this ritual:

> *Si tu veux obtenir d'elle quelques lueurs,*
> *Pose bien doucement, ta main sur son front pâle*
> *Et prononce bien bas le doux nom d'Ésenale !*
>
> If you would obtain from her some light,
> Place your hand very gently on her pale forehead
> And pronounce very softly the sweet name of Ésenale!
> (Flournoy, 1994[1899], p.100)

Flournoy obeyed. He writes, "For more than two years and a half, the imposition of the hand upon Hélène's forehead and the uttering of the name of Ésenale at the proper moment during the trance constitute[d] the "open sesame" of the Martian–French dictionary buried in the subliminal strata of Hélène's consciousness" (Flournoy, 1994[1899], p. 108). Ésenale had taught Hélène how to speak Martian. He was the translator of her Martian productions. He was at another level in the hierarchy of medium intermediates. Flournoy had to execute with Elise a vocal rite of passage for Flournoy to generate in himself the religious seriousness and awe and for Elise to become Hélène. The rule was one of *participation mystique*. Without empathy, no productions could occur.

Is it not powerful indeed to obtain from a glossolalic word the institution of a two-year ritual? Had the intuitive process been ineffective as a password, the rite would have been abandoned.

Magic words and power words were both *Einfälle* of neologisms. Both Freud and Jung, following the word association tests and the power-words of the patients, imitated the patients' leaning for etymology, although in diverse directions. In 1910 Freud gave a paper on "The antithetical meaning of primal words", where he emphasised the importance of linguistics for the interpretation of dreams (Freud, 1910e, p. 161). In his 1911 *Psychology of the Unconscious*, Jung rather favoured philology—not the word itself, but its perception. He was less interested in the word *per se* than in the word as a relationship. Both perception and relationship involved intuition, *Anschauung*. Linguistics, a modern view requiring thinking, needed to be excluded to understand primitive thinking. Jung did not look for any Martian phonetics, yet examined Hindu etymology. Bishop summarises one of Jung's examples:

> The phonetic resemblance between *mar* (Aryan, "to die"), *mère* (French, "mother"), *meer* (German, "see"), *mare* (Latin, "sea") prompts Jung to wonder, "Might it refer back to 'the great primitive idea of the mother' who, in the first place, meant to us our individual world and afterwards became the symbol of all worlds". (Bishop, 2004, p. 142)

Relating the hypnagogic visions of Miss Miller, Jung writes,

> Miss Miller felt that a name formed itself "bit by bit" . . . "Chi-wan-to-pel". As the author intimated, something similar to this belonged to her childish reminiscences. The act of naming is, like baptism, something exceedingly important for the creation of a personality, because, since olden times, a magic power has been attributed to the name, with which, for example, the spirit of the dead can be conjured. To know the name of any one means, in mythology, to have power over that one. (Jung, 1917a, p. 208)

Jung's emphasis on the significance of the name was right enough. Yet, instead of hearing the name "Chiwantopel", he heard and analysed the reminiscence of the girl who mentioned Mount Popocatepetl. After six pages of analysis, one being the phonetic analysis of "Popocatepelt", which Miss Miller did not utter in her vision, Jung concludes: "Chiwantopel . . . is a sort of human creation or birth by the anal route" (Jung, 1917a, p. 214).

Bit by bit, if we hear the *Einfall*, "Chi-wan-to-pel" uttered by an American girl could simply mean "she wants to peal", that is, "she wants to give forth loudly and sonorously". Again, Miss Miller's call would—anyway—be heard, through one of the most famous works of Jung, *The Psychology of the Unconscious*.

PART III

AFTER 1912: INTUITION IN THE UNCONSCIOUS

CHAPTER FIVE

Anschauung and archetype

Thanks to definitions, contextualisation (Part I), and the long but necessary explanations concerned with the limits and content of the under-conscious (Part II), Part III on Jung's psychology of the unconscious can appear clearly and concisely, whereas this area of Jung's psychology is often regarded as the most complex of all. I hope that my method of systematisation proves useful here, for that will seem, I believe, easy to grasp in this chapter relating to the most central issue in Jung's work, the correct understanding of Jung's notion of archetype.

The collective unconscious before Jung

Jung's central work, *The Psychology of the Unconscious*, was twice revised and reworked, *überarbeitet*, from its first eruption as a two-part article published in 1911–1912 to 1917, when it becomes a book, 1925, and, finally, 1952.[151] "Eruption" recalls the split between Freud and Jung, officially provoked by this publication, which contained Jung's characterisation of the later named "collective" unconscious. Jung's psychology of the unconscious, therefore, officially goes back to 1911.

Yet, if, on the one hand, Freud was not the only one to work within the scope of a personal unconscious (so were, at least, Jung's teachers Pierre Janet and Eugene Bleuler), Jung was not, on the other hand, the only thinker about the collective either.

The first point allows us to write again that Jung's psychology before 1911 is not, as is too often summarised, Jung's "Freudian period", as the longest part, Part II of this work, shows at length, but Jung's under-conscious psychology period, which has very little to do with Freud's work. Later, we shall study in detail how intuition rather than just libido issues provoked the split between Jung and Freud, as well as the central role played in the event by Henri Bergson's work. Freud, who had rightly sensed that psychopathologist Janet could threaten his collaboration with Jung, could not have presumed the extent of the influence over Jung not of Janet, but of Janet's friend and fellow philosopher, Bergson.

As for the idea of a collective sphere of the unconscious, Ellenberger traces the precise origin of the idea of the collective unconscious back to the work of the *Naturphilosoph* physician and painter Carl Gustav Carus, *Psyche*, published in 1864 (Ellenberger, 1970, pp. 207–210).[152] Jung, indeed, mentions in *Memories, Dreams, Reflections* having eagerly read Carus during his student years, as well as Eduard von Hartmann, whose *Philosophy of the Unconscious* was published in 1869 (Jung, 1995[1961/1963], p. 122). In addition, Frederic Myers, whose disciple was Théodore Flournoy, another of Jung's teachers and mentors, could not have worked without a collective dimension of the unconscious.[153]

As a result, Jung's publication of *The Psychology of the Unconscious* and subsequent split with Freud did not bring to life in the history of ideas *the* (or Jung's) collective unconscious but, rather, Jung's central contribution to this already discovered area of the unconscious. Theory emerged even later. Not until 1916 and 1917, in the *Collected Papers on Analytical Psychology*, did Jung offer theoretical distinctions between the personal and the collective unconscious, including their content, structures, and dynamics, and the different techniques for exploring them.[154]

Anschauung: *first definitions outside and inside psychology*

Archetypes, instincts, and intuition are the content, structures, and dynamics of Jung's collective unconscious. In this remote latency of consciousness, in the area of the "springs" of intuition, Jung employed the word *Anschauung* next to, and for, intuition. In *The Idea of the Numinous*, Bishop calls attention to the term *Anschauung* to reveal Jung's cultural inheritance from Goethe (Bishop, 2006, p. 125).[155] I will first place the term in Jung's environment and will then link it to the two key texts, *Psychological Types* and *Instinct and the Unconscious*.

To approach the term in a broader than Jungian, yet still precise, context, I translate from German into English the entry "Anschauung" of the brothers Grimms' *Deutsches Wörterbuch*, a classic German dictionary, which Jung must have known and used. A work of authority, the work undertaken by the linguists and famous fairy-tale writers in 1838 aimed to help create a German identity when a confederacy of states was not yet Germany.[156] Consequently, numerous quotations by German-speaking influential writers always follow short linguistic information to illustrate each word. Unsurprisingly, the thirteen references of the entry "Anschauung" are thus distributed: four quotations by Goethe, supplemented by three others in the correlated entry "Anschauen", seven quotations by Kant and six others for "Anschauen", and two quotations by Johann Gottlieb Fichte, a key philosopher between Kant and Hegel. The entry "Anschauen" also quotes the German-speaking Swiss physician Paracelsus, one of Jung's chief influences, next to quotations from the Bible. Through the mere mention of these names, readers accustomed to Jung's writings obtain a glimpse into his universe, his *Weltanschauung*, the unavoidable inherited *point de départ* of his world view.

This universe is wide. Let us compare, for example, Goethe's uses of *Anschauung* with that of Kant in two examples given by the Grimms:

> Goethe: For the first time, I learned to understand the difference between the natural melody of the nightingale's song and a hallelujah from human throats. I did not conceal my joy in this new "Anschauung" from my uncle.
>
> Kant: The "Anschauung" of this insight is bigger in mathematics than in the world wisdom. (Grimm & Grimm, 1854, vol. 1, p. 435)[157]

"Anschauung" is not polysemous here. Goethe and Kant evoke the same perception, the same capacity, intuition, in two typical and differentiated ways: the realm of the poet and that of the mathematician.

The Grimms give a third example, taken from the Old Testament, which unites and clarifies the first two: "Moses hid his face, for he was afraid to look at [*anschauen*] God (Ex. 3:6 RSV)". Exodus 3 deepens the reading of *Wilhelm Meister's Apprenticeship*. Wilhelm Meister learns. If Nature—the nightingale's song—is the direct expression of God, a human voice, even in the finest hallelujah, is not. The poet, however, is alone given to perceive, intuit, this difference. In addition, Moses perceives the presence of God but cannot—directly—look at, "anschauen", God. Now the link to Kant is possible, for God is Kant's humanly unreachable "noumenon". In Jung's psychology, God and noumenon become archetypes, and the way to reach them remains intuition, *Anschauung*.[158]

The term *Anschauung* appears in the chapter *Definitionen*, entry *Intuition*, of *Psychologischen Typen* in the *Gesammelte Werke*. Because of the spare style of lexicons, *Anschauung* is poorly transcribed in the English version of *Psychological Types*. The German reads: "Intuition (von *intueri* = anschauen)". The English translates: "Intuition (L. *intueri*, to look at or into)" (Jung, GW 6, par. 754, CW 6, par 770: the difference between the German and English paragraph numbers stems from the alphabetical order of the definitions). Jung's link to Latin is double-edged: albeit rich, it suggests nothing to non-Latin readers. The traditional Grimms' dictionary proposes three Latin synonyms for *anschauen*, one of which is, indeed, *intueri* (Grimm & Grimm, 1854, vol. 1 (original edition, p. 435): "A – BIERMOLKE".[159]

The English translation "to look at or into" proposed in Jung's *Collected Works* restricts both *anschauen* and *intueri* but tries to render the prefix *intu* [within] of *intueri* to give justice to intuition in the unconscious. A mere "into", however, cannot replace the immediate awareness of the German reader with regard to the inner unconscious *point de départ* of sight of the *Anschauung*. "To look into" presents the unconscious from the ego (as with an intuitive person's perceiving the unconscious thought of someone else) when *anschauen* starts from the collective, that is, from a *Weltanschauung*. In a lecture of 1923, Jung clarified his "to look at or into", talking of a "perception by way of the unconscious, or perception of unconscious contents" (Jung, CW 6, par. 899), but he did not edit his "definition" consequently.

The problematic issue of translation increases in Jung's psychology of the unconscious, where *Anschauung* first belongs. As I shall try to demonstrate later, when linked to the most fundamental notion in

Jung's psychology, that of the archetype, as in *Instinct and the Unconscious*, the significance of *Anschauung*, once translated, has been overlooked and underestimated. The English translators—and the French translators, too—simply misunderstood the term and missed the inherent link between archetype and intuition. By contrast, the familiarity of German readers with the term might explain their preference for the psychology of the unconscious concerning intuition.

Closer to Jung than the Grimms, Goethe, or Kant was Emilii Medtner, who, through one of his interventions at Jung's Psychological Club in 1919, also laid stress on the German term. Here is Magnus Ljunggren's portrait of Medtner:

> Emilii Medtner [1872–1936] was a central figure in the early twentieth-century Russian Symbolist movement. . . . Medtner made it his special mission to bind Symbolism closer to the German cultural legacy of Kant, Goethe, Nietzsche, and Wagner. . . . He also assumed the role of mentor and impresario for his brother, the composer Nikolai Medtner, and as a philosophical guide, intellectual stimulus and friend, he was particularly close to [the writer] Andrei Belyi. . . . When Symbolism disintegrated . . . Medtner entered an emotional crisis that was exacerbated by the outbreak of World War I and led him in August 1914 to begin psychoanalysis with Carl Gustav Jung in Zurich. . . . Medtner viewed Jung . . . as above all a brilliant artist. . . . As time went on Medtner became Jung's friend and colleague [Jung, who in the 1930s] appears to have been influenced by Medtner's ideas on race and his enthusiasm for Mussolini and Hitler. (Ljunggren, 1994, pp. 7–8)

This last piece of information might appear to be the reason for Medtner's falling into oblivion before Ljunggren's and Shamdasani's research about Medtner's influence on analytical psychology (see, for instance, Shamdasani, 2003, pp. 66–69). However, this does not seem to have been the case, since, among the figures present at the founding of Jung's Zürich School of Psychology following the split with Vienna, all other significant members of the Psychological Club underwent the same fate (as will be examined in Part V, section headed "Genesis: *Psychological Types* and the Zürich Club").

Among those figures who were significant concerning Jung on intuition, Medtner was remarkable for proving especially critical towards intuition.[160] His 1923 book *Über die sogenannte "Intuition," die ihr angrenzenden Begriffe und die an sie anknüpfenden Probleme*, in which he transcribed his reflections following the lectures at the Club, discussed the *"sogenannte Intuition"*, the "so-called intuition", as a reference to Jung's medical dissertation on the "so-called occult phenomena". For him, intuition could well be "played" with by mystics, spiritists, or any easy believers of new religious trends, but if it were to exist, then it could only be examined within the philosophical debate. There, exact—instead of absolute—methodology and terminology were the rule (Medtner, 1923, pp. 3, 11–18).

For Medtner, the word "intuition" presented two essential drawbacks. On the one hand, it belonged to a category of words such as *Gott* ("God") or *Geist* ("spirit"), which *einen Strahlenschein tragen* ("carry an aura") and *sind heilige Wörter* ("are holy words") (Medtner, 1923, p. 29). Consequently, just like the non-critiquable *"astralen" plane* of the spiritists, the term "intuition" was not open to criticism, which was the basic requirement of philosophy and, here, of the theory of knowledge (Medtner, 1923, p. 9).[161]

On the other hand, journalists could well borrow foreign terms, which Medtner designated as umbrella terms (*"Schammwörter"*, literally "sponge words"), empty terms, and as everyday terms (*Allerweltswörter*), such as "intuition". Philosophers needed accuracy (Medtner, 1923, p. 30). Latin, useful for technical terms, could not match German, "the remote language of the thinker", which was "dear and full of life". And Medtner concluded that "Intuition, in German, is called *Anschauung*" (Medtner, 1923, p. 30).

Jung used the term *Anschauung* for intuition in his psychology of the unconscious next to the concept of archetype. There, he was criticised for subsuming philosophy into psychology.

Dominants and primordial images as antecedents of archetypes

The notions of "dominants", primordial images (*Urbild*), and archetypes are close. Both the terms "primordial images" and "dominants" preceded "archetypes" and would reappear in Jung's later work, even after the use of "archetype", notably in Jung's works on alchemy (see, for example, Jung CW 8, par. 423). In 1917, Jung explains that, while progressing to consciousness, humankind simultaneously enriched the unconscious:

> The collective unconscious is the sediment of all the experience of the universe of all time, and is also an image of the universe that has been in process of formation for untold ages. In the course of time certain features have become prominent in this image, the so-called *dominants*. These dominants are the ruling powers, the gods; that is, the representation resulting from average regularities in the issue of the images that the brain has received as a consequence of secular processes. (Jung, 1917a, p. 432)

This extract theoretically met with the issues of the temporal and a-temporal aspects of the contents of the collective unconscious, which were always in the process of formation. Jung's evolutionism must be considered both chronologically and structurally because of the timelessness of the collective unconscious and its invariable influence on consciousness. Dominants were temporal—the result of the sedimentation of the collective unconscious—and a-temporal, the universal characteristic features (dominants) invariably observed from time immemorial.

Intuition explains this theoretical paradox. In *Psychology of the Unconscious* (1917a), Jung quotes a letter by the Swiss historian Jacob Burckhardt, which provides us with an example:

> What you are destined to find in Faust, that you will find by *intuition*. Faust is nothing else than pure and legitimate myth, a great primitive conception, so to speak, in which everyone can divine in his own way his own nature and destiny. Allow me to make a comparison. . . . There was a chord of the Oedipus legend in every Greek which longed to be touched directly and respond in its own way. And thus it is with the German nation and Faust (Jung, 1917a, p. 490, n. 42, my italics).[162]

Intuition links Oedipus to Greeks, Faust to Germans, and contemporaries such as Burckhardt's correspondent to Faust. Temporality and a-temporality coexist. As Jung commented on the letter, "every Greek of the classical era carried in himself a fragment of the Oedipus, just as every German carries a fragment of Faust" (Jung, 1917a, p. 40). Jung's "just as" contained the paradox of the future archetype through the analogical role of intuition. Albeit belonging to different eras, Faust and Oedipus were absolutely equivalent (they were "just as") through the common intuitive perception everybody had of them, that is, their archetype, universal and a-temporal. This is why Burckhardt referred his friend to intuition to understand Faust in the best possible way. Jung's example revealed his understanding of the archetype before its enunciation, but the reader of 1917 could neither fathom the notion of archetype through a too vague "just as" nor understand the hero as a "ruling power", a dominant.

The qualitative aspect that was lacking in the term "dominants" appeared in the term *Urbild*, "primordial image", used in conjunction with "dominants" in the years 1916–1917. Burckhardt again inspired Jung,[163] who borrowed the word *Urbild* from Burckhardt's work, frequently quoted in *The Psychology of the Unconscious*. In its theoretical counterpart, "The psychology of the unconscious processes" (1917b), Jung writes,

> In every individual, in addition to the personal memories, there are also, in Jacob Burckhardt's excellent phrase, the great "primordial images", the inherited potentialities of human imagination. They have always been potentially latent in the structure of the brain. The fact of this inheritance also explains the otherwise incredible phenomenon, that the matter and themes of certain legends are met with all the world over identical forms. (Jung, 1917b, p. 410)

In this extract, one can recognise Jung's archetype in its visual (the primordial *image*) aspect, an aspect that will always remain privileged by Jung. Jung continues to shift to the *primordial*:

> Further it explains how it is that persons who are mentally deranged are able to produce precisely the same images and associations that are known to us from the study of old manuscripts. I gave some examples of that in my book on "The Psychology of the Unconscious". I do not thereby assert the *transmission of representations*, but only of the *possibility of such representations*, which is a very different thing. (Jung, 1917b, p. 410)

While the "average regularities" of the dominants were too vague, "images", here, were inadequate. The German read not *Bild* but *Urbild*. As well as "potentialities", one could also read the too strong "inherited". Here, Jung faced a double critique: his assertion of the "(1) transmission of (2) representations".

"Representations" referred to the radical *Bild* in *Urbild*, that is, to "image" in "primordial image". *Bild* can be linked to *Bildung*, synonymous with *Kultur*, and, in turn, linked to *Bildungkraft*,[164] or collective conscious representations. At this point, we lose the universal and unconscious aspects of the representations. Instead, *Bild* (*Urbild*) referred to the two—unclearly as remote—linked terms "potential" and "possible" in this extract: *Bild* referred to unconscious representations.[165] However, only consciousness creates representation. This first critique has solid grounds and might have led Jung to the choice of the term archetype.

The second critique concerning the *transmission* of these images coerced Jung into rejecting the notion of the archetypal images as hereditary. "Primordial" had been wrongly grasped in its merely diachronic aspect. The term did not resolve the paradox of the peculiar temporality of the collective unconscious. Bishop restores the "status of the 'primordial'" in Jung's thought by placing the German prefix *Ur-* in its cultural context:

> [T]he prefix *Ur-* signifies, not simply that something is old – as, for example in the case of the *Urzeit* ['primeval times'] or even the word *ursprünglish* ('original') – but also that something is primary or fundamental: for example, when Goethe talks about the 'primordial phenomenon', or *Urphänomen*. (Bishop, 2008, p. 515)

The *Urphänomen* was one of the basic concepts of Romantic philosophy and of Schelling's *Naturphilosophie*. The *Urphänomen* was at the origin of the *Weltseele*, or "the world soul". Jung's *Urbild* and the subsequent term "archetype" are equivalent. Goethe, for example, "believed in the *Urplanze* (a primordial plant) as a model for all plants, of which each botanic species would partake to some degree" (Ellenberger, 1970, p. 203). In addition, Jung first imagined the archetype as a fundamental model outside of any hereditary considerations.

Bishop's two dimensions—historical and "primal"—allow the right reading of two examples where Jung used *Ur-* in *Psychology of the Unconscious* (1917a). Jung writes, "[T]he ancients had already placed εἱραμθένη (destiny) in relation to 'Primal light', or 'Primal Fire'" (Jung, 1917a, p. 496). If "the ancients" evoke history, "destiny" contains the idea of the fundamental and of the future: the a-temporal derived from the primordial, the timelessness of the archetype.

Here is the second, more developed extract:

> Anaxagoras developed the conception that the living primal power (*Urpotenz*) of νοῦς (mind) imparts movement, as if by a blast of wind, to the dead primal power (*Urpotenz*) of matter. . . . This νοῦς, which is very similar to the later conception of Philo . . . has rather the old mythological significance of the fructifying breath of the winds, which impregnated the mares of Lusitania, and the Egyptian vultures. The animation of Adam and the impregnation of the Mother of God . . . are produced in a similar manner. The infantile incest phantasy of one of my patient reads: "the father covered her face with his hands and blew into her open mouth". (Jung, 1917a, p. 492)

From Anaxagoras to Jung's patient there appeared the diachronic aspect of the *Urbild*, in this case the *Urpotenz*, the primal and ultimate power to give and retain life. Jung described the symbol of the fertile wind, the "fructifying breath" containing the primal power that similarly animated Adam, impregnated the Egyptian vultures, the Mother of God, and his patient. This similarity had nothing to do with chance but had everything to do with intuition, the analogical link embracing time and place, the direct unconscious and hereditary *perception* of the primordial image. This "image" was "potentially latent" in the unconscious and was nothing more in its nature—since belonging to the collective unconscious preceding any representation created by consciousness—than the wind, as transparent and direct as intuition, as empty as the archetype.

This example, through different eras, does reveal the heredity of the archetype, but that of the human function of intuition, the heredity of what Jung called the *"possibility* of such representations". But again, we find Jung, in 1917, trying and failing, with a too general term ("possibility", which later would become "tendency"), to express the specific nature of the archetype. "Possibility", "tendency" in psychology is a function. It is intuition, and its name in the unconscious is *Anschauung*.

The dependency of archetypes upon Jung's Anschauung

1919 saw the publication of "Instinct and the unconscious" and the first appearance of the term "archetype", suggested to Jung from a memory of Augustine.

ANSCHAUUNG AND ARCHETYPE   151

It is commonly perceived that the notion of archetype evolved in Jung's printings. The notion was rather variously expressed in numerous contexts and, therefore, led to confusion regarding its definition. Against this assumption, we will show that the term *Anschauung*, to be found together with "archetype" in "Instinct and the unconscious", highlighted as early as 1919 the difference between the archetype compared by Jung—in various contexts rather than chronologically—with the Platonic Idea and a matrix. The former has been wrongly associated with an early enunciation of the archetype, since the comparison with the Idea proves more static than that with a matrix.[166] The matricial metaphor resolves the issue of the articulation of the individual and the collective between the person and the archetype. The Platonic Idea merely emphasises the distance and the hierarchy between the individual and the collective. In contrast, the matrix reveals how the persons (1) can reach the collective (2) without losing their individuality. (1) and (2) can happen through intuition (*Anschauung*), as described by Jung in his first ever enunciation of the term "archetype" in his writings.

Problematically, I will show that only the German speaks of intuition. Let us examine five passages (correspondingly underlined) from this original German paragraph and its English translation:

> *Dazu kommen die a priori vorhandenen, das heißt mitgeborenen Formen <u>der Anschauung, der Intuition,</u> die* Archetypen *von Vahrnehmung und Erfassung, welche eine unvermeidliche und a priori determinierende Bedingung aller psychischen Prozesse sind. Wie die Instinkte den Menschen zu einer-spezifisch menschlichen Lebensführung veranlassen, so swingen die Archetypen die Wahrnehmung und <u>Anschauung</u> zu spezifisch menschlichen Bildungen. Die Instinkte und die Archetypen der Anschauung bilden das kollektive Unbewußte. . . .* (passage without the mention of either archetype or Anschauung) . . . *<u>Die Archetypen der Anschauung</u> haben dieselbe Qualität wie die Instinkte [die allgemein und gleichmäßig verbreitete <u>Erscheinung</u> sehen, welche mit der Individualität des Menschen nichts zu tun hat], sie sind ebenfalls kollektive Phänomene.*

In this "deeper" stratum we also find the a priori inborn forms <u>of "intuition"</u>, namely the archetypes of perception and apprehension, which are the necessary a priori determinants of all psychic processes. Just as his instincts compel man to a specifically human mode of existence, so the archetypes force his ways of perception and <u>apprehension</u> into specifically human patterns. The instincts and <u>the archetypes</u>

together form the "collective unconscious". . . . <u>Archetypes</u> have this quality in common with the instincts [to be a universal and regularly occurring <u>phenomenon</u> which has nothing to do with individuality] and are likewise collective phenomena. (Jung, *GW* and *CW* 8, par. 270)

In German, *Anschauung* and intuition are equivalent. Both identify the archetype. The grammatical analysis of the first, fourth, and fifth German underlined passages reveals either (1) the dependence of the archetype on *Anschauung* or (2) the identical character of archetypes and *Anschauung*.

In the first underlined passage, the German reads: *"mitgeborenen Formen der Anschauung, der Intuition"* to qualify the archetype. The comma separates the two *equivalent* terms *"Anschauung"* and *"Intuition"*. As for (1), the genitive *"der" Anschauung* is the complement of the noun "form". An adjective only qualifies a noun since this noun can stand without it. Conversely, a complement cannot be detached from the noun since the noun without the complement would not make any sense. *Anschauung* is the genitive complement of "[archetypal] forms". Therefore, grammatically, that is structurally, archetypes cannot exist without intuition as *Anschauung*. Whereas "inborn" only qualifies "[the archetypal] forms", "intuition" indicates the nature of the "forms", intuitive nature without which the forms are incomprehensible. In other words, archetype cannot be understood without intuition.

The sentence continues with another comma, expressing the equivalence between "inborn forms of 'intuition'", on the one hand, and "the archetypes of perception and apprehension", on the other. "Forms", thus, more clearly becomes "archetypes". Now *Anschauung* is directly genitive of "archetypes", as confirmed by the fourth and fifth equivalent passages in German: *die Archetypen* der *Anschauung* (I underline the genitive); *Die Archetypen der Anschauung*.

Standing against this precision of the original language is the inevitable loss caused by bad choices in translation. In English (1) *Anschauung* is not translated and (2) is signalled by the placement of "intuition" within quotation marks. The English term "intuition" exists. Consequently, placing "intuition" within quotation marks creates a false vagueness for a very specific (but not translated) term: *Anschauung*. When one reads the English paragraph, one immediately assumes that Jung is experimenting with a new but elusive idea, and the first appearance of a new term, archetype, confirms it. This impression, created by the English translation, is wrong. First, tracing as we have done the already long history of the archetype and second, looking in the Grimms' dictionary at the entry "Anschauung", reveals that this imprecision does not exist.

Thus, what Jung wanted to emphasise in his first use of the term was the intimate relationship between *Anschauung* and archetype. Archetype without *Anschauung* did not make sense. One could not fathom the nature of the archetype without linking the archetype to the function of intuition.

The lexical analysis confirms the grammatical analysis. None of the underlined passages translate the term *Anschauung*. We can see the suppression in the first passage. The second passage translates *Anschauung* as "apprehension". "Apprehension" can, at best, translate the term *Erfassung* of the previous sentence, but insufficiently qualifies the notion of *Anschauung*. *Anschauung* is not only a perception, a comprehension, or an apprehension, but an intuitive one. The fourth and the fifth passages both simply translated *Archetypen der Anschauung* into "archetypes". The suppression of *Anschauung* cannot be clearer. The French translation repeats this mistake (Jung, 1956[1919], p. 99, and so do all the others already mentioned.

Finally, to make clear that what has been lost in the bad translation is the inherent link between archetype and intuition, let us examine the final passage. *Erscheinung* is translated "phenomenon" in English. Whereas "phenomenon", such as "representation", or *Bildung*, previously studied automatically led the mind towards conscious realities, the dynamic and neutral term *Erscheinung* ("appearance") described the nature and the dynamics of the archetype, its unconscious origin, and its relationship to consciousness through intuition.

As early as 1919, Jung adequately described his archetypes. "Dominants" and "archetypes" were neologisms. *Urbild* and *Anschauung* were hardly translatable. "Intuition", in contrast, was clear and, most important, adequate. For German readers, *Die Archetypen der Anschauung* led to the very nature of the collective unconscious: empty, pre-formative, *a priori*, and pertaining to the mysteries of an unknowable state. It is not possible to study the origin and precise meaning of the term "archetype" the way we have done in the four sections of this chapter. However, a systematic translation of "the archetypes" into "the archetypes of intuition" would have properly introduced the significance and meaning of the notion of archetype in Jung's thinking. As we are reminded by Sonu Shamdasani, "the theoretical language that Jung was developing became reformulated and taken to different ends by those around him. This process of resignification has been central to the development of analytical psychology" (Shamdasani, 1999, p. 539). In face of this danger, the precision of intuition in the unconscious linked to Jung's central concept of archetype is precious indeed.

CHAPTER SIX

Archetype, intuition, instinct, and empathy (1)

Theoretical distinctions of contents: intuition and instinct

"Instinct and the unconscious" portrays the collective unconscious thanks to the three correlated notions of intuition, instincts, and archetypes. The following quotations, which appear (without my numbers) in this order in Jung's book, explain their different roles. Jung hardly ever attempted, or succeeded, at being as clear as he is here on such a complex matter. This is why the comments following the four extracts are only concerned with the intricacy and equal significance of the three notions.

> [1] Intuition ... resembles a process of perception but unlike the conscious activity of the senses and introspection the perception is unconscious. ... It is a process analogous to instinct with the difference that whereas instinct is the purposive impulse to carry out some highly complicated action, intuition is the unconscious purposive apprehension of a highly complicated situation.

> [2] Instincts are typical modes of action, and wherever we meet with uniform and regularly recurring modes of action and reaction we are dealing with instinct, no matter whether it is associated with a conscious motive or not.

[3] Archetypes are typical modes of apprehension, and wherever we meet with uniform and regularly recurring modes of apprehension we are dealing with archetypes, no matter whether its mythical character is recognised or not.

[4] In my view it is impossible to say which comes first – apprehension of the situation, or the impulse to act. It seems to me that both are aspects of the same vital activity, which we have to think of as two distinct processes *simply for the purpose of better understanding*. (Jung, 1956[1919], pars 269, 273, 280, 282, my italics)

Written in a parallel manner, [2] and [3] reveal the connection of instincts (patterns of behaviour) with action as well as the connection of archetypes with apprehension. Because [1] associates instinct with action and intuition with apprehension, the reader unites archetype and intuition. Therefore, the link between archetype and instinct seems not to be as direct as the link between archetype and intuition. In [4], however, Jung emphasises the uniting vitality of the psychic process, which leaves open the possibility of a closer link between instinct and archetype.

A pattern of behaviour is an act, the origin of which is an archetype. In other words, Jung never denied, albeit not altogether clearly, that archetypes can be instincts and instincts archetypes. In the 1945 "On the nature of the psyche" Jung writes,

It is therefore very natural to suppose that these factors [archetypes] are connected with the instincts and to inquire whether the typical situational patterns which these collective form-principles apparently represent are not in the end identical with the instinctual patterns, namely with the patterns of behaviour. (Jung, *CW 8*, par. 404)

The idea here is that one should not forget the inaccuracy of one's conscious apperception on probable simultaneous processes (instinct) and perceptions (intuition) of the collective unconscious (archetypes). Whether as forms or as functions, their interdependency is primary to their nature, as they do not "exist" yet.

Concerning the link between archetype and intuition, "Instinct and the unconscious" is remarkable for Jung's clear tribute to Bergson's philosophy.[167] Jung's praise of Bergson's clarity might partly explain that of Jung in this peculiar essay.

We previously examined a point of convergence between Jung's and Medtner's grasp of the term *Anschauung*, and we shall further (in Part V) appreciate his influence concerning types. In one of his 1919 lectures, Medtner distinguished among three kinds of oppositions to intuition. Singularly, his pair of "psychological" opposites between instinct and intuition did not directly inspire Jung. Yet, a close examination of Medtner's ideas, linked to those of another member of the Psychological Club, Maria Moltzer, brings to light another influence, this time on empathy (1).

In his lecture, Medtner successively described instinct inspired by Nietzsche, Bergson, and then Kant. Medtner first borrowed Nietzsche's aesthetics. Instincts and intuition are essentially comparable within art, through the art process. Art is a realm that is not, like science, universal. As a result, intuition is no science (Medtner, 1923, p. 48). Instinct, like intuition, is a *Trieb*, a "drive". Here, Medtner followed Bergson's evolutionism. Instinct appears before intuition in mankind's evolution. Intuition is more differentiated than instinct.[168] Contrary to instinct, intuition evolves next to the different "tastes" of the different civilisations.

Finally, following his favourite philosopher, Kant, Medtner differentiated between intuition and instinct, on the one hand, and *Vernunft*, or "pure reason", and *Verstand*, or "comprehension", on the other. Those two German terms will be described in detail later. Medtner, in this comparison, pitted the *naiven Monismus* point of view (such as Leibniz's), which he named the *primitive-intuitiv*, against the modern Kantian *Dualismus*, the root of which was the Logos (Medtner, 1923, pp. 49–50).

In 1916, Moltzer had already traced some phylogenetic dimensions of the origin of intuition, when she notably stated that intuition was the origin of religion and where she had quoted Lévy-Bruhl on *participation mystique* (Moltzer, 1916, Shamdasani, 1998, pp. 104, 118). Hence, in the last section of this chapter, titled "Jung's evolutionism: from empathy (1) to *Anschauung*", we must remember that Jung's evolutionism had been influenced by two members of the Psychological Club.

Identities of energies: libido and élan vital

Few studies hitherto have considered Bergson's influence on Jung. French philosopher Gilles Deleuze's publication, *Le Bergsonisme*, in

1966 might have encouraged studies on the relationship between Jung and Bergson, since Jung influenced Deleuze's reading of Bergson. In 1982, an American scholar, Pete Gunter, undertook a general investigation on how Bergson's philosophy stimulated Jung's philosophy in "Bergson and Jung". In 2006, philosopher Christian Kerslake analysed the affiliations among Kant's, Jung's, and Bergson's epistemologies. A British specialist on Bergson, John Mullarkey, saw a possible, albeit non-historical, link between Jung's archetypes and Bergson's 1911 *Creative Evolution*.[169]

In his 1984 article, "From somnambulism to the archetypes", Jungian analyst John Haule attempted to trace the French roots of Jung's psychology. Haule contextualised Jung's early work in the debate opposing associationists and dissocianists (see Chapter Two) such as Frédéric Paulhan (Haule, 1984, pp. 635–659). Like Bergson, Paulhan was an important figure in the psycho-philosophical debate in France at the turn of the twentieth century and in the following years. While Jung quotes Paulhan only on precise psychiatric issues, he more often refers to Bergson and on broader topics.[170]

We know how central to Freud and Jung's rift libido was. Whereas Jung decided to keep the term "libido" within his psychology, Freudian and Jungian libidos have little in common. By contrast, we will see that Jung equated his notion with Bergson's *élan vital*. Supported by Sonu Shamdasani and Pete Gunter's researches, I shall try to show the importance of Jung's Bergsonian background in the official break-up between Jung and Freud.

In Part I of *Psychology of the Unconscious*, Jung writes, "I am indebted to Rev. Dr. Keller of Zurich for calling my attention to Bergson's conception of the *durée créatrice* ['duration']" (Jung, 1917a, p. 496, n. 30), to be studied in the next section. A central notion of Bergson's "intuitionism", duration appeared as early as 1889 in *Time and Free Will*, Bergson's first major work written criticising Kant's categories. *Matter and Memory* appeared in 1896, followed, in 1907, by Bergson's third major opus, *Creative Evolution*. Winner of the Nobel Prize for Literature in 1927, Bergson was already famous in the psychological and philosophical circles frequented by both Jung and Freud when Jung discovered Bergson's philosophy. To my knowledge, Jung did not meet Bergson when he went to Paris in 1902–1903 to follow Janet's seminars, or later in 1907, but "by 1906," writes Gunter, "Jung was already familiar with certain of Bergson's ideas" (Gunter,

1982, p. 640). Rather than admitting to an influence on his psychology, Jung argued for a *simultaneous* similarity of thought with Bergson's philosophy.[171] Shamdasani confirms it by writing,

> The indications are that [Jung] read Bergson subsequent to developing his conception of the libido; the copy of Bergson's *Creative Evolution* in Jung's library is the 1912 German translation. His first reference to Bergson occurs in a letter to Loÿ in March 1913 . . . On October 8, 1912, in his presentation before the New York Academy of Medicine, while announcing that he proposed to liberate psychoanalytic theory from "the purely sexual standpoint," he claimed that libido could be understood as vital energy in general . . . [he added the following year while presenting the same paper in London] "or as Bergson's *élan vital*" (*CW* 4, §568). (Shamdasani, 2003, p. 227)

In 1914, Jung writes, "When I first read Bergson a year and a half ago I discovered to my great pleasure everything which I had worked out practically, but expressed by him in consummate language and in wonderfully clear philosophical style" (Jung 1917[1914], p. 351). "The date of this admission", comments Gunter, "is significant because it locates Jung's acquaintance with Bergson at the time he was struggling to free himself from his collaboration with Sigmund Freud" (Gunter, 1982, p. 638).

Letters confirm Gunter's point that Bergson, as the thinker of intuition who was the closest to Jung, would inevitably have separated Jung from Freud. In a letter to James Jackson Putnam dated 8 July 1915, Freud retrospectively complained,

> What I have seen of religious–ethical conversion has not been inviting. Jung, for example, I found sympathetic so long as he lived blindly, as I did. Then came his religious–ethical crisis with higher morality, "rebirth," Bergson and at the same time lies, brutality and anti-Semitic condescension towards me. (quoted in Hale, 1971, pp. 188–191)

Bergson belonged to what Jung called the "French School", one of the central interests of which was parapsychology and the origin of which could be traced, thanks to Ellenberger's work, to the Marques of Puységur (the "true founder" of mesmerism, in Charles Richet's terms) (see Ellenberger, 1970, p. 70).[172] In the letter above, Freud's associations of "religious–ethical" with "higher morality, 'rebirth'", and with "Bergson" allows us to understand Freud's second firm association in the following letter between intuition, divination, and revelation. Freud writes to Romain Rolland in 1936,

> There are no sources of knowledge of the universe other than the intellectual working-over of carefully scrutinized observations – in other words, what we call research – and alongside of it no knowledge derived from revelation, intuition or divination. . . . No new source of knowledge or methods of research has come into being. Intuition and divination would be such, if they existed; but they may safely be reckoned as illusions, the fulfilments of wishful impulses. (Freud, 1933a, SE 22, p. 159)

In 1920, Freud was already keen to repeat that he did not attribute any kind of credence to intuition as a method. He writes, "From what I have seen of intuition, it seems to me to be the product of a kind of impartiality" (Freud, 1920g, SE 18, p. 59; also quoted in Bishop, 2000, p. 127).

Whatever Freud's own interest in parapsychology (Bishop, 2000, pp. 102–139),[173] he considered it at the time "far beyond the original limits of psychoanalysis". However famous Charcot or Janet was, Freud was the first to create his school with practitioners entitled to follow his particular technique. Freud needed to make his potential heirs—and Jung was the first on the list—stand firm on the limits he set. Freud did not reject parapsychology, but he thought it was a danger for his young science. Intuition, or, rather, to use Freud's formulation, "revelation, intuition, or divination", thus represented the opposite of what Freud expected for the future of psychoanalysis.

What, then, did Bergson's theory offer Jung over and above that of Freud's? Gunter examines the elements of Bergson's philosophy to be found in Jung's psychology and relies on Jung's account concerning his (Jung's) single reading of Bergson's 1907 *Creative Evolution*.

This last point is of major importance and would need to be confirmed or refuted by further research, since, in *Time and Free Will* (1889), to Kant's unreachable "Intellectual Intuition", Bergson opposes duration. Kant is merely neutral in Jung's psychology of the unconscious. At stake is the status of the archetype, its accessibility by intuition beyond Kant's *phenomenon* and *noumenon*. Bergson's critique of Kant's philosophy of intuition reappears in *Creative Evolution*, yet in different terms, since Bergson is now at peace with Kant. In

1907, Bergson writes of Kant that he had opened the avenue for a "new philosophy". Without Kant's *formulation* of the unreachable Intellectual Intuition, writes Bergson, the old philosophy would have stayed a mere human intellectual–intuitive effort (see Bergson, 2008 [1892–1893], p. 10).[174]

"[W]ith *Creative Evolution*", writes Gunter, "the human unconscious becomes suprapersonal. There is in each of us the memory of a biological past which far antedates our individual lives" (Gunter, 1982, p. 637). Bergson's "suprapersonal" and Jung's "collective" unconscious are interchangeable. Less obvious to grasp is Bergson's "memory of a *biological* past" and its link to Jung's work as a psychologist.[175]

I have tried to show that the inheritance of the archetypes, instead of describing any inherited images, corresponded to the inheritance of the human function of intuition. Bergson's memory of a biological past corresponds to Jung's inheritance of the patterns of behaviour, not through intuition, but through instinct, even though it is hardly possible to distinguish between instinct, intuition, and archetype in the unconscious. Jung writes that "instincts are typical modes of actions . . . archetypes are typical modes of apprehension [this apprehension being intuition] . . . it is impossible to say which comes first . . . both are aspects of the same vital activity" (Jung, *CW 8*, pars 273, 280, 282). This description belongs to these "other ways of explanations", writes Jung,

> deriving from Bergson's philosophy, [which] have recently been put forward, laying stress on the factor of intuition . . . we speak of intuition as an 'instinctive' act of comprehension. It is a process analogous to instinct, with the difference that whereas instinct is a purposive impulse to carry out some highly complicated action, intuition is the unconscious, purposive apprehension of a highly complicated situation. (Jung, *CW 8*, par. 269)

In Bergson's philosophy, "memory" refers to the faculty of remembering other lives (human, then animal, then vegetal) through intuition. Evolution from the vegetative to the instinctive—animal in this context—and intelligent levels, together with their present interpenetration in all species, was possible thanks to the vital impetus, the *élan vital*, the nature of which was neither psychic nor organic and had no definite nature, as shown by this conclusive statement in Bergson's third chapter of *Creative Evolution*:

All the living hold together, and all yield to the same tremendous push [the vital impetus]. The animal takes its stand on the plant, man bestrides animality, and the whole of humanity, in space and in time, is one immense army galloping beside and before and behind each of us in an overwhelming charge able to beat down every resistance and clear the most formidable obstacles, perhaps even death. (Bergson, 1911[1907], p. 286)

In Jung's opinion, the vital impetus possessed the strong energetic character of pushing the living ahead that he did not see in Freud's libido, which was turned to the past, to the childhood of the individual. For Jung, the life of the psyche was future-directed and, thus, allowed the presence of intuition. That Jung's psychology of the unconscious is future-orientated appears in his writing on dream. In 1916, Jung writes, "The occurrence of prospective dreams cannot be denied", and he continues, "dreams are often in a much more favourable position than consciousness with regard to prognosis" (Jung, CW 8, par. 493).

Identities of processes: intuition and duration

Introduced as early as *Time and Free Will* in Bergson's work, duration (*durée créatrice*) reappears in *Creative Evolution*, linked this time to the collective, a "data"—or a "given", if we translate literally the French "donnée" appearing in the sub-title, *Essai sur les données immédiates de la conscience*—which was not considered by Bergson in 1889. Gunter explains how, for Bergson, intuition is a "method"—the experience—of thinking[176] in duration, which reflects the continuous flow of reality. This continuity of time is the time within, composed of the untouched sum of all "memories" linked by intuition in the suprapersonal unconscious (collective memory unlimited by a single lifetime). Commonly referred to as reality, time without, or "spatialised time", does not, in fact, possess this wholeness and exactitude that intuition provides, as time without is perceived by the filter of consciousness.

Bergson assigned to intuition of the world within (the *durée*) a better collective rightness than our personal consciousness of the world experienced without. In *Creative Evolution* he writes,

> [M]any agreements are possible, while there is only one truth. Intuition, if it could be prolonged beyond a few instants [in consciousness], would not only make the philosopher agree with his own thought, but also all philosophers with each other. (Bergson, 1911 [1907], p. 251)[177]

In Jung's psychology, Bergson's system corresponded to the "reality" of the psyche and to the *Anschauung*, which alone reached the archetypes of the collective unconscious. The flow of this inner, true, reality was the creative aspect of duration, itself linked to the vital impetus. Bergson's flow becomes Jung's psychic process of individuation,[178] as portrayed in *Psychology of the Unconscious* in the following extract, where Jung quotes Bergson:

> In the Egyptian Book of the Dead, Tum is even designated as a he-cat, because as such he fought the snake, Apophis. The encoiling also means the engulfing, the entering into the mother's womb. Thus time is defined by the rising and setting of the sun, that is to say, through the death and renewal of the libido. The addition of the cock again suggests time, and the addition of implements suggests the creation through time. ("Durée créatrice," Bergson.) (Jung, 1917a, pp. 314–316)

Jung turned this rightness of intuition to his anthropological (with no vegetative and animal stages, such as in Bergson's *Creative Evolution*) evolutionism (see next section), as the best possible recourse each time humanity had had to face a significant transformation, either collective or personal. When humans experienced a passage from life to death or from childhood to adulthood, they turned to the world within to let the *creative* duration operate.

In *The Book of the Dead*, Tum's death occurred. Tum had to join the underworld (the collective unconscious). On his way to this world he would have—literally, for the Egyptians, at least—to fight a snake: for this reason, implements and a cock (creation) were left by his side. Bergson's time in the suprapersonal unconscious is qualitative and no longer spatial. Tum was no longer amid his people (spatial time of consciousness) and the underworld would lead him to the (deprived of spatial constraints) collective time, where he would then be able to meet the gods and ancestors. This quality of Bergson's collective time was translated in Jung's psychology into primordial images such as "the entering into the mother's womb", which is an amplification of the "encoiling" of the snake. The truth of Bergson's intuition, of the *durée créatrice*, was translated into efficiency, the living character of the symbols for Tum and of the rites for his contempories.

The sexual aspect of the libido was just one, and not the single or even the main, theoretical issue which divided Jung and Freud in the 1910s. Bergson's intuitionism offered Jung a link to the collective dimension of the unconscious. As will be seen in Part V, it also helped him build his psychology of consciousness.

Jung's evolutionism: from empathy (1) to Anschauung

The link that Jung implied in his writings between *Einfühlung*, here empathy (1), and *Anschauung* reveals how the intuitive significance that we emphasised in the "Socrates" *Einfall*—a significance which existed in similar examples within the tests—must have impressed him as early as 1907.

In 1911, Jung sought the psychological significance of the "primitive" mentality with regard to that of the moderns, as revealed by his chapter, "The two kinds of thinking" in the first part of *Psychology of the Unconscious*. There, Jung opposed the directed thinking of moderns, which he linked to consciousness, to the thinking-in-images of "primitives", which he linked to the unconscious and to dreams in moderns. As Segal writes, "'primitive' peoples think as they do because they live in a state of unconsciousness" (Segal, 2007, p. 635). The origin of consciousness for Jung was the unconscious. In the collective unconscious everything was present but nothing, from either nature or humanity, was differentiated. "Primitives" experienced a first stage of differentiation: the psychic alterity with nature or between themselves. Yet, their empathic tendency to identify themselves with the external world as a mechanism of defence remained. "[The objects]", writes Jung, "have a direct psychic effect upon [the primitive] producing what is practically a dynamic identification with the object" (Jung, CW 6, par. 495).

Instead of fighting the elements of the external, "primitives" identified themselves with them. A man could be a mountain, or a lake, and another lake could be a woman, and this woman could be a man, such as an ancestor. This represented the most intuitive as well as the firmest possible link between humanity and nature—that is, between the potential consciousness of the "primitive" and the collective unconscious. This was empathy in its purest form. At the same time, by failing to integrate the whole outer world within themselves, "primitives" intuited, perceived through this unsuccessful rapport with nature, the primal idea of god: power. Nature was a force "out there" beyond their control.

"Primitives" called all that was out of the reach of empathy by a generic term such as *mana* or *Melungu*, some power or energy upon which everything depended. *Mana*, a notion first used by the anthropologist R. H. Codrington in 1891 in *The Melanesians*, designated, writes Paul Bishop, "a supernatural force that emanates from certain magic individuals, a quasi divine, primal, vital force . . . such as [emanates from] sorcerers, witches, werewolves, and the like" (Bishop, 2008, pp. 509–510). In 1917, Jung showed how vast the notion could be:

> [T]his notion comprises the idea of soul, spirit, God, health, physical strength, fertility, magic power, influence, might, prestige, curative remedies, as well as certain states of mind which are characterised by the setting loose of affects [thus when empathy disappears]. Among certain Polynesians "Melungu" (that is this primitive concept of energy) is spirit, demoniacal being, magic, prestige. (Jung, 1917a, p. 413)

The power of the sorcerers forecasted that of god, the fear of whom gave rise to the religious rites and later, in the Western world, for instance, within a more and more conscious, rational religion, the dogma. Jung described this chronological process two years later in "Instinct and the unconscious":

> Intuitional activity can be observed most easily among primitives. There we constantly meet with certain typical images [witches, sorcerers, and the like] and motifs [rites] which are the foundations of their mythologies. These images are autochthonous and occur with great regularity; everywhere we find the idea of a magic power or substance, of spirits and their doings, of heroes and gods and their legends. In the great religions of the world we see the perfection of those images and at the same time their progressive incrustation with rational forms. (Jung, *CW 8*, par. 278)

While *mana* described a relationship, "gods", which appeared later, described a concept, and, thus, a progress from the unconscious to consciousness.

The perfection of the primordial images through time allowed the progress of humankind to consciousness. Yet, the loss of religion for moderns implied what Jung called the loss of their soul, the neurotic moving away of consciousness from the unconscious. No longer connected by *Einfühlung* to the images and motifs of the collective unconscious, mankind gained the more and more elaborated levels of consciousness, intelligence, and rationality, but at the expense of his closeness to his soul, to his instincts. What was initially *Einfühlung*, or empathy in its strongest sense, would became *Anschauung*, another form of intuition, which, rather than connecting a mere potential consciousness, an under-consciousness, to the collective unconscious, would link a differentiated consciousness to archetypes.

PART IV

AFTER 1913: INTUITION IN JUNGIAN AND POST-JUNGIAN PRACTICE

CHAPTER SEVEN

Intuitive methods and empathy (2)

Introduction

Empathy in the unconscious, we have called empathy (1). The form of intuition that is present in the empathy that appears in the under-conscious, we call empathy (2). Empathy (2) is mostly present in the consulting room, alongside and linked to the phenomenon of transference, to be examined in the fourth section of this chapter. Intuition also occurs in Jungian and post-Jungian practice during two specific activities: active imagination, and the constructive method. It is difficult to know which, in practice, of these two arose first. Most important is that Jung practised them long before writing on them, and when he did so, he emphasised that those methods could hardly be theorised. Practice and theory, for Jung, were distinct. This chapter deals with method, and the next chapter, very different, essentially treats of theory. The first two sections of this chapter explain the constructive method and active imagination. A longer third section acts out both techniques through Aniéla Jaffé's *Memories, Dreams, Reflections* and invites an understanding of Jung's take on myth.

Intuition in the constructive method

In the mid 1910s, Jung defined the constructive method *vis-à-vis* Freud's "analytic method" and as the psychological equivalent of Bergson's "intuitive method".[178] Shamdasani writes,

> What Jung [when he read Bergson for the first time around 1912] had discovered through clinical work had been confirmed by Bergson's philosophy, and specifically indicated two points of convergence: that between his concept of *hormé* [Jungian libido] and Bergson's *élan vital* [as seen earlier], and between his constructive method and Bergson's intuitive method. (Shamdasani, 2003, p. 128)[179]

During the same period, Jung, in 1914, explained in a lecture given in London that,

> in its immediate results, the constructive method does not produce anything that could be called a scientific theory. It traces, rather, the psychological path of development in a given individual, as I tried to show in my book *Wandlungen und Symbole der Libido*". (Jung, CW 3, par. 422)

"Traces" and "path" remind us of the symbols that trace "the way of what is to come", the opening words of *The Red Book*. The principle—understanding the symbols—and the goal—one's individuation—are equivalent.

Jung continues by developing his theory of the symbol. A symbol is a possibility, a key to a potential resolution of a present psychological conflict. It is a hunch that individuals can either catch or miss. The symbol can be perceived if the person understands which is the healthier psychological way to choose, whatever the sacrifice, and whatever one's former expectations. From one accepted—Jungians employ the term "integrated"—symbol to the other, persons create the way of their individuation, away from the collective expectations and away from their own prior expectations about the collective. This new attitude opens new and unexpected doors.

Jung pits his theory of the symbol against Freud's theory of the sign:

> The analytic–reductive method has the advantage of being much simpler. It reduces everything to known basic principles of a very

simple nature. The constructive method, working with highly complex material, has to build up towards an unknown goal. (Jung, CW 3, par. 423)

The unknown goal is each person's individuation, hence, unknown to anybody, even to the persons themselves. What Jung does here is to oppose Freud's psychoanalysis to a theory of the symbol, the core of the constructive method. Whereas the sign points to the personal and to the past of the patients, the symbol paves the way to their future. In that sense, the symbol is intuitive by nature.[180]

According to Jung, Freud's method was limited and potentially harmful. In the first of the *Two Essays on Analytical Psychology*, Jung writes,

> I have indicated above the justification as well as the limitation of this procedure [the analytic–reductive method]. It breaks down at the point where the dream symbols can no longer be reduced to personal reminiscences or aspirations, that is, when the images of the collective unconscious begin to appear. It would be quite senseless to try to reduce these collective ideas to anything personal – not only senseless but positively harmful, as painful experience has taught me. (Jung, CW 7, par. 122)

As soon as the psychologist can find a referent to the dream material in the patient's life, we are dealing with a sign. Any other "highly complex material" indicates that the origin of the symbol is the collective unconscious and that the method must change. The second step of the constructive method is "amplification"—as opposed to "reduction". In the lecture "The theory of psycho-analysis"m delivered at Fordham University in New York in 1912, Jung used the example of baptism and of the historian to clarify his purpose:

> Suppose, for instance, we did not understand the meaning of the baptismal rite practised in our churches today. The priest tells us: baptism means the admission of a child into the Christian community. But this does not satisfy us. Why is the child sprinkled with water? In order to understand this ceremony, we must gather together from the whole history of ritual, that is, from mankind's memories of the relevant traditions, a body of comparative material culled from the most varied sources:

1. Baptism is clearly a rite of initiation, a consecration. Therefore we have to collect all memories in which any initiation rites are preserved.
2. The act of baptism is performed with water. For this special form another series of memories must be collected, namely, of rites in which water is used.
3. The person to be baptised is sprinkled with water. Here we have to collect all those rites in which the neophyte is sprinkled, immersed, etc.
4. All reminiscences from mythology, folklore, as well as superstitious practices, etc., have to be recalled, in so far as they run in any way parallel to the symbolism of the baptismal act. (Jung, CW 4, par. 330)

In Jung's example, baptism represents the dream material. The priest who defines baptism in terms of his contemporary practice is like the psychologist who uses the analytic–reductive method. His grasp of baptism, since limited to the present time, is "very superficial and one-sided" (Jung, CW 4, par. 331). In contrast, the historian who contextualises baptism, initiation, or sprinkling water in any past mythology or religion is like the psychologist who uses the constructive method. Both the historian and the analytical psychologist start with collecting data, which Jung calls—as revealed by his example above—"highly complex material", before he makes any sense of the dream in the consciousness of the dreamer.

Jung's hypothesis is that the origin of the dream material can be any time and anywhere in the collective unconscious and that nobody can anticipate this origin before amplification begins. To understand a dream when one starts from consciousness (that is, after the dream has occurred in the collective unconscious), one must first try to re-create the scene of the dream in its context, in its time and place in the collective unconscious. This re-creation is amplification—that is, the necessary amplification from consciousness to the collective unconscious.

The difference between the size and importance of consciousness and that of the collective unconscious in some dreams in this example is equivalent to the distinction made by Bergson between the time without, the time of the clock, and the time within, the *durée créatrice* available through intuition. Mathematically, with Jung's "amplification" and "construction", one adds, with Freud's "analysis", one reduces. This is why Jung in a contemporary statement of 1914 equated his constructive method with Bergson's intuitive method.

In a statement about Friedrich Nietzsche, whose thinking, as we shall see in Part V, inspired Jung's types, Jung expresses what links amplification with intuition. According to Jung,

> Nietzsche as an intuitive simply touches upon a thing and off he goes. He does not dwell upon the subject, though in the long run one can say he really does dwell upon it by amplification. But he does not deal with things in a logical way, going into the intellectual process of elucidation; he just catches such an intuition on the wing and leaves it, going round and round amplifying so that in the end we get a complete picture but by intuitive means, not by logical means. (Jarrett, (1988)[1934–1939], p. 1083, quoted in Huskinson, 2004, pp. 115–116)

Here, Jung at once unites Bergson with Nietzsche. According to Jung, Bergson merely thought intuition, whereas Nietzsche was "absolutely identical with intuition" (Huskinson, 2004, p. 115).[181]

The constructive method was not limited to dream material. It could also be employed with visions, as we shall see is the case with active imagination. But the difference between active imagination and the constructive method was that the constructive method remained in the consulting room, whereas active imagination could be used by Jung's patients themselves. Jung was aware of the danger of this situation. Some visions could torment his patients, or leave some of them in a state of illusion of grandeur, like many of his former schizophrenic patients.[182] As we shall see in the next section, the courage required by active imagination did not consist in letting one go down to the dark areas of the collective unconscious, but, rather, coming back from them to integrate the visions in order to make one's way, in order to understand and create one's individuation.

With *The Red Book*, Jung turned his terrifying intuitive visions into symbols and created analytical psychology. Schizophrenic patients and their own visions would never reawaken fear in Jung. Psychology gained much through Jung's experience of pathological cases. As psychiatrist Caspar Toni Frey-Wehrlin writes, "the fantasy of a psychotic compared to that of a neurotic or of anyone else, is like a fresco compared to a copperplate engraving" (Fierz, 1991, p. 7). Psychiatry lost Jung, but his work at the Burghölzli inspired, and continues to inspire, advances in research into schizophrenia.[183]

Intuition in active imagination

Swan (2008, p. 190) reframed Jung's use of active imagination in context. "When Jung worked with the technique of active imagination himself from 1912–1918, he was working with a tradition with a long-standing history and, in that sense, it is not a technique that he discovered". Intuitive tools, means, and under-conscious states that favoured intuition, such as automatic writing, crystal-gazing, hypnagogia (the twilight state occurring just before one falls asleep and which is rich in visions), were used by Jung and other experimenters.[184] Among Jung's predecessors was Myers, who called "the mythopoetic function" the "unconscious tendency to weave fantasies" (Ellenberger, 1970, p. 314) that could incite "a kind of colloquy between a conscious and an unconscious self" (Myers, 1885, pp. 24–25) through mythic and poetic symbols. This function inspired Jung's dialogical active imagination, when the experimenter makes one of his other voices appear to engage in a dialogue with it, like Jung with Philemon and all the characters of *The Red Book*.

Jung equated the term "fantasy" with that of "imagination". The singular "imagination" described for him the "activity of the mind in general . . . simply the direct expression of psychic life" (Jung, CW 6, par. 722). Active fantasies, or else active imaginations, were symbols seeking to "trace out a line of future psychological development" (Jung, CW 6, par. 726). This search followed the principles of the constructive method by bringing into play varied and creative tools.

An important auxiliary of individuation, the method of active imagination, was that of encountering or confronting consciousness with the unconscious. During the process, fantasies appeared, underconsciously "produced" by intuition. Ambiguous, Jung's formulation shows how symbols were at once created and appeared, at once individual and collective. Jung writes,

> Active fantasies are the product of intuition, i.e., they are evoked by an attitude directed to the perception of unconscious contents, as a result of which the libido immediately invests all the elements emerging from the unconscious and, by association with parallel material [drawing, writing, sculpture, dance, etc.], bring them into clear focus in visual form. (Jung, CW 6, par. 712)

This method attempts to convert symptomatic contents of the unconscious into symbolic forms in consciousness. The symbol adjusts the symptom in the natural progression of the psychic life. This co-operation of consciousness with the unconscious is called the "transcendent"—or "religious"—function of the psyche. The emerging symbol represents the third—transcendent—term, which assimilates the blockage of the complex to use and overcome it.

As explained by the Jungian analyst and dance therapist Joan Chodorow, "active imagination has two parts or stages: First, letting the unconscious come up; and second, coming to terms with the unconscious [where] consciousness takes the lead" (Chodorow, 1997, p. 10). During the second phase, all four functions of consciousness are necessary to understand the significance of the symbol in one's life. Yet, only intuition in the first stage creates and apprehends the symbol in the under-conscious.

This capacity of intuition is stressed in the contemporary correspondence between Hans Schmid-Guisan and Jung about types, to be studied in Part V. Beebe comments,

> The way he [Jung] stresses that intuition, though irrational, can yet be a potential source of new understanding – the thinking and feeling of the future – seems to reflect what he has learned in the course of the active imaginations recorded in *Liber Novus*. There, as we now know, he had written that "my soul gave me ancient things that pointed to the future. She gave me three things: The misery of war, the darkness of magic, and the gift of religion" (Jung, 2009, p: 306). All these irrational sources of insight are intuitive ways the unconscious has of informing the conscious mind. (Beebe & Falzeder, 2013, p. 24)

When Jung emphasised the role of the three other functions, he pointed to the importance of the acceptance by all facets of the conscious personality of the new element, an acceptation without which reaching another stage, adopting a new attitude, would be impossible. In this future-orientated psychology, understanding the symbol and understanding its significance were allied, but each function had a distinct role and that of intuition was primary.

We remember that the under-conscious was the most favourable condition for intuition to appear. In his 1916 theoretical essay "The transcendent function", Jung states,

> The method of "active imagination" hereinafter described, is the most important auxiliary for the production of those contents of the unconscious which lie, as it were, immediately below the threshold of consciousness and, when intensified, are the most likely to irrupt spontaneously into the conscious mind. (Jung, *CW 8*, par. 130)

In this extract, Jung describes (1) intuitive contents and (2) the first stage of active imagination. For example, in *The Red Book*, Jung names one chapter, after his conditioning himself in an under-conscious state, "The incantations". When people formulate incantations, they temporarily forget their environment. In psychological terms, they let their intuitive function go anywhere to make images and sounds appear, that is, elements that belong to archetypes. By his association with fourteen paintings, as we shall see, those elements, for Jung, were brought into clear focus in visual forms, adjusting Jung's complex in the progression of his psychic life. The incantation read,

> Christmas has come. The God is in the egg. I have prepared a rug for my God, an expensive red rug from the land of morning.
>
> He shall be surrounded by the shimmer of magnificence of his Eastern land.
>
> I am the mother, the simple maiden, who gave birth and did not know how.
>
> I am the careful father, who protected the maiden.
>
> I am the shepherd, who received the message as he guarded his herd at night on the dark fields. (Jung in Shamdasani, 2009, p. 284 and image 50)

The associated painting notably contains the symbols of the first verse of the song: the egg, Christmas, the red, and the Eastern land. This fiftieth image of *The Red Book* evokes India rather than any Western traditional representation of the Nativity. This is an example of Jung's project, embodied in *Liber Novus*, to understand what *his* myth was. As Shamdasani explains, "what the work develops or portrays is what I call Jung's *private* [and therefore individual] cosmology" (Shamdasani, 2010, p. 39, my italics). Following the death of his father, Jung's religious preoccupation became, in the mid 1910s, an autonomous "complex". The "symptom" of this complex was the failure to resolve the vital, existential, question formulated by Jung: if the Christian myth is not mine, then what is my myth?[185]

Christmas with an egg in the Eastern land pictured—well before words, and perhaps even without words—an image of *Jung's* myth. In essence, Christmas represented the earlier symptom. The egg was the rebirth to the personal myth. The entire picture of "Christmas with an egg in the Eastern land" had turned a symptom for Jung—Christianity—into a living symbol. This series of pictures represented Jung's process to his myth, and Jung's unconscious brought conscious renunciation of Christianity. This was the beginning of "what was to come" for Jung: the start of his individuation.

A paradigm: Jaffé's Mythosanschauung in Memories, Dreams, Reflections

As a paradigm of Jung's theory, Jaffé's *Memories, Dreams, Reflections* (*MDR*) helps us clarify major theoretical entries of intuition and develop in a drawn-out metaphor the intuitive part of both the constructive method and active imagination. Jaffé is an essential link between Jungian and post-Jungian practice. When, in Part III, we could only explain the *Anschauung*, the intuitive function, thanks to theory and examples, *MDR* provides us with the two intermediary stages of the paradigm and the case. Jaffé's *Mythosanschauung*, or "case Jung", is theoretically faithful to both Jung's theory of *Anschauung* and his theory of myth. Likewise, if Jaffé's fable is not Jung's life, the centrality of Jung's childhood "secrets" (*Geheimnisse*) in *MDR* rhetorically and aesthetically exposes the four functions and brings the readers to esotericist realms through Jaffé's psychological amplification.

MDR is not Jung's autobiography. It is not Jung's assistant and follower Aniéla Jaffé's biography, either. The first three chapters, which cover childhood, school and student years, and the last two chapters, "Late thoughts" and "Retrospect", were actually written by Jung but heavily edited by Jaffé. The rest of the book was written by Jaffé from the protocols of their encounters, and the entire book was published after Jung's death. As Shamdasani notes, the posthumous character of the publication opened the door to the editor's censorship regarding some the dark periods of Jung's life.[186] Letters also reveal that Jung himself was critical of Jaffé's "auntification", as

Maillard analyses when she writes of Jaffé's reworking as a "monumentalisation".[187]

MDR is a psychobiography—a biography where Jaffé links Jung's life to his psychology—and I will try to show that it is Jaffé's *Mythosanschauung*—a biography where the author connects Jung's life, Jung's psychology, and, crucially, the readers, thanks to myth and intuition (*Anschauung*). "Myth" here must be understood in a Jungian sense. Jung's psychology embraces a theory of myth and myth is used by Jungian analysts in a specific way. As Segal elucidates,

> A myth [for Jung] is not merely a myth in its own right. It is a myth for someone. The meaning of a myth is more than its general meaning for all humanity. One must understand the person or the society to understand the myth: "So it is with the individual images [in a myth]: they need a context, and the context is not only a myth but an individual anamnesis". (Segal, 1998, p. 13, quoting from Jung's "The psychological aspect of the Kore", in *The Archetypes and the Collective Unconscious*, 1981, p. 189)

To get from life to myth, the individual passes by one or several archetypes. The encounter of one archetype in one's life is a necessary step of individuation as well as a passage of the utmost importance. In the consulting room, this passage is achieved by anamnesis. When some complex—or archetype—significantly appears in one client's dreams, for instance, the analyst helps the client "amplify" the motif within a myth. As a result, the client realises the meaning of *his or her* complex. The reason for that success is the intuitive nature of the link, able to keep absolutely intact both the collective and the individual meaning of the archetype, and, by amplification, of the myth.[188]

Jaffé's particular talent—her intuition and insight into Jung's entire work—is that link between Jung's life and Jung's psychology, and also the link to the reader in *MDR*. The readers are not clients ready to come to terms with complexes. In the two anonymously directed dimensions of writing, myth and intuition work on the reader thanks to elaborate rules of composition. Rowland (2005, p. 3) reads *MDR* as a "mythography":

> Such a form of writing [Jung's] cannot help being, in part, literary. This is not to allege that Jung was, or considered himself to be, the author of fiction. Rather, its psychology needs to be understood in

terms of its aesthetic qualities. And these qualities, in the Jungian approach, do not detract from its identity as 'psychology'; they are basic to it.

Just as religion has hagiographies, written not by people later canonised, but by their followers, so myth can, indeed, have mythographies. Jung had devotees. Marie-Louise von Franz, Jung's closest follower, was, therefore, the person most suited to express in 1975 Jung's "myth in our time", her own phrase (von Franz, 1975[1972]).[189] Yet, when von Franz and Jaffé describe Jung's personal—that is, conscious and individuated—myth, the reader enters *MDR* through the collective, unconscious, and, therefore, powerful dimension of the myth.[190]

The first rule of composition of a mythography by followers or assistants paradoxically consists in the mythographer's creation of a personal myth by being intuitively embedded in the collective and powerful dimension of that same myth. Jaffé had been Jung's secretary for decades. She sometimes answered his mail on his behalf because, writes Shamdasani, "at the outset, Jung trusted her ability to 'assume his "I",' and to represent it to the outer world" (Shamdasani, 1995, p. 122).

This situation finds an echo in a different literary genre. The historical novelist Robert Graves subtly opens *I, Claudius* by revealing the intuitive confusion of authors, which reinforces the individual and collective—mythical—*I* of the title. Graves describes the relationship existing between the mythographer—Graves in reality, as well as "Polybius" in the book, *called* "Polybius" by Claudius after the name of the famous historian (one part of Graves' real function)—and the hero of the myth—Claudius, deified Roman emperor and a professional writer in reality (like Graves), as well as Graves in the book, since the book is written in the first person:

> I [Claudius] dictated most of the first four volumes to a ... secretary [Polybius] and told him to alter nothing as he wrote ... but I admit that nearly all the second half of the work, and some chapters at least of the first, were composed by this same fellow ... from material that I gave him. And he modelled his style so accurately on mine that, really, when he had done, nobody could have guessed what was mine and what was his. (Graves, (1986)[1934], pp. 9–10)

Paralleling Claudius and Polybius with Jung and Jaffé is possible and allows us to understand why *I, Claudius* and *MDR* were both bestsellers. Both books were written not by authors, but by mythographers, not by a single mind, but by a collective psyche linked by *Anschauung* with intuitive hands.

Rowland further identifies eight applied methods for *MDR* to appear as a non-linear narrative: a thematic organisation, the use of repetitions and substitutions, the use of metaphors, spatiality, ritual, monumentality, reading, and myth (Jung's references to the Bible) (Rowland, 2005, pp. 33–35). Those eight methods belong to *ekphrasis*, the second rule, for us, of composition of *MDR*.

Ekphrasis in classical myth—a sudden change in the rhythm of the narration; a narration pause emphasising a long description or a motif, visual or otherwise—is a rhetorical form, used to serve either political figures through advantageous descriptions or the authors themselves.[191] In *MDR*, Jaffé's "political figure" is Jung.

Let me first explain what an *ekphrasis* is, using a classic poetic example. Our analysis will reveal how, in this case, *ekphrasis* serves the author.

Ovid's apparent digression in the *Book X* of his *Metamorphoses* from the verses 85 to 105, where he lists twenty-seven kinds of trees, in fact not only is central to the song, but also is most important to Ovid's *oeuvre* itself.

One of the recurrent topics of the *Metamorphoses* is the failure of hopes, crystallised, frozen, in a metamorphosis of a (divine-)human form (the Roman anthropomorphic gods and goddesses) into an animal, a plant, or a rock. *Book X* and *XI*, exceptionally, spare their main characters, Orpheus and Eurydice, from this fate. The poet and his beloved spouse cannot suffer metamorphoses because Orpheus must remain (half-)human in order to testify, to sing, these metamorphoses. The twenty-seven trees, like all the other natural elements that witness Orpheus's complaint when he returns alone from Hades, all belong, writes Ovid, to the "[human–divine] crowd" (*M. X*, 106) that used to live before the metamorphoses. Only the elected poet has access to this time. Where everybody sees trees—that is, previous human–divine forms—the poet is bound to see the crowd of the "olden days".

Orpheus's fate is the never-ending mourning of the poet. From Ovid to Stéphane Mallarmé, the poet's distress remains identical. It is the agony of the messenger between two worlds, two times, between the absolute and the particular. Mallarmé describes himself centuries later as "a queer person probably condemned to wear mourning for the inexplicable Penultimate" (Cohn, 1987, p. 7) as the next-to-last glorious poet, but never possibly the last one. The poets Mallarmé and Ovid both sing the eternal complaint of the sons of Orpheus, the (archetypal) Poet, themselves.

Those twenty verses of the *Book X* are composed in order for the readers to stop following a linear story and stare at a picture that will remind them of the role of the poet announced in the opening line of the *Metamorphoses*: "My soul is wrought to sing of forms transformed to bodies new and strange" (*M.* I, 1). *Ekphrasis* here presents Ovid in the most advantageous facet possible for him, that of the Poet, whose work is that of an elected missionary.

Jung is no poet, but a psychologist. In *MDR*, the links from psychologist to Psychologist are myth and *Anschauung* and Jaffé's literary means is *ekphrasis*. For Rowland, *MDR* is "a means of representing [Jung]'s inner life and his work as united", a "work between life-history . . . and the desire to shape that history in order to construct an *argument* . . . for [Jung']s unique psychological perceptions" (Rowland, 2005, pp. 25, 31). Rowland's use of the term "perceptions" recalls *schauen*. This "unity" is Jaffé's *Mythosanschauung*: a system where life and work correspond to each other, not by narrative, time, or causality, but by a form of meaningful chance, which Jung names synchronicity.

Restricted to *MDR*, synchronicity is Jaffé's first powerful underlying rhetorical form of *ekphrasis*. Aesthetically, between an archetype and its realisation in consciousness, there is the symbol. Between myth and life there is synchronicity.[192] The nature of both links (symbol and synchronicity) is *Anschauung*, intuition. Synchronicity unites *Welt*- with *Mythosanschauung*. Metaphorically, one's *Weltanschauung* is the pupil of the eye, which is the *Mythosanschauung*.

For example, Jaffé–Jung is telling a story of a statuette of a man, "the old Stückelberger", from the eighteenth century, which had buckled shoes . . . which in a strange way [Jung] recognised as [his] own . . . and that he could still feel on [his] feet". Then Jaffé–Jung writes, "Often in those days I would write the date 1786 instead of 1886, and each time this happened I was overcome by an inexplicable nostalgia" (Jung, 1995[1961/1963], p. 51).

Here, the *Mythosanschauung* is situated in the eighteenth century, with the old doctor Stückelberger, a real citizen of Basel. The *Weltanschauung* is Jung's reality a century later, where he could feel the shoes on his feet. Between *Mythos* and *Welt* many symbols manifest themselves, such as a shoe, a buckle, and a century. These symbols can be, within Jung's psychology, intuitively amplified at length and can reveal endless meanings.

Two synchronicities also manifest themselves in a "strange" and "inexplicable"—that is, a-causally—way: (1) Jung does feel the shoes, (2) Jung mistakes 1786 for 1886.[193] "Why so?" is not the question Jaffé wishes the readers to ask themselves in the face of such uncommon events or sensations as "because" implies a cause–effect relationship. Jaffé, rather, wishes the readers to be "impressed", as Jung himself had been impressed: this way they *participate* in the myth through their own intuition, their own *Anschauung*, which ultimately does not belong to anybody but is, instead, collective. They do not observe a myth. They are inside it.

We recall how Ovid had used a classical form of poetic *ekphrasis*, that is, the resonance of one passage with another crucial passage of the poem, in this case, the opening lines. The opening words of the prologue of *MDR* are: "My life is a story of the self-realisation of the unconscious" (Jung, 1995[1961/1963], p. 17).[194] This sentence compels advancing in the story through the (Jungian) symbol. It brings on *ekphrasis* and prevents any fluid linearity of narration. To borrow Jungian analyst Gaillard's expression, symbols are the "vectors" of *MDR*'s "scenarios" (Gaillard, 2003, p. 575).

At once, the multi-faceted aspect of the symbols explain Gaillard's "constant and insistent surprise" each time he "go[es] back to it [*MDR*], a book [he] supposedly know[s] well" (Gaillard, 2003, p. 575). Each aspect of each symbol corresponds to one situation in a life and, thus, appeals to the reader. Poetry uses the same means: words are the poet's symbols and vectors. They affect the poet and, in turn, the reader, each new reader with a new *Weltanschauung*, each new situation with another one.

The sentence announces Jung's introverted viewpoint: his need to make the unconscious conscious and the consequent direction and depiction of Jung's story from inside to outside. These opening words, the crux of the book, outline and structure Jung's memories and dreams and introduce his reflections.[195]

Jaffé's narration of Jung's story consists of several episodes, which form the chapters of *MDR*. Their respective endings each validate the opening "My life is a story of the self-realisation of the unconscious". This circular *ekphrasis* is an aesthetic version of Jung's psychological circumbulation, such as his way of turning around a complex in dreams through the various forms of its expression.

In the first three chapters as well as in the last one before the five pages of "Retrospect", this circular form of *ekphrasis* aims at emphasising "the secret" (*das Geheimnis*).

At the prominent position of the end of the first chapter, Jung writes, "This possession of a secret had a very powerful formative influence on my character; I consider it the essential factor of my boyhood" (Jung, 1995[1961/1963], p. 37). Then, at the end of the second chapter, "School years", Jung once again, albeit not directly, evokes the secret: "I could not explain to myself what this essential thing was . . . this was something I could not fathom" (Jung, 1995[1961/1963], p. 102). At the end of the third chapter, "Student years", Jung describes psychiatry as "the longed-for opportunity to obtain a deeper insight into the psyche" (Jung, 1995[1961/1963], p. 134) or again, the first great opportunity and step to realising the unconscious.

Jung's secret, in fact, corresponds to a *series* of secrets previously described by the author, but the use of the singular here is meaningful. The single story that Jaffé wishes to tell is that of the self-realisation of the unconscious. *The* secret is the single and best possible way that the unconscious has yet found to express itself. In Jaffé's *Mythosanschauung*, the secret is one, yet multi-faceted, Jungian symbol. It is Jung's way to his myth. Jung's myth, which was then unconscious as Jung was a boy, is so important that it cannot find room in Jung's life. *Ekphrasis*, this time, directly serves Jung, the main character of the fable, the hero of Jung's theory of myth.

Jaffé reuses the same emphasis towards myth and the secret in the last chapter of *MDR*, "Late thoughts". "Late thoughts" is divided into three parts. Only the first one deals with myth. Jung's life is behind him. What used to be in childhood a source of turmoil—the opposition between myth and life—now seems resolved. *Mythos-* and *Weltanschauung* have become one. The readers enter Jung's personal, individuated myth. The penultimate part begins as follows: "There is no better means of intensifying the treasured feeling of individuality than the possession of a secret which the individual is pledged to guard" (Jung, 1995[1961/1963], pp. 374–375). The word "secret" is then used eight times in the first page, and its significance is explained for *all* in the way it had been explained for Jung. The secret, as the central symbol between life and myth, now becomes the essential means to the readers' own individuation.

When Jaffé writes that the possession of a secret has been "the essential factor of [Jung's] boyhood", one must understand that the factor rather possessed him. In Jaffé's *Mythosanschauung*, the hero's way to the realisation of the unconscious is not an easy one.

In Jung's theory, children live in a less conscious state than adults. They chiefly have perceptions (sensations and intuitions). Apperceptions (thoughts and feelings) only come with self-awareness. Jung's *MDR*'s life displays the rule.

At age twelve in 1887, Jung had such a first experience of ego-consciousness. On his way to school, he "had the overwhelming impression of having just emerged from a cloud" (Jung, 1995[1961/1963], p. 49). The cloud symbolises the world of the unconscious, whereas Basel and the school represents the harsh world of consciousness (see Wehr, 1988, p. 37). For the first time Jung felt "authority" in himself. Before this moment, things used to "happen", being barely sensed by the nearly unconscious boy.

Psychobiography and *Mythosanschauung* again need disentanglement as Jaffé ventures, thanks to the central figure of myth—the hero—through the four psychological functions. This boy who can sense—who has sensations—I refer to as Carl. The boy who can feel and think—and can therefore say "I"—is Number 1. The intuition that leads Carl—and that after age twelve fights against the nascent "I" of Number 1—is represented through the character of Number 2 as well as through various other apparitions (hallucinations, visions).

The tale is played out between the worlds of the unconscious and consciousness and the transitional-magical under-conscious. Carl is nearly unconscious, whereas Number 1 is conscious. Both are one and the same hero. Number 2 is felt as "other". He needs a progressive integration in order to ensure the passage from Carl to Number 1.[196]

Unlike Number 1's, Number 2's authority seems firm. Rather than a deliverance, the birth of Number 1 in 1887 appeared as the beginning of troubles for the protagonist of the story. Jaffé describes

Number 1 as "the [consciously apprehended, apperceived] schoolboy who could not grasp algebra and was far from sure of himself", whereas Number 2 was "the Other", "a high authority, a man not to be trifled with . . . an old man who lived in the eighteenth century" (Jung, 1995[1961/1963], p. 50).

Number 1's fight for life consisted, then, in Number 1's realisation of the merely ghostly nature of Number 2. In the *Mythosanschauung*, Number 2's "authority" refers to "charisma", "charm", and the power of this charm, all together seductive and frightening.[197] This power on boy Carl in turn corresponds to Jung's numinous in the psychobiography. By contrast, Number 1's "authority" refers to "author" and (unique) identity. While Number 1 is conscious of being "Jung", Number 2 is an archetype—presumably of the magus, guide, or wise old man—the presence of which is revealed through multiple symbols.[198]

These symbols reveal two kinds of intuition. First, their presence implies the (unconscious) *Anschauung* between Number 2 and Number 1. Second, they are under-conscious apparitions. In the case of "the old Stückelberger" from the eighteenth century, for instance, we encounter a sensual kind of apparition, or else a counter-apparition. The real statuette of the Baselian becomes an apparition as Jung enters his shoes, or rather—and this trance is common in fairytales—Jung enters the under-conscious state by fitting the (archetypal guide) old Stückelberger's shoe.[199] Statuette and shoes become transitional objects (psychobiography) as well as magical instruments (*Mythosanschauung*) to enter wonderlands.

Other under-conscious apparitions are visual. Jaffé depicts at length visions that only Jung's intuition could have possibly perceived while Carl had to pay the bill with negative uncanny impressions. It is not Carl, for example, but Jung's intuition that could see through his mother one "faintly luminous, indefinite figure whose head detached itself from the neck and floated along in front of it, in the air, like a little moon". The vision followed: "Immediately another head was produced and again detached itself. This process was repeated six or seven times" (Jung, 1995[1961/1963], pp. 33–34). Another night, Carl saw "the glowing blue circle about the size of the full moon, and inside it moved golden figures which [he] thought were angels" as he stood, head bent back over the rail of his child's bed, while his father held him during an attack of "pseudo-croup" (laryngeal obstruction) (Jung, 1995[1961/1963], p. 34).

For Carl, who could merely sense and not also think, those visions were linked to the "unbreathable" atmosphere of the house. No explanation was given by Jung's intuition. Number 1 was not yet born to think or evaluate. Instead, Jung's intuition showed and pictured, and Carl tangibly connected. He connected heads–circles–moon by their shape, and connected luminosity–gold–angels by their colour and light. When sick, or when "things incomprehensible and alarming were happening at night" (Jung, 1995[1961/1963 in English, p. 33), he could grasp only that something was wrong, and his compensatory unconscious faculty comprehended his sensations to get a head full of angels.

This intuitive and sensitive co-operation through the associations (appearing here with the distinctive connecting rule, –) that the boy made naturally during his childhood constitute the work of analogy—or association—required by the patients during active imagination and the constructive method.

I shall try to show how, through Jaffé's narrative of Jung's secrets, one can easily recognise the four functions and Jung's first stage of the constructive method through the analogies (indicated once more with the connecting rule).[200]

As in dreams, where the recurrent patterns are confronted by the patient and the analyst, "the secret" kept coming back in Jung's *MDR*'s childhood. These secrets might have indeed been central in Jung's real life, but the way Jaffé told them serves the two purposes announced earlier. They allow the readers (1) to enter Jaffé's system by displaying Jung's psychobiograph and (2) to enter Jaffé's *Mythosanschauung* through the realm of esotericism, to be examined next, a mutual interest of Jung and Jaffé.

Bishop noticed this emphasis accorded to the secret in Jung's *MDR*'s childhood. With him, we observe that Jung's first secret stemmed from his dream "of a giant, subterranean ritual phallus which he came to associate with 'the [secretly distrusted] dark Lord Jesus' and . . . [the hidden] fear incited by the sight of the black robes of a Catholic Jesuit priest". This dream and its associations Jung considered *"mein erstes großes Geheimnis"*, "my first great secret" (Bishop, 2003, p. 329).

His dream appeared at the end of a series of Carl's perceptions. First was a strong vision (sight): his father, the pastor of the vicarage, was wearing black robes during funerals. The parental explanation that Lord Jesus had *taken* the buried man to himself was hardly visualised by the boy.

Next came the acoustic perception of Jung's mother's evening song:

> Spread out thy wings, Lord Jesus mild,
> And take to thee thy chick, thy child.
> If Satan would devour it,
> No harm shall overpower it,
> So let the angel sing!
> (Jung, 1995[1961/1963], pp. 24–25)

Jesus, who took buried people to himself, was now comforting Jung in a very strange way. Carl "understood [heard] at once" that Satan liked eating *Küechli* (Basler term for "little cake", mistaken by the boy for the real term of the song, *Küchlein*, "chick").[201] To protect "children-cakes" from Satan's appetite, Lord Jesus ate them, *took* them, as he took those people buried in big holes. Here the association between "eating" and "taking" reveals the absence of Number 1's rational functions. Eventually came the sight of the Jesuit, a term already heard by Carl from his father, who himself wore black robes.

Here follow the sensitive and intuitive associations that provoked Carl's fear, escape, and hiding in the attic. The first analogy was visual: the man in black robes—Jung's father in black robes during funeral. The second analogy was acoustic: *Jesuit–Jesus*. This sight, once associated with all other perceptions, amounted to the fear that (1) this Jesuit–Jesus–father in black would (2) bury in a hole–eat (3) Karl–*Küechli* little cake. All these associations led to Jung's dream. Jung's phallus dream, where a "tree trunk ... made of skin ... on top of which was something like a rounded head" stood erected on a throne was the last avatar of the series Karl's father in black–the Jesuit–Jesus and, by association, "the man-eater" (Jung, 1995[1961/1963], p. 27) of Karl–*Küechli*.

Jung's "second great secret", writes Bishop,

> was a small wooden manikin, which he carved as a seven- or eight-year-old out of the end of a ruler, coloured black with ink, and placed, together with a special stone, in a pencil-case which he kept hidden under one of the roof-beams in the attic. (Bishop, 2003, p. 329)

We can visually connect the manikin painted black–father in black–Jesuit–Jesus–tree trunk and (visually as well as acoustically) stone–throne (*Stein–Stuhl*). These associations allow a plastic understanding of Jung's "first attempt, still unconscious, to give *shape* to the secret" (Jung, 1995[1961/1963], p. 37, my italics). This sentence, crucial to understanding the plastic connection between all the black and oblong elements previously depicted by Jaffé falls, once more, just before the end of a chapter, here the first one.

What Bishop called the third vision appeared just after Jung's first experience of ego-existence at the age of twelve and illustrated the difficult birth of Number 1. On a sunny day of summer, Jung contemplated the cathedral of Basel and started imagining: "The world is beautiful and the church is beautiful, and God made all this and sits above it far away in the blue sky on a golden throne and . . ." (Jung, 1995[1961/1963], p. 52). This fragment of vision was another hallucination of Carl, first stopped by some opposing feelings of Number 1. Then a tormenting collaboration between Carl's associations and Number 1's syllogisms began leading three days later to the delivery, with immense relief, of the whole picture:

> I gathered all my courage, as though I were about to leap forthwith into hell-fire, and let the thought come. I saw before me the cathedral, the blue sky. God sits on His golden throne, high above the world – and from under the throne an enormous turd falls upon the sparkling new roof, shatters it, and breaks the walls of the cathedral asunder. (Jung, 1995[1961/1963], p. 56)

It was as if Number 2 had eventually given its definitive shape to the secret: the shape of the manikin on his stone, now God on his throne. The black colours of the robes had disappeared to be replaced by God's white gown. The manikin box, such as the man's coffin, reappeared in the role and shape of the walls of the cathedral, sacred containers broken by God's turd, associated with Jung letting his thought come. "Grace" had come upon Jung together with, writes Bishop, "'die Ahnung [the intuition] daß Gott etwas furchtbares sein könnte [that God could be something terrible] and Jung believed that he had experienced nothing less than 'ein furchbares Geheimnis' [a terrible secret]" (Bishop, 2003, p. 331).

Just as the little boy Carl could not have rationally grasped the reason that he had seen several heads of his mother at once, so the teenager was unable to provide any rational explanation for his vision of God defecating on the cathedral of Basel. Instead, he was given the *intuition* that God could be something terrible. Jaffé's insistence on the irrational functions at once (1) reminds us of Jung's theory that the rational functions appear later in life and (2) describes the first stage of the analogical work of the constructive method. When Jaffé writes that "I [Jung] cannot recall in my boyhood ever having *thought* [my italics] of the possibility of a connection between Lord Jesus – or the Jesuit in the black robe – the men in frock coats and top hats standing by the grave, the gravelike hole in the meadow, the underground temple of the phallus, and my little man in the pencil-case", she emphasises that the connection in question was not one of any rational kind. While Jung-Number 1 never *thought* of a connection (at that time), the boy connected all the elements, thanks to his functions of sensation and intuition, and carved the manikin.

Carl's secrets are embedded not only in Jung's psychology, but are also set in Jaffé's *Mythosanschauung*. In Jaffé's "fable", to use one term in the prologue, Jung is the hero. The theorist of myth, Robert Segal, describes Jung's *general* views on hero myths, which I will link to Jaffé's description of *Jung*'s childhood by using brackets:

> Jung's psychological interpretation of hero myths makes the symbolized not persons but parts of the mind [such as the various functions, in our case]. Like the myth of the child, the myth of the hero symbolizes at once an archetype and, even more, the psychological life cycle. The birth, childhood, and adolescence of the hero [in our case, the first three chapters of *MDR*] symbolize the emergence and development of the ego and of ego consciousness [Number 1, in our case], which is consciousness of the difference between oneself and the external world [as, in our case, Jung felt "authority" in himself as he emerged from the cloud of the natural life in Laufen to join the external city-world of Basel]. (Segal, 1998, p. 145)

Clearly, Jung in *MDR* is not only a boy. He is an archetypal hero as well. One can also recognise a hero by his dual birth. Like all heroes, Carl has two mothers. This is possible through the magic of Jung's mother's Personality Number 1 and Personality Number 2. In Jung's theory of myth, we read, "One of the mothers is the real, human mother [such as, in *MDR*, the mother who, for instance, 'spent several months in a hospital in Basel' (Jung, 1995[1961/1963], p. 23)], the other is the symbolical mother; in other words she is distinguished as being divine, supernatural, or in some way extraordinary [like the mother that Carl sees with several heads at once]" (Jung, CW 5, par. 495). Jaffé writes,

> I was sure that she [Jung's mother] consisted of two personalities, one innocuous and human, the other uncanny. This other immerged only now and then, but each time it was unexpected and frightening. She would then speak as if talking to herself, but what she said was aimed at me and usually struck to the core of my being, so that I was stunned to silence. (Jung, 1995[1961/1963], p. 66)

Jung's mother's words struck to the core of Carl's being because (his) Number 2 was linked by intuition to his mother's Personality Number 2.[202] Only a "high authority not to be trifled with" could equal in nature a voice that stunned to silence.

Myth, for Jung, "expresses psychic facts and situations, just as normal dream does or the delusion of a schizophrenic. It describes, in figurative form, psychic facts whose existence can never be dispelled by mere explanation" (Jung, CW 18, par. 1362, and in Segal, 1998, p. 72). If Jung's MDR boyhood resembles a dream, then we understand why Jaffé does not "dispel" any of Jung's secrets, but, instead, uses constructive method to transfer their "spell" to the readers. I have described the analogical stage of the method. I shall now describe Jaffé's work of amplification.

Passing from boy to hero is the first necessary amplification from consciousness to the collective unconscious. Yet, a single archetype cannot alone recreate a myth. Now this hero needs a realm. A writer on esotericism, Jaffé was able to amplify Jung's secrets to create the uncanny atmosphere of the *Mythosanschauung* (see, for example, Jaffé, 1979, 1986, 1989.

All three secrets resemble features of the secrets of the esoteric literature. From the single term "secret", Jaffé actually deploys three distinct features. By circumbulating around a single word, she unfolds several of its meanings from a distant past and a distant place in the unconscious. She brings her readers into her amplification. In Jung's *MDR*'s childhood, the secret is not only emphasised, it is amplified, as in Jung's constructive method.

Jung's first and second secrets are comparable with esoteric secrecy. Carl's concealed distrust of Jesus and fear of the Jesuit amounted to the hidden manikin and to the phallus dream. The carving of the manikin, the stone and the sheets of paper put in the box, all had for Jung "the character of a solemn ceremonial act" and fell under a necessary (not of any whimsical nature) secrecy. "It was an inviolable secret which must never be betrayed, for the safety of my life depended on it. Why that was so I did not ask myself. It simply was so" (Jung, 1995[1961/1963], p. 37). As for the dream, Jung considered, writes Jaffé, that through it he had been "initiated into the secrets of the earth" (Jung, 1995[1961/1963], p. 30).[203]

A boy can hardly be thus initiated. In contrast, at such a young age, a hero has to be. These acts are comparable with, for example, "the most important secret from the ancient world [which] without any doubt was the experience of the Mysteries of Eleusis" (de Jong, 2006, p. 1052).[204] In Athenian law, revealing the Mysteries was a sin punishable by death. Jung's "secrets of the earth", intrinsically mysterious, in other words, hidden from everyone, and, thus, first to himself, appeared to Carl as being imperatively and primarily kept hidden from his parents. Through the Athenian rituals, candidates, first novices, underwent several ordeals leading to grades. Carl's initiation into the secrets of (Mother) Earth was the experience of a *spiritual* birth that he had to keep hidden from his *biological* parents.[205] Next to the amplification of the secret in some attic to a ritual act of initiation into a secret society or an ancient world, we find a second amplification of the dual birth of the hero. Jaffé describes Jung's rebirth from Mother Earth, thereby displaying Jung's theory of libido, symbolically returning to the womb of the archetypal mother (see Segal, 1998, pp. 145–173; for direct examples, see Jung, *CW 5*, notably pars 251, 297–299, 309–312, 493–496, 508–511, 538–540, 553, *CW 7*, par. 160, *CW 12*, pars 437–441, *CW 14*, par. 756, *CW 18*, pars 191–197). This oath of secrecy "was an initiation into the realm of darkness. My intellectual life had its unconscious beginnings at that time" (Jung, 1995 [1961/1963], p. 30). Secrecy ensured Jung's most important sense of intellectual and spiritual belonging. Jung's conscious mission, his intellectual life, was the result of this early rebirth.

Jung's third vision falls under two other kinds of esoteric secret: (1) an ineffable—no longer solemn and hidden like the manikin—experience resulting in (2) the access to gnosis. Gnosis is not knowledge but, as defined by Faivre (1994, p. 19), "an activity that can accede to a special mode of knowledge". This special mode of knowledge is no ordinary knowledge acquired in all consciousness, but, instead, an intuitive revelation that strikes the individual in a second state. It is also called "true learning" because the revelation will change the attitude of the individual forever. What is learnt through gnosis is awe. What is perceived is ineffable. What is perceived is, rather, absolutely mysterious than secret (hidden).

The vision of God defecating on the cathedral did not provide Jung merely with a sense of origin, but, rather, elevated him to the second grade of his initiation by giving him access to gnosis through the *numinosum* (Fanger, 2006, p. 1055, explains the Gnostic aspect of "true learning"). "Grace", also used by Jung in this episode, rendered the positive side of this numinous effect.

Jung did not acquire any—subsequently—rationally explicable knowledge from this experience, but only intuited gnosis. His thinking function was of no use. Jaffé does not refer to it. She does not explain the vision or its origin, but relates that this was Jung's *Ahnung* (intuition, premonition) "that God could be something terrible" (Jung, 1995[1961/1963], p. 30). The most important things in the life of (solitary and exceptional) heroes need no explanation, but always have consequences:

> From that moment on, when I experienced grace, my true responsibility began . . . My entire youth can be understood in terms of this secret. . . . Thus the pattern of my relationship to the world was already pre-figured: today as then I am a solitary, because I know things and must hint at things which other people do not know, and usually do not even want to know. (Jung, 1995[1961/1963], pp. 56–58)

Albeit ineffable, Carl's intuitive revelation was clear enough for him to realise that he had experienced "what [his] father [the pastor] had not understood [as Paul Jung had not experienced God's wrath]" (Jung, 1995[1961/1963], p. 56). In contrast, Jung's father had chosen for his son the path of—or had been guided by—those who had *thought* religion instead of living in God's obedience and awe. As dangerous as his experience had proved to be, hero Jung had been able to come back from his vision in the collective unconscious to his life in consciousness, whereas his father had lost the meaning of his life as a pastor: his faith. Amplified in the fable *MDR*, hero Carl's relationship to his father might enlighten Jung's real experience. As Jung sometimes concludes, to what degree this amplification can be true "is a matter of taste".

Empathy (2): intuition and transference

It is no secret for any psychologist or psychoanalyst that the link which united the protagonists of both hypnotism and spiritism, sometimes called the rapport, heralded transference and countertransference. When Freud and Jung alike, for instance, admitted that transference represented the alpha and omega of their practice, they pointed to the centrality of the unconscious, pre-conscious, and under-conscious relationship that unites patient with analyst. Yet, Freudian and Jungian transference have strong dissimilarities, to be traced in their antecedents of the nineteenth century (Shamdasani, 2001, pp. 10–13).[206]

Among the various methods used to reach the under-conscious of the patients, we can, for our purpose, distinguish between those which retain intuition and sometimes stop a specific access to the unconscious (to be studied first), and those which try to favour intuition and the access to the unconscious (to be studied second). These distinctions are theoretical. In practice, several methods were used at once. Moreover, the names given to these methods were numerous. Different names described the same methods. Similar names described various phenomena.[207] It is, therefore, with caution that I distinguish here between the two families of methods: "suggestion", which retains intuition, and "auto-suggestion", which develops intuition. Myers explains the origin of the confusion between the methods:

> These words bring no true solution; they are mere names which disguise our ignorance. We do not know either *why* a subject obeys any suggestion which may be made to him, or *how* he obeys it. [In some cases] suggestion is merely equivalent to self-suggestion. (Myers, 1903, pp. 153–154)

We remember how intuition was at home in the in-between state of the under-conscious. There, in contrast, feeling, thinking, and sensation appear distorted, since they do not belong to the subject, who either is reacting rather than acting, or else is passive rather than active. People *react* under the sway of an exterior power when the first method is used—with hypnotism, for instance. People are *passive* when they let intuition act with the second method—auto-suggestion, somnambulism, for instance.

The first methodological family stemmed from Mesmerism. Myers writes,

> *Mesmerism* is the oldest widely-recognised word for a large group of phenomena. The name need imply nothing more than the fact that Mesmer was the conspicuous introducer of many of the phenomena to the European public. But it is also specially used to imply something of his theory [implying the presence of the Mesmeric fluid] of their production ... The term *Animal Magnetism* implies a somewhat different theory. The term *Hypnotism*, when first started by Braid, was again meant to imply a theory of the genesis of these phenomena, but it is now [in 1900] generally used with no theoretical implication. (Myers, 1903, p. xviii)

A contemporary (from 2009) definition of hypnosis allows the connecting of all the terms italicised by Myers, even though their theoretical backgrounds vary. Hypnosis is "an artificially induced alteration of consciousness characterised by increased suggestibility [state of uncritical compliance with influence or uncritical acceptance] and receptivity to direction. See also Mesmerism, an early term for hypnosis" (Bhatia, 2009, pp. 195, 399 for "suggestibility": the different theorectical backgrounds do not concern the methods or intuition).

The artificial induction of the patient by the therapist into the under-conscious state is both central and common to all these methods. This induction itself is named "suggestion", "hypnosis", or "fascination". As contemporary hypnotherapist James Hall describes, "at a time 'hypnosis' largely meant an authoritative stance for the hypnotist and an acquiescent attitude for the patient. The 'doctor' maintained his position of prestige, and suggestions were characteristically given as if from on high" (Hall, 1989, p. 19). From fascination, where patients had to focus their attention on something, to suggestion, where patients' attention was derived from their own words, thoughts, or feelings, as in the next example, the goal of the manipulation was the dissociation of the mind.

Janet called this means the *rétrécissement du champ de conscience*, the "narrowing of the field of consciousness". Here is how Janet described one suggestion of his:

It is enough, in order to provoke some intelligent manifestations [links], to determine phenomena that would be related to those that the patient still perceives, to enter, so to speak, in the dream. As Justine utters, "The cholera, it is going to take me . . .", I answer her, "Yes, it holds you by the right leg", and here she is, violently withdrawing her right leg. (Janet, 1898, p. 160, translated for this edition)[208]

Janet's manoeuvre is not authoritative, as in hypnosis, but suggestive. The result is identical: one part of Justine's mind will be focused on the leg-cholera while Janet will address another area of her mind. The part of Justine's mind able to focus is the superior zone of her mind, consciousness, which is now "occupied" by Justine's *idée fixe* of being a cholera victim, anaesthetised enough with the leg for the second, under-conscious level to be reached. Thereby, Janet narrowed Justine's field of consciousness.

The therapeutic aim of such experiences was to relieve patients from traumas. Janet compared his work with that of exorcists.

Achille had another "fixed idea": he thought he was possessed by the devil. His negative "reverie" became strong enough to create complete hallucinations and delirium. After several consultations, Janet discovered that Achille had cheated on his wife. "Although the patient seemed to be a possessed person, his pain is the emotion of remorse . . . the devil is the embodiment of their [the possessed people] regrets, of their remorse, of their terrors, or of their vices" (Janet, 1898, p. 401, translated for this edition).[209] Against possession, Janet applied a sort of modern exorcism, which he qualified as a "moral science as a treatment" (*une science morale comme traitement*) and which consisted in *withdrawing* the fixed idea. Janet wrote that it was Achille's memory of his infidelity that he needed to make forgotten, since forgetting is the condition of progress, of life itself (we recognise Bergson's influence here) (Janet, 1898, p. 401).

Achille, thus, had no access to the intuitive links among his hallucinations, his delirium, and the fact that he cheated on his wife. Janet blocks this intuitive access by manipulating memory, thus trying to delete Achille's fixed idea that he is the devil. If, in the best case, the patient is cured, he does not know why.

Likewise, Marie, at the age of thirteen, was put into a cold bath by one of her parents in order to stop her periods. This traumatic event had been "withdrawn" in a session by Janet and "replaced" with the memory of a normal menstruation (Janet, 1903, p. 431).

In Justine's case evoked earlier, Janet was temporarily successful, yet he had substituted her panicky fear of cholera for an (undesired) hilarity over the comic Chinese military general, "Cho-lé-ra"[210] (invented by Janet) (Janet, 1898, p. 475; Haule, 1984, p. 642).

Therefore, with his patients, Janet explains that,

> He [Janet, the one who "directs" the patient] has organised resolutions, beliefs, emotions. He has helped the subject attach to his/her personality images and sensations. Moreover, he has built this system of thoughts around a specific hub, which is the memory and the image of his/her person. The subject has brought with him/her in his/her mind a new synthesis, somewhat artificial and very fragile, on which emotion has easily exerted its disorganising power. (Janet, 1898, pp. 475–476, translated for this edition)[211]

Suggestion has been substituted for the fixed idea. Problematically, the therapist has removed neither its *raison d'être*, meaning that the original symptoms could still reappear, nor the effect of the suggestion on the patient: dependence upon the doctor.

Janet called this dependence "electivity", "adoption", and the "need for guidance (or direction)". It could take the various forms of "a tender feeling, often close to love, adoration, and fear" (Binet, 1897, p. 667). "Transference and counter-transference are the major precautions to be noted in the practice of hypnotherapy", writes hypnotist Hall, "their major fantasy themes are of control, dependence, or seduction (both hetero- and homosexual)" (Hall, 1989, p. 89). Hall differs from the Freudian single association of sexual desire with transference by naming seduction as one out of three manifestations. In addition, in "L'influence somnambulique et le besoin de direction", Janet taught how the physician must know the nature of the rapport in order to sever the patient from the sway of suggestion at the end of the cure. Love and erotic passion constituted only one aspect of the rapport, which was based, above all, on the patients' "need to be directed" (*le besoin de direction*) (see Janet, 1887, pp. 113–143). Following the treatment, the patients had to learn how to become independent again, without support from the doctor and away from his presence and suggestions, which were felt as protective.

Both Freud and Jung used and abandoned hypnosis in their practice of psychoanalysis. Hypnosis and psychoanalysis methods had been introduced into the Burghölzli. In 1886, director August Forel, the predecessor of Jung's first teacher, Eugen Bleuer, introduced hypnosis, and it was his successor, Bleuler, who allowed the use of psychoanalysis (Shamdasani, 2001a, p. 6). Freud stopped using hypnosis because of what he saw as the libidinal at work behind it. Yet, the erotic bond did not disappear with psychoanalysis. Freud thought it necessary to analyse and resolve the transference neurosis—that is, the projection of the oedipal complex on to the person of the analyst. The same reason disturbed Jung as well, added to the fact that Jung wished the patient and himself to know *why* the manipulation had worked in removing symptoms, which was not the case. Jung distinguished hypnosis from suggestion. Given the unconscious nature of suggestion, of transference, and of countertransference, it was, for him, "impossible to rule out the role of suggestion" (Shamdasani, 2001a, p. 13).

The prestige and, therefore, the power of the doctor and the suggestion, which is given as if from on high, were maintained when theoretically framed in the oedipal complex of the client, who, by projecting on to the person of the analyst the authority of the father, held himself in the role of the child.

Transference through analytical psychology incorporated both Janet's and Freud's approaches. The power of the analytical psychologist did not suddenly disappear with Jung. Yet, against this unilateral position of control of the analyst over the patient, the intuitive and shared dimension of the phenomenon clearly appeared with Jung.

The etymology of the German term *Einfühlung*, which Jung sometimes used to designate transference—our empathy (2)—proves useful. The radical *fühl* refers to feeling, as well as the erotic bond. The prefix *ein-*, as in *einwärts* ("inwards"), and like *ein* ("one"), refers to intuition. The doctor and the patient, the analysand and the analyst, are one in empathy, in the shared created space of their underconscious and unconscious.

Again, we are in 1913, and Jung wishes to differentiate his approach to transference from Freud's. In an important letter to Doctor Loÿ, he depicts this twofold character of the *Einfühlung*:

> The patient's libido fastens on the person of the analyst in the form of expectation, hope, interest, trust, friendship, and love. The transference first produces a projection of infantile fantasies, often with a

predominantly erotic tinge. At this stage it is, as a rule, of a decidedly sexual character, even though the sexual component remains relatively unconscious. But this emotional process serves as a bridge for the higher aspect of empathy [*Einfühlung*] . . . an intimacy based not on the existence of sexual or power factors but on the value of personality. That is the road to freedom which the analyst should show his patient. (Jung, *CW 4*, par. 663)

Here, Jung first describes Freud's infantile erotic bond to the person of the analyst. He then evokes the "road to freedom", which reminds us of Jung's "way of what is come", of individuation through "the value of personality", as well as Janet's "need to be directed", from which the patient must be severed. The intimacy, if not based on sexual or power factors, is created thanks to intuition. In other words, the link exists through under-conscious rendered conscious, yet always *analogical* expectations, hopes, and interests between analyst and patient. What is minimised with intuition is the position "as if from on high" of the doctor.[212]

Before the end of the treatment, patients must reach and come to terms with their complexes or archetypes, helped on their way by the analyst, who is playing the role of the third and guide between consciousness and the unconscious. For a man, this guide (projected on to the person of the analyst), or psychopomp, to the unconscious is the anima, that Jung concretely called his "soul" in *Liber Primus*.[213]

The soul is the first character of *The Red Book*. Jung belongs, and is a slave, to "the spirit of this time" when he encounters his soul, or "the spirit of the depths from time immemorial and for all the future" (Shamdasani, 2009, p. 229).[214] In the role of the projected anima in Jung's surroundings in 1914 might have been Antonia Wolff.[215] She was analysed by Jung and later became an analyst herself. By so doing, she would have participated in Jung's own anamnesis. Charet noticed that Antonia Wolff, "almost as a medium, helped Jung see his images [those of *The Red Book*] and talked with them . . . she mediated Jung's mind and intuitive ideas directly, for she had been part of their creation from the unconscious" (Charet, 1993, p. 257). Among the omissions of *MDR*, and, therefore, among the passages that Jung did tell to Aniéla Jaffé, is the one where Jung describes his relationship with Toni Wolff. Although in darker terms than Charet's, Jung evoked the same unconscious area, writing "that he had infected her with his experience, which was awful and terrible, and that she got drawn into it and was equally helpless" (Shamdasani, 1995, p. 125).

If Wolff famously became Jung's mistress, a sheer intuitive relationship of *Einfühlung* gave rise to another of Jung's most important works. *Psychology of the Unconscious* analysed the fantasies of Miss Miller, whom Jung never met. As Jung describes, "I had to realise then that in Miss Miller I was analysing my own fantasy function" (McGuire, 1989[1925], p. 28). To do this, Jung employed, writes Haule (1984, p. 654), "Goethe's *Faust* as a bridge between Miss Miller's "Number 2" and his own Number 2". Jung did not picture here a sexual link, but instead a strong empathy.

If empathy (2) could be mixed with, or sometimes hindered by, links of power or by links of a sexual nature, its apparition could, in contrast, be favoured by self-induced trance during spiritist sessions.

Trance as "a state of focused attention and diminished sensory and motor activity [impulse to action]" (Bhatia, 2009, p. 435), or as a "narrowing of the field of consciousness" in Janet's terms, reflects the hypnotist's perception of trance, not that of a somnambulist in a self-induced trance. Self-induced trance could also be called self-suggestion, "a suggestion conveyed by the subject himself from one stratum of his personality to another, without external intervention" (Myers, 1903, p. xxi), in Myers' terms this time.

Whereas hypnotists perceived the new state as a mere reduction of the former one, the practitioners who experimented with somnambulists or medium spirits, without denying this aspect, added that the new state at once opened the subject to other perceptions and enabled new capacities.

For example, such privative as well as additive effects were analgesia (insensibility to pain) on the one hand, hypersensitivity on the other. Intuition played a central role in these additive effects such as hypermnesia and hyperpromethia. Evoked by Jung in his medical dissertation, hypermnesia was an "over-activity of the memory, a condition in which past acts, feelings, or ideas are brought vividly to the mind, which, in its natural condition, has wholly lost the remembrance of them" (Myers, 1903, p. xvii, quoting Tuke, 1892). Myers defined hyperpromethia as a "supernormal power of foresight attributed to the subliminal self as a hypothesis by which to explain premonitions" (Myers, 1903, p. xvii).

The focus on diminution during hypnosis accounted for the dispossession by the subjects of their will. The subjects' attention was, indeed, focused only on the external suggestion of the hypnotist. By contrast, medium spirits would claim that they were possessed by the spirits of dead people, an additive effect—their capacity to hear, see, or contact dead people—enabled by trance. This belief influenced the way empathy operated between the participants of the sessions, freeing the medium from the exclusive suggestion of a single hypnotist.

Before the end of the nineteenth century, self-induced trance became a common *modus operandi*. Yet, even in previous periods, spirits already represented a third element preventing the power of the hypnotist. As observed by the historian Priska Pytlik, in hypnotism the relationship depended upon the power of suggestion, whereas in spiritism, the first relationship linked the medium and the realm of the spirits. If the hypnotist believed in spirits, his relationship with the medium was reinforced (see Pytlik, 2005). The spirits—and not the hypnotist—played the role of the third, of the guide, that of the analyst, which I previously described as being between the consciousness and the unconscious of a patient.

William Goodheart, James Hillman, and Susan Rowland have emphasised the role of creativity during the spiritist sessions that Jung attended with his cousin (Goodheart, 1984, pp. 23–34); Hillman, 1976, pp. 132–133; Rowland, 2009, pp. 701–704). All three researchers analysed that Helene Preiswerk's spirits not only embodied Helene's sub-personalities, but also represented some "interpersonal unconscious realities of both Jung and Helly . . . not autonomous, but interactionally determined" (Goodheart, 1984, p. 27). I described this collective, as well as spontaneous character, in Chapter Two, as *folie à plusieurs*.

Charet also reminds us of the same collective interactive empathy through the example of the clairvoyant of Prevost:

> Frau Hauffe [Kerner's seeress] created quite a sensation and was visited by philosophers such as [Johann Joseph] Görres, [Franz von] Baader, [Friedrich W. J.] Schelling, G. von Schubert, [Adam K. A.] Eschenmayer, and the theologians David Strauss and [Friedrich] Schleiermacher who came repeatedly to see her and discuss her revelations. (Charet, 1993, p. 31)

Frau Hauffe's first gift was indeed empathy. The exceptional quality of her visions stemmed partly from the fact that she was surrounded by great and many favourable minds that she could reach by intuition, sometimes amounting to telepathy. As Jung himself remarked concerning the cases of somnambulistic heightened performances,

> The somnambulist not only incorporates every suggestive idea into himself, he actually lives himself into the suggestion, into the person of the doctor or observer ... Frau Hauffe's relation to Kerner is an excellent example of this. So it is not surprising that there is in these cases a high degree of concord of associations [such as what happens] on thought-transference. (Jung, *CW 1*, par. 148)

Empathy (1) and (2) treat of intuition in our relationship to others. So does intuition in consciousness, as psychological types depict attitudes in consciousness and aim at the comprehension of one's and the others' inklings, of everybody's natural limits to the understanding of the other.

PART V

AFTER 1921: INTUITION IN JUNGIAN AND POST-JUNGIAN CONSCIOUSNESS

CHAPTER EIGHT

Psychological types

Introduction

Part I (Chapter Two) of this work developed the context of the birth of intuition in Jung's beginning—rather than early, perhaps—psychology. With the appearance of Jung's psychology of consciousness, we reach another stage in Jung's writing, the context changes. Jung is no longer anybody's pupil, and the debates of the end of the nineteenth century have faded. Some Jungian constants remain, however, such as the priority given to experience. In addition, we would rather not forget all that which Jung has already discovered concerning intuition in the under-conscious and in the unconscious, as they provide the perspective to, and help the understanding of, his psychology of consciousness.

Psychological Types coincided with the writing of *The Red Book*. From approximately 1913 to 1921, the date of the publication of *Psychological Types*, Jung went through the most fertile, if also perhaps most painful, period of his life. Jung's psychology of consciousness depends upon his psychology of the unconscious. Since, ordinarily, a reader of the book tends to infer unconscious processes from conscious observation—a mistaken habit which Jung's constant claims of empiricism supplied—misapprehension inevitably occurs.[216] *Psychological Types* epitomises this misunderstanding. It creates spontaneous typologists ignorant of Jung's overall psychology, and it repels some analytical psychologists themselves. As revealed by its structure—nine chapters out of ten treat how typology has been thought of in realms as various as history, philosophy, or religion—the work *Psychological Types* is, above all, theory. Inapplicable directly, the book becomes comprehensible once Jung's psychology of consciousness and of the unconscious are understood. Ideally, types and functions are (only) used by analysts.

The historical genesis of types—a new context here of the birth of intuition—represents another way of grasping their real complexity. We will examine it after delineating the fundamental structures and dynamics of the types and functions.

General structures and dynamics of consciousness

Jung's psychology of consciousness describes and explains behaviour in consciousness. The basic functions from which Jung's typology derives—thinking, feeling, sensation, and intuition—characterise four of the seven contents likely to appear in consciousness. The other three are the volitional processes, the instinctual ones, and dreams (Jung, *CW 8*, par. 292).[217] Since the nature of dreams remains unknown, it is a matter of convenience, for Jung here in his theoretical *The Structure of the Psyche* (1927), to count them within consciousness. Theoretically speaking, archetypes can also appear in dreams. Thus, dreams can be examined in the psychology of the unconscious as well. Dreams can also be characterised as a means from the unconscious to consciousness and, accordingly, belong to the underconscious, too.

The complex opposition between will and instinct in consciousness allows the distinction of intuition from the psychological terms generally associated with it. Contrary to instincts in the unconscious, instinctual processes in consciousness can be independent from intuition.[218] Sexual instincts, when conscious, for example, can or cannot be linked to intuition. Equating the immediate representation one has of the strong term "will" with "volitional processes" can be misleading. Fantasies, for instance, belong to volitional processes. They are, thus, the opposite of instincts and are distinct from dreams and from intuition. When one *makes* fantasies, one *has* intuitions.[219] As created, fantasies do not possess the authenticity and the certainty of intuitions. "Wrong" intuitions do not appear in Jung's work: what would be wrong in such a case would be the person's judgement or thought. Intuition and the capacity of judgement or of thinking are not linked.

Jung often depicted the four basic functions of consciousness this way: "The essential function of sensation is to establish that something exists, thinking tells us what it means, feeling what its value is, and intuition surmises whence it comes and wither it goes" (Jung, *CW 6*, par. 899)[220]

A psychological type (*Typus*) is characterised by a general, common attitude (*Einstellung*) of consciousness. It is "an *a priori* orientation to a definite thing . . . a readiness of the psyche to act or react in a certain way" (Jung, *CW 6*, par. 687). Whereas a function can describe an action, a type describes the condition facilitating the action. The type is a structure. The function is its dynamics. Which function one most relies on determines an individual's type. The designation "intuitive type", for instance, refers to the dominant, or first, function of the individual's consciousness. Opposite to this first function stands the inferior function. Jung describes it as "archaic". It expresses itself in the language of the unconscious, where it mostly remains. The inferior function of the intuitive type is sensation. The second and third functions are the auxiliary ones: they are the two rational functions of an irrational type, or the two irrational ones of a rational type. Hence, feeling and thinking are, for the intuitive type, the second and third functions. The hierarchy depends on the most frequent use of one or the other function. Yet, the two auxiliary functions are less opposed among themselves than is the leading function *vis-à-vis* the inferior one.

Translated into psychological terms, the first function, as the one most visible, clear, and prominent in consciousness, is the one most differentiated. The second function, which is rational for irrational types and vice versa, is the one necessary complement in consciousness. The fourth and third functions are more frequently complementary to the two first ones in the unconscious. Inferior functions, including the second one, can also remain unconscious and, thus, provoke one-sided behaviour in consciousness.

This structure evolves within the dynamics of the psyche. Differentiation is a process that supposes a progressive or rapid emerging of one function from the unconscious into consciousness. During childhood, the irrational functions prevail in consciousness. That is why, for instance, the child is prone to know that something is wrong with his mother or father without having any rational clue, which, even if present, he would perhaps not be able to grasp. During one's teens, or even adulthood, the initially differentiated function is not necessarily the one that becomes the dominant one. Schools or universities mostly require thinking tasks, even though not all students are the corresponding types.

The differentiation of the functions also evolves both qualitatively and quantitatively. A feeling type may, through experience, improve judgements. An extraverted intuitive type may learn to recognise intuitions systematically in order to follow them. Even if someone's type is fixed in adulthood, the differentiation of the functions, other than the first one, continue in order for the individual to adapt to external situations and inner demands, and to allow a better understanding of the other and of oneself. Differentiation is a natural psychic progression. Therapy helps its comprehension, or even its process, when blockages occur.

Genesis: Psychological Types *and the Zürich Club*

During the elaboration of *Types*, Jung developed his understanding of intuition and of his psychology as a whole. Like a puzzle constituted by thoughts, experience, reading (we remember that Jung notably discovered Bergson a little bit earlier), and, last but not least, debates at the Zürich Club, Jung was in the process of getting a first big picture of his psychology. If, concurrently, *The Red Book* provided Jung with *prima materia*, discussions and lectures gave him words, which articulated concepts.

Opposites structure types and functions. Their reconciliation and overcoming constitute their dynamics. This is also true in both Jung's psychology of the unconscious and in Jungian practice. From active imagination to transference, the psychological progress to individuation passes by the comprehension of a third entity, the symbol which unites opposites. In other words, types do not only constitute a part of Jung's psychology, but mirror and bind all of Jung's system in 1921.

The pair extraversion–introversion forms the first (chronologically) opposition that struck Jung. A shift occurred when Jung discovered a second major opposition, that which opposed the rational functions and types (feeling and thinking that were already present in Jung's scheme) to some new irrational functions and types. Huskinson decribes how Jung renders the origin of his discovery in *Types*:

> This new set of psychological functions Jung claims to have derived directly from Nietzsche: "Nietzsche's concepts [the Apollinian and Dionysian] thus lead us to the principles of a third and fourth psychological type, which one might call 'aesthetic' types as opposed to rational types (thinking and feeling). These are the intuitive and sensation types" (Jung, 1921, par. 240). (Huskinson, 2004, p. 101, quoting Jung, *CW 6*, par. 240)[221]

Eighty per cent of *Psychological Types* consists in commenting on sources. Jung, therefore, never claimed to have invented types. Yet, if Tertullian, Abelard, Spitteler, Schiller, James, and Nietzsche, among other great figures, is overtly quoted and used, Jung, with few notable exceptions, did not acknowledge contemporaries much. By studying the organisation of Jung's Zürich Club, Shamdasani discovered that, in fact, *Types* was not the result of a solitary journey:

> It is important then to grasp that Jung's work on psychological types represented the summation of collective research. . . . Hans Schmid showed Jung that extraversion was not necessarily correlated with feeling, Toni Wolff was instrumental in introducing the functions of sensation and intuition, and finally intuition was dealt with critically by Emil Medtner. According to Jung's son, Franz Jung, Jung met on a regular basis with a sort of committee consisting of Emil Medtner, Toni Wolff, Adolf Keller, and some theologians, which worked together in the preparation of *Psychological Types*. (Shamdasani, 2003, p. 69)[222]

Jung did not mention this committee in *Types*, yet wrote of his gratitude to Schmid-Guisan in his introduction and credited Maria Moltzer with the discovery of the intuitive type. The following text uses the work of those persons to show their influence on the shaping of Jung's types, starting with Hans Schmid-Guisan in 1915, Maria Moltzer in 1917, and Emilii Medtner in 1919, as all three collaborations have hitherto received no, or few, academic comments. I am not aware of any work by Reverend Adolf Keller. Finally, Toni Wolff's publication on types, because it is already known by scholars, will be treated in the next section.

The correspondence between Jung and his friend the psychiatrist Hans Schmid-Guisan—thirteen letters on types from 1915 to 1916—reveals the building of Jung's theory out of hypotheses and wandering. In his introduction to *Types*, Jung wrote that he had chosen not to publish the correspondence to avoid confusion. I found one reason that could have stopped Jung from publishing the letters. There Bergson's "irrational"—or, rather, Jung's view of Bergson's use of the notion—is raised by Jung. We previously saw how pivotal in Jung's final scheme is the distinction between rational and irrational types and functions. The way the term "irrational" appears in the letters is confusing indeed because (1) Jung does not use Bergson's term and (2) he does not describe "irrational" here in the way he will describe it in *Types*.[223]

In 1915, Jung distinguished only two opposite types of behaviour in consciousness. Those were the extraverted–feeling pole, on the one hand, and the introverted–thinking pole, on the other. With the idea borrowed, by Jung's account, from Bergson's idea of the irrational, each attitude was described as "irrational" (Iselin, 1982, p. 39) *vis-à-vis* the other.

One of the pivots of Bergson's thinking, rightly intuited by Jung, was the discrepancy between the perception of the unmediated "given" and the mediation of the intellect on things. Bergson's philosophy is intuitionist. What allows the immediate perception of the given—or, rather, of "that which gives"—is intuition (Bergson, 2001 [1888]). Whereas Bergson writes of *immédiat* (not mediated), Jung writes of "irrational". By so doing, Jung mistakenly thinks he uses Bergson's term.[224] In any case, Jung used Bergson's idea and his claim that Nietzsche's Apollinian and Dyonysian description inspired his irrational types was unfair to Bergson.

Let us come back to Jung in June 1915. Then, the "irrational" did not describe the opposition between feeling and thinking, on the one hand, and intuition and sensation, on the other, as in Jung's final scheme, but instead described a general *relationship* between opposites. The confusion comes from the fact that, then, only feeling and thinking existed. Those that would become the rational functions behaved at that moment "irrationally" among themselves.²²⁵ From those confusing reflections in progress, Jung retained that which constituted a second opposition next to the first of extraversion–introversion, that of irrational–rational.

Later in the correspondence, in a letter dated November 1915, Jung established closer parallels between the notion of rational and his future definitive rational functions and between rational and the "adapted" functions. Jung no longer described types of persons, but individuation. At the same time, he linked "irrational" with "unconscious", that is, with unconscious before individuation. If the irrational became conscious, then it was associated with "projection" because those elements of the non-adapted functions, instead of being seen for what they were, were (inaccurately) projected on others (all these elements will appear in the table presented below).

The content of that letter by Jung is extremely rich. It contains tabular material, which is reproduced here. It also contains a formally written part, to be commented on later, where Jung describes one of his dreams to Schmid.²²⁶

Introverted:

Conscious *Thinking* as the logical rational function (adapted and generally accepted).

Feeling as gradations of feeling subordinated to thinking and as an emotional reaction to what has been discerned through thought; *weak* with respect to external effect.

Sensation as a strongly (excessively) expressed organ function.

Uncs. *Feeling* as sporadic INTUITION = a complex of emotion with undeveloped thought-content. Undeveloped, and therefore archaic, symbolic, ambiguous, phenomenological, irrational, actus purus naturae, only defectively formulable and graspable by the intellect, projected.

I Extraverted:

Conscious *Feeling* as the logical (logical to the feelings) – rational function (adapted and generally accepted).

Thinking as the intellectual processes subordinated to feeling and as a reaction to what has been felt (discerned through feelings); *weak* with respect to external effect.

	Sensation, subordinated to feeling, weakly expressed (or even distorted) organ function.
Uncs.	*Thinking* as sporadic INTUITION = Complex of thoughts with undeveloped content in terms of feeling and sensation. Other attributes as above. (Iselin, 1982, pp. 109–110, translated for this edition: I placed "Intuition" in upper case for the sake of clarity)[227]

In this first draft by Jung, as well as throughout the correspondence, extraversion and introversion were described in the way that they would remain in *Psychological Types*. Introversion and extraversion are historically and hierarchically primary in Jung's scheme. Jung writes, "we must treat the introverted and extraverted types as categories over and above the function-type" (Jung, CW 6, par. 836). Conversely, following this table, intuition last appeared hierarchically to Jung as having the status of a function and type next to thinking, feeling and sensation. Sensation appeared last chronologically.[228] In 1915, intuitions were only *sporadic* and were wedged in between the unconscious of both introverted and extraverted types. This is important for functions, on the one hand, and for types, on the other.

Even though provisional, the table shows one stable and crucial aspect of the function of intuition with regard to the three others: *its specific relationship to the unconscious*. As stated by John Beebe as he introduces the correspondence, "here Jung takes pain to make clear that he now sees intuition as the guiding principle of the unconscious" (Beebe & Falzeder, 2013, p. 24). Now acknowledged as function, intuition remains difficult to grasp in consciousness, where it has no proper existence. In *Types*, paragraph 770, where one finds the definition of intuition in consciousness, Jung writes, "The peculiarity of intuition is that it is neither sense perception, nor feeling, nor intellectual inference, although it may also appear in these forms" (Jung, CW 6, par. 770). Connected to the table, where the mere "sporadic intuitions" remain unconscious in each type, the quotation gains its true meaning. Jung is close to writing the impossible statement that intuition does not exist in consciousness. At best, it is invisible. In the same paragraph, Jung designates *Anschauung*, writing that intuition "is the function that mediates perceptions *in an unconscious way*". Understanding this coherence between intuition in the unconscious and in consciousness is a theoretical challenge, but it allows for a three-dimensional reality rather than a two-dimensional table.

Unlike undifferentiated thought, feeling, and sensation, which are all stuck in the unconscious, undifferentiated intuition can be stuck in conscious material because of its inherent unconscious nature. To use a useful figure of speech, intuition proceeds to consciousness through a double differentiation, first by appearing in the conscious and then, if necessary, by provoking one's awareness. An illustration of this process appears in the letter that Jung sent to Schmid-Guisan that contains the table.

Jung describes, in a letter of 6 November 1915 to Schmid-Guisan, a dream in which "[he] was standing in [his] garden and had dug open a rich spring of water that gushed forth. Then [he] had to dig another deep hole, where [he] collected all the water and conducted it back into the depths of the earth again" (Adler & Jaffé, 1973, p. 32). Jung's dream illustrates this singularity of the function of intuition. The water (intuition) sprang from earth (the unconscious) but was conducted back to earth by him. Albeit conscious, intuition was not yet differentiated. Jung interprets the dream by writing, "True understanding seems to be one which does not understand, yet lives and works" (Adler & Jaffé, 1973, p. 32). The sentence depicts the work of intuition in natural individuation as well as Jung's own intuition processing to the elaboration of his theory of types. This dream follows his table, where intuitions were stuck in the unconscious of two provisional types. Six years after the letter, Jung's theory, once differentiated, would understand, comprehend, and differentiate intuition in consciousness. Until then, it remained in the safe place of the dreamer's garden.

To express his idea of "true understanding," Jung tells Schmid-Guisan,

> Once when Ludwig the Saint visited the holy Aegidius incognito, and as the two, who did not know each other, came face to face, they both fell to their knees before each other, embraced and kissed - *and spoke no words together*. Their gods recognised each other, and their human parts followed. (Adler & Jaffé, 1973, p. 32)

We could, *mutadis mutandis*, link Jung's story to Jung's encounter with Bergson's thought, since we may recall that Jung used Bergson's "irrational" to build his table. Their gods in the unconscious, intuition, that is, for Jung through the *Anschauung*, certainly met. Yet, the story ends where Jung, instead of staying silent, spoke to Schmid-Guisan in

1915 and then *apparently* (that is, through his first words to Guisan) misunderstood Bergson's irrational in the table containing only two functions, without intuition. In 1921, however, Jung's "true understanding" of Bergson's irrational is patent: it became the pivotal idea of *Psychological Types*.

In 1916, Moltzer delivered two papers at the Zürich Club. According to Shamdasani, who published them, they are notably "significant for understanding the genesis of some of Jung's signature concepts . . . of particular interest in this regard is the presentation of her concept of the intuitive type", which Jung reworked in order to develop his own model (Shamdasani, 1998c, p. 104). As we shall see, Moltzer's presentation denotes a fine mind and clear thinking.

Moltzer's paper "The conception of the libido and its psychic manifestations" allows, for instance, the understanding of the link between Jung's function of intuition, the religious function, and their contemporary manifestation through active imagination in *The Red Book*. Moltzer writes,

> The tendency of individualization also contains a collective element which arises in the half conscious, half unconscious function which we call intuition [here Moltzer also describes Jung's first stage of active imagination]. Intuition . . . tries to solve a given problem and create an adaptation in bringing together these half conscious and half unconscious elements [in Jung's scheme, by creating and carrying the symbol to consciousness]. (Shamdasani, 1998c, p. 108)[229]

"This adaptation", continues Moltzer, "coincides neither with the extraversion nor the introversion tendency—it contains elements of both. Therefore I am inclined to accept a third type which uses mainly this intuitive function in its adaptation to life" (Shamdasani, 1998c, p. 108), This second extract shows (1) where Moltzer and Jung differ as well as (2) the specificity, the primary role, of intuition among the four types in Jung's scheme. That which Moltzer depicts and retains for a single type—her intuitive type—Jung uses for his four types. The collective element of the religious function of the psyche and the step forward in individuation are not, in Jung's theory, the privileging of the intuitive type.

A second point of Moltzer's proposition is not at odds with Jung's intuitive type, but is, rather, specifically hers. Moltzer distinguishes three kinds among the intuitive type: "those who are more inclined towards thinking", "those who are more inclined towards action", and, finally, "the artists, who are able to assimilate the unconscious and bring it to its full value" (Shamdasani, 1998c, p. 116).

The points of convergence between Moltzer's paper and Jung's *Types* can be caught in some sentences or parts of sentences. Moltzer writes, for instance, that "intuition seems first to manifest itself in the age of childhood . . .", and elsewhere, "in these times of human agony, the saving work can be found through the help of intuition" (Shamdasani, 1998c, p. 109–110).[230] In the first case, Moltzer asserts the precedence of intuition over the rational functions, as Jung does. In the second case, she describes the redeemer (or, in her words, intuition "in its perfection") in a way similar to Jung's depiction of the saviour and of the prophet.

Two last points of Moltzer's paper, which are part of her last subsection, "On identification", present salient remarks, for they do not offer a link between her intuitive type and Jung's but, rather, provide a link between her function of intuition and two other facets of intuition in Jung's work that I have previously described: the *Anschauung* and empathy.

Bearing in mind Jung's description of intuition in the unconscious studied earlier, the *Anschauung*, let us compare it to this statement of Moltzer, who writes, "Intuition stands at the threshold of consciousness and introversion of the function leads of itself to the pictures within the unconscious" (Shamdasani, 1998c, p. 117). Here, again, Molzer's explanation, perhaps because she puts intuition to the fore, is extremely clear and makes it easy for us to grasp the co-operation between the dynamics of libido (through introversion) and the function of intuition in reaching the archetypal image.

Concerning empathy, Moltzer helps us connect the two notions of empathy (1) and (2) in another short and clear statement:

> [The patient] does not know the symbolic value of his identification [empathy (1)], and usually thinks he must model his thoughts and actions according to the concrete personality with whom by means of his identification, he is one [empathy (2)]. The consequence of this assumption is that he fails to understand his problem and continues to project upon others, that which he ought to find in himself. (Shamdasani, 1998c, p. 118)

Transference, in Jung's theory, overlooks this identification with the analyst, empathy (2). Following Moltzer explanation, his role consists in making clear to the patient the passage between the concrete unconscious identification, empathy (1), and the symbolic attachment of the patient to the attributes of the object of empathy, rather than to the object itself.

Based on archives and historical research, Shamdasani has proposed that Moltzer—rather than Spielrein, as suggested by Kerr— inspired Jung's notion of anima, central in his theory of transference (see Shamdasani, 1995, p. 128, 1998a, pp. 16, 69).[231] The topic and quality of Moltzer's "On the conception of the unconscious" may be considered another clue in favour of Shamdasani's hypothesis.

I introduced Emilii Medtner in the chapter concerning the *Anschauung*. Among the persons from the Zürich Club who debated intuition with Jung, Medtner might have been the most critical of all.[232] On that matter, his views were nearly as radical as those of Freud, for whom intuition simply did not exist. It was not Freud's ideas, however, that interested Medtner, but essentially Kant's, and, to a lesser extent, the thought of the pre-Socratics, Goethe, and Schiller.

In 1923, Medtner wrote the essay *Uber die sogenannte "Intuition", die ihr angrenzenden Begriffe und die an sie anknüpfenden Probleme* ("On so-called 'Intuition', its adjacent concepts and relevant problems"). He qualified his words on the basis of some considerations raised during the debates that had followed Jung's 1916 lecture at the Club on the belief in spirits. Medtner's reference in his title to Jung's title, *On the Psychology and Psychopathology of the So-Called Occult Phenomena: A Psychiatric Study*, announces the author's position by putting occult phenomena and intuition on the same level.

Whereas Moltzer intended in her paper, "The conception of the libido and its psychic manifestations", to comment critically on certain issues of Jung's *Psychology of the Unconscious*, Medtner's, through its use of Kant's gnosology and frequent reference to *Dreams of a Spirit Seer*, appears to be a reply to Jung's Zofingia Lectures.[233]

By relying on Kant's theory of knowledge, Medtner aimed at proving that Jung's audience at the Club had gone too fast in conceiving of intuition as "a knowledge organ, able to function independently and validly".[234] According to Medtner, intuition was not an organ (*Erkenntnisorgan*) but a function (*Erkenntnisfunktion*) (Medtner, 1923, p. vii). Instead of being independent, this knowledge function and its validity depended upon its *Wertung* ("assessment"). There was no knowledge without validation (Medtner, 1923, p. vii).[235] There was no absolute knowledge but exact knowledge, and "where ignorance was rejected [by intuition, which supposedly provided absolute knowledge], there was no room for exactitude", the proper criterion of gnosology (Medtner, 1923, p. 13, translated for this edition).[236] As sciences, biology, and psychology had probably offered valuable contributions (notably their recent thought on evolutionism), yet gnosology remained a matter of philosophy (Medtner, 1923, p. 7).[237] As a function, intuition was valuable, yet the intuitive *Eingebung* ("inspiration") was only the jolt at the start of a thought, for instance, not the thought itself (Medtner, 1923, p. 22).[238]

In October 1919, still in the context of his papers on the topic of intuition, Medtner dedicated a lecture to Kant's "intellectus archetypus". We remember that Jung's seminal lecture *Instinct and the Unconscious*, where Jung used the term "archetype" for the first time, was also delivered in 1919, but in July. Even though Jung's lecture preceded Medtner's, the men carried on a correspondence with each other and met at the Club. They might have debated the issue together before both gave their papers. My earlier insistence on the significance of intuition in the appearance of the "archetype" in Jung's thought is here confirmed by the context of its (intuition's) numerous occurrences in the discussions, which went beyond types.

At stake with Kant's intellectus archetypus was the differentiation between the archetype (Jung's) and the archetypal image. In his lecture, Medtner insists on Kant's hierarchy between *Verstand* ("comprehension") and *Vernunft* ("reason", or "intellectual comprehension"). Medtner quotes Kant, who writes that we owe sensation to the ability to distinguish opposites and that we could not think without comprehension. In addition, just as thinking without content would be empty, intuitions without concepts would be blind ["Anschauungen ohne Begriffe sind blind"] (Medtner, 1923, p. 31, translated for this edition).[239] Two levels, therefore, appear: that of sensation, called "perception" by Medtner, and that of intellectualisation (Medtner, 1923, p. vii).[240]

In Kant's gnosology, intuition belongs to both. On the one hand, we find the "intellectus ectypus [which] derives its knowledge of objects directly from passive intuitions of things-in-themselves unmediated by the forms of intuition and the synthetic activity of the understanding". On the other hand, we have the "intellectual archetypus [which] is productive in its thinking, creating the objects of its knowledge through the act of thinking them" (Chadwick & Cazeaux, 1992, p. 256). According to Medtner, the object which is self created is the symbol. But symbol there is. No direct access to the things-in-themselves (such as God—or the archetype in Jung's psychology) is possible as claimed, for instance, by the mystics (Medtner, 1923, p. 67).[241] This debate over direct or indirect access still continues today between specialists in Jung and esotericists.

When, for example, he examines the relationship between Jung's psychology and mysticism, Schlamm (2006) sees no contradiction in Jung as "a post-religious or detraditionalised mystic as well as a scientist" (p. 7). Jung's active imagination, which connects the unconscious to consciousness to make images appear, is investigated by Schlamm,[242] who reframes active imagination in the field of esotericism and gives the term "mystic" a new perspective, different from the mystic aspiration to meet God directly.

Schlamm writes,

> Henri Corbin demonstrated that the spiritual organ of imagination, accessing during the liminal period between sleep and waking experiences of the *mundus imaginalis* located between the spiritual (formless) and material levels of reality, was central, rather than marginal, to the spiritual journeys of many [mystics]. (Schlamm, 2006, p. 11)

If we "detraditionalise" and translate this experience in Jungian terminology, we describe, indeed, active imagination. The "liminal period"—and *mundus imaginalis*—becomes the under-conscious, and the "spiritual organ of imagination" able to form images, auditions, and paranormal experiences is intuition in the unconscious, the *Anschauung* perceiving the content of archetypes.

Schlamm here opposes Faivre's view of what would distinguish the mystical from the esoteric: mediation. Whereas, for Faivre, there is no mediation between the mystics and God because what is being sought is an immediate union (Faivre, 1994, p. 12),[243] for Schlamm, these images are intermediaries between the mystic and God. Between Faivre's and Schlamm's position, we find the unstable status of the term "intermediary".

"[I]ntuitive revelation ... opens the imaginal [the *mundus imaginalis*] for us: Gnosis is inner vision", writes Faivre, who uses "gnosis" in its general sense of knowledge not separated from sacred wisdom, the origin of Truth being God. When entering the imaginal, the disciple reaches gnosis by "(true) imagination" (Faivre, 1994, p. 21). Likewise, Jung's active imagination pictures intuition as translating the content of archetypes into images, auditions, or paranormal experiences. Jung maintained that translation did not mean creation, or, in other words, that the images, the symbols, appeared. Like true imagination, intuition for Jung does not create, but instead reveals. This view frames Jung's claim not to be an artist. The truth obtained from God or from the archetype (the content inside the archetype) during esoteric or Jungian active imagination is prior to the form, to the temporary and intermediary image in which it appears. Jung's view also is close to Medtner's symbolism (see Medtner, 1923, pp. 60–73).

Medtner's last point concerns intuition and typology. *Angeregt durch* ("stimulated by") and, following Schiller's twofold typology opposing the sentimental and the naïve poet, Medtner created the following scheme:

I. Intuitive–Discursive.
   A gnoseological contrast.
II. Intuitive–Instinctive.
   A psychological contrast.
III. Intuitive–Speculative.
   A thinking–typological contrast.
   (Medtner, 1923, p. 31, translated for this edition)[244]

In *Psychological Types*, Jung used Schiller's typology from his 1795 essay "Uber die äesthetische Erziehung des Menschen" (translated as "On the aesthetic education of man") to associate the (Schiller) naïve poet with an extraverted sensation type and the sentimental poet with an introvert intuitive type (Jung, *CW 6*, pars 213–219). As remarked by Shamdasani, "Medtner noted that he was not sure if what he had to say was connected with analytical psychology or not", yet, "in the discussion following this lecture, Jung spoke of another contrast, intuitive–perceptive, which he made for his own use" (Shamdasani, 2003, p. 69, quoting Medtner, 1923, pp. 33, 49). The debate, therefore, in any case had proved fruitful for Jung.

Beyond morality and reason—that is, beyond that which an individual obtains from the rational functions—Jung had "directly" read of Nietzsche's aesthetic types. This had led him to the discovery of the irrational types: the Apollinian–intuitive type and the Dionysian–sensation type. If Jung did not, indeed, directly use Medtner's gnosological or psychological contrasts, debates and emulation at the Zürich Club did inspire him. In addition, that Jung read Nietzsche is obvious, but he might also have discussed his ideas at the Club. Second, Jung mentions Nietzsche as the only thinker who directed his thought towards the irrational types (Jung, CW 6, par. 240).[245] After having examined the correspondence between Schmid and Jung concerning Bergson and the central notion of "irrational", to use Jung's own terms, I can state that this is false. In fact, many people contributed to the elaboration of Jung's types, some in building hypotheses, others in proposing their hermeneutics, and, finally, yet others in using them in their practice during Jung's life and after his death, as we shall see now.

Critiques of, and variants to, Jungian types

Among Jung's hermeneuts, we find many women, including Marie-Louise von Franz, Cary Baynes, Anièla Jaffé, and Antonia Wolff. All four women had been Jung's assistants and have published on intuitive and esotericist topics.[246] We see here the variants and critiques that clarify or add to the role of intuition in Jung's typology.

Valuable critiques of Jung's typology have been made by Jungian feminists. They have raised the issue of contradictions between some of Jung's concepts and his typology, notably, between types and the notion of anima.

We saw with Medtner and Motzer that alternatives to Jung's ideas on types and functions regarding intuition had been proposed as early as their conception. Moltzer, however, did not publish her work and Medtner's publication focuses on gnosology and philosophical matters rather than on psychological types.

Present at the Zürich Club and, as seen, "instrumental in introducing the functions of sensation and intuition", Wolff published her own discoveries concerning women and typology (1995[1934], pp. 77–90).[247] Wolff's "Structural forms of the feminine psyche" distinguishes four types of woman: the Mother, the Hetaira (or companion), the Amazon, and the Medium. Wolff specifies,

The *mother* is caring and protective, giving, instructive, [her negative aspects are] a tendency to interfere in their [husband, children, friends, etc.] development. . . .

The *hetaira*'s function is to awaken the man's individual psychic life and to lead him through and beyond his male responsibilities into his total personality. . . . For the hetaira, relationship is decisive. Everything else—social security, position, etc.—is irrelevant. . . .

The *Amazon* is independent of the male, because her development is not based on a psychological relationship with him. The conscious values he represents are hers, too. . . . The amazon is also in danger of abusing human relationships by treating them as "business" or as vehicle for her career. . . .

The *medial woman* [or the medium] is immersed in the psychic atmosphere of her environment and the spirit of her times, but above all, in the collective (impersonal) unconscious. . . . As the elements involved are unconscious, she generally lacks the discernment to perceive them or the language to express them adequately. (Wolff, 1995[1934], pp. 80, 82, 84–87)

Wolff's typology does not challenge the universality of Jung's types, but "adds" to them. Where Jung focuses on attitudes, Wolff is interested in relationship. Except for the independent Amazon–sensation type, whose development is not based on any relationship, a specific link to the world, every type of woman is depicted through relationships. The medium and the Amazon bear traits of "Jung's" irrational (perceptive) types as opposed to the mother and the hetaira, who resemble the apperceptive and rational types, who are good at judging, thinking, assisting, etc.[248] Yet, Wolff does not write of "rational", but of "personally connected to", such as the hetaira, who cares for her—and her surrounding's—personal development. Wolff does not write of "irrational", but of "impersonally connected to", such as the independent Amazon, for whom persons are almost (impersonal) objects.

To put it another way, Jung's typology is directed inwards. It answers the question "who I am (now)?" and "knowing it, what can I do to adapt myself to the current reality?" When used by a woman, Wolff's typology goes in the opposite direction. She wonders, "what is the situation?" and "knowing it, which attitude in me now is the most appropriate to use?"

Later feminist "re-visions of Jungian thought" have been critical of Wolff's emphasis on the relationship (Lauter & Schreier Rupprecht, 1985).[249] While paying Wolff tributes for her work in imposing woman distinctively from man in types, some feminists insist that Wolff describes the woman almost exclusively with regard to the role she holds *vis-à-vis* the man. Lauter writes on Wolff's medial type,

> It is the medial woman's task to find an "objective language" to express the meaning of the collective unconscious. I do not doubt that such a figure exists, but it still correlates better with well-known images of the muse who inspires others than with the images of women who are themselves inspired or otherwise empowered to act. (Lauter in Lauter, & Schreier Rupprecht (Eds.), 1985, p. 74)

Wolff's depiction of the intuitive–medial woman's relationship to man strangely recalls Jung's depiction of his relationship with Toni Wolff. Wolff has been described as a muse for Jung, but she was not perhaps a woman empowered to act and to inspire her own work over and above his. We remember, indeed, that Jung had told Jaffé about his "confrontation with the unconscious", that "he had infected her [Toni Wolff] with his experience, which was awful and terrible, and that she got drawn into it and was equally helpless" (Shamdasani, 1995, p. 125). With Wolff, we read, as in an echo, of the medial woman that "she will often embody the impersonal side of his [the man's] anima and will thus unwittingly drag him into a chaotic whirlpool in which she too will be swept away" (Wolff, 1995[1934], p. 87).

Wolff also proposes that her types of woman correspond to anima figures (archetypal images) for men. The relationship described is no longer that of a woman in the world, but that of a man in the psyche (Wolff, 1995[1934], p. 80).[250] Wolff justifies this swap from consciousness to the unconscious by explaining that whereas a man is "dualistic by nature" [as society imposes on him a rupture between his social persona and his intimate anima], a woman, "on the other hand, is by nature conditioned by the soul and is thus more consistent" (Wolff, 1995[1934], pp 77–78).[251] Wolff's explanation is subtle and consistent with her entire article. Yet, she paves the way to the all too easy parallel between real woman and anima, which notably leads to stereotypes.

Rowland noticed this "displacement" in *MDR*:

> The theoretical formation of the concept of the anima is described in the autobiography as generated from a mediumistic contact with a feminine *voice* within his own mind. At this point of the building of a psychology, "women," or more precisely "the feminine," are displaced from medium to anima. (Rowland, 2002, p. 19, my italics, used to emphasis the voice pattern that we can link with a motor *Einfall*, as seen in Chapter ??)

Rowland's critique, like Lauter's, is not theoretical, but political. Before examining theoretical critiques of Jung's types related to intuition, we must recall Jung's thought on the anima and animus. They are as important to the differentiation of types as intuition is. Intuition is necessary for, and always permits, individuation. In contrast, the anima/us both hinders and allows individuation, depending upon— to simplify matters—the stage of psychic evolution of the patient. Analytical psychologist Daryl Sharp summarises the four stages of the animus:

> Jung described four stages of animus development in a woman. He first appears in dreams and fantasy as the embodiment of physical power . . . In the second stage, the animus provides her with initiative and the capacity for planned actions. He is behind a woman's desire for independence. . . . In the next stage, the animus is the "word," often personified in dreams as a professor or clergyman. In the fourth stage, the animus is the incarnation of spiritual meaning [mediating] between a woman's conscious mind and the unconscious. (Sharp, 1991, p. 24)

Sharp depicts only the positive action of the animus, yet he depicts the four stages in detail. Now, with Jung, we see both positive and negative aspects of the anima and then of the animus from projection to psychopomp. Jung writes,

> [The anima] is always the a priori element in moods, reactions, impulses, and whatever else is spontaneous in psychic life . . . The anima is a factor of the utmost importance in the psychology of a man wherever emotions and affects are at work. She intensifies, exaggerates, falsifies, and mythologizes all emotional relations with his work and with other people of both sexes . . . when the anima is strongly constellated, she softens the man's character and makes him touchy, irritable, moody, jealous, vain, and unadjusted. (Jung, CW 9(ii), pars 57, 144)

Jung writes that just "as the anima produces *moods*, so the animus produces *opinions* [which] rest on prior assumptions", He continues,

> No man can converse with an animus for five minutes without becoming the victim of his own anima. Anyone who still had enough sense of humour to listen objectively to the ensuing dialogue would be staggered by the vast number of commonplaces, misapplied truisms ... shop-soiled platitudes of every description interspersed with vulgar abuse and brain-splitting lack of logic. (Jung, CW 9(ii), par. 29)

At the same time, writes Jung,

> in the fourth stage, as Sophia (called Wisdom in the Bible), a man's anima functions as a guide to the inner life, mediating to consciousness the content of the unconscious. She cooperates in the search for meaning and is the creative muse in an artist's life. (Jung, CW 16, par. 361)

Jung's portraits of the main aspects of the anima and animus, especially in the first stage, do not correspond to each other. Commonplaces and truisms are Logos' lures. Irritation and moods are Eros' snares. Jung's theory is gendered. This fact was emphasised and became the hub of numerous critiques after Jung's death, in post-Jungian publications.

Another strongly intuitive woman was Christiana Morgan. Jung portrayed her visions and their role regarding types in seminars that he delivered in the 1930s. In 1997, Claire Douglas, who introduced the two-volume work *Visions*, shows how Jung's use of his notion of the animus as linked to Logos cannot fit the visions of the intuitive–thinking type Morgan. "Equally disturbing", writes Douglas, "is Jung's insistence that Morgan's animus serves Logos rather than Eros, when her material [her visions] so clearly points to Eros as the principle behind many of her animus figures" (Douglas, 1997, p. xxvi). As an intuitive–thinking type, Morgan's unconscious was filled with sensation–feeling content. The contradiction with a logos–animus for any woman of such type—Jung's type, too, but Jung is a man[251]—indeed disqualifies the notion of animus thus pictured.

Later, in 1971, von Franz involuntarily revealed the same contradiction when she described the role of the fourth function. Von Franz writes, "One can say that the inferior function always makes the bridge to the unconscious. It is always directed towards the unconscious and the symbolic world" (p. 7). This fundamental and intuitive role of psychopomp describes that of the anima/us, therefore, neither erotically nor logically tinged, but simply gendered. This intuitive role exists next to *any* fourth function. This role points, above all, to the specificity of intuition with regard to all three other functions: its privileged relationship to the unconscious. Jung writes of the "imaginative activity of the fourth function—intuition, without which no realisation is complete" (Jung, GW 16, par. 492). Symbolically speaking, von Franz thus pretends that she knows the sex of the angels.

Specificities of introverted and extraverted intuitive types

Jung's theory, some examples in his writing, and, most of all, the analysis of the variants and critiques of Jung's typology, allow me now to suggest some clarifications concerning the hermeneutics of Jung's types (and of their existence after Jung) regarding intuition and the specific individuation of the two intuitive types.

Introverted intuitive types like Jung are different from extraverted intuitive types. They do not perceive the same present and future. While extraverted intuitive types are fast, "continually scenting out new possibilities" (Jung, CW 6, par. 658), introverted intuitive types are slow. They need their secondary extraverted function to realise any intuition.

Here, Wolff's typology proves useful. We could use it to describe the extraverted intuitive type's intuition as "personal" and, therefore, instantly useful (for him). In contrast, the intuition of the introvert intuitive type is "impersonal" and is lost in consciousness. Wolff describes the medial woman (or the medium) as a person who lacks "discernment" (Wolff, 1995[1934], p. 88). So is the intuition of the introverted intuitive person. It lacks direction. If not transformed into, and directed by, a thought or a feeling, this intuition simply is not, and simply does not become, anything in consciousness.

The system of the Myers–Briggs's typology, which first distinguishes perceptive types from apperceptive ones before analysing the four functions, shows how Jung's difference between extraverted and introverted types has guided studies on types (Beebe, 2004, pp. 100–101). More recently, the work of Beebe has echoed this fundamental distinction. He writes that for an introverted intuitive type, the extraverted intuitive type (and vice versa) archetypally represents his or her "opposing personality", which is "often more like a symptom than like a dashing enemy on a black horse" (Beebe, 2004, p. 107).

We can imagine that intuitive persons could all be inclined towards, or gifted at, several paranormal activities. Yet, their perceptions or intuitive results would not be obtained through the same means. Intuitive capacities, or phenomena such as telepathy, which Jung recognised, are differently perceived by introverted and extraverted types. Were introverted individuals to explain telepathy, for example, they would emphasise the (natural) unconscious link between subjects. By contrast, extraverted intuitive individuals would stress one's capacity to read someone's mind or identify an unseen playing card.

I shall try to show, with examples, that the individuation of intuitive types implies intuition in opposite ways. Extraverted types, I think, can be aware of inner "signs", such as apparent inaccurate statements in dreams. Introverted types are more likely to receive strange lessons from outside. Synchronicities and numinosities represent such signs for both types, but extraverted types are, rather, likely to live inner numinosities (in dreams), whereas introverted types meet them in the outer world.

Jaffé reports how Jung narrates two important passages of his life and individuation. Against chronology, the first one is a near death experience (NDE), remembered by Jung, the introverted intuitive, as an *out*put of his body. In 1944, after a heart attack, and receiving oxygen, Jung had extraordinary numinous (external) visions, where "high up in space" he could see the world. The second one, earlier in time, marks the no less important rift with Freud at the beginning of the 1910s. Whatever Jaffé's or Jung's lyricism, this is a concrete dream (filled with sensation) of a *house* in 1909 that signalled Jung's own nascent psychology (Jung, 1995[1961/1963], pp. 182–183, 320–329). An extraordinarily interesting dream, it was not of any extraordinary nature.

I suggest a parallel with synchronicity. A series of internal and external events linked by synchronicity could happen to intuitive persons, but the last and alerting event—or the single one—would be exterior concerning introverted intuitive types, who live ordinarily blindly in the world, and internal for extraverted intuitive types, who pay little or no attention to their dreams.

If we ask, for example, extraverted intuitive types how they became aware of their first function, the person would probably answer with an inner phenomenon. In contrast, an introverted intuitive type would rather remember an exterior sign, revelation, or call. Here is how the extraverted intuitive John Beebe discovered his own superior function:

> My discovery of my superior function, intuition, came in the first year of my analysis. . . . While I was in the midst of reiterating these complaints [of depression], my analyst asked: "Do you ever dream when you're depressed?" It was as if a light had been turned on in a dark room. . . . In a flash I knew that what I was superior at – dreaming – . . . I was an intuitive type. (Beebe, 2004, p. 92)

Beebe's example reveals another striking opposition between introverted and extraverted intuitive individuals. Beebe realised that his leading function was intuition "in a flash". Let us now remember Jung's visions before the First World War. Jung never realised that he had dreamed of the war, let alone that he was intuitive. For more than six months, the fear of being schizophrenic, painting, and the practice of active imagination had been necessary for him to differentiate his first function, intuition.[253]

In Jung's case, what first emerged was a natural (conscious) opposition to (unconscious) intuition, the problematic *double* differentiation of intuition. If the *function* of intuition does not necessarily need to be differentiated to be effective, as we previously saw in Jung's dream of the dormant waters described in a letter to Schmid, intuitive persons, intuitive *types*, need individuation, and, thus, particularly the difficult differentiation of their first function.[254] To realise their unconscious functions, introverted intuitive types need to get or have a palpable or sometimes crude reality just before their eyes.

A final example on dreams. It is commonly admitted that everybody needs to get rid of his or her own projections to meet people in the external world properly. Members of a couple must ideally differentiate the person they live with from the archetypes and complexes of the Mother, the Father, the anima and the animus. Dream analysis can help, but, while for seven types out of eight, the task consists in linking elements of external reality with their symbols in dreams, it consists, for introverted intuitive types, in the opposite work.

Let us imagine that a mother complex affects one member of a couple. If that person is not an introverted intuitive type, the member will be informed of this complex through symbols in dreams such as a frightening animal, or a *cul de sac*. Once, say, the frightening animal is recognised as such, and its projection on to the real mother, the real wife or husband is *removed*, and the complex loses its power. If that person, in contrast, is an introverted intuitive type, the person will dream of his or her *real* mother more frequently. The task then consists in trying to find, in the series of dreams, the "quality"[255] of the mother. By so doing, the literal mother in the dream becomes symbolic. Once the symbol or the quality—over-/under-protection, for instance—is recognised, it can then be *added* to the real mother outside and acknowledged as the complex that had been projected on to the real wife or husband (outside).

This example is confirmed by Fierz's statement: "In cases of psychosis or near psychosis, dreams should be understood directly from the images they contained, rather than interpreted" (1991, p. 9). Fierz was one of the rare persons trained by Jung who became a psychiatrist. Like Jung, he worked with schizophrenic patients at the Burghölzli hospital. The main problem encountered with psychotic cases is that of communication since the schizophrenic patient—such as the introverted type, but pathological—is trapped in the unconscious. Yet, that person's dream is more likely to speak literally than in a language of symbols. In such a concrete and direct way can be read Jung's thrice repeated dreams of 1914, where he saw "the whole of Lorraine and its canals frozen and the entire region totally deserted by human beings" (Jung, 1995[1961/63], p. 200).

Jung's own struggle with the recognition of his type and with his individuation shows how particular and difficult this task is for introverted intuitive types, whose natural tendency is doubly unconscious. An introvert intuitive type is like a person whose head is full of images. Schlamm recalls that

> for Jung, the descent into the unconscious is frequently located in both the intrapsychic and exterior worlds. While Jung acknowledged the value of wholly intrapsychic descents into the unconscious . . . he was equally engaged with unconscious contents mediated by the material world. (Schlamm, 2008, from manuscript).

More than any other types, introverted intuitive individuals need, at any cost, to hang on to external reality and to keep their feet firmly planted on the ground. Finding equivalents between the content of their unconscious images and the exterior world is crucial for their individuation and a constant effort to produce. As Jung did all his life, they would rather be assisted in this task by friends, family, or colleagues in order to sharpen their discernment, in order constantly to be able either to validate or to invalidate their images with the reality.

To close this chapter, I would like to use a metaphor in harmony with my hermeneutics of the primary role of intuition in Jung's theory of consciousness. Jung rejected the term "categories" to designate types because, for him, the dynamics of types and functions (individuation) were as important as their setting. Consider the human hand. The thumb is intuition in the unconscious, *Anschauung*. The four other fingers are the four functions, intuition included. Each time a person discovers a new function, using it more regularly by "differentiating" it in consciousness, the person performs many flicks with one finger *and* with the thumb to get used to this new aptitude. The thumb on the hand is as central as intuition is in Jung's functions and types. Beyond the other three functions, it has a primary status.

A final reflection in order not to forget the limitations of theory. Gunter reminded us that Jung was not the first thinker to have had imagined a typology. This remark Jung acknowledged easily (Gunter, 1982, pp. 636–637). Other critics, however, did give the reader or the user of Jung's psychology a real benefit of hindsight. A colleague of Jung at the Burghölzli, Karl Abraham, joined the Freudian side after the rift between Jung and Freud. Falzeder informed Shamdasani of one anecdote, which I will mention here. Absorbed in his typology, as well as in the collective unconscious, Jung, at least for Freud and Abraham, seemed to have lost the sense of any reality outside this frame. Jung had typed both Adler and Freud as introverted and extraverted, while he considered himself introverted. On 13 July 1917, Freud wrote to Abraham that Jung "seems to have gone beyond the crude conversion into theory of the fact that he came across myself and Adler. We meet in the 'archaic'" (Shamdasani, 2003, p. 73).

If, hitherto, Jung had openly criticised Freud for the vicious circle that Freud had created by diagnosing nearly all of his colleagues with neurosis, Freud, this time, subtly replied with a similar vicious circle, this time created by Jung, that everybody could be diagnosed from the "archaic", that is, from anything stemming from the collective unconscious. A cigar sometimes is nothing but a cigar. Types inform us of the multi-perceptive aspect of life. They should not impede our judgement.

PART VI

LATE JUNG, EMPATHY (3), AND THE NATURE OF INTUITION

CHAPTER NINE

Suggestions for further research

Part VI is as short as it is complex, for it constitutes a theoretical platform that synthesises the whole book in order to introduce the difficult notion of empathy (3) and, most important, to foster further research on intuition, ideally both theoretical and practical.

For Jung, as for any other theorist of psychology, the gap between theory and practice is large enough to create contradictions. This is especially true concerning the notion of empathy, *Einfühlung*, which I described in this work as empathy (1), empathy (2), and mentioned as empathy (3). In my first study, *Sur Jung et le Yi King*, I had written in my epilogue that I wanted to develop my research for a better understanding of the term *Einfühlung*. This research is unfinished, for the notion of empathy (3) is linked to synchronicity and the objective psyche, one of the last topics of research undertaken by Jung and pursued by Marie-Louise von Franz.[256]

Through my readings, I can state that the objective psyche enables us to make a real system of Jung's psychology. Nevertheless, I am not yet capable of putting this understanding into clear words. Instead of elaborating, therefore, I summarise in this very short chapter as a starting point for further research.

I, and, most significantly, others have defined synchronicity, the acausal connection, elsewhere.[257] Synchronicity describes a link of equivalence between two events, objects, an object and a person, etc. that causality cannot explain. For instance, someone dreams of a beetle and, as the dreamer relates the dream to her psychoanalyst—Jung in this case—a beetle enters the consulting room. The link between the beetle in the dream and that of the real beetle is acausal and, instead of meaningful, is synchronistic.

In this work, I am only attached to the notion that I named "empathy (3)", or *intuition* in synchronicity, which I shall soon define in context *vis-à-vis* empathy (1) and (2) for a better understanding.

Twelve categories of intuition exist in Jung's work.

Four categories stem from the unconscious:

- empathy (1),
- *Anschauung*,
- *Mythosanschauung*,
- *Weltanschauung*.

Four categories, or sub-categories, stem from the under-conscious:

- psychological intuitions
- extra-ordinary intuitions,
- among which are the religious intuitions
- and the scientific kinds of intuitions.

Two categories stem from consciousness:

- the type and
- the function of intuition.

And two categories stem from practice:

- empathy (2),
- empathy (3).

From description to (first elements of) analysis, let us propose four other categories, the fourfold scheme of the *nature* of intuition. Intuition is:

1. A function leading to knowledge and the knowledge itself (such as psychological intuitions, scientific intuitions, *Anschauung*, and *Mythosanschauung*).
2. A function leading to gnosis and gnosis itself (such as extraordinary intuitions and religious intuitions).
3. A relationship (such as the intuitive function, empathy (1), (2), and (3)).
4. A language (such as the intuitive type and *Weltanschauung*).

Intuition as (4), a language, describes the limitations of intuition exactly as expressed in the punishment of the Tower of Babel.[258] The ultimate learning of types is fraught with reservations. No one ever has the exact same experience as someone else. Both collective (*Weltanschauung*) and personal (types) hindrances prevent the creation of a general truth in the field of the humanities that would be comparable to scientific objectivity.

On the opposite side of the spectrum lie (1) knowledge and (2) gnosis. How, then, can knowledge and gnosis "appear"—if we follow the status of intuition: intuition does not *exist*, intuition *is* not, intuition *appears*—in a sceptical system?[259] Which kind of phenomenology can resolve the apparently impossible equation?

Intuition as (3), a relationship, provides the solution. Here we find the theoretical contribution of synchronicity to Jung's systematic psychology. Intuition as a function and as a relationship constitutes Jung's single definition of intuition because the intuitive function is present in the unconscious, the under-conscious, consciousness, and in practice. Jung's (single) definition of intuition is, thus, extremely concise and requires going through with a fine-toothed comb for years.

In the same category (intuition as a relationship), we find the three empathies that all depict an intuitive relationship of identity. Empathy (1) treats of the identity shared between a tree and some ancestor, for instance, or else the very identity of everything that is consistent with the state of total unconsciousness.[260] Empathy (2) brings the reader into the fountain, where both the analyst and the patient bathe, sharing identical unconscious to conscious thoughts and complexes. Empathy (3) materialises the rupture of time, where inner objects of worry, for instance, appear in front of our eyes, just like hallucinations, yet are observable by all. Against the objective fact of science, which just is with no reason to be, "objective" synchronicity appears meaningful and meaning warrants precise objectivity.

If we trace the two ends of synchronicity, we have a person's subjective consciousness on the one hand, and the objective psyche on the other, or else Self (not just the world, but the world of the past, present, and future). The economy of synchronicity is just like that of libido, compensative. The quality of synchronicity is that of the archetype. The link between the two ends is, therefore, the *Anschauung* between consciousness and the archetype. Because the archetype in question is that of completeness, the Self, we employ the term empathy (3). Synchronicities are symbols of the Self, of the totality. Unlike symbols of archetypes, which often manifest once, or more than once but repeatedly, synchronicities appear *in pairs* from one end of the spectrum to the other, repeating not themselves through symbols, but the range of their completeness through opposite and similar pairs of symbols.

In the example of the beetle, the symbol is opposite (one beetle in the dream, the other in consciousness) and similar (the same beetle). In this case, the range of completeness from consciousness to the collective unconscious is the direction that the patient has to follow if she wants to pursue her analysis with Jung. The range of completeness is the meaning and its impetus, naturally displayed by the two functions of the psyche at once, compensation and imagination.

Objectivity in synchronicity is not, as in science, indifferent to our human state of life and death. In contrast, or perhaps by enantiodromia (the pre-Socratic principle of the return to the opposite that was appreciated by Jung), objectivity arises from the most restricted space that objectivity can imagine and the biggest space that subjectivity can create. To use an image, when scientific objectivity is the perimeter of the circle and its content, objective synchronicity is the line that forms its diameter from the centre (collective unconscious) to one point in the circle (personal consciousness). This meeting point between objectivity and subjectivity is one ray of a rainbow, a holograph. If the line is intuition, empathy (3), the bigger the line (that is, the bigger the difference between one-sided conscious attitude and opposite, unconscious *Streben* (striving)), the bigger the effect, the clearer the meaning, the more objective the learning, the knowledge, the gnosis (at the centre of the circle, where knowledge is both personal and collective). We have solved the equation. There is no need of general truth, of indifferent general objectivity, when our minds can create personalised objectivity. Or so the modern world looks.

The synchronistic phenomenology not only assesses, after Husserl, that conscience is the conscience of something—and thereby gives meaning to that something—but that, paradoxically, the most subjective conditions of that conscience create objectivity. Those conditions do not produce indifferent objectivity (as in science), but objectivity "on demand", just as the simple use of the Internet via personal computers generates personal objective advertisement—that is, the same advert that everybody *could* receive, but that people actually receive because they have typed the relevant words into an Internet search engine. Synchronicities are as objective as they are subjective, a double character soon to become a very common aspect of things in a connected world where little is left undiscovered.

APPENDIX I: INDEXATIONS OF "-INTUITION"

Table I(1). German and English index-linking in Jung's *Collected Works* of "-intuition", "-intuitive", "-intuitive type". *Sources*: Niehus (1994); Glover and Forryan (1979).

Corresponding volumes of the *Gesammelte Werke* and *Collected Works* of C. G. Jung	Index-linked paragraphs of *Intuition, Intuiren* (s. a. *Funktion*) *Intuitiv* *Intuitiver Typus*	Index-linked paragraphs of Intuition(s) as function (see function) Intuitive Intuitive type
1		168
2		
3	423, 452, 539	539
4		490
5		546
6	7, 103–104, 117, 123, 171, 184 195, 219, 238, 240, 242, 252–254 281, 316, 524, 540, (591), 603, 605, 608, 610–615, 630, 637, 654–663, 668–669, 678, 702, 727, 754–757, 762, 782, (792), 797, 817, 828, 835, 899–900, 913, 951, 953–954, (957), 983–984*	7,103–104, 117–118, 143*n*, 148*n*, 219, 240, 242, 244, 252*n*, 254, 540, 610–615, 655–663, <u>770–773</u> (Def.) [*754–7 in G.*], 899–901, 951, 953–954, 983*

(continued)

240   APPENDIX I

Table I(1). (continued)

Corresponding volumes of the *Gesammelte Werke* and *Collected Works* of C. G. Jung	Index-linked paragraphs of *Intuition, Intuiren* (s. a. Funktion) *Intuitiv* *Intuitiver Typus*	Index-linked paragraphs of Intuition(s) as function (see function) Intuitive Intuitive type
7	64*n*, 505	64*n*, 107, 151, 270, 296, 505
8	92, 175, 257, 259, 269 (*Definition der*), 270, 277, 279, 292, 396, 594, 825, 863, 865, 948	98, 257, 269–270, 277–278, 292, 594, 863
9(i)	245, 425, 504, 541, 693, 697	504, 541
9(ii)	237	
10	23, 25, 393, 626, 657, 774, 903–904, 916, 918, 924	25, 574, 626, 657, 774, 916, 918
11	69, 245, 446, 804, 818, 821, 1015	69, 245–6, 446, 784, 804, 818
12	148–149, 152(T), 175, 305	148–149, 153, 175, 305, 517
13	7, 207, 309, 458	1–2, 7, 36, 44–45, 59, 207–208
14(i)**	*218*	
15	9, 31, 41, 173	148
16	59, 486, 492, 532	59, 77*n*, 194, 345, 486, 492
17		
18	24–26, 53–54, 89, 420, 461, 489, 502–503, 512, 573, 576–577, 780, 1114, 1157, 1198, 1259, 1282, 1818, 1820	24–26, 33, 53–54, 89, 110, 502–503, 576–577, 779–780

* Figures in italic only relevant for the corresponding language (here due to alphabetical order).

** The Swiss volumes 14(i) and 14(ii) represent the English–American Volume 14: paragraphs do not correspond.

Table I(2a). Common (German and English) index-linking.

Corresponding volumes of the *Gesammelte Werke* and *Collected Works* of C. G. Jung	Paragraphs index-linked in both German and English editions*
3	539
6	7, 103–104, 117, 219, 240, 242, 252, 254, 540, 610–615, 655–663, 770–773, 899–900, 951, 953–954, 983*
7	64*n*, 505
8	257, 269–70, 277, 292, 594, 863
9(i)	504, 541
10	25, 626, 657, 774, 916, 918
11	69, 245, 446, 804, 818
12	148–149, 152–153, 175, 305
13	7, 207
16	59, 486, 492
18	24–26, 53–54, 89, 502–503, 576–577, 780

* German paragraphs appearing in alphabetical order in Volume 6 have been converted here into their corresponding chapters in English.

Table I(2b). German additional index-linking.

Corresponding volumes of the *Gesammelte Werke* and *Collected Works* of C. G. Jung	Paragraphs index-linked only in the German edition
3	423, 452
6	**123****, 171, 184, 195, 238, 253–254, 281, 316, 524, (591), 603, 605, 608, 630, 637, 654, 668–669, 678, 692, 712, (722), 731, 787, 812, 823, 832, 835, 913, (957), 984*
8	92, 175, 259, 269, 279, 396, 825, 865, 948
9.(i)	245, 425, 693, 697
9.(ii)	237
10	**23****, 393, 903–904, 924
11	821, 1015
13	309, 458
14*	224
15	9, 31, 41, 173
16	532
18	420, 461, 489, 512, 573, 1114, 1157, 1198, 1259, 1282, 1818, 1820

* German paragraphs appearing in alphabetical order in Volume 6 have been here converted into their English correspondent chapters, such as the German paragraph of Volume 14.(i) into the English Volume 14.
** Bold means the term "intuition"—or associated terms—do not appear in the paragraph.

Table I(2c). English additional index-linking.

Corresponding volumes of the *Gesammelte Werke* and *Collected Works of* C. G. Jung	Paragraphs index-linked only in the English edition
1	168
4	490
5	546
6	118, **143n****, 148*n*, 244, 901
7	107, 151, 270, 296
8	98, 278
10	574
11	246, 784
12	517
13	1–2, 36, 44–45, 59, 208
15	148
16	77*n*, 194, 345
18	33, 110, 779

** Bold means the term "intuition"—or associated terms—do not appear in the paragraph.

APPENDIX II: CW AND GW 6, INDEXING OF "-INTUITION" IN CHAPTER TWO

Table II(1). Compared index-linking of CW and GW 6, Chapter 2

	Index linking of Volume 6, Chapter 2 paragraphs 101 to paragraph 222	Corresponding names of the entries and sub-entries of the index-linked paragraphs***
Paragraphs index-linked in both German and English editions	103	G. *Intuition—bei Goethe* E. Intuition—in Schiller
	104	G. *Intuitivismus* E. Intuition—in Schiller
	117	G. *Intuition—bei Schiller* E. Intuition—in Schiller
	219	G. *Intuition—bei Schiller and—und Objekt* E. Intuition—and object
Paragraphs forgotten in both German and English editions*	169, 188, 192, 211	
Paragraphs index-linked only in the German edition	**123****	*Intuition—bei Schiller*)
	171	*Intuition—bei Schiller*),
	184	*Intuition*
	195	*Intuition—bei Schiller*
Paragraphs index-linked only in the English edition	118	Intuition—in Schiller
	143n**	Intuitive type— extraverted feeling
	148*n*	Intuitive type— introverted thinking)

* "Forgotten" as the term "intuition" or its corollaries appear in the chapter, but are not selected.

** Bold is used when the term "intuition" or its corollaries do not appear in the paragraph selected.

*** G. for German and E. for English.

NOTES

1. In an interview with Ann Casement, Sonu Shamdasani declared that his recent study of the *Red Book* [to publish it] had changed his views on Jung's work (Shamdasani, 2010, p. 35).
2. In this work "esotericism" refers to Antoine Faivre's sixfold paradigm of "a group composed of specific historical currents", which are transversal rather than marginal *vis-à-vis* established religions (Faivre, 1992, p. 7). Kocku von Stuckrad's identification of the "two dimensions of an esotericist discourse, [namely] the claims of higher knowledge and ways of accessing this 'truth'", also fits Jung's approach to the esotericist phenomena as well as Jung's as the creator of new discourses (see Von Stuckrad, 2005a, p. 78).
3. To identify a few of those contributions see Faivre (1992), Hanegraaff (1995), Riffard (2001), Von Stuckrad (2003, 2005a,b). The authors themselves refer to other authors in their works.
4. On Jung's "personal equation" *vis-à-vis* his metapsychological attempt to identify types and functions, see Shamdasani (2003, pp. 72–99). In this work, Shamdasani argued that the personal equation could contradict the generality of types.
5. I have tried, as often as possible, to distinguish between spiritism (that refers to the technique or the experience of sessions) and the religious movement of Spiritualism.

6. As seen earlier, Jung himself has been described as a thinker of the esotericist discipline—notably by Antoine Faivre (Faivre, 1992, p. 10). There is no period of Jung's writing without esotericist work, that is, works about esotericist topics.
7. To protect the privacy of their patients, physicians write of "cases" in order not to mention their names. That Helene Preiswerk was Jung's cousin provoked arguments between the paternal and the maternal side of Jung's family. See the historian Henri Ellenberger's analysis in the section headed "Experiencing intuition through spiritist séances and *Liber Novus*" in Chapter Two.
8. "Images" refers to *Anschauung* and the radical *schauen*, "to see". The nature of the psyche was essentially imaginal for Jung. Yet, we could write of archetypal sounds, tastes, touches, and smells, or write of acts deriving from instincts.
9. On Jung's use of Lévy-Bruhl's expression, see Segal (2007, pp. 635–658).
10. Jung follows the tenets of the Romantics and of the *Naturphilosophie*. See Todorov, 1982[1977].
11. See, notably, the first part of Jung's [1911] *Wandlungen und Symbole der Libido* in Jung [1917] *CW B*. The constructive method first appeared in Jung's (1916) *La structure de l'inconscient*.
12. Individuation is a never-ending process. An individuated person would be, following Jung's view, a Chinese wise man, or Nietzsche's _bermensch, for instance, who would be in possession of a form of intuition that we call empathy (3) (see Figure 2 in Chapter Three and Part V. Empathy (3) is the intuition contained in synchronicity, as is described by Jung in his later work in relation to his notion of Self, or the archetype of wholeness (and not that of perfection). Psychologically, the consciousness of the Chinese wise man or that of the "Overhuman" would not be equivalent to the collective unconscious, but his consciousness would have access to it through intuition, that is, through the archetypes of intuition. On Jung's reading and use of Nietzsche regarding wholeness, see Huskinskon (2004). On intuition and synchronicity, see Pilard (2010).
13. See, notably, the further references to Emilii Medtner, Antonia Wolff, and Maria Moltzer.
14. About the various kinds of Jung's biographies, see Shamdasani's *Jung Stripped Bare by His Biographers, Even*. The title announces the author's point of view on the poor exactitude of the establishment of facts so far.
15. I thank Sonu Shamdasani for his loan of Medtner's (1923) *Über die sogenannte "Intuition", die ihr angrenzenden Begriffe und die an sie anknüpfenden Probleme. Vorgetragen im Psychologischen Klub, Zürich*

MDCCCCCIXX von Emil Medtner (Moscow; Zürich, Musagetes). Moltzer wrote two lectures published and introduced by Sonu Shamdasani in Shamdasani (1998c).

16. Jaffé's (1963[1958]) *Apparitions and Precognitions* contains a foreword by Jung and it is a strict Jungian explanation of intuitive phenomena, such as Jaffé's (1979) *Apparitions: An Archetypal Approach to Death, Dreams and Ghosts*. Jung might not have been as cautious as Jaffé in her analysis.
17. It is appropriate here to indicate that, so far, I have never come across any definition of intuition in a Jungian glossary. Jung gives a proper definition of intuition in 1921, which we will examine in detail in Chapter Two.
18. Christian McMillan's PhD, undertaken at Essex University through the Centre for Psychoanalytic Studies, is co-directed by Matt ffytche and Roderick Main, himself a specialist in Jung on synchronicity. The final title of the thesis, which will take place in November 2014, is "The 'Image of Thought' in Jung's Whole Self: a critical study".
19. *Liber Novus* had not been published when I began this work. My analysis of that *Summa* will evolve, or, at least, gain in depth in the future.
20. McGuire writes, p. 123, "On March 20, 1947, the contracts between Kegan Paul and the Foundation was signed in Washington … Kegan Paul was in charge of the editorial preparation, Bollingen paid the bill".
21. Sonu Shamdasani is the general editor and co-founder of the Philemon Foundation, the goal of which is to bring to publication all of the works of C. G. Jung.
22. The German as well as English entries for "intuition", "intuitive", and "intuitive types" have been collected here. For the sake of clarity, the tables concerning other German entries linked to intuition, the translation of which could not appear in the English index (because the terms are untranslatable), have been excluded. Complex cross-checking has confirmed the analysis proposed in my indices that *concerning intuition* German-writing editors tend to favour Jung's psychology of intuition, whereas English-writing editors tend to favour Jung's psychology of consciousness.
23. By German, I mean German language, but I refer to the Swiss indexing. By English, I mean English language, and I refer to the Anglo-American editing of the *General Index*. This comparison could not be done with French and Italian languages: there is no French collected works by Jung and the Italian *C. G. Jung Opere* do not contain either a general index or the corresponding chapters that link English and German works. Concerning Jung's bibliography and the correspondences of his work between languages, see the systematic work of Juliette Vieljeux (2004).

24. The German independent entries *"Intuitionismus"* and *"Intuitivismus"* are assembled under the German subject entry *"Intuition"* (in the English index, they fall under the word entry "Intuition"). The general indexation (volume 20) refers to corresponding English and German paragraphs. Each volume's indices refer to pages. English *Volume 19* and German *Band 19* featured C. G. Jung's general bibliography, outdated now.
25. To be more precise, whereas the German *Gesamtregister* index links the definition of intuition to Volume 8, paragraph 269 of the *Gesammelte Werke*, the English *General Index* guides the reader to the paragraphs 770–773 of Volume 6 of the *Collected Works* (see Appendix I, Table 1: German and English paragraphs overlap).
26. After eight virtually identical reprintings of the book, Jung decided in the 1940s to revise the set of definitions for the ninth edition. But in a "letter to Rascher of 1 February 1949", reports Bishop, "Jung wrote that he had in fact decided not to undertake the promised 'Umarbeitung' [re-engineering]", for the task required to be carried out for years to come and because Jung ultimately wanted to leave the book in its old form, much to Rascher's regret. Instead, new entries were added and "intuition" is not one of them. See Bishop (1998a, p. 264).
27. Jung 1950[1921], CW., 6, pars 672–844, pars 770–773 for the entry "Intuition".
28. Jung's comparison stems from his debate with Emilii Medtner, see Part V, section headed "Genesis: *Psychological Types* and the Zürich Club".
29. See Shamdasani (2005), Chapter Three in particular, and Pilard (2010, pp. 69–79).
30. Bishop (1998a, pp. 269–272). In the 1950s, the Genevan Editions du Mont Blanc titled *L'Homme à la découverte de son âme*, the foreword was styled "Foreword and *translation*" by R. Cahen. In the 1960s, the editor, Payot, changed it to "Foreword and *adaptation*". In the 1980s, the Parisian publisher Albin Michel added "entirely *revised*". See, too, Huskinson (2013, pp. 64–80).
31. Kirsch (2000, p. 158) specifies that Cahen-Salabelle was analysed by Jung.
32. In Jung (1951[1943], p. 18, translated for this edition):

> Pour notre compte, nous nous sommes efforcé d'apporter une traduction à la fois fidèle et souple. La pensée de l'auteur s'exprime souvent en de tels raccourcis que pour en rendre la 'substantifique moelle' il faut un peu l'expliciter, la commenter. Nous nous sommes efforcé de ne transcrire aucune pensée, si

complexe et profonde soit-elle, sans la revêtir d'une expression qui puisse être immédiatement accessible au lecteur cultivé. Quand nous nous heurtions à une difficulté de traduction, nous nous demandions: 'comment aurions-nous dit cela en français,', 'comment les choses se passent-elles dans la réalité et la pratique analytique?', et la solution linguistique jaillissait.

33. Jung, 1951[1943], pp. 18–19. Translated for this edition from the French:

Si Jung ne s'est jamais piqué d'être écrivain, nous ne sommes devenu traducteur que par nécessité, pour aider à une meilleure connaissance de l'âme humaine, à une compréhension approfondie des malades et de leur conscience malheureuse et troublée ... la rénovation médicale et sociale promue par la psychologie médicale moderne doit triompher. C'est pourquoi, nous semble-t-il, il faut oser. Car la psyché humaine tolère mal de végéter.

34. Jung, *GW 6*, par. 834 (Rascher) and Jung, *GW 6*, par. 754 (Walter). Because of the alphabetical order of the entries, there cannot be any correspondence with the English paragraphs.
35. Letter from Jung to Michael Fordham of 18 April 1948 (Shamdasani, 2007, p. 184).
36. Jung, *GW 20*, p. 101. Two other sub-entries (*–Zielrichtung der* ("the aim of" the *Einfälle*), and *Einfallsreihen* ("chains of associations") have been removed here for the sake of clarity. They will be dealt with in Part II, Chapter Four, section headed "Intuition from pathological *Einfälle* to general *Einfall*".
37. My derivation of the adjective "imaginal" from Henry Corbin's concept of the imaginal will not be discussed further. It is useful mainly in this context of defining terms outside of their contexts as a first approach. This imaginal nature can arguably be challenged by Jung's late hypothesis of the objective psyche in place of that of the collective unconscious.
38. Jung, *CW 6*, pars 808–811. Jung was particularly interested in the privileged relationship that the Catholics had maintained with Mary and highly valorised it in a late work, *Answer to Job*, in Jung, *CW 11*, pars 552–758. Jung also studied the psychology of the Eucharist, seeing a religious analogue in the link of faith between the Christians and the body of Christ and the intuitive and instinctive link between a human being and the archetype. See, notably, Jung, *CW 6*, pars 96–100 on the controversy about the Holy Communion between Zwingli and Luther, and, more broadly, on sacrifice, Jung, *CW 11*, pars 296–448.

39. I italicised "personally" to emphasise the fact that what is reached is not the archetype in itself, but the archetypal image or the pattern. The archetype in itself, derived from Kant's *Ding an sich*, is a mere concept.
40. Jung, for instance, in *CW17*, par. 198, explains that "for the practical work of dream analysis one needs a special knack and intuitive understanding [*Einfühlung*]".
41. By "metapsychology", I refer to Jung's notion of the objective psyche. *Psychological Types* was a metapsychological attempt, which led to emphasising the "personal equation" (see Shamdasani, 2003, pp. 29–87) of any psychology. Synchronicity can be read as a hypothetical alternative.
42. Jung also describes empathy in aesthetics in *CW 6*, pars 484–504.
43. A complex is the pathological archetype analogue, however mild the pathology is. Normal people have complexes. The goal of analytical psychology is not the exploration of archetypes inside (provided that these are "inside"), but psychological progression. This is why Jung employed the terms archetypes and complexes as theoretical equivalents.
44. Jung, *CW 6*, pars 770–773. (The third sentence has been modified thanks to the German original. The English reads, "Everything, whether outer or inner objects or their relationships, can be the focus of this perception." The object of the focus is too important to be presented in a dependent clause within commas.) The German (*GW 6*, pars 834–835) reads,

> *Intuition* (von intueri-anschauen) ist nach meiner Auffassung eine psychologische Grundfunktion. Die I. ist diejenige psychologische Funktion, welche Wahrnehmungen *auf unbewusstem Wege* vermittelt. Gegenstand dieser Wahrnehmung kann alles sein, äussere und innere Objekte oder deren Zusammenhänge. Das Eigentümliche der I. ist, dass sie weder Sinnesempfindung, noch Gefühl, noch intellektueller Schluss ist, obschon sie auch in diesen Formen auftreten kann. Bei der I. präsentiert sich irgend ein Inhalt als fertiges Ganzes, ohne dass wir zunächst fähig wären, anzugeben oder herauszufinden, auf welche Weise dieser Inhalt zustande gekommen ist. Die I. ist eine Art instinktiven Erfassens, gleichviel welcher Inhalte. Sie ist, wie die *Empfindung*, eine *irrationale* Wahrnehmungsfunktion. Ihre Inhalte haben, wie die der Empfindung, den Charakter der Gegebenheit, im Gegensatz zu dem Charakter des "Abgeleiteten", "Hervorgebrachten" der Gefühls- und Denkinhalte. Die intuitive Erkenntnis hat daher ihren Charakter von Sicherheit und Gewissheit, der SPINOZA vermochte, die "scientia intuitiva" für die höchste Form der Erkenntnis zu halten.* Die I. hat diese Eigenschaft mit der

Empfindung gemein, deren physische Grundlage Grund und Ursache ihrer Gewissheit ist. Ebenso beruht die Gewissheit der I. auf einem bestimmten psychischen Tatbestand, dessen Zustandekommen und Bereitsein aber unbewusst war. Die I. tritt auf in *subjektiver* oder *objektiver* Form; erstere ist eine Wahrnehmung unbewusster psychischer Tatbestände, die wesentlich subjektiver Provenienz sind, letzere eine Wahrnehmung von Tatbeständen, die auf subliminalen Wahrnehmungen am Objekte und auch durch sie veranlassten subliminalen Gefühlen und Gedanken beruhen. Es sind auch *konkrete* und *abstrakte* Formen der I. zu unterscheiden, je nach dem Grade der Mitbeteiligung der Empfindung. Die konkrete I. vermittelt Wahrnehmungen, welche die Tatsächlichkeit der Dinge betreffen, die abstrakte I. dagegen vermittelt die Wahrnehmung ideeller Zusammenhänge. Die konkrete I. ist ein reaktiver Vorgang, indem sie aus gegebenen Tatbeständen ohne weiteres erfolgt. Die abstrakte I. dagegen benötigt, wie die abstrakte Empfindung, eines gewissen Richtungselementes, eines Willens oder einer Absicht.

Die I. ist neben der Emfindung ein Charakteristikum der infantilen und primitiven Psychologie. Sie vermittelt dem Kinde und dem Primitiven gegenüber dem stark hervortretenden Empfindunseindruck die Wahrnehmung der mythologischen Bilder, der Vorstufen der *Ideen*. Die I. verhält sich kompensierend zur Empfindung und ist, wie die Empfindung, die Mutterstätte, von wo sich Denken und Fühlen als rationale Funktionen entwickeln. Die I. ist eine irrationale Funktion, obschon viele I. nachträglich in ihre Komponenten zerlegt werden können, und somit auch ihr Zustandekommen mit den Vernunftgesetzen in Einklang gebracht werden kann. Jemand, der seine allgemeine Einstellung nach dem Prinzip der I., also nach Wahrnehmungen über das Unbewusste orientiert, gehört zum *intuitive Typus*.** Je nach der Verwertung der I. nach innen, ins Erkennen oder innere Anschauen, oder nach aussen ins Handeln und Ausführen kann man introvertierte und extravertierte Intuitive unterscheiden. In abnormen Fällen tritt eine starke Verschmelzung mit und eine ebenso grosse Bedingtheit durch Inhalte des kollektiven Unbewussten zu Tage, wodurch der intuitive Typus äussert irrational und unbegreiflich erscheinen kann.

*Ähnlich BERGSON.

**Das Verdienst, die Existenz dieses Typus entdeckt zu haben, gebührt M. Moltzer.

45. Jung, *CW A*, pars 1–142. Jung opposes materialism with both the scientific study of the immaterial and Spiritualism, the belief in spirits.
46. By "occult", I am referring to Jung's expression "occult phenomena", which he used to title his MD dissertation written in 1902, yet based on experiences that are contemporary to the Zofingia Lectures. Under the umbrella term "occult" (Latin "hidden, secret"), Jung describes practices more than theories. For a complete definition, see Hanegraaff (2006).
47. Von Franz emphasises in her introduction how Jung felt lonely and misunderstood in his student years and, therefore, by his audience. Thus, she dismisses the possibility that further discussions following the talks with the members of the club could have been of use to Jung. This statement is also at odds with Jung's mention during his second lecture that a previous "first-rate talk" devoted to hypnotism had taken place before his own. See Jung, *CW A*, par. 125.
48. Patrick Vandermeersch writes, "In those days, there was nothing peculiar about such a topic. Somnambulistic states were then a privileged field of study and phenomena such as table-turning and spiritism were not uncommon" (Vandermeersch, 1991, p. 45).
49. Hence my differentiation between Spiritualism (the religious movement) and spiritist séances (the practice by either believers or scientists, or amateurs). In French-speaking continental Europe, Spiritualism becomes *spiritisme*.
50. Jung mentions "Papa DuBois-Reymond" and von Franz adds a note to explain that DuBois-Reymond founded the modern science of electrophysiology, which in turn had a huge impact on psychology against vitalistic theories (Jung, *CW A*, par. 14*n*).
51. The birth of psychology as a science has been traced at various moments of history. In his *Discovery of the Unconscious*, Ellenberger (1970) proposes the shift (from religion) occurred with Franz Anton Mesmer, soon followed by his disciple, the Marques of Puységur, Shamdasani elects Wundt and W. James the popes of the discipline in his *Jung and the Dream of Modern Psychology: The Dream of a Science* (2003). In both cases, as elsewhere (see, for instance, Carroy (1991), we observe chronological turning from the immaterial study of the psyche (such as Puységur and James) to the material study of the psyche (such as Mesmer and Wundt), or the other way around. This confrontation forms a regulating debate of the discipline, of its schools and personalities. It has various implications (see Chapter Four, section headed "Associations: between Janet and Freud"), from the most general to the most technical. As did many psychologists, Jung aimed at conciliating matter and spirit.

52. A third branch was devised by Wundt to deal with issues of individual psychology, that of ethnopsychology, or *Völkerpsychologie*.
53. This approach was later challenged in favour of a post-critical reading of *Dream*.
54. Using the list of books that Jung borrowed from the University of Basel as a student, a list established by Sonu Shamdasani, Eugene Taylor quotes Johann Passavant, who wrote on animal magnetism, Du Prel, and Carl Eschenmayer, who wrote on "demon possession, mysticism, and the supernatural, as did Joseph Görres, while Justinus Kerner had described the *Seeress of Prevorst*" (Taylor, 2012). All these readings confirm that Jung knew not only the contemporary context of the "immaterial", but also its history.
55. "Contre le spiritisme" was the title of Vogt's third and last paper during the conference. See Vogt (1901a, p. 656). The original text of Piéron's report is:

> Théodore Flournoy, à propos de sa belle analyse du langage dit 'martien' du medium Hélène Smith, fut appelé à parler avec tact du spiritisme dans une des séances générales, mais des spirites trop convaincus intervinrent dans une section que présidait le Nancéen Bernheim, intitulée 'Hypnotisme, suggestion et questions connexes' et ils provoquèrent de vives réactions : Hebinghaus se déclara 'scandalisé' et Oskar Vogt éleva une protestation énergique 'contre le spiritisme'.

Flournoy's work will be analysed in more detail later.
56. See, for instance, Oskar Vogt, "Valeur de l'hypnotisme comme moyen d'investigation psychologique", *IIe Congrès International de l'Hypnotisme* (Paris, 1900), Paris, Vigot, 1902. Vogt was German and trained at the University of Jena, but his wife, Cécile Vogt-Mugnier, was a French neurologist.
57. In the original French, Flournoy's comments are:

> ... études si compromettantes, comme chacun sait, qu'on n'en parle volontiers qu'à mots couverts, et qu'un Congrès qui se respecte, tel que le nôtre, lorsqu'il ne réussit pas à leur fermer complètement sa porte, les dissimule prudemment sous l'ingénieuse rubrique des *Questions connexes*. Nul plus que moi n'admire l'art délicat de sauver les apparences. Mais puisque nous sommes entre nous, vous me pardonnerez d'appeler un chat un chat et d'avouer que sous les questions connexes se dérobent en réalité le spiritisme, l'occultisme et autres bêtes noires de la psychologie scientifique contemporaine.

58. In his foreword to Flournoy's *From India to the Planet Mars* (1994), Shamdasani describes the shift of the subject of science from the medium to the child. See also Carroy (1991).
59. Jung's MD dissertation copied Flournoy's *From India*. Jung's *Psychology of the Unconscious* started from Flournoy and from Miller's article "Quelques faits d'imagination créatrice", published in 1906.
60. Falzeder attributes the failure of psychoanalysis to reach academia and psychiatry in Europe to Freud's failure to convince Bleuler—rather than anybody else, Jung included—of his "cause" (itself defended as "truth" by Freud's followers).
61. Morality was at the centre of Janet's work, such as in Janet (2007[1919]).
62. I refer here to Carroy (1991), a historical work on "the subjects of science", which triggered this crucial identity issue. I am differentiating this issue from the other, arguably close, of the nicknames given to patients in order to protect their actual identity.
63. I agree with Falzeder's view that both Bleuler and Freud—rather than just Freud—were spiritual fathers to Jung and that it must have been hard for Jung to find his own way as someone different from both men (see Falzeder & Beebe, 2007, p. 363).
64. For a brief historical account of dissociation psychology, see Haule, 1984, pp. 635–639. Haule reminds us that if—as Jung announces in *CW 7*, par. 76—Freud wrote of "split-off ideas", it was to reframe them from an associationist point of view.
65. Jung wrote his dissertation once he was employed at the Burghölzli hospital under Bleuler's direction. Bleuler had no prejudice towards the scientific study of spiritist mediums.
66. Jung (1961 in German/1988), p. 379. The text was translated into English by Shamdasani in Flournoy (1994[1899], p. ix). In 1966, the text was translated into French by Cahen-Salabelle, and was published in Jung (1966[1961]. Analyst Joan Chodorow recalls (Chodorow, 1997, p. 7) one quotation by Jung concerning the relationship between analysand and analyst: "The English verb, 'to look at', does not convey this meaning, but the German *betrachten*, which is an equivalent, means also to make pregnant".
67. Bergson's original text reads,

> Ce qui caractérise la psychologie scientifique française, c'est qu'elle s'appuie surtout sur la pathologie tandis que la psychologie allemande s'attache davantage aux recherches de laboratoire et aux mensurations pratiquées sur des personalités normales.

68. Moskowitz, Schäfer, and Dorah propose the possibility of Jung distorting reality to please Freud in that instance (Moskowitz, Schäfer, and Dorahy, 2009, p. 46). I disagree, and believe that Jung was truly disappointed.
69. See, for instance, Jung's letters in French written to Edouard Clarapède (archives of the University of Geneva). Jung's French mistakes are infrequent, yet, when he was very busy, as was the case at the Burghölzli, he wrote to his Swiss colleague in German (see, notably, Jung's letter to Claparède of 22 January 1906).
70. Jung (1897), *Handschriften und Autographen der ETH - Bibliothek, C. G. Jung Manuskripte*, HS 1055:1a, "*Spiritische Experimente*", p. 1, translated for this edition. Jung also names the participants: "Walze, Fex, Icarus, Stengel, Joseph [and then another participant, the name of whom I could not read, perhaps Kneipp, or some indication about Fex]".
71. In the first of the *Zofingia Lectures*, Jung also promotes curiosity as an adequate attitude: "no doubt all of us asked ourselves questions whose import transcends the confines of any single discipline and which must be of the most vital interest to every educated person" (Jung, CW A, par. 12).
72. Jung (1897), *Handschriften und Autographen der ETH - Bibliothek, C. G. Jung Manuskripte*, HS 1055:1a, "*Spiritische Experimente*", p. 2.
73. Jung (1897), *Handschriften und Autographen der ETH - Bibliothek, C. G. Jung Manuskripte*, HS 1055:1a, "*Spiritische Experimente*", p. 2. Jung writes, "Walze: 2 maliges neigen soll Ja 3 maliges Nein bedeuten".
74. Ibid., p. 1, translated for this edition. I could not read the exact "message" of the "spirit"; therefore, I relied on Walze's explanation pp. 3, 4.
75. Jung (1897), *Handschriften und Autographen der ETH - Bibliothek, C. G. Jung Manuskripte*, HS 1055:1a, "*Spiritische Experimente*", p.1, translated for this edition. I could not read the exact "message" of the "spirit"; therefore, I relied on Walze's explanation.
76. Jung (1897), *Handschriften und Autographen der ETH - Bibliothek, C. G. Jung Manuskripte*, HS 1055:1a, "*Spiritische Experimente*", p. 4.
77. Jung (1897), *Handschriften und Autographen der ETH - Bibliothek, C. G. Jung Manuskripte*, HS 1055:1a, "*Spiritische Experimente*", p. 5, translated for this edition, and Holy Bible New Century Version (which gives a whole sentence instead of just one part in the Revised Standard Version).
78. Von Franz specifies:

> David Friedrich Strauss, Protestant theologian and author of an influential *Life of Jesus*, included reviews of the books of the

spiritualist physician Justinus Kerner about Kerner's observations of a woman who saw and conversed with benign and malign spirits and produced knocking and other phenomena of the "poltergeist" type in the presence of witnesses. (Jung, *CW A*, par. 73*n*)

79. See Jung, *CW 18*, pars 697–740; McGuire (1974)[1909], p. 215, Letter 138J; McGuire (1989)[1925], pp. 3–12; *CW 18*, pars 746–756; Adler & Jaffé (1973)[1946], p. 432; *CW 8*, pars 570–600; *CW 18*, pars 757–781; *CW 18*, pars 782–789; Jung (1995)[1961/1963], p. 155.
80. Zumstein-Preiswerk, S., *Stefanie Zumstein-Preiswerk. Materialen zu "C. G. Jungs Medium. Die Geschichte der Helly Preiswerk." Munschen 1975*, Wissenschaftshistorische Sammlungen der ETH-Bibliothek, 1991.
81. Zumstein-Preiswerk, S., *Stefanie Zumstein-Preiswerk. Materialen zu "C. G. Jungs Medium. Die Geschichte der Helly Preiswerk." Munschen 1975*, Wissenschaftshistorische Sammlungen der ETH-Bibliothek, 1991, p. 7.
82. Zumstein-Preiswerk, S., *Stefanie Zumstein-Preiswerk. Materialen zu "C. G. Jungs Medium. Die Geschichte der Helly Preiswerk." Munschen 1975*, Wissenschaftshistorische Sammlungen der ETH-Bibliothek, 1991, p. 8.
83. Zumstein-Preiswerk, S., *Stefanie Zumstein-Preiswerk. Materialen zu "C. G. Jungs Medium. Die Geschichte der Helly Preiswerk." Munschen 1975*, Wissenschaftshistorische Sammlungen der ETH-Bibliothek, 1991. When published in 1975, *C. G. Jungs Medium* had a Foreword by Heinrich Balmer. Henry Ellenberger must have allowed the publisher, Kindler, to use his name and one key sentence from *Die Entdeckung des Unbewußten* (The Discovery of the Unconscious), pointing to the significance of Jung's experiments with his cousin for analytical psychology, for the cover of the book.
84. Zumstein-Preiswerk, S., *Stefanie Zumstein-Preiswerk. Materialen zu "C. G. Jungs Medium. Die Geschichte der Helly Preiswerk." Munschen 1975*, Wissenschaftshistorische Sammlungen der ETH-Bibliothek, 1991, pp. 11–13.
85. In Bellini's opera, Amina is about to marry the man she loves, Elvino, in their village. Caught in the room of another man, she tries to explain to Elvino that she was in a somnambulistic state. Everybody believes her, except for Elvino, who will need to witness Amina in a dangerous position on a bridge while in a state of somnambulism to trust her. All opera libretti are not that simple, but this one reveals how the "story" is never all that opera is about, but merely a part of a much greater whole.
86. Because the book is the experience itself, its content will be studied in later chapters. Sonu Shamdasani's footnotes in *The Red Book* clarify the correspondences with the *Black Books*.

87. The *Gesamtregister* indicates where Jung refers in the *GW* to "unterbewusst das Unterbewusste (Unterbewusstsein), and unterbewusste" (gen.). Nineteen entries appear. This number might seem important compared, for instance, with the entry "Bergson", which only counts fourteen entries. Yet, the entry "unterbewusst" must instead be compared, for example, to the entry "unbewusst" (unconscious), which contains more than a hundred times the number of the entry "unterbewusst". Here are the entries: *GW 2*, pars 323, 330, 451; *GW 4*, pars 576, 619; *GW 5*, par. 670; *GW 8*, pars 352, 362, 369, 383, 385; *GW 9i*, pars 40, 433; *GW 11*, pars 769, 775; *GW 18*, pars 16, 798, 818, 893. See Jung (1994), *GW 20*, p. 457.
88. The extract from Richet's report on the First International Congress of Psychology in the original French:

> *Inconscience*: Etat de l'esprit dans lequel il n'y a pas de conscience, c'est-à-dire où les actes et idées ne sont pas perçues par le *moi*, ou bien s'effacent de la mémoire au fur et à mesure qu'elles se manifestent. Le travail intellectuel qui préside à ces actes est probablement de même nature que le travail intellectuel conscient. Il peut y avoir des *consciences multiples* qui coïncident chez le même individu, c'est-à-dire des *personalités multiples* ; ces consciences multiples peuvent être successives ou simultanées. Dans ce cas, il y a une inconscience partielle et non totale. L'état d'inconscience totale est d'état de fatalité psychologique ; car la délibération suppose la conscience, c'est-à-dire la simultanéité dans l'esprit de plusieurs idées qui peuvent se balancer et se combattre.

89. Janet preferred the term subconscious to unconscious, but he described *several* subconscious states through the dissociated states of his patients in *L'automatisme psychologique*. Freud differentiated unconscious from the intermediary area he called the preconscious, central in his shift in 1923 to the tripartite model of the mind. See Sandler, Holder, Dare, et al. (1997). Myers and Flournoy both used the term "subliminal", but Flournoy equated it with both "subconscious" and "unconscious" and, to a great extent, with "conscious". See Flournoy, 1994[1899], p. 9.
90. Janet presented the same text (revised) the following year at the VIth International Congress of Psychology in Geneva, 3–7 August 1909. The extract is translated for this edition from the French:

> Les études sur l'inconscient sont fort anciennes : ce sont des études de métaphysique sur la possibilité d'une intelligence

différente de l'intelligence humaine, indépendante de la conscience et de ses conditions telles que nous les constatons en nous-mêmes. Les recherches sur *le subconscient* sont au contraire beaucoup plus récentes : ce sont des études purement psychologiques qui ont pris naissance à propos des difficultés que soulevait l'interprétation de certains troubles mentaux tout particuliers. Le mot 'subconscient' si l'on s'en tient à la signification que je lui donnais quand j'en ai proposé l'usage en 1889, se borne à résumer les caractères singuliers que présentent à l'observateur certains troubles de la personnalité.

91. Both Bergson and Janet remained lifelong high school teachers of philosophy. Students entering the Ecole Normale Supérieure sign a contract, which stipulates that their studies are paid and that, in return, they have to teach once their studies are over. Janet was the author of books of philosophy for high school students, such as Janet (1902).
92. The extract from Bergson's letter in the original French reads,

Il faut d'abord mettre à part la psychologie, qui s'est constituée en science indépendante et qui ne veut se solidariser avec aucun système philosophique. Elle est représentée principalement par Ribot, Pierre Janet, Binet, Dumas, etc. ; elle a ses revues spéciales et ses chaires spéciales. Ce qui caractérise la psychologie scientifique française, c'est qu'elle s'appuie surtout sur la pathologie tandis que la psychologie allemande s'attache davantage aux recherches de laboratoire et aux mensurations pratiquées sur des personnalités normales.

93. Janet's text is available in French online at: http://classiques.uqac.ca/classiques/janet_pierre/janet_pierrehtml.
94. The British definition of "hysteria" given by the *Encyclopedia Britannica* was reported in Myers (1903) and read, "A disordered condition of the nervous system, the anatomical seat and nature of which are *unknown to medical science*, but of which the symptoms consist in well-marked and very varied disturbances of nerve-function" (p. xviii, my italics). The physical origin of hysteria for Charcot was, by contrast, taken for granted.
95. One of Ellenberger's sources is Myers, who writes, "Mesmerism foreshadowed hypnotic suggestion and psycho-therapeutics" (1903, p. xxiv).
96. "Dissolutive" meant decay, "evolutive" progress (italics added to link "subliminal" to "sublime").

97. The dichotomy that is emphasised here does not prevent the actual convergences between animal magnetism, on the one hand, and magnetic sleep, on the other. "A number of representatives of German romantic *Naturphilosophen* eventually came to see the cornerstone of the 'physico-psycho-spiritual' structure of the human being as they imagined it", writes Faivre (2008, p. 192, translated for this edition).
98. Sociologist Bertrand Méheust proposes the differentiation between hypnologists (*hypnologues*) and magnetists, on the one hand, and psychists and psychologists, on the other, as a strong dynamic in the history of "the unconscious". Through this, he aims to acknowledge and continue Ellenberger's work on the "discovery–history of the unconscious". See Méheust (1999, vol. 1, pp. 122–124). Likewise, Borch-Jacobsen differentiates between "allopathic" (hypnotists who want to eradicate the trance and its origin, hysteria) and "homeopathic", "traditional" approaches, which cultivate the content of the trance. See Borch-Jacobsen in Chertok (1971, p. 211, quoted by Shamdasani in Flournoy (1994[1899], p. xxiii).
99. Myers (1890, p. 191), reviewing Janet's book, in Shamdasani (1993, p. 129).
100. Myers (1884, pp. 218–219), in Shamdasani (1993, p. 129).
101. Concerning the primitive period influenced by the French philosopher turned anthropologist Lucien Lévy-Bruhl, see Segal (2007, pp. 635–658).
102. Jung's *Answer to Job* can be read as the confrontation with the Godhead (for both Shamdasani and Bishop).
103. Bergson's influence on Jung with regard to Bergson's notion of vital impetus on Jung's dynamics of the unconscious is to be found in Jung's *On Psychic Energy* (*CW 8*, pars 1–130).
104. Jung was particularly interested in this state through his study of Eastern wisdom. In the Foreword to *The Psychology of Kundalini Yoga. Notes of the Seminar given in 1932* (2001b), Shamdasani writes, "Kundalini Yoga presented Jung with . . . an account of the developmental phases of higher consciousness".
105. Mancini & Faivre (2012).
106. They were only privately published in 1916.
107. Jung's letter to Alphonse Maeder, who psychologically acknowledged prognostic dreams in 1912, is dated 19 January 1917.
108. Flournoy reuses the term "automatist" to describe Hélène Smith.
109. On this topic, see Faivre (2003).
110. For example in the medieval list of the *Manual of Astral Magic* (Kieckhefer) (see Tanger, 2006, p. 622).

260　NOTES

111. We remember that grandfather Preiswerk believed his daughter, Jung's mother, was gifted with second sight. The verb "afflicted" was frequently associated with intuition by Jung, who, intuitive himself, considered intuition to be "a curse and a gift".
112. Offering a sociological, psychological, or historical motive for the belief in any irrational phenomena (such as communication with the dead) would not prove the existence or non-existence of the phenomenon itself. To use the familiar expression, the "genetic fallacy" would consist here in mistaking what has been offered as the motive for the proof of the non-existence of the phenomenon.
113. This is Kuehn's translation from the German (2001, p. 172). The first English translator of Kant used, rather, a "free rendering of the German, the outspokenness of which [wa]s hardly bearable in English". He thus preferred "holy inspirations ... simply caused by a disordered stomach" in Kant (1900[1766], p. 84).
114. Du Prel's "non-antagonist" or "mystical" reading of *Dreams*, commonly held in Jung's time, was based on Kant's favourable review of Swedenborg's work in his *Lectures on Metaphysics* (1788). Im (2011, pp. 72–73), reminds us that there Kant writes: "The thought of Swedenborg is in this quite sublime. He says the spiritual world constitutes a special real universe ... Now when the hindrance of sensible intuition is once removed, then we see ourselves in this spiritual world" (104–105/1928: 298–299). "Yet," writes Im, "[scholar] Lind attempts to reject the view that Kant's opinion of Swedenborg in the *Lectures* is not different from that in *Dreams* [and thus Kant's tone is there too ironic]".
115. In German, Jung, 1961, p. 101.
116. In 1966, the Congress on the Origins of Gnosticism in Messina examined the criteria and the terms common to the various forms of Gnosticism to establish a definition of the religion of knowledge.
117. *Ahnungen* and *Vorahnungen* are equivalent in meaning.
118. Jeromson quotes Jung, *CW 13*, par. 31*n* and par. 37.
119. Shamdasani also quotes Jung, *CW 9(i)*, par. 691.
120. Roderick Main quotes the *Terry Lectures* in Jung, *CW 11*, pars 3–168.
121. For Otto's and Jung's distinctive uses of the term, read Huskinson, 2006, pp. 200–212.
122. LR stands for *Livre Rouge* and RB for *Red Book*. Translated for this edition from the French:

> L'expression même de 'l'à-venir' (*das Kommende*) et de sa voie (*der Weg des Kommenden*) est bien distincte de celle, plus commune, de 'l'avenir' (*die Zukunft*), présente elle aussi dans les textes du *Livre*

Rouge, même si elles sont bien en rapport l'une avec l'autre. Et de fait elles apparaissent parfois comme antinomiques : l'avenir, au sens d'une représentation du futur, n'est pas ce qui intéresse le locuteur du *Livre Rouge*. Il faut, dit-il, 'le laisser à ceux qui sont de l'avenir' (LR, p. 306). Il ne s'agit pas de se projeter dans un futur, objet de toutes les attentes, au détriment de l'instant présent, mais de revenir à l'essentiel : 'Je retourne dans la petitesse du réel, car c'est cela le noble chemin, la voie de l'à-venir' (LR, p. 306).

123. C'est à travers le symbole que peut être perçu l'à-venir, ce qui n'est pas encore, mais qui fait déjà l'objet de presentiment intuitif (*Ahnung*), ce sont les symboles qui tracent cette 'voie de l'à-venir', tandis que les signes (Zeichen) n'évoquent que le déjà connu dont le sens est fixé. Aussi le *Livre Rouge* formule-t-il, sous le revêtement poétique qui est le sien, une théorie du symbole qui sera développée dans les *Types Psychologiques*, dont le travail est en préparation durant ces mêmes années. . . . 'Lorsqu'on accepte le symbole, c'est comme si s'ouvrait une porte qui mène dans une nouvelle pièce dont on ignorait l'existence' (LR, p. 311). La 'vie symbolique' dont il est ici question est d'abord celle de l'individu engagé sur la voie que Jung, dans le cadre de sa psychologie, appellera 'individuation', et qui désigne un processus d'émancipation du sujet qui échappe, de ce fait, aux déterminations collectives.

124. This is true even in the secular sense offered by Homans (1979, p. 91), who writes,

> Jung's personal identity as a founder of a new psychology . . . was threefold: psychologist (originator of a new theory and critic of Freud), social critic and moralist (commentator on the predicament of modern man), and prophet (critic of traditional Christianity).

Homans' definition of "prophet" is rather closer to "theologian", or "scholar".

125. I agree with Roderick Main, as we shall see in Part IV, who adds,

> The emphasis here on the positive, prospective tendency of apparently pathological symptoms foreshadows Jung's later ideas on compensation and individuation, while the practice of consciously interacting with fantasy images prefigures his method of active imagination.

126. Jung referred to this paper later, in *CW 7*, par. 252.

127. The C. G. Jung Papers Collection of the ETH Zürich contains the inventory as well as actual studies on association psychology, among which is the original work carried out at the Burghölzli.
128. Aschaffenburg and Kraepelin's distinction corresponds to Categories 1 and 2 of Jung's classification below, and Ziehen's complexes correspond to Jung's complex-constellation-type without concealment, or II (α) (αα) in Jung's summary.
129. Jung indicates that he quotes Munsterberg, 1892, p. 7.
130. This French influence is to be found in Jung's psychodynamics, described in Jung's *On Psychic Energy* as well as in Jung's *Types*, the *fonction du réel* being precisely what intuition lacks and that which the three other functions have. See Gunter, 1982, pp. 650–651.
131. Janet's text in the original French is:

> les opérations psychologiques qui permettent à l'humanité d'entrer en contact avec la réalité, d'agir sur elle, et de saisir son existence avec certitude. La fonction du réel, avec les opérations de la volonté, le sentiment du réel, le sentiment du présent, tient la première place dans la hiérarchie des phénomènes psychologiques.

132. Jacques Lacan was also a student of the Parisian École Normale Supérieure.
133. Whereas intuition as a function, as a link, and, by extension, as a language is always singular, only intuition as a result, that is, when visible, patent, bears the plural.
134. This is a literal translation from the French in Rimbaud, 1895[1870–1871], p. 7 in order to keep the term "latent", which can be linked to the under-conscious state. The French reads: "A noir, E blanc, I rouge, U vert, O bleu: voyelles / Je dirai quelques jours vos naissances latentes".
135. Distraction sometimes led to the failure of the test, since some subjects were simply occupied with the distraction.
136. Jung's theory never refuted Freud's lapsus. But what is for Freud a *missed* deed, which *hides* an unconscious desire, appears to Jung as the *direct* expression of intuition (provided that Jung does not separate personal and collective unconscious, a later achievement: I would not apply the term "intuition" as the link to a complex of the personal unconscious in the way Jung linked the archetype with *Anschauung*, but what appears as historically odd is theoretically defendable.
137. Haule's thought matches that of Shamdasani, who quotes Haule in Shamdasani, 1998b, p. 122.

138. I showed in Pilard, 2010, p. 17 how Jung's work alternates bold hypotheses and strong reservations. It reappears here in the opposite word association tests carried out before 1906 and *Dementia Praecox*, just as previously between the *Zofingia Lectures* and Jung's *So-called Occult Phenomena*.
139. Words composed with *Vorstellung* have been included, such as *Vorstellungablauf*, which is, problematically, not a "process of ideation", or, as we shall see, *Vorstellungsverbindung*, which is not a "combination of ideas", and *Vorstellungsreihe*, which is not a "sequence of ideas" either.
140. The recent publication by Beebe and Falzeder of the Jung–Schmid correspondence of 1915 twice corroborates my point as they notice on page 82, note 117, that "Jung appears to be using representation or imagination (*Vorstellung*, which implies a mental picture) as a synonym for what he came to call the intuitive function in his mature typology" and on page 123, note 209, "again representation [Vorstellung] is being seen as the fourth function beyond feeling, thinking, and sensation: Intuition had not yet been conceived as the name for this function".
141. Jung writes *Dieses schöne Beispiel* ("This beautiful example"). Hull translates "This example". Concerning the other mistranslations see, for instance, pars 24 and 54.
142. We also recognise intuition in the form of *Anschauung* here.
143. Hull translates *flachen* into "superficial" to describe the "course of association".
144. Anagogy is the interpretation of Scriptures to extract their spiritual meaning.
145. It is regrettable that Jung omitted to report the repetitions. The (here sixth) *Einfall*, "is the highest ground-pedestal", will be examined later.
146. If one looks at the table of contents, the section "continuous association" appears as a short sub-section of "A-Wish-fulfilment". In fact, it runs throughout A, B, and C, to stop only before "D-Summary".
147. In 1909, hence probably inspired by these *Machtwörter*, Freud would write of the unconscious power of some word over the patient in his famous case of the "Rat Man" (Freud, 1909d).
148. Hull translates *durch Neuheiten auf allen Gebieten* into [secretly] "on account of novelties of all descriptions" [is unfortunately . . .].
149. Amended by me where Hull translates *Vorstellungen* into "ideas" and *Unter der Konstellation einer Spiritistischen Überzeugung werden leich auch Ansätze zu neuen Sprachen gemacht* into "In mediumnistic circles attempts are sometimes made at inventing new languages".

150. In German, Jung wrote "Oeleum" [oleum]. We might recall how he had also written "wena" [vena]. To avoid confusion, I write "oleum".
151. *A Study of the Transformation and Symbolism of the Libido: A Contribution to the History of the Evolution of Thought* is the title of the 600-page book published in 1917. In 1952, the title becomes *Symbols of Transformation: An Analysis of the Prelude to a Case of Schizophrenia*.
152. Matthew Bell reminds us that Jung quoted Carus twenty-two times in the *CW*. See Bell, 2010, p. 158 (in Nicholls & Liebscher, 2010).
153. We saw that Myers notably worked on telepathy—the term he himself coined in 1882 (see Myers, 1903, p. xxii)—which implies a collective, shared unconscious. See Shamdasani, 1993, p. 111, concerning the agreement between William James and Myers on telepathy and the problematic "boundaries of our individuality" (James' expression in "Notes on automatic writing" (1889).
154. Jung speaks (in a lecture) for the first time of "impersonal or suprapersonal" "collective psyche", "collective mind", and "collective soul" in 1916 in *The Structure of the Unconscious*. See Jung, *CW 7*, par. 456.
155. The root *anschau-* or even *schau-* (*schauen*, "to see") appears elsewhere in Bishop's articles on Jung or on other German-writing authors. Earlier, I defined the "numinous" and its difference from intuition.
156. Germany as a nation was declared after the French defeat in the Franco-Prussian War of 1871. Jung's grandfather, C. G. Jung the elder, was imprisoned for having demonstrated in favour of a united Germany in 1817. See Wehr, 1988, p. 15.
157. The Grimms quote in old German:

    GOETHE (1795–96), *Wilhelm Meisters Lehrjahre (19, 136)*: ich lernte den unterschied zwischen dem gesang der nachtigall und einem hallelujah aus menschenkehlen erst kennen, ich verbarg meine freude über diese neue anschauung meinem oheim nicht.

    KANT (1781), *Kritik der reinen Vernunft (1, 85)*: die anschauung dieser erkentnis ist in der mathematik gröszer als in der weltweisheit. (Translated for this edition and revised by Greg Richter, Department of English and Linguistic, Truman State University, who noted that the Grimms' translation was edited down to exactly what was in the original German.)

158. The representation we have of the object, for Kant, is its "phenomenon". The object in itself is its "noumenon", a limiting concept. Our knowledge of it is, therefore, only negative. A positive knowledge of the noumenon would require the "intellectual intuition" that Kant

characterises as outside of human capacity, as beyond the accessible "sensory intuition". There, Jung introduces his notion of synchronicity, the meeting point, for him, between the noumenon and the phenomenon—or between the archetype and its image—where chance is out of the picture. Kant refutes intellectual intuition, Jung gives examples of its manifestation in his synchronicities, or "meaningful coincidences".

159. The two other synonyms are *aspicere* and *contemplari*. "*Aspicere*: to catch sight of, spot; to look at; to inspect, look over; to look in the eye; to visit; to consider; to picture; *contemplari*: to observe, survey, gaze on, contemplate; *intueri*: to look at, gaze at; to consider, take into consideration; to look up to, have regard for; to keep an eye on, to examine visually, inspect", in Traupman, 1995, pp. 68, 116, 229).
160. Those figures were particularly significant in Jung's psychology of consciousness and, therefore, will be introduced in Part V.
161. Medtner exposed Kant's gnosiology. He did not refute Kant's interest in soteriology, yet linked it to Kant's morals.
162. Letter to Albert Brenner published by Hans Brenner in the Basel *Jahrbuch* in 1901.
163. Jacob Burckhardt taught in Jung's Gymnasium in Basel.
164. This term is different from *Einbildunskraft*, "true imagination", which is linked to Jung's collective unconscious through Goethe's aesthetics for example (see Bishop, 1999, pp. 425, 438). But *Einbildunskraft*, even more than *Anschauung*, exclusively belongs to the German culture. See Faivre, 1996, Volume 1, p. 189). It is noticeable that this is the third time that the prefix "Ein" is strongly linked to intuition in Jung's thought.
165. Jung's "potential" here can be linked to his defintion of intuition in his 1928 essay "The structure of the psyche", in *GW 8*, par. 292: "Intuition, as I conceive it, is one of the basic functions of the psyche, namely perception of the possibilities inherent in a situation". My next example will show this relationship between the archetype and intuition as a potential.
166. Jung compares the archetype with the Platonic Idea in essays that were written as late as 1954, such as in "On the nature of the psyche" (see *CW 8*, par. 388), whereas, for example, the matrix appears in Jung's *Terry Lectures* of 1937 (see *CW 11*, par. 107).
167. Jung's general tribute to Bergson would be slightly less glowing two years later in *Psychological Types* (see Jung, *CW 6*, par. 540). There, Jung writes, "Bergson's method is not intuitive but intellectual". A reader who is familiar with Bergson's philosophy can appreciate Jung's statement, yet Jung's projection is equally appreciable. See my further

comparison between Nietzsche and Bergson on that same issue in Part IV.

168. Medtner writes, "Die Intuition, philogenetisch betrachtet, ist ein unendlich differenzierter Instinkt" (Medtner, 1923, pp. 48–49).

169. Personal correspondence informed me of (1) Mullarkey's link and (2) of a PhD research in progress at Essex University on the topic of the relationship between Jung and Bergson.

170. The *Gesamregister* counts three entries for "Paulhan" (among which two notes) and fifteen for "Bergson".

171. Gunter writes of "a line of influence running from Bergson's through Jung's analytical psychology [a function which] helped Jung in directions in which he was already going". Many minds met in that period. That same clearness Jung had already met with—this time in the flesh—through the philosopher and psychologist William James. In 1909, during his trip to the USA with Freud, Jung reports, in a letter to Virginia Payne of 23 July, that he had been "tremendously impressed by the clearness of his [James'] mind and the complete absence of intellectual prejudices" before adding "my discussions with William James were chiefly about this subject [parapsychology] and about the psychology of religious experience" (Adler & Jaffé, 1973), p. 531). Not only style, therefore, but also content, for Jung, united James and Bergson.

172. Charles Richet considered Franz Mesmer the "initiator" of Mesmerism and his French compatriot Puységur the true "founder" of what is now named hypnotism.

173. In Jung, 1995[1961/1963], p. 178, Jung wrote that Freud "recognised the seriousness of parapsychology".

174. I paraphrase Bergson in *L'évolution créatrice* and use Panero's 2008 first publication and introduction to Bergson's *Cours de psychologie de 1892–1893 au lycée Henri-IV*.

175. In a letter to Dr Loÿ in March 1913 (Jung, CW 4, par. 665), Jung comments on the "determinants that produce culture" by referring to "Bergson's excellent criticism on this respect" and equates what he (Jung) calls "biological duty" with some determinants inherent to the *psyche*.

176. Mullarkey (2008, p. 597) analyses that intuition, for Bergson, is a "superior empiricism" and that we owe to Bergson the idea that the "true empiricism" is the "true metaphysics".

177. Bergson's "truth" of intuition also bears resemblance to Jung's later formulation of the objectivity of the psyche.

178. Evoking both Bergson and Jung's intuition, Kerslake (2006) writes, "Individuation occurs when the imagination, faced with problematic

Ideas, attempts to invoke the power of intuition". The notion of individuation, central to Jung's psychology, will be examined in more detail in Chapter Eight, which deals entirely with psychological types. Here what is emphasised is the move from personal consciousness to the collective unconscious, which is the general direction of individuation.

179. See the chapter on "Bergson, intuition, instinct, archetypes". Jung writes, "I realise that my views are parallel with those of Bergson ... [and then adds] my constructive method corresponds to his intuitive method" (Jung, 1917[1914], p. 351).

180. Jung writes,

> The essence of the symbol consists in the fact that it represents in itself something that is not wholly understandable, and that it hints only intuitively at its possible meaning. . . . To understand a symbol we need a certain amount of intuition which apprehends, if only approximately, the meaning of the symbol that has been created, and then incorporates it into consciousness. (Jung, CW 6, par. 171).

When Jung writes "approximately", he is not describing any vagueness of intuition, but its relation to the infinite scope of the symbol, understood in a Goethean approach.

181. When Jung criticised Bergson's so-called intuitive "method" by stating that no experience was implied in the method, he, according to me, underestimated Bergson's thought. Bergson's method was, indeed, intellectual, yet his ambition was to change humanity's *habit*. Bergson worked and wrote for his generation and became as famous as Jung or Nietzsche in his time. Today, however, no one can apply Nietzsche's philosophy (and that was not Nietzsche's intention). Nietzsche never wrote of any programme; there will never be any *Ubermensch* to be found anywhere. In contrast, time could bring the changing of *habit* described by Bergson.

182. For a more precise description of the dangers of active imagination, see Jung, *CW 8*, par. 130.

183. The need of psychology, or psychotherapy, for schizophrenia—settled on by Eugen Bleuler rather than by Jung—created a proper psychotherapy for schizophrenia that began in the 1930s. An extensive bibliography of the literature of that field can be found in Lysaker and Silverstein, 2009.

184. Crystal-gazing is, for Myers, "the act of looking into a crystal, glass ball, or other *speculum*, or reflecting surface, with the object of inducing

hallucinatory pictures. The pictures, of course, exist in the mind and not in the crystal" (Myers, 1903, p. xvi).
185. Concerning Jung naming Christianity a myth, see Segal, 1998.
186. Shamdasani called his study of the editing of *MDR* "Memories, dreams, omissions" (1995). See also his book, *Jung Stripped Bare by His Biographers, Even* (2005).
187. With no less wit than Shamdasani, Christine Maillard called her study "Le livre de Madame Jaffé, ma vie de C. G. Jung: remémoration, légitimation, monumentalisation" (2002). Freudian analyses of Jung's childhood in *MDR* also point to what is missing in Jung's *MDR*, see, for instance, Golberg, N. (1990) and Feldman, B. (1992). As well, Winnicott's fine and cathartic (see Sedgwick, 2008) book review of *MDR* in 1964 in the *International Journal of Psychoanalysis* includes "Jung did not see", or "Jung did not connect this to", or else "all this [some psychoanalytic work] seems to be ignored in Jungian writings, and we cannot afford to ignore anything that is valid".
188. We could add the numinous effect to the reason for the success of the method.
189. In Charet (1993, pp. 201–202), Charet characterises von Franz's biography as a "hagiography" but of a "higher order" than Hannah's *Jung: His Life and Work* (1976). In the same vein, Gaillard evokes the possibility of "the creation of an explanatory myth [by Jung, or Jaffé concerning *MDR*] cobbled together in the aftermath" (2003, p. 574). While Charet uses the term "hagiography" in a secularised mode, I am referring to saints' hagiographies. My term *Mythosanschauung* includes Gaillard's "explanatory myth", but as a single cause among many others. See Shamdasani's bibliography on the relationship between *MDR* and hagiography (1995, p. 135, notes 19 to 26).
190. Jung's personal myth was built from the *psychological* assimilation of the somehow exhaustive quantity of myths studied in *Psychology of the Unconscious* as well as from the realisation that the Christian myth was not his.
191. There is not a single definition of "ekphrasis", even in classic literature, but as many definitions as there can be of "myth". See, for example, Charbonnier, 2009; Fowler, 1991; Heffernan, 2004).
192. My "There is", although clear, is inadequate to express symbols and synchronicity. Both "emerge" from a situation where objects and people are actors and re-actors. Synchronicity and (Jungian) symbols have neither essence nor existence. They both express and impress a relationship.

193. Jung had his first ego-experience in 1887, a date itself linked to one of Jung's dreams of Goethe—who himself probably wore buckled shoes—during which the date 1787 appeared.
194. Christian Gaillard's semantic as well as traduction comments on this sentence are worth reading (Gaillard, 2003, pp. 576–579, 590–591), but do not concern our purpose here.
195. By the same token, the sentence induces the contours and the intention of Jaffé's selection of memories.
196. By "progressive", I refer to the journey of the hero, where this "other" is integrated at the very end.
197. "Charm" is to be understood in an esotericist sense, such as a "spell". See Federici Vescovini (2006).
198. My "Jung" (with quotation marks) is a reminder that we find ourselves in the amplification of the myth of Jung's childhood, or else at the paradigmatic level. "Jung" is "hero Jung".
199. Zipes, a specialist in fairy-tales recalls that

> in the period following World War II, Aniéla Jaffé, Joseph Campbell, and Marie-Louise von Franz charted the links between archetypes, the collective unconscious, and fairy tales, while Julius Heuscher and Bruno Bettelheim focused on Oedipal conflicts from neo-Freudian positions in their analyses of some Grimm's tales. (Zipes, 1999, p. 78).

Jaffé, therefore, is at home when she amplifies Jung to hero Jung. Stückelberg's role is (rhetorically) that of Philemon, Jung's guide through the journey of *The Red Book*, itself aesthetically comparable to Mephisto for Faust in Goethe's *Faust* or Virgil for Dante in the *Divine Comedy*.

200. The description of the four functions in Part I is sufficient to allow understanding of this chapter. The stress is put on the difference between the archetypal–mythical and real perceptions.
201. This indication is not present in the English *MDR*, but in the French translation of Roland Cahen (Jung, 1973[1961/1966, p. 29).
202. Since we are in the collective unconscious, we could also describe the link between Jung's and his mother's Number 2 as a *coniunctio*, the alchemical sacred marriage, used by Jung to describe transference and countertransference in *The Psychology of the Transference*. Partly intuitive, this link brings the reader, as if in a consulting room, into Jung's unconscious.
203. Main (2004, p. 167), has noted that, just as in Hermetic circles or societies, transmission from teacher to disciple is the core of the practice of analytical psychology.

204. I write "comparable with" to show the strength of Jung's feeling, and the close relationship to be found here between his life and Hermeticism. Relationship does not mean identity. Following Segal (1995), and Shamdasani (1998a), I disagree with the general thesis of Richard Noll, who wrote of an *actual* secret cult organised around Jung (Noll, 1994).
205. Mircea Éliade expresses the palpable and authentic character of this *experience*: "Initiation is equivalent to a basic change in existential condition; the novice emerges from his ordeal endowed with a totally different being from that which he possessed before his initiation; he has become another" (Eliade, 1958, p. x).
206. After suggestion divided Freud and Jung, Freud conceded, "It is absolutely exact that psychoanalysis also works with suggestion as other therapeutic methods do" (Freud, *SE 11*, p. 54).
207. The historian Jacqueline Carroy (1991, pp. 179–236), studies the theoretical and historical links between all the "suggestive therapies" of the end of the nineteenth century and shows how close were the various methods of hypnosis (Charcot, Bernheim) and of suggestion (Janet, Gabriel Tarde, Gustave Le Bon, Freud's psychoanalysis). In contrast, even though her analysis of auto-suggestive therapies was not as developed as that of the suggestive therapies, she clearly distinguished between hypnotic and spirit "cultures" (pp. 19–21, 42–43). What she called "voluntary subjects" and "unconscious artists" also shared traits with the spirit medium practising auto-suggestion (pp. 88–96).
208. The French original reads:

    Il suffit, pour provoquer des manifestations intelligentes, de déterminer des phénomènes en rapport avec ceux que la malade perçoit encore, d'entrer pour ainsi dire dans le rêve. Au moment où Justine s'écrie : « le choléra, il va me prendre ... » , je lui réponds : « oui, il te tient par la jambe droite », et la voici qui retire violemment sa jambe droite.

209. The original French is: "Quoi que le malade semble un possédé, son mal, c'est l'émotion du remords ... le diable est l'incarnation de leurs regrets, de leurs remords, de leur terreur ou de leurs vices".
210. This is an example of the phenomenon called "symptom substitution", which still constitutes a theoretical objection to hypnotherapy. It is a "phenomenon in which a set of symptoms that are removed directly in therapy, without regard for the unconscious conflicts responsible for their formation, are replaced by new symptoms". See also Bhatia, 2009, p. 402.

211. The original French reads:

> [Le directeur] a organisé des résolutions, des croyances, des émotions, il a aidé le sujet à rattacher à sa personnalité des images et des sensations. Bien plus il a échafaudé tout ce système de pensée autour d'un centre spécial qui est le souvenir et l'image de sa personne. Le sujet a emporté dans son esprit une synthèse nouvelle, passablement artificielle et très fragile, sur laquelle l'émotion a facilement exercé sa puissance désorganisatrice.

212. In *The Psychology of Transference*, Jung would use one picture of the *Rosarium Philosophorum*, where the King and the Queen both enter the bath to illustrate that single level between patient and analyst.
213. In using "concretely", I recall the practical aspect of *The Red Book*, which contains no theory.
214. We recognise both the archetypal and the intuitive ("for all the future") nature of the soul in action. In the French note on the translation of *The Red Book*, Maillard recalls Jung's use of the German term *wirklich* as well as his famous expression "Wirklich ist was wirkt!" "Is real that which is effective!" (as here is the soul). See Shamdasani (2009), *The Red Book*, p. 225.
215. Antonia Wolff might not have been the only person to carry the projection of Jung's anima in this period of his life. When I study the relationship between types, individuation, and anima in Part V, I also mention the role of Maria Moltzer.
216. Alfred Adler's psychology of consciousness is at least for the same reason "still yet to be reckoned with" (see Taylor, 1996, p. 549). Taylor here agrees with Ellenberger, who specifically describes in his 1970 *Discovery of the Unconscious* the works of Janet, Freud, Jung, and Adler in a similar form (one entire chapter dedicated to each psychologist).
217. Jung included dreams in consciousness and wrote of their unconscious origin (see, for example, Jung, *CW 8*, pars 294, 532).
218. We remember how archetype, instinct, and intuition were close, sometimes almost indistinct, in the unconscious. There is no such issue in consciousness, where instincts and intuition coexist and can be analysed through palpable results, which science, or the expertise of psychiatry, examine (through renewed forms of Jung's word association tests, for example).
219. In *CW 11*, par. 69, Jung writes,

> In uttering this word [intuition] most people have an agreeable feeling, as if something has been settled. But they never consider

that you do not *make* an intuition. On the contrary, it always comes to you; you *have* a hunch, it has come of itself, and you only catch it if you are clever or quick enough.

220. A Christian equivalent of this description can be found in Aquinas:

> When I say 'Let there be Light' and speak of corporeal light, it pertains to the literal sense [sensation]. If 'Let there be Light' is understood as 'let Christ be born in the Church' it pertains to the allegorical sense. If it is understood as 'let us be illumined in our intellects [thinking] and inflamed in our affections [feeling]' it pertains to the moral sense. If it is understood as 'let us be introduced to glory through Christ' it pertains to the anagogical sense [intuition]. (Aquinas, 1953, Volume 1, p. 621)

Jung, like—and possibly after—Aquinas, unites feeling and thinking. Aquinas associates intellect and affection through morality. Jung differentiates the functions of perceptions (intuition and sensation) from the functions of apperception (thinking and feeling). Aquinas's affection–morality unity can also be found in Jung's association between feeling and value.

221. Nietzsche's Apollinian and Dyonisian types will be re-examined in comparison with Emilii Medtner's types.
222. I have already mentioned Adolf Keller, when Jung wrote in *Psychology of the Unconscious*, "I am indebted to Rev. Dr. Keller for calling my attention to Bergson's conception of *durée créatrice*".
223. Concerning Bergson and the irrational, see also Shamdasani, 2003, p. 77.
224. Jung writes in his letter to Schmidt-Guisan of the 14 June 1915, "Von *Bergson* nämlich bekam ich der Begriff des *Irrationale*". See Iselin, 1982, p. 39.
225. Schmid showed Jung how, therefore, opposite types could not agree with each other. To overcome those innate different attitudes, Jung linked types to individuation.
226. The written part of the letter, without the table, can be found in the selected *Jung's Letters* (1973, Volume 1) edited by Gerhard Adler and Aniéla Jaffé. The entire correspondence between Schmit and Jung is now available in the Philemon editions.
227. The translation aims at rendering the fact that Jung was writing notes. For a more "written" translation, see Falzeder, 2013, pp. 136–137). The translator, Ernst Falzeder, missed the last line devoted to sensation in "Introverted; Conscious". The original in German of the passage follows:

Introvertiert:

Bewußt   *Denken* als logische rationale Function (adaptiert u. allgemeingültig).

Fühlen als dem Denken untergeordnete Gefühlstöne und als emotionale Reaction auf denkend Erkanntes, in Bezug auf äußere Wirkung *schwach*.

Empfindung als stark (übermäßig) ausgeprägte Organfunction.

Unbewußt *Fühlen* als sporadisches Intuieren = ein Complex von *Emotion* mit *unentwickeltem*

Gedankengehalt. Weil unentwickelt, darum archaisch, symbolisch, sweideutig, phaenomenal,

irrational, actus purus naturae, intellectuell nur mangelhaft formulier- und erfaßbar, *projiciert*.

Extravertiert:

Bewußt *Fühlen* als logisch (gefühlslogisch) - rationale Function (adaptiert u. allgemeingültig).

Denken als dem Fühlen untergeordnete intellectuelle Vorgänge und Reaction auf Gefühltes (fühlend Erkanntes). In Bezug auf äußere Wirkung *schwach*.

Empfindung, in Unterordnung unter das Fühlen, schwach ausgeprägte (bis gestörte) Organfunction.

Unbewußt *Denken* als sporadisches *Intuieren* = Complex von *Gedanken* mit unentwickeltem Fühl-

und Empfindungsgehalt. Übrige Attribute wie oben.

228. In 1957, Jung writes, answering Richard I. Evans:

> Now mind you, these four functions were not a scheme I had simply invented and applied to psychology. On the contrary, it took me quite a long time to discover them. Take the thinking type for example as I thought my type to be. Of course, that is human, is it not? ... and so after a while I discovered that there are intuitive types. They gave me much trouble. It took me over a year to become somewhat clear about the existence of the intuitive types.

This quotation shows how Jung indeed struggled with the intuitive type. See Evans (1976)[1964], pp. 103, 190–200.

229. Later in her paper, Moltzer uses the symbol of the "Redeemer, whom analytically, we find in the transcendent [religious] function" (Shamdasani, 1998c, p. 110).
230. Moltzer develops the topic of intuition preceding the rational functions in the larger context of the evolution of mandkind rather than that of the child in her second paper, "The relation between the Zurich school and the Club". The convergences with Jung's ideas are, in this second context, less easy to find. As noticed by Shamdasani (2003, p. 71), Moltzer developed the idea of intuition as a "phylogenetically earlier mode of adaptation" that Jung did not retain. Yet, those ideas (1) resemble Jung's first chapter on the two kinds of thinking in *The Psychology of the Unconscious*, which Moltzer read and commented on, but (2) can also be read as thoughts that preceded Jung's reading and appropriation of Lévy-Bruhl's *participation mystique*.
231. Shamdasani writes, "In the transcripts [of *MDR*, when he evokes the woman who inspired in him the notion of anima], Jung adds a small but telling detail—that the woman in question was Dutch. The one Dutch woman in Jung's circle at this time was Maria Moltzer". See Kerr, 1993, for his hypothesis.
232. Medtner was especially critical towards intuition. I do not mean that the other members mentioned earlier were not critical. They, too, nourished the debate on types. Moltzer, for instance, had expressed in 1916 her concern about the contemporary reduction of Jung's psychology into typology in the same way that the sexual, she believed, had diminished Freud's psychoanalysis.
233. Medtner's sometimes ironical tone also resembles Jung's in the Zofingia Lectures.
234. Medtner writes, "Der springende Punkt aller Erörterungen schien mir die "Intuition" gewesen zu sein, und zwar in der Qualität eines meistens fraglos zugegebenen Erkenntnisorgans, das selbständig und gültig zu funktionieren vermag" (Medtner, 1923, p. iii).
235. Medtner writes, "Es gibt aber keine Erkenntnis ohne Wertung, sonst hätte sie keine Gültigkeit". Against intuition, Medtner uses Kant's argument against spirits. Kant does not argue that spirits do not exist because we cannot prove it. Kant knows that there is no means to know if spirits exist or not. The theory of knowledge is a philosophical matter and, as such, it belongs to a relative system where absolute knowledge has no standing. However, *Wertung* ("validation") has, and the objects of study must be open to criticism.
236. Medtner writes, "wo aber das Nichtwissen (wie im Okkultismus) verworfen ist, dort gibt es keinen Platz für die Exaktheit".

237. Medtner writes, "Die biologische (eigentlich psychophysiologische und neuerdings psychoanalytische) Untersuchung des Erkenntnisvermögens hat ihren Sinn und Zweck, der aber weder mit der gnoseologischen zusammenfàllt, noch die letztere je zu ersetzen imstande sein wird".
238. Medtner writes, "Die sogennante 'intuitive Eingebung' ist ein Blitz; ein starker und heller Intellekt wird von diesem Blitz nicht betroffen".
239. Medtner writes, "Kant sagt: 'Ohne Sinnlichkeit würde uns kein Gegenstand gegeben und ohne Verstand keiner gedacht sein. . . . Gedanken ohne Inhalt sind leer, Anschauungen ohne Begriffe sind blind'".
240. Medtner writes, "Wahrnehmung ist noch lange keine Erkenntnis" ("Perception is by no means knowledge").
241. Medtner writes, "Eine unvermittelte Aussage ist unmöglich" ("An unmediated enunciation is impossible").
242. I exclude here the corporeal forms of active imagination, such as "authentic movement", where acts replace images through a direct transformation in consciousness of (unconscious) instincts. See Keller-Jenny, in Swan, 2011.
243. Faivre's distinction was, to quote him, "merely a practical one. Indeed, there is sometimes a great deal of esotericism [in mystics and viceversa]".
244. Medtner writes,

> Diese drei Paare sind folgende:
> I. Intuitiv–Diskursiv.
>   Ein gnoseologischer Gegensatz.
> II. Intuitiv–Instinktiv.
>   Ein psychologischer Gegensatz.
> III. Intuitiv–Spekulativ.
>   Ein denk-typologischer Gegensatz.

245. Jung only mentions Nietzsche, whose poetic thinking he contrasts to the intellectual thinking of Bergson. According to Jung, compared with Nietzsche's experience, Bergson's *"méthode intuitive"* is only intellectual.
246. I have already mentioned von Franz and Jaffé's interests. Baynes translated the *I Ching*, or *Book of Changes*, from German to English as well as Jung's introduction to the work on synchronicity.
247. And I quote again Shamdasani, 2003, p. 69.
248. The Amazon is also opposite to the medial woman, for she "has no patience or understanding for anything that is undeveloped or nascent", which is precisely the realm of the intuitive–medial woman. See Wolff, 1995[1934], p. 85.

249. "Feminine re-visions of Jungian thought" refers to the title of the compendium *Feminist Archetypal Theory: Interdisciplinary Re-visions of Jungian Thought*.
250. Wolff writes that her four types "also correspond to aspects of a man's anima".
251. We must, of course, contextualise Wolff's text, which was written in 1934.
252. Jung was an introverted intuitive type with thinking as complementary function. (John Beebe, personal correspondence, confirmed by some inferences to Jung's statements such as seen earlier with Evans.)
253. Jung's function of intuition did not exist yet in 1914. Incubation, debates, and time must be added to the factors that led Jung to the discovery of his type. That which I want to emphasise is the disparity between Beebe's "flash" (in consciousness) and Jung's slow but large vision. We are describing two very distinct intuitions.
254. The dormant waters represented Jung's unconscious intuition of the whole scheme of his typology before the introduction of the irrational types. The waters (Jung's *Anschauung*), therefore, did not need Jung's ego (consciousness) to work their way to Jung's awareness. Jung writes, "As a rule these inner processes [the creative intuitions] have the peculiarities of being subliminal, i.e., unconscious, in the first place and of reaching consciousness only gradually" (Jung, CW 7, par. 270).
255. Concerning the relationship between the quality and the archetype see Maillard, 1993, pp. 68–70, 87–88.
256. I refer the reader to von Franz's excellent (1993) *Projection and Re-Collection in Jungian Psychology*, where the author logically and metaphorically reconnects empathy (1) and empathy (3) in order to explain the problematics of projections and transference, which I named empathy (2).
257. Roderick Main's work, especially that of 2004, particularly addresses synchronicity's definition.
258. As expressed, too, in Lacan's structuralism. The sole exception, outside of discourse, is James Joyce's sinthome. See www.lacaninireland.com for an English translation of Lacan's Seminar XXIII.
259. On the status of intuition, the theological work of Jean-Luc Marion is most helpful and would constitute a great topic for further research on the topic of intuition.
260. As depicted in alchemist Gerhard Dorn's *Unus Mundus*, another source for Jung. See, for instance, Jung, CW 10, par. 780.

REFERENCES

Archives

Handschriften und Autographen der ETH - Bibliothek
C. G. Jung Manuskripte
eth - 22067 - 01
1897 vgl. GW 1 S. 28–31
Spiritische Experimente
Sitzungen: I vom 19.3
   II vom 22.3
   IV vom 18.8 1897
xMS (xerokopierte Manuskript) 8 S. v
HS 1055: 1a
1898
Aufzeichnungen über positive, relative und negative Kräfte
Fragment
MS S. 151–154
+ Diagr. -Bl.
Hs 1055: 469
D 1905 e
GW 18, 4
Über spiritistische Erscheinungen (nach einem Vortrag am 5. Febr. Im
   Bernoullianum) In/ Basler Nachrichten Nov. 1905
Photok. d. Drucks 6 S. v
Hs 1055: 543
Wissenschaftshistorische Sammlungen der ETH-Bibliothek, 1991
*Stefanie Zumstein-Preiswerk. Materialen zu "C. G. Jungs Medium. Die
   Geschichte der Helly Preiswerk."* Munich 1975

Adler, G., & Jaffé, A. (Eds.) (1973). *C. G. Jung Letters*. London: Routledge and Kegan Paul.

Agazzi, E., & Pauri, M. (2000). *The Reality of the Unobservable: Observability, Unobservability and Their Impact on the Issue of Scientific Realism*. Berlin: Springer.

Aldridge, A. O. (1975). *Voltaire and the Century of Light*. Princeton, NJ: Princeton University Press.

Aquinas, T. (1953). *Galatas*, c. 4, lecture 7. Rome: Marietti.

Armand, T. (1896). Le Congrès international de Psychologie à Munich. *Revue néo-scolastique, 12*: 428–433.

Bair, D. (2004). *Jung: A Biography*. London: Little, Brown.

Bazin, N., Lefrere, F., Passerieux, C., Sarfati, Y., & Hardy-Baylé, M. C. (2002). Formal thought disorders: French translation of the thought, language and communication assessment scale. *Encephale, 28*(2): 109–119.

Beebe, J. (2004). Understanding consciousness through the theory of psychological types. In: J. Cambray & L. Carter (Eds.), *Contemporary Perspectives in Jungian Analysis* (pp. 83–115). Hove: Brunner-Routledge.

Beebe, J., & Falzeder, E. (Eds.) (2013). *The Question of Psychological Types. C. G. Jung - Hans Schmid-Guisan Correspondence*. Princeton, NJ: Princeton University Press.

Bell, M. (2010). Carl Gustav Carus and the science of the unconscious. In: A. Nicholls & M. Liebscher (Eds.), *Thinking the Unconscious. Nineteenth-century Thought* (pp. 156–172). Cambridge: Cambridge University Press.

Bergson, H. (1910). Letter of 12 April to Vitalis Norström. In: Bergson (2002), *Correspondances* (p. 347). Paris: Presses Universitaires de France.

Bergson, H. (1911)[1907]. *Creative Evolution*. London: Macmillan.

Bergson, H. (2001)[1888]. *Essai sur les données immédiates de la conscience*. Paris: Presses Universitaires de France.

Bergson, H. (2002). *Correspondances*. Paris: Presses Universitaires de France.

Bergson, H. (2008)[1892–1893]. *Cours de psychologie de 1892–1893 au lycée Henri-IV*. Milan: Archè.

Berrios, G. E. (1999). Falret, Séglas, Morselli, and Masselon, and the 'language of the insane'. *Brain and Language, 69*(1): 56–75.

Bhatia, M. S. (2009). *Dictionary of Psychology and Allied Sciences*. New Delhi: New Age International.

Binet, A. (1897). [Review]. Sommeil, rêves et cas pathologiques. *L'année psychologique, 4*(4): 667.

Bishop, P. (1998a). On the history of analytical psychology: C. G. Jung and the Rascher Verlag: Part 1. *Seminar, 34*(3): 256–279.
Bishop, P. (1998b). On the history of analytical psychology: C. G. Jung and the Rascher Verlag: Part 2. *Seminar, 34*(4): 364–387.
Bishop, P. (1999). The birth of analytical psychology from the spirit of Weimar Classicism. *European Studies, XXIX*: 417–440.
Bishop, P. (2000). *Synchronicity and Intellectual Intuition in Kant, Swedenborg, and Jung.* New York: Edwin Mellen Press.
Bishop, P. (2003). C. G. Jung and '*Naturmystic*': The early poem '*Gedanken in einer Frühlingsnacht*'. *German Life and Letters, 56*(4): 327–343.
Bishop, P. (2004). Speaking of symbols: affinities between Cassirer's and Jung's theories of language. In: C. Hamlin & J. M. Krois (Eds.), *Symbolic Forms and Cultural Studies* (pp. 127–156). New Haven, CT: Yale University Press.
Bishop, P. (2006). The idea of the numinous in Goethe and Jung. In: A. Casement & D. Tacey (Eds.), *The Idea of the Numinous* (pp. 117–136). London: Routledge.
Bishop, P. (2008). The timeliness and timelessness of the "archaic": analytical psychology, "primordial" thought, synchronicity. *Journal of Analytical Psychology, 53*: 501–523.
Bishop, P. (2010). Review of Jung's *The Red Book: Liber Novus. International Journal of Jungian Studies, 2*: 160–166.
Boag, S. (2006). Freudian repression, the common view, and pathological sciences. *Review of General Psychology, 10*: 74–86.
Borch-Jacobsen, M. (2001). Making psychiatric history: madness as *folie à plusieurs*. *History of the Human Sciences, 14*(2): 19–38.
Brach, J.-P. (2006). Intermediary beings III: Renaissance. In: W. J. Hanegraaff (Ed.), *Dictionary of Gnosis and Western Mysticism* (pp. 623–628). Boston, MA: Brill Academic.
Butts, R. (1986). *Kant and the Double Government Methodology: Supersensibility and Method in Kant's Philosophy of Science.* Dordrecht: D. Reidel.
Carroy, J. (1991). *Hypnose, suggestion et psychologie: L'invention de sujets.* Paris: Presses Universitaires de France.
Chadwick, R. F., & Cazeaux, C. (Eds.) (1992). *Immanuel Kant, Critical Assessments: Kant's Critique of Pure Reason.* London: Routledge.
Charbonnier, S. (2009). Poétique de l'ekphrasis et rhétorique de l'image dans la Rome de Léon X. *Camenae*. Available at: www.paris-sorbonne.fr/IMG/pdf/Charbonni.pdf [accessed on 1 October 2014].
Charet, F. X. (1993). *Spiritualism and the Foundations of C. G. Jung's Psychology.* Albany, NY: State University of New York Press.

Chodorow, J. (1997). *Jung on Active Imagination*. London: Routledge.
Claviere, J. (1898). L'audition colorée. *L'année psychologique*, 5(5): 161–178.
Cohn, R. G. (1987). *Mallarmé's Prose Poems: A Critical Study*. Cambridge, Cambridge University Press.
De Jong, A. (2006). Secrecy I: Antiquity. In: W. J. Hanegraaff (Ed.), *Dictionary of Gnosis and Western Mysticism* (pp. 1050–1054). Boston, MA: Brill Academic Publishers.
De Saussure, F. (1903)[1972]. *Course in General Linguistics*, C. Bally, R. Harris, A. Sechehaye (Trans.). London: Duckworth.
Deleuze, G. (1966). *Le Bergsonisme*. Paris: Presses Universitaires de France.
Deveney, J. P. (2006). Spiritualism. In: W. J. Hanegraaff (Ed.), *Dictionary of Gnosis and Western Mysticism* (pp. 1074–1082). Boston, MA: Brill Academic.
Douglas, C. (Ed.) (1997). Jung, C. G. *Visions: Notes of the Seminar given in 1930–1934* (two volumes). Princeton, NJ: Princeton University Press.
Edelman, N. (2001). Régine Plas, Naissance d'une science humaine: la psychologie. Les Psychologues et le 'merveilleux psychique', collection Carnot, Paris, Presses universitaires de Rennes, 2000, 175 pp, in *Revue d'histoire du XIXe siècle*, p. 22.
Eliade, M. (1958). *Rites and Symbols of Initiation (Birth and Rebirth)*. London: Harvill Press.
Ellenberger, H. F. (1970). *The Discovery of the Unconscious. The History and Evolution of Dynamic Psychiatry*. London: Fontana Press, 1994.
Ellenberger, H. F. (1991). The story of Helene Preiswerk: a critical study with new documents. *History of Psychiatry*, ii: 41–52.
Evans, R. I. (1976)[1964]. *Jung on Elementary Psychology: A Discussion between C. G. Jung and Richard I. Evans*. London: Routledge and Kegan Paul.
Faivre, A. (1992). *L'Ésotérisme*. Paris: Presses Universitaires de France.
Faivre, A. (1994). *Access to Western Esotericism*. Albany, NY: State University of New York Press (two volumes in French).
Faivre, A. (2003). Sir Arthur Conan Doyle et les esprits photographiés. *Ethnologie Française*, XXXIII(4): 623–632.
Faivre, A. (2008). 'Éloquence magique', ou descriptions des mondes de l'au-delà explorés par le magnétisme animal: au carrefour de la *Naturphilosophie* romantique et de la théosophie chrétienne (première moitié du XIXe siècle). *Aries*, 8: 191–228.
Falzeder, E. (Trans.) (2013). *The Question of Psychological Types: The Correspondence of C. G. Jung and Hans Schmid-Guisan, 1915–1916*. Princeton, NJ: Princeton University Press.

Falzeder, E., & Beebe, J. (Eds.) (2007). The story of an ambivalent relationship: Sigmund Freud and Eugen Bleuler. *Journal of Analytical Psychology*, *52*: 343–368.

Fanger, C. (2006). Secrecy II: Middle Ages. In: W. J. Hanegraaff (Ed.), *Dictionary of Gnosis and Western Mysticism* (pp. 1054–1056). Boston, MA: Brill Academic.

Federici Vescovini, G. (2006). Magical instruments. In: W. J. Hanegraaff (Ed.), *Dictionary of Gnosis and Western Esotericism* (pp. 744–747). Boston, MA: Brill Academic.

Feldman, B. (1992). Jung's infancy and childhood and its influence upon the development of analytical psychology. *Journal of Analytical Psychology*, *37*: 255–274.

Fierz, H. K. (1991). *Jungian Psychiatry*. Einsielden: Daimon.

Flournoy, T. (1901). Observations psychologiques sur le spiritisme. *IVe congrès international de psychologie, tenu à Paris du 20 au 26 août 1900 sous la présidence de Théodule Ribot. Compte-rendu des séances et textes des mémoires publiés par les soins du docteur Pierre Janet* (pp. 100–125). Paris: Alcan.

Flournoy, T. (1907). Automatisme téléologique anti-suicide: un cas de suicide empêché par une hallucination. *Archives de Psychologie*, *VII*: 113–137.

Flournoy, T. (1994)[1899]. *From India to the Planet Mars: A Case of Multiple Personality with Imaginary Languages*. Princeton, NJ: Princeton University Press, 1994.

Fowler, D. P. (1991). Narrate and describe: the problem of ekphrasis. *Journal of Roman Studies*, *81*: 25–35.

Freud, S. (1894a). Neuro-psychoses of defence. S.E., 3: 43–70. London: Hogarth.

Freud, S. (1898b). The psychical mechanism of forgetfulness. S.E., 3: 289–297. London: Hogarth.

Freud, S. (1899a). Screen memories. S.E., 3: 301–322. London: Hogarth.

Freud, S. (1900a). *The Interpretation of Dreams*. S.E., 4–5. London: Hogarth.

Freud, S. (1901b). *The Psychopathology of Everyday Life*. S.E., 6. London: Hogarth.

Freud, S. (1909d). *Notes upon a Case of Obsessional Neurosis*. S.E., 10: 153–149. London: Hogarth.

Freud, S. (1910e). The antithetical meaning of primal words. S.E., 11: 155–161. London: Hogarth.

Freud, S. (1920g). *Beyond the Pleasure Principle*. S.E., 18: 59. London: Hogarth.

Freud, S. (1933a). *New Introductory Lectures on Psycho-analysis. S.E.*, 22: 159. London: Hogarth.

Freud, S., with Breuer, J. (1895d). *Studies on Hysteria, S.E.*, 2. London: Hogarth.

Gadamer, H.-G. (1975)[1960]. *Truth and Method*. New York: Seabury Press.

Gaillard, C. (2003). On defining words, some scenarios and vectors in the 'autobiography' of C. G. Jung. *Journal of Analytical Psychology, 48*: 571–591.

Galton, F. (1883). *Inquiries into Human Faculty and its Development*. London: Macmillan.

Glover, J. M., & Forryan, B. (1979). *General Index to the Collected Works of C. G. Jung*. London: Routledge and Kegan Paul.

Goodheart, W. B. (1984). C. G. Jung's first patient: on the seminal emergence of Jung's thought. *Journal of Analytical Psychology, 29*: 1–34.

Graves, R. (1986)[1934]. *I, Claudius*. Harmondsworth: Penguin.

Grimm, J., & Grimm, W. (1854). *Deutsches Worterbuch* (Volume 1). Leipzig: Hirtzel.

Gunter, P. A. Y. (1982). Bergson and Jung. *Journal of the History of Ideas, 43*(4): 635–652.

Hanegraaff, W. J. (1995). Empirical method in the study of esotericism. *Method and Theory in the Study of Religion, 7*(2): 99–129.

Hanegraaff, W. J. (2006). Occult/occultism. In: W. J. Hanegraaff (Ed.), *Dictionary of Gnosis and Western Esotericism* (pp. 884–889). Boston, MA: Brill Academic.

Hale, N. G., Jr. (Ed.) (1971). *James Jackson Putnam and Psychoanalysis*. Princeton, NJ: Princeton University Press.

Hall, J. A. (1989). *Hypnosis: A Jungian Perspective*: New York: Guilford Press.

Hannah, B. (1976). *Jung: His Life and Work: A Biographical Memoir*. New York: Putnam.

Haule, J. R. (1984). From somnambulism to the archetypes: the French roots of Jung's split with Freud. *Psychoanalytic Review, 71*(4): 635–659.

Heffernan, J. A. W. (2004). *Museum of Words: The Poetics of Ekphrasis from Homer to Ashbery*. Chicago, IL: University of Chicago Press.

Hewison, D. S. (2006). Case history, case story: an enquiry into the hermeneutics of C. G. Jung. *Journal of Analytical Psychology, 40*(3): 383–403.

Hillman, J. (1976). Some early background to Jung's ideas. *Spring*, 123–136.

Hogenson, G. B. (2012). Review of Sherry, J. (2010) *Carl Gustav Jung, Avant-Garde Conservative*, New York: Palgrave MacMillan. *Journal of Analytical Psychology*, 57(2): 258–260.
Homans, P. (1979). *Jung in Contents. Modernity and the Making of a Psychology*. London: University of Chicago Press.
Huguelet, P., Nicastro, R., & Zanello, A. (2002). Influence of attention on an auditory-verbal learning test in schizophrenic patients. *Encephale*, 28(4): 291–297.
Huskinson, L. (2004). *Nietzsche and Jung*. Hove: Routledge.
Huskinson, L. (2006). Holy, holy, holy: the misappropriation of the numinous in Jung. In: A. Casement & D. Tacey (Eds.), *The Idea of the Numinous* (pp. 200–212). London: Routledge.
Huskinson, L. (2013). Housing complexes. Redesigning the house of psyche in light of a curious mistranslation of C. G. Jung appropriated by Gaston Bachelard. *International Journal of Jungian Studies*, 5(1): 64–80.
Im, S. (2011). *A Study of Kant's "Dreams of a Spirit-Seer": Kant's Ambiguous Relation to Swedenborg*. Massachusetts: UMI.
Iselin, H. K. (1982). *Zur Entstehung von C. G. Jungs "Psychologischen Typen". Der Briefwechsel zwischen C. G. Jung und Hans Schmid-Guisan im Lichte ihrer Freundschaft*. Aarau: Sauerländer.
Jaffé, A. (1963)[1958]. *Apparitions and Precognitions: A Study from the Point of View of C. G. Jung's Analytical Psychology*. New York: University Books.
Jaffé, A. (1979). *Apparitions: An Archetypal Approach to Death, Dreams and Ghosts*. Irving, TX: Spring.
Jaffé, A. (1986). *Religiöser Wahn und Swarze Magie: Das Tragische Leben der Anna Kingsford*. Eisiedeln, Switzerland: Daimon.
Jaffé, A. (1989). *Was C. G. Jung a Mystic? And Other Essays*. Eisiedeln, Switzerland: Daimon.
Jahoda, G. (2005). Theodor Lipps and the shift from 'sympathy' to 'empathy'. *Spring*, 41(2): 151–163.
James, W. (1889). Notes on automatic writing. *Proceedings of the American Society for Psychical Research*.
James, W. (1905)[1902]. *The Varieties of Religious Experience*. London: Longmans, Green [reprinted London: Penguin, 1986].
Janet, P. (1886). Les actes inconscients et le de doublement de la personnalité pendant le somnambulisme provoqué. *La Revue Philosophique*, XXII(II): 577–592. Available at: http://classiques.uqac.ca/classiques/janet_pierre/janet_pierrehtlm

Janet, P. (1887). L'influence somnambulique et le besoin de direction. *Revue Philosophique, XLIII*(I): 113–143.
Janet, P. (1889). *L'automatisme psychologique: Essai de psychologie expérimentale sur les formes inférieures de l'activité humaine*. Paris: Alcan.
Janet, P. (1898). *Névroses et idées fixes*. Paris: Alcan, two volumes.
Janet, P. (1902). *Manuel du baccalauréat de l'enseignement secondaire classique moderne, classes de philosophie et de première-lettres*. Paris: Nony.
Janet, P. (1903). *Les Obsessions et la psychasthénie*. Paris: Alcan, two volumes.
Janet, P. (2004)[1895–1934]. *Leçons au Collège de France (1895–1934)*. Paris: L'Harmattan.
Janet, P. (2007)[1919]. L'action morale, l'utilisation de l'automatisme. In: *Les médications psychologiques*. Paris, L'Harmattan.
Jarrett, J. L. (Ed.) (1988). *Nietzsche's Zarathustra: Notes of the Seminar given in 1934–1939. C. G. Jung*. Princeton, NJ: Princeton University Press.
Jastrow, J. (1908). *La subconscience*, préface de M. le Dr Pierre Janet. Paris: Alcan.
Jeromson, B. (2012). The genesis of Jung's first mandala: unanswered questions. *Jung's History*, 2(2): online, Philemon Foundation. Available at https://www.philemonfoundation.org/resources/jung_history/volume_2_issue_2/the_sources_of_systema_munditotius.
Jung, C. G. (1917)[1914]. The content of the psychoses. In: *Collected Papers on Analytical Psychology*, C. E. Long (Ed.). London: Tindall and Cox.
Jung, C. G. (1917a). *Psychology of the Unconscious: A Study of the Transformations and Symbolisms of the Libido. A Contribution to the History of the Evolution of Thought*. London: Kegan Paul, Trench, & Trubner.
Jung, C. G. (1917b). The psychology of the unconscious processes. In: *Collected Papers on Analytical Psychology*, C. E. Long (Ed.). London: Tindall and Cox.
Jung, C. G. (1919). Instinct and the unconscious. *British Journal of Psychology*, 10(1): 15–23.
Jung, C. G. (1950)[1921]. *Types psychologiques*, Y. Le Lay (Trans.). Geneva: Georg.
Jung, C. G. (1951)[1943]. *Psychologie de l'inconscient*. Geneva: Georg.
Jung, C. G. (1953–1983)[1902–1972]. *Collected Works*, 20 vols. London: Routledge and Kegan Paul.
Jung, C. G. (1956)[1919]. *Instinct et inconscient*, Y. Le Lay (Trans.). Geneva: Georg.
Jung, C. G. (1957)[1916]. *The Transcendent Function*, A. R. Pope (Trans.) [Pamphlet]. Zurich: Student association, C. G. Jung Institute.

Jung, C. G. (1960–1983)[1902–1972]. *Gesammelte Werke*, 20 vols. Olten und Freiburg im Breisgau: Walter.

Jung, C. G. (1961). *Erinnerung, Träume, Gedanken von C. G. Jung*, A. Jaffé (Ed.). Olten and Freiburg im Breisgau: Walter.

Jung, C. G. (1966)[1961]. *"Ma vie". Souvenirs, rêves et pensées. Recueillis et publiés par Aniéla Jaffé*, R. Cahen (Trans.). Paris: Gallimard, 1973.

Jung, C. G. (1979). *General Index to the Collected Works of C. G. Jung* (volume xx of the *Collected Works*). London: Routledge and Kegan Paul.

Jung, C. G. (1983)[1896–1899]. The Zofingia Lectures, C.W., A. London: Routledge and Kegan Paul.

Jung, C. G. (1989)[1934–1939]. *Nietzsche's Zarathustra: Notes of the Seminar Given in 1934–1939*, two volumes. London: Routledge.

Jung, C. G. (1994). *Gesamtregister* (volume xx of the *Gesammelte Werke*). Solothurn und Düsseldorf: Walter).

Jung, C. G. (1995)[1961/1963]. *Memories, Dreams, Reflections*, A. Jaffé (Ed.). London: Fontana Press.

Jung, C. G. (1997)[1896–1899]. *Die Zofingia-Vorträge*. Zürich: Walter.

Jung, C. G., & Cahen-Salabelle, R. (2013)[1915–1916]. Foreword. In: *The Question of Psychological Types: The Correspondence of C. G. Jung and Hans Schmid-Guisan, 1915–1916*, E. Falzeder (Trans.). Princeton, NJ: Princeton University Press.

Kant, I. (1900)[1766]. *Dreams of a Spirit-Seer Illustrated by Dreams of Metaphysics*, E. F. Goerwitz (Trans.). London: Swan Sonnenschein.

Kant, I. (1996)[1794]. *Religion Within the Limits of Reason Alone*, T. Greene & H. Hudson (Trans.). Cambridge: Cambridge University Press.

Kast, V. (1980). *Das Assoziationexperiment in der therapeutischen Praxis*. Stuttgart: Bonz, Fellbach.

Kerner, J. (1845)[1829]. *The Seeress of Prevorst, Being Revelations Concerning the Inner Life of Man, and the Inter-diffusion of a World of Spirits in the One We Inhabit, Communicated by Justinus Kerner*, C. Crowe (Trans.). London: J. C. Moore.

Kerr, J. (1993). *A Most Dangerous Method. The Story of Jung, Freud and Sabina Spielrein*. New York: Knopf.

Kerslake, C. (2006). Insectes et inceste. Bergson, Jung, Deleuze. *Multitudes*, 25(2): 31–51.

Kirsch, T. B. (2000). *The Jungians*. London: Routledge.

Kraepelin, E. (1883–1899). *Compendium der Psychiatrie* (6th edn revised). Leipzig: A. Abel.

Kraepelin, E. (1987). *Memoirs*, H. Hippius, G. Peters, & D. Ploog (Eds.). Berlin: Springer.

Kraepelin, E. (1992). The manifestations of insanity, D. Beer (Ed. & Trans.). *History of Psychiatry*, 3: 504–508.

Kuehn, M. (2001). *Kant: A Biography*. Cambridge: Cambridge University Press.

Kugler, P. (2002). *The Alchemy of Discourse: Image, Sound and Psyche*. Einsieldeln: Daimon.

Lauter, E., & Schreier Rupprecht, C. (Eds.) (1985). *Feminist Archetypal Theory: Interdisciplinary Re-visions of Jungian Thought*. Knoxville, TN: University of Tennessee Press.

Lévy-Bruhl, L. (1923). *Primitive Mentality*. London: George Allen.

Ljunggren, M. (1994). *The Russian Mephisto. A Study of the Life and Work of Emilii Medtner*. Stockholm: Gotab.

Lysaker, P. H., & Silverstein, S. M. (2009). Psychotherapy of schizophrenia: a brief history of the potential to promote recovery. *Clinical Case Studies*, 8: 417–423.

Maillard, C. (1993). *Du Plérome à l'Etoile: Les 'Sept Sermons aux Morts' de Carl Gustav Jung*. Nancy: Presses Universitaires de Nancy.

Maillard, C. (2002). Le livre de Madame Jaffé, ma vie de C. G. Jung: remémoration, légitimation, monumentalisation. *Cahiers Jungiens de Psychanalyse*, 104: 79–97.

Maillard, C. (2011). La voie de l'à-venir. Du discours prophétique dans Livre Rouge de C. G. Jung. *Cahiers Jungiens de Psychanalyse*, 134: 119–131.

Main, R. (2004). *The Rupture of Time. Synchronicity and Jung's Critique of Modern Western Culture*. Hove: Brunner-Routledge.

Mancini, S., & Faivre, A. (Eds.) (2012). *Des mediums: techniques du corps et de l'esprit dans les deux ameriques*. Paris: Imago.

Marini, A., Spoletini, I., Rubino, I. A., Ciuffa, M., Bria, P., Martinotti, G., Banfi, G., Boccascino, R., Strom, P., Siracusano, A., Caltagirone, C., Spalletta, G. (2008). The language of schizophrenia: an analysis of micro and macrolinguistic ability and their neuropsychological correlates. *Schizophrenia Research*, 105(1–3): 144–155.

McGuire, W. (Ed.) (1974)[1909]. *The Freud/Jung Letters*. Cambridge, MA: Harvard University Press.

McGuire, W. (1982). *Bollingen: An Adventure in Collecting the Past*. Princeton, NJ: Princeton University Press.

McGuire, W. (Ed.) (1988)[1974]. *The Freud/Jung Letters*. Cambridge, MA: Harvard University Press.

McGuire, W. (1989)[1925]. *Analytical Psychology. Notes on the Seminar Given in 1925*. Princeton, NJ: Princeton University Press.

Medtner, E. (1923). *Über die sogenannte "Intuition", die ihr angrenzenden Begriffe und die an sie anknüpfenden Probleme. Vorgetragen im Psychologischen Klub, Zürich MDCCCCIXX von Emil Medtner*. Moscow: Musagetes.

Méheust, B. (1999). *Somnambulisme et médiumnité. Volume 1: Le défi du magnétisme*. Paris: Les Empêcheurs de tourner en rond.

Monahan, P. A. (2009). C. G. Jung: Freud's heir or Janet's? The influence upon Jung of Janet's dissociationism. *International Journal of Jungian Studies, 1*(1): 33–49.

Montesquieu, C.-L. de S. de (2004)[1721]. *Persian Letters*. London: Penguin Books.

Moskowitz, A., & Heim, G. (2011). Eugen Bleuler's *Dementia Praecox or the Group of Schizophrenia* (1911): a centenary appreciation and reconsideration. *Schizophrenia Bulletin, 37*(3): 471–479.

Moskowitz, A., Schäfer, I., & Dorahy, M. J. (Eds.) (2009). *Psychosis, Trauma and Dissociation*. John Wiley.

Mullarkey, J. (2008). Breaking the circle: élan vital as performative metaphysics. In: F. Worms (Ed.), *L'Évolution créatrice 1907–2007: épistémologie et métaphysique Annales bergsoniennes IV* (pp. 591–600). Paris: Presses Universitaires de France.

Munsterberg, H. (1892). *Beiträge zur experimentellen Psychologie*, IV. Freiburg: J. C. B. Wohr.

Myers, F. W. H. (1884). On a telepathic explanation of so-called spiritualistic phenomena. *Proceedings of the Society for Psychical Research*, 217–237.

Myers, F. W. H. (1885). Automatic writing II. *Proceedings of the Society for Psychical Research*.

Myers, F. W. H. (1903). *Human Personality and its Survival of Bodily Death* (two volumes). London: Longmans, Green.

Nicholls, A., & Liebscher, M. (2010). *Thinking the Unconscious. Nineteenth Century German Thought*. Cambridge: Cambridge University Press.

Nicolas, S. (2004)[1895–1934]. Preface. In: Janet (2004)[1895–1934], *Leçons au Collège de France (1895–1934)*. Paris: L'Harmattan.

Niehus, L. (1994). *Gesamtregister*. Solothurn: Walter.

Noll, R. (1994). *The Jung Cult: Origins of a Charismatic Movement*. Princeton, NJ: Princeton University Press.

Obler, L. K., & Albert, M. L. (1985). Historical note: Jules Séglas on language in dementia. *Brain and Language, 24*(2): 314–325.

Pelletier, M. (1904). *L'Association des idées dans la manie aiguë et dans la débilité mentale*. Paris: J. Rousset.

Piéron, H. (1954). Histoire succincte des Congrès internationaux de Psychologie. *L'année psychologique*, 54(2): 397–405.

Pilard, N. (2010). *Sur Jung et le Yi King: Intuition et Synchronicité dans la préface de C. G. Jung au* Livre des Changements. Milan: Archè.

Pytlik, P. (2005). *Okkultismus und Moderne: Eine Kulturhistorisches Phänomen und seine Bedeutung für die Literatur um 1900*. Paderborn: Ferdinand Schöningh.

Richet, C. (1889). *Rapports et compte-rendus sommaires. Congrès international de Psychologie*.

Riffard, P. (2001). L'ésoterisme nous apprend-il quelque chose? In: R. Caron (Ed.), *Ésotérisme, gnoses et imaginaires symbolique: Mélanges offerts à Antoine Faivre* (pp. 807–818). Leuven: Peeters.

Rimbaud, A. (1895). *Poésie complète*. Paris: L. Vanier.

Roelcke, V. (1997). Biologizing social facts: an early 20th century debate on Kraepelin's concepts of culture, neurasthenia, and degeneration. *Culture, Medicine and Psychiatry*, 21(4): 383–403.

Rossi, P. (2009). Kant's philosophy of religion. *Stanford Encyclopaedia of Philosophy*. Available at: http://plato.stanford.edu/entries/kant-religion/ [accessed on 3 October 2014].

Rowland, S. (2002). *Jung: A Feminist Revision*. Cambridge: Polity Press.

Rowland, S. (2005). *Jung as a Writer*. Hove: Routledge.

Rowland, S. (2009). Ghost and self: Jung's paradigm shift and a response to Zinkin. *Journal of Analytical Psychology*, 54: 697–715.

Rudolph, K. (1998). *Gnosis: The Nature and History of Gnosticism*. Trowbridge: Cromwell Press.

Sandler, J., Holder, A., Dare, C., & Dreher, A. U. (1997). *Freud's Models of the Mind*. Madison, CT: International Universities Press.

Schlamm, L. (2006). C. G. Jung's visionary mysticism. *Harvest: Journal for Jungian Studies*, 52(1): 7–37.

Schlamm, L. (2007). C. G. Jung and numinous experience: between the known and the unknown. *European Journal of Psychotherapy and Counselling*, 9(4): 403–414.

Schlamm, L. (2008). C. G. Jung: Gnostic or Kabbalist? In: R. Gilbert (Ed.), *Knowledge of the Heart: Gnostic Movements and Secret Traditions* (pp. 132–142). London: Ian Allen.

Schopenhauer, A. (2000)[1851]. *Parerga and Paralipomena*, E. F. J. Payne (Trans.). Oxford: Clarendon Press.

Sedgwick, D. (2008). Winnicott's dream: some reflections on D. W. Winnicott and C. G. Jung. *Journal of Analytical Psychology*, 53: 543–560.

Segal, R. (Ed.) (1992). *The Gnostic Jung: Selections from the Writings of C. G. Jung and His Critics*. Princeton, NJ: Princeton University Press.
Segal, R. (1995). Critical notice on Noll, Richard, *The Jung Cult: Origin of a Charismatic Movement*. *Journal of Analytical Psychology*, 40: 597–608.
Segal, R. (Ed.) (1998). *Jung on Mythology: Key Readings*. London: Routledge.
Segal, R. (1999). Is analytical psychology a religion? Rationalist and romantic approaches to religion and modernity. *Journal of Analytical Psychology*, 44: 547–560.
Segal, R. (2007). Jung and Lévy-Bruhl. *Journal of Analytical Psychology*, 52: 635–658.
Shamdasani, S. (1993). Automatic writing and the discovery of the unconscious. *Spring*, 53: 100–131.
Shamdasani, S. (1994). Foreword. Encountering Hélène: Théodore Flournoy and the genesis of subliminal psychology. In: Flournoy, T. (1899). *From India to the Planet Mars* (pp. xi–li). Princeton, NJ: Princeton University Press.
Shamdasani, S. (1995). Memories, dreams, omissions. *Spring*, 57: 115–137.
Shamdasani, S. (1998a). *Cult Fiction: C. G. Jung and the Founding of Analytical Psychology*. London: Routledge.
Shamdasani, S. (1998b). From Geneva to Zürich: Jung and French Switzerland. *Journal of Analytical Psychology*, 43: 115–126.
Shamdasani, S. (1998c). The lost contributions of Maria Moltzer to analytical psychology. Two unknown papers. *Spring*, 64: 103–120.
Shamdasani, S. (1999). Is analytical psychology a religion? *In statu nascendi*. *Journal of Analytical Psychology*, 44: 539–545.
Shamdasani, S. (2000). Misunderstanding Jung: the afterlife of legends. *Journal of Analytical Psychology*, 45: 459–472.
Shamdasani, S. (2001a). The 'magical method that works in the dark': C. G. Jung, hypnosis, and suggestion. *Journal of Jungian Theory and Practice*, 3: 5–17.
Shamdasani, S. (Ed.) (2001b). *The Psychology of Kundalini Yoga. Notes of the Seminar given in 1932*. Princeton, NJ: Princeton University Press.
Shamdasani, S. (2003). *Jung and the Making of Modern Psychology: The Dream of a Science*. Cambridge: Cambridge University Press.
Shamdasani, S. (2005). *Jung Stripped Bare by His Biographers, Even*. London: Karnac.
Shamdasani, S. (2007). The incomplete works of Jung. In: A. Casement (Ed.), *Who Owns Jung?* (pp. 173–188). London: Karnac.
Shamdasani, S. (Ed.) (2009). *The Red Book: Liber Novus*. New York: W. W. Norton.

Shamdasani, S. (2010). Sonu Shamdasani interviewed by Ann Casement. *Journal of Analytical Psychology*, 55: 35–49.
Sharp, D. (1991). *Jung Lexicon*. Toronto, Canada: Inner City Books.
Shoja, M. M., & Shane Tubbs, R. (2007). The disorder of love in the canon of Avicenna (A.D. 980–1037). *American Journal of Psychiatry*, 164: 228–229.
Stein, M. (2006). On the importance of numinous experience in the alchemy of individuation. In: A. Casement & D. Tacey (Eds.), *The Idea of the Numinous* (pp. 34–52). Hove: Routledge.
Swan, W. (2008). C. G. Jung's psychotherapeutic technique of active imagination in historical context. *Psychoanalysis and History*, 10(2): 185–204.
Swan, W. (Ed.) (2011). *Memoir of Tina Keller-Jenny: A Lifelong Confrontation with the Psychology of C. G. Jung*. Lancaster: Spring Journal Books.
Tanger, C. (2006). Intermediary Beings II: Middle Ages. In W. L. Hanegraaff (Ed.), *Dictionary of Gnosis and Western Esotericism* (pp. 619–623). Boston (MA): Brill.
Tart, C. (Ed.) (1968). *Altered States of Consciousness*. New York: Wiley [reprinted New York: HarperCollins, 1990].
Taylor, E. (1996). The new Jung scholarship. *Psychoanalytic Review*, 83(4): 547–568.
Taylor, E. (2012). Jung on Swedenborg, Revividus. *Jung History*, 2(2). Available at: philemonfoundation.org/resources/jung_history/volume_2 issue_2/jung-on-Swedenborg [accessed on 1 October 2014].
Titchener, E. B. (1910). *A Textbook of Psychology*. New York: Macmillan.
Todorov, S. (1982)[1977]. *Theories of the Symbol*. Ithaca, NY: Cornell University Press.
Traupman, J. C. (1995). *Latin and English Dictionary*. New York: Bantam Books.
Treitel, C. (2004). *A Science for the Soul: Occultism and the Genesis of German Modern*. Baltimore, MD: Johns Hopkins University Press.
Tuke, D. H. (1892). *Dictionary of Psychological Medicine*. London: J. and A. Churchill.
Van den Broek, R. (2006). Intermediary Beings I: Antiquity. In: W. J. Hanegraaff (Ed.), *Dictionary of Gnosis and Western Esotericism* (pp. 616–619). Boston, MA: Brill Academic.
Vandermeersch, P. (1991). *Unresolved Questions in the Freud/Jung Debate on Psychosis, Sexual Identity and Religion*. Leuven: Leuven University Press.
Vezzoli, C., Bressi, C., Tricarico, G., Boato, P., Cattaneo, C., Visentin, U., & Invernizzi, G. (2007). Methodological evolution and clinical application

of C. G. Jung word association experiment: a follow-up study. *Journal of Analytical Psychology*, 57(2): 89–108.
Vieljeux, J. (2004). *Jung, Catalogue Chronologique des Ecrits*. Paris: Hors-série des *Cahiers jungiens de psychanalyse*.
Vogt, O. (1901a). Contre le spiritisme. *IVe congrès international de psychologie, tenu à Paris du 20 au 26 août 1900 sous la présidence de Théodule Ribot. Compte-rendu des séances et textes des mémoires publiés par les soins du docteur Pierre Janet* (pp. 656–660). Paris: Alcan.
Vogt, O. (1901b). La psychologie du sentiment. *IVe congrès international de psychologie, tenu à Paris du 20 au 26 août 1900 sous la présidence de Théodule Ribot. Compte-rendu des séances et textes des mémoires publiés par les soins du docteur Pierre Janet* (pp. 254–263). Paris: Alcan.
Vogt, O. (1901c). L'anatomie du cerveau et la psychologie. *IVe congrès international de psychologie, tenu à Paris du 20 au 26 août 1900 sous la présidence de Théodule Ribot. Compte-rendu des séances et textes des mémoires publiés par les soins du docteur Pierre Janet* (pp. 403–407). Paris: Alcan.
Voltaire (2003)[1759]. *Candide, or Optimism*, H. Morley (Trans.). New York: Barnes and Noble Classics.
Von Franz, M.-L. (1971). The inferior function. In: *Jung's Typology* (pp. 1–72). London: Spring Books.
Von Franz, M.-L. (1975)[1972]. *C. G. Jung, His Myth in Our Time*. Zürich: C. G. Jung Foundation.
Von Franz, M.-L. (1983). Introduction to Jung's *Zofingia Lectures. C.W., A*, xxiii–xxv.
Von Franz, M.-L. (1993). *Projection and Re-Collection in Jungian Psychology: Reflections of the Soul*, W. H. Kennedy (Trans.). Peru, IL: Open Court.
Von Stuckrad, K. (2003). Discursive study of religion: from states of the mind to communication and action. *Method and Theory in the Study of Religion*, 15: 255–271.
Von Stuckrad, K. (2005a). Western esotericism: towards an integrative model of interpretation. *Religion*, 35: 78–97.
Von Stuckrad, K. (2005b). *Western Esotericism. A Brief History of Secret Knowledge*. London: Equinox.
Weber, M. M., & Engstrom, E. J. (1997). Kraepelin's 'diagnostic cards'. The confluence of clinical research and preconceived categories. *History of Psychiatry*, 8(31): 375–385.
Wehr, G. (1988). *Jung: A Biography*. Boston, MA: Shambhala.
Williams-Hogan, J. (2006). Swedenborg, Emanuel. In: W. J. Hanegraaff (Ed.), *Dictionary of Gnosis and Western Esotericism* (pp. 1096–1105). Boston, MA: Brill Academic.

Winnicott, D. W. (1964). Review of C. G. Jung's *Memories, Dreams, Reflections*. *International Journal of Psychoanalysis, 45*: 450–455.

Witzig, J. (1982). Théodore Flournoy: a friend indeed. *Journal of Analytical Psychology, 27*(2): 131–148.

Wolff, T. (1995)[1934]. Structural forms of the feminine psyche. *Psychological Perspectives, 31*(1): 77–90.

Zipes, J. D. (1999). *When Dreams Come True: Classical Fairy Tales and their Tradition*. New York: Routledge.

Zumstein-Preiswerk, S. (1975). *C. G. Jungs Medium. Die Geschichte der Helly Preiswerk*. Munich: Kindler.

INDEX

active imagination, xvi, 13, 17, 36, 57, 93, 169, 173–177, 186, 208, 214, 218–219, 227, 261, 267, 275
Adler, G., 8, 11, 52, 58, 213, 229, 256, 266, 271–272
affect, xv, 49, 57, 71, 78, 165, 223, 228
Agazzi, E., 131
Albert, M. L., 125
Aldridge, A. O., 71
anima, 14, 111, 198, 216, 220, 222–225, 227, 271, 274, 276
anxiety, 11, 74, 95–96, 105, 133
Aquinas, T., 272
archetypes, xiv, 14, 17–18, 54, 111, 123, 142, 144, 146, 150–153, 155–156, 158, 161, 163, 166, 176, 178, 198, 206, 218–219, 227, 236, 250, 267, 269
  of intuition, xv, 153, 246
  symbols of, 236
Armand, T., 29

Bair, D., 69, 102, 112
Banfi, G., 125
Bazin, N., 125
Beebe, J., xvii–xviii, 33, 175, 212, 225–227, 254, 263, 276
behaviour, 32, 101, 114, 206–207, 210
  patterns of, xiv, 14, 156, 161
Bell, M., 264
Bergson, H., xv, xviii, 10–11, 14–15, 19–20, 24, 29, 32–34, 36–37, 48, 51, 54, 108, 142, 156–164, 170, 172–173, 195, 208, 210, 213–214, 220, 254, 257–259, 265–267, 272, 275
Berrios, G. E., 125
Bhatia, M. S., 194, 199, 270
Binet, A., 30, 36–37, 47–48, 95–96, 196, 258
Bishop, P., xviii, 3–4, 8–10, 54, 63, 72, 75, 84–85, 96, 136, 143, 149, 160, 165, 186–188, 248, 259, 264–265
Boag, S., 106

Boato, P., 111
Boccascino, R., 125
Borch-Jacobsen, M., 40, 259
Brach, J.-P., 64
Bressi, C., 111
Breuer, J., 34
Bria, P., 125
Butts, R., 72

Cahen-Salabelle, R., 8–10, 248, 254, 269
Caltagirone, C., 125
Carroy, J., xviii, 49, 252, 254, 270
Cattaneo, C., 111
Cazeaux, C., 218
Chadwick, R. F., 218
Charbonnier, S., 268
Charcot, J.-M., 26–28, 36, 47, 49–51, 53, 160, 258, 270
Charet, F. X., 198, 200, 268
Chodorow, J., 175, 254
Ciuffa, M., 125
Claviere, J., 109
Cohn, R. G., 181
complex, 17–18, 105, 107–108, 114–115, 117, 121, 125, 127, 175–176, 178, 186, 198, 227–228, 235, 250, 262
    autonomous, 176
    emotionally charged, 104
    feeling-toned, 114
    mother, 228
    Oedipus, 14, 197
    of grief, 126
    Paris, 37
    sexual, 114, 126
    theory of, 31
    thought-, 130, 212
    under-conscious, 99
    universal, 101
    Vienna, 37
conscious(ness) (*passim*) *see also*: Jung, C. G., unconscious(ness)
    absence of, 49
    activity, 155
    apperception, 156
    awareness, 49
    co-, 52
    collective, 149, 161
    comprehension of, 55
    differentiated, 166
    ego-, 184, 189
    half-, 101–102
    human, 25
    individuation in, 55
    intuition in, xiii, xv, 5, 7, 16, 18, 201, 213
    life, 52
    margin of, 52
    mind, 175–176
    non-, 107
    observation, 205
    of humanity, 14
    personal, 162, 236, 267
    potential, 165
    pre-, 15, 193, 257
    process, 107
    realities, 153
    repression, 104
    restricted, 49
    restriction of, 52
    semi-, 100
    state, 53
    sub-, 15, 46, 48–53, 88, 99, 107, 257
    subjective, 236
    super-, 53
    threshold of, 52, 176, 215
    under-, 12–13, 15, 17–18, 21, 36, 46, 54–58, 65, 99, 102, 104, 106–107, 109–110, 121–124, 126–127, 131–133, 135, 141, 166, 169, 174–176, 184–185, 193–195, 197–198, 205–206, 218, 234–235, 262

Dare, C., 257
De Jong, A., 191
De Saussure, F., 127
Deleuze, G., 157–158

development(al), 86, 221
   animus, 223
   ego, 189
   historical, 62, 77
   of analytical psychology, 154
   path of, 170
   personal, 221
   phase of, 98, 259
   psychological, 125, 174
Deveney, J. P., 24
disorder, 258, 260
   mental, 32
   of love, 102
   of the nervous system, 102
   personality, 48–49
Dorahy, M. J., 34, 255
Douglas, C., 57, 224
dream, xv–xvi, 61, 72, 74, 86, 89–90, 93, 111, 115, 120, 127, 130, 162, 164, 172, 178, 182–183, 186–187, 190–191, 195, 206–207, 211, 213, 223, 226–228, 234, 236, 268–269, 271
   analysis, 102, 227, 250
   day-, 55
   distorted, xv
   interpretation of, 121, 136
   material, xv, 70, 171–173
   phallus, 187, 191
   precognitive, 12–13, 17, 55
   prognostic, 259
   prophetic, 62, 68, 90
   prospective, 162
   symbols, 171, 227–228
   unfulfilled desires, xv
   waking, 15
   world of, 112
Dreher, A. U., 257

Edelman, N., 48
ego, 82, 92, 107, 129, 144, 189, 276
   see also: conscious(ness), development(al)
   -centred, 105, 109
   -centric, 103–105

   -existence, 188
   -experience, 269
Eliade, M., 270
Ellenberger, H. F., xviii, 28–29, 43–44, 49–50, 52, 97, 102–103, 142, 159, 174, 246, 252, 256, 258–259, 271
empathy, xiii, xv–xvi, xviii, 14, 16–18, 20–21, 45, 54, 128–129, 133, 136, 157, 164–166, 169, 171, 193, 197–201, 215–216, 233–236, 246, 250, 276
Engstrom, E. J., 32
esoteric, xii, xiv, 24, 54–55, 58, 64, 76, 91, 177, 186, 190–191, 218–220, 245–246, 269, 275
Evans, R. I., 273, 276
extravert, 6–7, 18–20, 208–212, 214, 218, 225–227, 229, 243, 251

Faivre, A., xviii, 54, 56, 67, 82, 128, 191, 218–219, 245–246, 259, 265, 275
Falzeder, E., xvii, 33, 175, 212, 229, 254, 263, 272
Fanger, C., 192
fantasy, 17, 36, 89, 122, 173–174, 196, 199, 206–207, 223, 261
   infantile, 197
Federici Vescovini, G., 269
Feldman, B., 268
Fierz, H. K., xviii, 173, 228
Flournoy, T., 12, 14–15, 21, 24–25, 27, 29–36, 45, 47, 51, 79, 88, 97–99, 102, 107, 111, 135–136, 142, 253–254, 257, 259
Forryan, B., 239
Fowler, D. P., 268
Freud, S. (*passim*)
   analysis, 14, 170, 172, 268
   cited works, xv, 27, 33, 106, 111, 121, 136, 270
   libido, 15, 17, 158, 162
   and mental hospitals, 112
   on dreams, xv, 127

on free association, 12, 111
on hypnosis, 196–197
on repression, 34, 99, 106
Rat Man, 263
rift with Jung, xv, 34, 141–142, 158–159, 164, 226, 229, 270
teachings of, 31
theories, xv, 31, 34, 114, 170

Gadamer, H.-G., 43
Gaillard, C., 182, 268–269
Galton, F., 47, 101–102
Glover, J. M., 239
Gnostic(ism), 15, 55, 79, 81–85, 260
 aspect, 192
 character, 67, 82
 foundation, 121
 system, 82
 teachings, 55
 theories, 81
Goodheart, W. B., 200
Graves, R., 179
Grimm, J., 143–145, 153, 264, 269
Grimm, W., 143–145, 153, 264, 269
Gunter, P. A. Y., 158–162, 229, 262, 266

Haanegraaff, W. J., 62, 245, 252
Hale, N. G., Jr., 159
Hall, J. A., 194, 196
Hannah, B., 268
Hardy-Baylé, M. C., 125
Haule, J. R., 108, 111, 158, 196, 199, 254, 262
Heffernan, J. A. W., 268
Heim, G., 32
Hewison, D. S., 43
Hillman, J., 200
Hogenson, G. B., 25
Holder, A., 257
Homans, P., 261
Huguelet, P., 125
Huskinson, L., xviii, 92, 173, 209, 248, 260

hypnotism, 25–26, 28–30, 49–50, 53, 62, 65, 110, 193, 194, 196, 199–200, 252, 259, 266
hysteria, 27, 49–52, 114, 129, 258–259
 subjects, 96

Im, S., 260
instinct(ive), 14–15, 17, 20, 106–107, 130, 142, 151–152, 155–157, 161, 166, 206–207, 246, 267, 271, 275
 apprehension, 19
 unconscious, 20
 link, 249
 loss of, 130
 sexual, 206
 survival, 99
 vacillation, 73
introvert, xvi, 6–7, 17–20, 182, 209–212, 214–215, 219, 225–229, 243, 251, 272
intuition (*passim*) *see also*: archetypes, conscious(ness), object(ive), unconscious(ness)
 abstract, 19–20
 centrality of, xiii
 certainty of, 19
 concrete, 19–20
 expressions of, 109
 extra-ordinary, 234
 intellectual, 15, 75, 118, 160–161, 264–265
 multi-disciplinary, xii
 notion of, xi, xvii, 5, 155
 peculiarity of, 18, 212
 perception of, 118
 philosophy of, 160
 polymorphic aspect of, xi
 processes of, 5
 psychological, xiv, 234–235
 religious, 234–235
 scientific, 234–235
 sensory, 88, 265
 sporadic, 212
 theory of, 46

Invernizzi, G., 111
Iselin, H. K., xvii, 210, 212, 272

Jaffé, A., xvii–xviii, 13, 44, 52,
    57–58, 112, 169, 177–186,
    188–192, 198, 213, 220, 222,
    226, 247, 256, 266, 268–269,
    272, 275
Jahoda, G., 14
James, W., 14–15, 24, 26–29, 32–33,
    35, 47, 51–52, 88, 159, 194, 200,
    209, 252, 264, 266, 276
Janet, P., xiv, 12, 14–15, 17, 24, 29,
    31–34, 36–37, 46–49, 51–53, 56,
    97, 102, 106–111, 122, 142, 158,
    160, 194–197, 199, 252, 257–259,
    262, 270–271
  cited works, 33, 36, 49, 108,
    195–196, 254, 258
Jarrett, J. L., 173
Jastrow, J., 47–48
Jeromson, B., 81, 85–86, 260
Jung, C. G. (*passim*) *see also*: Freud
  cited works, xiii, 11–12, 14, 25, 31,
    35–36, 61, 66, 76, 78, 86, 112,
    136, 147–150, 153, 159, 163,
    165, 175, 181–192, 226, 228,
    246, 248–249, 254, 257, 260,
    266–267, 269
  libido, 17–18, 158, 191
  on dreams, xv, 17, 271
  psychology of
    consciousness, xiii–xiv, xvi,
      5–7, 16, 18, 20, 54–55, 57–58,
      206
    unconsciousness, xiii–xiv, xviii,
      5–6, 11, 18, 20–21, 54, 57,
      141–142, 160, 206
    under-conscious, xiii, 11, 18, 46,
      51, 54, 57–58, 141–142
  synchronicity, 16, 54, 181, 247,
    275
  theories, xiii, xvii, 5, 53–54, 58, 105,
    184, 189, 213, 216, 224–225,
    229

Kant, I., 15, 25–26, 62, 68–78, 81, 118,
    143–145, 157–158, 160–161,
    216–217, 250, 260, 264–265,
    274–275
Kast, V., xviii
Kerner, J., 15, 26, 42, 68, 82–83,
    200–201, 253, 256
Kerr, J., 216, 274
Kerslake, C., 158, 266
Kirsch, T. B., 248
Kraepelin, E., 32, 34, 103, 113–114,
    262
Kuehn, M., 70, 73, 76, 260
Kugler, P., 122–123

Lauter, E., 222–223
Lefrere, F., 125
Lévy-Bruhl, L., xiv–xv, xviii, 16, 157,
    246, 259, 274
libido, 17–18, 55, 142, 157–159,
    163–164, 174, 191, 214, 216, 236
  dynamics of, 215
  Freudian, 15, 17, 162
  Jungian, 17, 170
Liebscher, M., 264
life (*passim*) *see also*: conscious(ness)
  after death, 57, 72
  -altering, 70
  battle for, 78
  conception of, 92
  cycle, 189
  elixir of, 134
  everyday, 114, 133
  experience of, 92
  -history, 181
  inner, 181, 224
  intellectual, 191
  mid-, 69
  moral, 87
  natural, 189
  precariousness of, 73
  precious, 134
  psychic, 174–176, 221, 223
  -sphere, 83
  supernatural, 87

symbolic, 91, 126–128
tree of, 124
vision of, xii
young, xvii
Ljunggren, M., 145
Lysaker, P. H., 267

Maillard, C., xviii, 58, 90–91, 178, 268, 271, 276
Main, R., xviii, 54–55, 61, 88, 97–98, 247, 260–261, 269, 276
Mancini, S., 56, 259
Marini, A., 125
Martinotti, G., 125
McGuire, W., 3–4, 33, 37, 101, 113, 199, 247, 256
Medtner, E., xviii, 16, 145–146, 157, 209, 216–220, 246–248, 265–266, 272, 274–275
Méheust, B., 259
Monahan, P. A., 31, 49
Montesquieu, C.-L. de S. de, 71
Moskowitz, A., 32, 34, 255
Mullarkey, J., 54, 158, 266
Munsterberg, H., 26, 47, 103, 107, 262
Myers, F. W. H., 15, 21, 24, 30, 34–35, 46, 50–53, 56–57, 63, 65, 67, 97, 102, 142, 174, 193–194, 199, 225, 257–259, 264, 267–268

Nicastro, R., 125
Nicholls, A., 264
Nicolas, S., 36–37
Niehus, L., 239
Noll, R., 270

object(ive), xii, 16, 18–19, 33, 40, 43, 65, 77, 90–91, 124, 127–128, 164, 216–218, 224, 234, 236–237, 243, 250, 264, 267–268
impersonal, 221
inner, 18, 235, 250
intuition, 20
language, 58, 222

meaning, 104
of empathy, 216
precise, 236
psyche, 233, 236, 249–250, 266
reaction, 103, 110
synchronicity, 236
transitional, 185
type, 104–105, 108
Obler, L. K., 125
occult, 23, 31, 62–63, 76, 252
literature, 82
movement, 26
phenomena, 13, 27, 45, 54, 62–63, 76, 146, 216, 252
philosophy, 62–63, 75
practices, 17
qualities, 62
science, 63

Passerieux, C., 125
Pauri, M., 131
Pelletier, M., 120–123, 125–126, 133
Piéron, H., 29–30, 47, 253
Pilard, N., xi, 246, 248, 263
Preiswerk, H., xiv, 17, 35, 40–41, 43–44, 81, 83–84, 86, 95–96, 99–101, 117, 200, 246
Preiswerk, S., 41–42, 61, 260
projection, 197, 211, 223, 227–228, 265, 271, 276
passive, 91
Psychological Club of Zürich, xvi, 145, 157
Pytlik, P., 28, 200

repression, xiv, 12, 15, 17, 34, 55, 99, 105–106, 109–111, 114 see also: conscious(ness)
memory, 114
sexual, 97
Richet, C., 24, 29, 47, 159, 257, 266
Riffard, P., xii, 245
Rimbaud, A., 85, 109, 262
Roelcke, V., 32
Rossi, P., 70

Rowland, S., 178, 180–181, 200, 222–223
Rubino, I. A., 125
Rudolph, K., 83

Sandler, J., 257
Sarfati, Y., 125
Schafer, I., 34, 255
schizophrenia, 34, 89, 113–114, 122, 124–126, 129–130, 173, 190, 227–228, 264, 267
Schlamm, L., xviii, 54–55, 218, 228
Schmid-Guisan, H., xvii, 175, 209–211, 213, 220, 227, 263, 272
Schreier Rupprecht, C., 222–223
Sedgwick, D., 288
Segal, R., xviii, 54–55, 58, 83, 87–88, 164, 178, 189–191, 246, 259, 268, 270
self, 35, 46–47, 86, 128, 218, 236, 246–247 see also: unconscious(ness)
 -awareness, 184
 -cure, 51
 -experience, 13
 -induced, 17, 49, 51, 96, 199–200
 -irony, 116
 -realisation, 182–183
 -respecting, 30, 86
 -satisfied, 128
 single, 34
 -spirit, 100
 subliminal, 199
 -suggestion, 15, 193, 199
sexual, 198, 274 see also: complex, instinct(ive), repression
 aspect, 164
 character, 198
 component, 198
 desire, 196
 homo-, 196
 intercourse, 115
 link, 199
 manifestations, 115
 nature, 45, 199

standpoint, 159
theory, 31, 34
Shamdasani, S., xiii–xiv, xviii, 4, 8, 10–11, 25, 32, 38, 46, 50, 53, 57, 86, 88–92, 106, 109, 112–113, 117, 145, 154, 157–159, 170, 176–177, 179, 193, 197–199, 209, 214–216, 219, 222, 229, 245–250, 252–254, 256, 259–260, 262, 264, 268, 270–272, 274–275
Shane Tubbs, R., 102
Sharp, D., 223
Shoja, M. M., 102
Shopenhauer, A., 30, 68
Silverstein, S. M., 267
Siracusano, A., 125
somnambulism, 15, 17, 35, 49, 51, 84, 86, 95, 97–98, 131, 135, 158, 194, 199, 201, 252
 artificial, 28, 50
 attack, 100
 classic, 132
 semi-, 100–101
 states, 28, 256
Spalletta, G., 125
spiritist, xiv, 24, 28–31, 45, 51, 70, 75, 81, 100–101, 146, 193, 200, 245, 252
 circles, 24, 31, 85
 convictions, 132
 experience, xvii, 38, 44–45, 79
 experimentation, 41
 literature, 40
 mediums, 254
 phenomena, 24, 40, 61
 process, 96
 séances, 13, 35, 38, 246, 252
 sessions, xiv, 15, 17, 39–40, 51, 64, 132, 199–200
spiritual(ism), 23–24, 27, 29–31, 36, 38, 41–43, 45, 50, 64–65, 78, 218, 245, 252
 belonging, 191
 birth, 191
 crisis, 69

fathers, 254
forces, 83
friend, 66
growth, 86
journeys, 218
intermediary, 64
meaning, 223, 263
organ of imagination, 218
phenomena, 61, 101
psychic-, 51
science of, 31
state of health, 70
tutors, 64
world, 69, 260
Spoletini, I., 125
Stein, M., 188
Strom, P., 125
Swan, W., 46, 174, 275
Swedenborg, E., 15, 69–76, 260
symbol(ic), xv, 6, 55, 57, 77, 86, 91–93, 115, 120–122, 124, 127, 129, 131, 133–134, 136, 145, 150, 164, 170–176, 181–185, 189, 191, 208, 211, 214, 218–219, 227–228, 236, 261, 267–268, 274 *see also*: archetypes
attachment, 216
central, 184
dimension, 124
dream, 171, 228
indistinct, 121
language of, 228
life, 91, 126–128
living, 177
mother, 190
of transformation, 17
poetic, 174
primitive, 123
relationships, 121
theory of, 170–171
value, 215
world, 225

Tanger, C., 259
Tart, C., 55–56

Taylor, E., xviii, 25, 51–52, 253, 271
telepathy, 53, 62, 66–67, 201, 226, 264
Titchener, E. B., 14, 29
Todorov, S., 246
transference, xvi, 17, 20–21, 45, 65, 169, 193, 196–197, 208, 216, 269, 276
counter-, 17, 193, 196–197, 269
neurosis, 197
successful, 16
thought-, 201
Traupman, J. C., 265
Treitel, C., xviii, 25–26, 28
Tricarico, G., 111
Tuke, D. H., 199

unconscious(ness) (*passim*) *see also*: conscious(ness), instinct(ive), Jung, C. G.
aspects, 149
collective, xiv–xvi, 13, 17, 19, 46, 53, 58, 121, 124, 129, 141–142, 147, 149–150, 152–153, 155–156, 163–166, 171–173, 190, 192, 221–222, 229–230, 236, 246, 249, 262, 264–265, 267, 269
compensatory, 186
conflicts, 270
contents, 174
deepest, xiii
functions, 227
human, 161
identification, 216
images, 229
intuition, xiv, 5, 7, 13, 161, 215, 227, 276
mind, 28
personal, xiv, 46, 55, 122, 142, 262
supra-, 162–163
process, 148, 205
psychic data, 19
realities, 200
representations, 149
self, 174

Van den Broek, R., 64–65
Vandermeersch, P., 252
Vezzoli, C., 111
Vieljeux, J., 247
Visentin, U., 111
Vogt, O., 29–30, 47, 253
Voltaire, 71–75
Von Franz, M.-L., xviii, 7–8, 23–24, 179, 209, 220, 224–225, 233, 252, 255, 268–269, 275–276
Von Stuckrad, K., 245

war, 34, 85, 88–89, 227
   First World, 75, 88–89, 145, 227
   misery of, 175
   pre-, 89
   Prussian, 264
   Second World, 8, 269
Weber, M. M., 32
Wehr, G., 41–42, 69, 173, 184, 264
Wilhelm, R., xi, 66
Williams-Hogan, J., 69–70
Winnicott, D. W., 268
Witzig, J., 32, 35–36
Wolff, T., xvii–xviii, 198–199, 209–210, 220–222, 225, 246, 271, 275–276

Zanello, A., 125
Zipes, J. D., 269
Zumstein-Preiswerk, S., 44, 256